Scribal News in Politics and Parliament, 1660–1760

T0385762

Scribal News in Politics and Parliament, 1660–1760

Edited by

ROBIN EAGLES

and

MICHAEL SCHAICH

WILEY

for

THE PARLIAMENTARY HISTORY YEARBOOK TRUST

John Wiley & Sons

Registered Office
John Wiley & Sons Ltd, The Atrium, Southern Gate, Chichester, West Sussex, PO19 8SQ, UK

Editorial Offices
101 Station Landing, Medford, MA 02155, USA
9600 Garsington Road, Oxford, OX4 2DQ, UK
The Atrium, Southern Gate, Chichester, West Sussex, PO19 8SQ, UK

For details of our global editorial offices, for customer services, and for information about how to apply for permission to reuse the copyright material in this book please see our website at https://www.wiley.com/WileyCDA/Brand/id-35.html.

Wiley also publishes its books in a variety of electronic formats. Some content that appears in print may not be available in electronic books.

Library of Congress Cataloging-in-Publication data is available for this book

ISBN 9781119912163

A catalogue record for this title is available from the British Library
Set in 10/12pt Bembo
by Aptara Inc., India
Printed and bound in Singapore
by C.O.S Printers Pte Ltd

1   2022

CONTENTS

NOTES ON CONTRIBUTORS

Davide Boerio obtained a dual PhD in early modern history from the University of Teramo and University College Cork in 2018 with a thesis titled 'News, Network and Discourses during the Neapolitan Revolution of 1647–48 and Its Aftermath'. His research focuses on the production, circulation, reception and control of political information in the early modern period. He has held several doctoral and post-doctoral research fellowships related to the history of communication awarded by American, Italian and European research agencies. In January 2020 he joined the EUORNEWS project on the history of early modern news, sponsored by the Irish Research Council, where he is the post-doctoral researcher and research co-ordinator.

Ugo Bruschi is associate professor of medieval and modern legal history in the department of Legal Studies at the University of Bologna. He began his career as an archivist and then joined academia, publishing widely on medieval notaries and on the relationship between Church and State in the 16th and 17th centuries. British constitutional and political history in the long 18th century has been his main field of research. He is currently working on premiership and the cabinet system in 18th-century Britain, and on the perception that Italian diplomats in London had of the British polity. He is the author of *Rivoluzioni silenziose: l'evoluzione costituzionale della Gran Bretagna tra la* Glorious Revolution *e il* Great Reform Act (2014).

Leith Davis is professor in the English department and director of the Centre for Scottish Studies at Simon Fraser University. She is the author of *Acts of Union: Scotland and the Negotiation of the British Nation, 1707–1832* (1999) and *Music, Postcolonialism and Gender: The Construction of Irish Identity, 1724–1874* (2005) as well as co-editor of *Scotland and the Borders of Romanticism* (2004), *Robert Burns and Transatlantic Culture* (2012) and the *International Companion to Scottish Literature of the Long Eighteenth Century* (2021). Her new book, *Mediating Cultural Memory in Britain and Ireland from the 1688 Revolution to the 1745 Jacobite Rising,* is forthcoming with Cambridge University Press.

Brendan Dooley currently professor of renaissance studies at University College Cork, previously taught at Harvard, Notre Dame and Jacobs University, Bremen. He works on the histories of culture and knowledge with reference to Europe and especially to Italy and the Mediterranean world. Publications include *Angelica's Book and the World of Reading in Late Renaissance Italy* (2016), *A Mattress Maker's Daughter: The Renaissance Romance of Don Giovanni de' Medici and Livia Vernazza* (2014), *The Social History of Skepticism* (1999), and, as editor, *The Dissemination of News and the Emergence of Contemporaneity in*

Early Modern Culture (2010). He is also principal investigator of the EURONEWS Project (www.euronewsproject.org) engaged with analysing the early manuscript sources of news.

Robin Eagles is editor of the *House of Lords 1660–1832* section at the History of Parliament. He was one of the principal contributors to *The History of Parliament: The Lords 1660–1715* (2016) and is now overseeing the next part of the project covering 1715–90. He is the author of *Francophilia in English Society, 1748–1815* (2000), has published an edition of *The Diaries of John Wilkes, 1770–1797* (2014) and was co-editor with Coleman Dennehy of *Henry Bennet, Earl of Arlington, and His World: Restoration Court, Politics and Diplomacy* (2020).

Markman Ellis is professor of 18th-century studies at Queen Mary University of London. He is the author of *The Politics of Sensibility: Race, Gender and Commerce in the Sentimental Novel* (1996), *The History of Gothic Fiction* (2000), *The Coffee-House: A Cultural History* (2004), co-author of *Empire of Tea* (2015), and the editor of *Eighteenth-Century Coffee-House Culture* (2006) and *Tea and the Tea-Table in Eighteenth-Century England* (2010). He is currently working on sociability and intellectual culture in London in the mid 18th century, focusing especially on the Hardwicke and Bluestocking circles.

Rachael Scarborough King is associate professor of English at the University of California, Santa Barbara. She is the author of *Writing to the World: Letters and the Origins of Modern Print Genres* (2018) and editor of *After Print: Eighteenth-Century Manuscript Cultures* (2020). Her work focuses on the literature and media of the long 18th century, with particular interests in newspapers, periodicals and letters.

Charles Littleton is a senior research fellow in the *House of Lords 1660–1832* section of the History of Parliament and also serves on the editorial committee of the *Huguenot Society Journal*. He has published articles on the estate bills of the earls of Derby and on the Bennet family, barons Ossulston and earls of Tankerville, deriving from his work for the section. His contribution in this volume comes from his research for the 1715–90 project, but he was initially directed to the activities of the diplomatic residents Bonnet and L'Hermitage from an interest in the Huguenot diaspora. He has also published work on Abel Boyer's parliamentary reporting.

Kate Loveman is an associate professor in English at the University of Leicester. She works on 17th- and 18th-century literature and history, with particular interests in reading habits, collecting and information networks. Her publications include *Samuel Pepys and His Books: Reading, Newsgathering, and Sociability, 1660–1703* (2015) and *Reading Fictions, 1660–1740: Deception in English Literary and Political Culture* (2008). She has also edited a selection of Samuel Pepys's diary for Everyman (2018).

Jason Peacey is professor of early modern British history at UCL. He is the author of *Politicians and Pamphleteers: Propaganda in the Civil Wars and Interregnum* (2004), *Print and Public Politics in the English Revolution* (2013) and *The Madman and the Churchrobber: Law and Conflict in Early Modern England* (2022). He also edited *The Regicides and the Execution of Charles I* (2001) and *The Print Culture of Parliament, 1600–1800* (2007), and *Making the British Empire, 1660–1800* (2020). With Chris R. Kyle he edited *Parliament at Work* (2002) and *Connecting Centre and Locality: Political Communication in Early Modern England* (2020). With Robert G. Ingram and Alex W. Barber he edited *Freedom of Speech, 1500-1850* (2020). He is currently working on Anglo–Dutch relations in the 17th century.

Alasdair Raffe is a senior lecturer in history at the University of Edinburgh, where he has taught since 2013. He specialises in the religious, political and intellectual history of 17th- and 18th-century Scotland. His monograph, *The Culture of Controversy: Religious Arguments in Scotland, 1660–1714* (2012), won the Hume Brown Prize for the best first book in Scottish History. He is also the author of *Scotland in Revolution, 1685–1690* (2018). His most recent publications concern the development of religious pluralism in 18th-century Scotland.

Michael Schaich is deputy director of the German Historical Institute London and teaches early modern history at the University of Munich. He specialises in 17th- and 18th-century British and German history. Among his most recent publications are two volumes of collected essays: (with Andreas Gestrich), *The Hanoverian Succession: Dynastic Politics and Monarchical Culture* (2015) and (with Matthias Pohlig), *The War of the Spanish Succession: New Perspectives* (2018). He is currently working on the transmission of information from London to various German courts in the late 17th and early 18th centuries.

Edward Taylor works on the media and political culture, in both English and Latin, in early modern Britain. He has been a post-doctoral research fellow at UCL since 2019, as part of Dr Victoria Moul's Leverhulme-funded project, 'Neo-Latin Poetry in English Manuscript Verse Miscellanies, c. 1550–1700'. He originally trained as a historian, completing his BA in History (2008–11) and MPhil in early modern history (2011–12) at Clare College, Cambridge, before taking the Graduate Diploma in classical studies at KCL (2013–14), during which he studied Latin and Greek. He worked on his PhD, 'Commenting on the News: The Serial Press and Political Culture in Britain, 1641–c. 1730', at the University of Warwick (2015–19), where he was supervised by professor Mark Knights. He has also worked and volunteered at a range of historical institutions, including the British Library (Sloane Printed Books Project), Hampton Court Palace and Dr Williams's Library.

ABBREVIATIONS

Add. MS(S)	Additional Manuscript(s)
ASFi	Archivio di Stato, Florence
ASGe	Archivio di Stato, Genoa
ASMo	Archivio di Stato, Modena
ASTo	Archivio di Stato, Turin
ASVe	Archivio di Stato, Venice
BEUMo	Biblioteca Estense Universitaria, Modena
BL	British Library, London
Bodl.	Bodleian Libraries, Oxford
CJ	*Commons Journals*
CSP Dom.	*Calendar of State Papers, Domestic Series*
CSP Ven.	*Calendar of State Papers, Venetian*
CTB	*Calendar of Treasury Books*
CUL	Cambridge University Library
E.H.R.	*The English Historical Review*
ESL	Early Stuart Libels https://www.earlystuartlibels.net
Folger	Folger Shakespeare Library, Washington
GStA PK	Geheimes Staatsarchiv Preußischer Kulturbesitz, Berlin
HLQ	Huntington Library Quarterly
HMC	Historical Manuscripts Commission (reports)
HPC 1690-1715	*The History of Parliament: The House of Commons 1690–1715*, ed. Eveline Cruickshanks, Stuart Handley and D.W. Hayton (5 vols, Cambridge, 2002)
HPL 1660-1715	*The History of Parliament: The House of Lords 1660–1715*, ed. Ruth Paley (5 vols, Cambridge, 2016)
LJ	*Journals of the House of Lords*
n.s.	new series
NLA	Niedersächsisches Landesarchiv, Hanover
NLS	National Library of Scotland
NRS	National Records of Scotland
OED	*Oxford English Dictionary*
Oxf. DNB	*The Oxford Dictionary of National Biography*
PA	Parliamentary Archives
Parl. Hist.	*Parliamentary History*
POAS	Poems on Affairs of State
P&P	*Past & Present*
RO	Record Office
SP	State Papers
TNA	The National Archives [of the U.K.]
UL	University Library

Preface

ROBIN EAGLES AND MICHAEL SCHAICH

This volume has grown out of a one-day conference held between the History of Parliament and the German Historical Institute London (GHIL), on 14 December 2018, 'Scribal News and News Cultures in Late Stuart and Early Georgian Britain'. The editors are grateful to the directors of the History of Parliament and GHIL for their support for the event, and to all of the contributors for their participation. A number of them are contributors to the present volume. The editors would also like to thank *Parliamentary History* for its encouragement for the volume and, in particular, Dr Richard Gaunt and Dr John Cooper for their editorial oversight and Sarah Worrall and Ajay Patel for preparing the manuscript for publication. The editors would also like to thank the Parliamentary Art Collection (and in particular Melanie Unwin and Helen Taylor) for permitting the use of the image of Westminster Hall on the cover. Dr Clyve Jones had originally planned to produce a collection examining reporting of parliament 'before Hansard'. This volume has taken some inspiration from that project, but has taken it forward in a different direction by focusing solely on manuscript news reporting and how that remained a feature of the parliamentary and political sphere well into the 18th century.

Introduction

ROBIN EAGLES AND MICHAEL SCHAICH

1

The importance of print for English (and British) politics during the late Stuart and early Georgian period has been recognised for some time. Scholars have devoted considerable attention to the role of newspapers in creating a space for the continuous discussion of politics; they have explored the effects of pamphlets and partisan journals on the politicisation of the reading public, especially during the 'age of party';[1] and they have discussed print's impact upon and coverage of the most important political venue of the time, parliament. There have been two previous special issues of this journal devoted to the topic: *Parliament and the Press, 1689–c.1939*, edited by Karl Schweizer, and *The Print Culture of Parliament, 1600–1800*, edited by Jason Peacey.[2]

By comparison, manuscript forms of communication are still not as well understood as print media, whether with respect to parliamentary proceedings or the political scene more generally.[3] To be sure, manuscript (or scribal) news is certainly not an unknown quantity. It has attracted the interest of scholars working on early modern Europe, especially for the 16th and early 17th centuries.[4] In the British context, there has been a considerable amount of research on 'manuscript circulation' and its formative role in the creation of a (polarised) public sphere in the early Stuart period.[5] But the later epochs are less well

[1] See, among others, *News, Newspapers, and Society in Early Modern Britain*, ed. Joad Raymond (1999); Hannah Barker, *Newspapers, Politics and English Society, 1695–1855* (Harlow, 2000); Joad Raymond, *Pamphlets and Pamphleteering in Early Modern Britain* (Cambridge, 2003); Edward Taylor, 'John Tutchin's Observator, Comment Serials, and the Rage of Party in Britain, 1678 – c.1730', *Historical Journal*, lxiii (2020), 862–84.

[2] *Parliament and the Press, 1689–c.1939*, ed. K.W. Schweizer (Edinburgh, 2006); *The Print Culture of Parliament, 1660–1800*, ed. Jason Peacey (Edinburgh, 2007).

[3] Philip Baker has recently published on parliamentary diaries in the early Stuart period. While these were often compiled for the personal instruction of the member of parliament taking the information down, sometimes they were an aid for 'communicating it to a wider audience': Philip Baker, ' "But Private Notes for My Own Memory?" Parliamentary Diaries, Parliamentary History and the Politics of Information in Early Stuart England', *Parl. Hist.*, xxxix (2020), 405–22.

[4] From the wealth of literature on 16th and early 17th-century '*avvisi*' see Mario Infelise, 'From Merchants' Letters to Handwritten Political Avvisi: Notes on the Origins of Public Information', in *Cultural Exchange in Early Modern Europe*, vol. iii, ed. Francisco Bethencourt and Florike Egmond (Cambridge, 2007), 33–79; Filippo de Vivo, *Information and Communication in Venice: Rethinking Early Modern Politics* (Oxford, 2007), ch. 2; *Die Fuggerzeitungen im Kontext: Zeitungssammlungen im Alten Reich und in Italien*, ed. Katrin Keller and Paola Molino (Vienna, 2015); Andrew Pettegree, *The Invention of News: How the World Came to Know About Itself* (New Haven, CT, 2014), 96–116.

[5] For the early Stuart period see for example Richard Cust, 'News and Politics in Early Seventeenth-Century England', *P&P*, cxii (1986), 60–90; Harold Love, *Scribal Publication in Seventeenth-Century England* (Oxford, 1993); Ian Atherton, ' "The Itch Grown a Disease": Manuscript Transmission of News in the Seventeenth Century',

served. As recently as 2018, Rachael King stated: 'The continuing presence and prominence of manuscript news in the Restoration and eighteenth century remains a footnote in the story of the rise of the newspaper'.[6] This holds true until today. Following on from earlier studies on the secretaries of state's management of news, the significance of handwritten media for Restoration political culture is slowly being recognised.[7] Yet for many scholars the permanent lapse of the licensing laws in England in 1695 and ensuing eruption of print media, as well as the publication of a long-lasting newspaper in Scotland in 1699, sounded the death knell for scribal publications. Manuscript newssheets and scribal poetry, two of the main handwritten genres of political discourse, seemed a thing of the past, finally surpassed by cheaper, more efficient and more widely available newspapers and journals. Only recently have historians and literary scholars like Alex Barber, Rachael King, Markman Ellis and Christopher Reid started systematically to critique this assumption. In doing so they have built on the work of Henry L. Snyder and Jeremy Black, who in the 1970s and 1980s highlighted the continuing significance of scribal news well into the 18th century.[8]

The present volume seeks to expand on these efforts and take forward our understanding of scribal news in the 17th and 18th centuries. It focuses on the topical reporting of political developments in Britain in a variety of handwritten genres, mainly during the period from 1660 to 1760 with occasional forays into the early 17th century. Although it covers politics more broadly, taking in events such as the Great Fire of London (1666) or the Jacobite uprising of 1715, and dealing with processes of political information gathering by actors ranging from the English government under Charles II to a Scottish Presbyterian minister to individual English politicians such as Philip Yorke, at the heart of this volume is the coverage of parliament. Parliament and scribal news remain an under-researched field,

---

[5] *(continued)* in *News, Newspapers and Society*, ed. Joad Raymond (1999), 39–65; S.A. Baron, 'The Guises of Dissemination in Early Seventeenth-Century England: News in Manuscript and Print', in *The Politics of Information in Early Modern Europe*, ed. Brendan Dooley and S.A. Baron (2001), 41–56; Noah Millstone, *Manuscript Circulation and the Invention of Politics in Early Stuart England* (Cambridge, 2017). A fuller body of reference can be found in the footnotes to the contributions to this volume.

[6] R.S. King, ' "All the News That's fit to Write: The Eighteenth-Century Manuscript Newsletter" ', in *Travelling Chronicles: News and Newspapers from the Early Modern Period to the Eighteenth Century*, ed. S.G. Brandtzaeg, Paul Goring and Christine Watson (Leiden, 2018), 96.

[7] J.G. Muddiman, *The King's Journalist, 1659–1689* (1923); Peter Fraser, *The Intelligence of the Secretaries of State and their Monopoly of Licensed News, 1660–1688* (Cambridge, 1956); Atherton, ' "The Itch Grown a Disease" ', 52–6; Alan Marshall, *Intelligence and Espionage in the Reign of Charles II, 1660–1685* (Cambridge, 2003); Jason Peacey, 'Managing Dutch Advices: Abraham Casteleyn and the English Government, 1660–1681', *Media History*, xxii (2016), 421–37; Jason Peacey, ' "My Friend the Gazetier": Diplomacy and News in Seventeenth-Century Europe', in *News Networks in Early Modern Europe*, ed. Joad Raymond and Noah Moxham (Leiden, 2016), 420–42; Lindsay O'Neill, 'News and the Personal Letter, or the News Education of Theophilus Hastings, 7th Earl of Huntingdon, 1660–71', in *Connecting Centre and Locality: Political Communication in Early Modern England*, ed. C.R. Kyle and Jason Peacey (Manchester, 2020), 193–208. See also Mark Goldie discussing the resemblance of Roger Morrice's *Entring Book* to newsletters, *The Entring Book of Roger Morrice 1677–1691* (7 vols, Woodbridge, 2007), i, 109–16.

[8] H.L. Snyder, 'Newsletters in England, 1689–1715, with Special Reference to John Dyer – A Byway in the History of England', in *Newsletters to Newspapers: Eighteenth-Century Journalism*, ed. D.H. Bond and W.R. McLeod (Morgantown, WV, 1977), 3–19; Jeremy Black, *The English Press in the Eighteenth Century* (Pennsylvania, 1987); A.W. Barber, ' "It Is Not Easy What to Say of our Condition, Much Less to Write It": The Continued Importance of Scribal News in the Early 18th Century', *Parl. Hist.*, xxxii (2013), 293–316; R.S. King, 'The Manuscript Newsletter and the Rise of the Newspaper, 1665–1715', *HLQ*, lxxix (2016), 411–37; King, ' "All the News That's fit to Write" '; Markman Ellis, 'Thomas Birch's "Weekly Letter" (1741–66): Correspondence and History in the Mid-Eighteenth-Century Royal Society', *Notes and Records* lxviii (2014), 261–78; Christopher Reid, 'Reporting by Letter: The 2nd Earl of Hardwicke and his Parliamentary Correspondents', *Parl. Hist.*, xxxix (2020), 239–54.

which is surprising given the prominence of parliamentary proceedings in all sorts of hand-written reportage.[9] There were few other topics that resurfaced with such regularity and were treated as extensively as the affairs in the Lords and Commons. It has even been suggested that parliament's fractious relationship with the public helped to secure the survival of scribal news after the ascendancy of newspapers.[10] And although this may not be the whole truth, as King has argued, and we should not overestimate the amount of detail conveyed in many forms of handwritten news especially as far as the contents of speeches and debates were concerned,[11] parliament sitting in private was certainly a major contributing factor to the business model of scribal news. Despite repeated encroachments on parliamentary privilege by early journalists such as Abel Boyer in the period between roughly 1700 and 1740, newsletters remained arguably the only media that could provide reliable, regular and continuous access to the debates within the two Houses before parliamentary reporting in print was conceded by the Commons after the groundbreaking Printers' Case in 1771.[12] But although parliament was undoubtedly a staple of scribal news throughout our period, parliament's relationship with manuscript hasn't been addressed in the same way as print's relationship has. We still don't know nearly enough about how parliamentary information ended up in scribal news, which aspects of parliamentary business were reported and which weren't, how parliament as a whole or the two chambers individually were portrayed to various audiences, and how reliable manuscript parliamentary reporting was at all. These are only some of the issues to be addressed in this volume.

For this purpose, the scope of the term 'scribal news' is deliberately broad to encompass the ill-defined and constantly shifting nature of manuscript reporting about politics that was characteristic of the period.[13] Contemporary practitioners, observers and commentators of the political process did not differentiate between various forms of manuscript reporting, nor did they privilege one form over the other. They tried to get hold of as much information as possible and relied for their consumption of topical news on whatever was available to them: private letters which, apart from personal communication, contained the latest gossip about events in the political world; regular letters of intelligence sent by a client to his or her patron, where the information offered reaffirmed the social bond between recipient and sender; commentary on political events and actors in the form of manuscript verse; commercial newsletters written by professional newsmongers and distributed via a subscription service; letters of news composed primarily by merchants stationed abroad, which circulated in coffeehouses and other public places as well as among friendship groups and professional

---

[9] The pervasiveness of parliamentary reporting in scribal news has been acknowledged among others by Atherton, '"The Itch Grown a Disease"', 46. Where more detailed attention has been paid to manuscript reportage of parliament, it has tended to be in the context of specific types of business; technical aspects of parliament, for example the privilege exercised by the Lords to issue formal written protests; or for high profile events like impeachments. See for example Clyve Jones, 'The Opening of the Impeachment of Robert Harley, Earl of Oxford, June to September 1715: The "Memorandum" of William Wake, Bishop of Lincoln', *eBLJ* (2015), Article 4; Jones, 'Dissent and Protest in the House of Lords, 1641–1998: An Attempt to Reconstruct the Procedures Involved in Entering a Protest into the Journals', *Parl. Hist.*, xxvii (2008), 309–29; Jones, '"Party Rage and Faction" – the View from Fulham, Scotland Yard and the Temple: Parliament in the Letters of Thomas Bateman and John and Ralph Bridges to Sir William Trumbull, 1710–1714', *British Library Journal*, xix (1993), 148–80.

[10] Barber, '"It Is Not Easy What to Say of our Condition, Much Less to Write It"', 295, 303–7.

[11] See Rachael King's article in this volume and King, '"All the News That's fit to Write"', 109.

[12] For the Printers' Case see P.D.G. Thomas, *John Wilkes: A Friend to Liberty* (Oxford, 1996).

[13] A similar argument is made by Atherton, '"The Itch Grown a Disease"', 41.

networks; and finally, diplomatic despatches of various kinds that were distributed, often in digested form, among government ministers, courtiers and, sometimes more widely, among members of the social elites. Scribal news as understood in this volume is thus a protean term that comprises a variety of handwritten news media including scribal poetry, private correspondence, and despatches by diplomatic actors as well as the more commonly known commercial newsletters.

The writers of scribal news likewise resist easy categorisation. Among the newsmongers and intelligencers of the day we find a wide spectrum of social figures. We encounter entrepreneurs such as John Dyer and William Wye, who ran highly efficient operations employing numerous scriveners and producing hundreds of copies of a newsletter each post day. We also come across literary hacks and early journalists such as Abel Boyer, who in addition to writing journals and other print works, recycled parts of the information they gathered in handwritten services for individual patrons and were reminiscent of their later Grub Street colleagues. In addition, there were (often anonymous) authors using poetry to enter the political arena and express their (mostly critical) view of king and government: clerks in Whitehall or journalists in government pay who produced 'official' newsletters for a select audience; and junior diplomats termed agents, residents or correspondents who occupied a peculiar position on the borderline between journalism and diplomacy and supplied foreign courts with regular updates on occurrences in their place of residence.

The abundance of genres and characters that populated the world of manuscript should not blind us to the fact, that scribal news never functioned in isolation from and independently of topical print. As has been observed before,[14] and is also evident in the contributions to this volume, manuscript and print were deeply intertwined.[15] Throughout the 17th century scribal news developed in response to trends in the area of print and vice versa. Newspapers and newsletters learned from each other how to organise their information by using paragraphs, banner headings or datelines. The credibility and authority of one medium also depended to a large extent on the waxing or waning fortunes of the other, as Jason Peacey demonstrates in this volume and Ian Atherton has argued in a separate article.[16] In a more immediate sense, recipients often received scribal news not on its own but in the same post with newspapers, journals and tracts. They read manuscript and print alongside each other, comparing information from both media and constructing their view of the world based on what they learnt from handwritten as well as printed sources.[17] This applied not only to individual readers but also to the intelligence gathering of governments: the mail coming in from diplomats and foreign correspondents of all hues comprised print publications alongside the main handwritten despatch. In a similar vein, print and manuscript media drew on each other as sources: many newsletters extracted information from newspapers while print journalists excerpted scribal news. During the

---

[14] Most effectively by King, 'Manuscript Newsletter' and ' "All the News That's fit to Write"'.

[15] Some manuscript newsletters cited what was being reported in the press, which suggests that subscribers found such a digest useful. See, for example, Bodl., MS. Eng. hist. c. 1040, f. 29, where the newsletter drew its readers' attention to reports in the *Daily Courant*.

[16] Atherton, ' "The Itch Grown a Disease"', 46–56.

[17] Sometimes newsletter writers had to offer alternative additional material when the usual sources proved disappointing. In October 1722 William Wye annotated one of his newsletters, 'Sr ye Last Gazette having little or no news In it I send you instead of it ye House of Comons Addresse'. Bodl., MS Rawl. C. 151, f. 6v.

first half of the 18th century, provincial newspapers regularly based part of their coverage on what they learnt from their handwritten counterparts. Finally, the ability of print and scribal news to exist in tandem is evident on the production side: manuscript verse could appear in print too, and the editors of newspapers often doubled as purveyors of scribal news or moved from one medium to the other.[18]

There was also a close link between scribal news and the sphere of the spoken word. Newsletters, despatches and manuscript verse were read aloud, and in the case of poems also sung, in coffeehouses and taverns, at princely courts or at informal gatherings such as the 'Hardwicke Circle'. Rumour and gossip also found their way into scribal news of all shades. Many a news story was based on off-the-record conversations with ministers, clerks and secretaries, members of parliament and other political actors. Significantly for this volume, parliamentary speeches were one of the most reported oral news items in handwritten reports connecting the culture of debate in Westminster with a wider reading public.

It is this multi-layered landscape of manuscript, oral and print, of private, contractual and international news coverage, that provides the common framework within which the articles in this volume are written. At the same time the chapters in this collection approach the main topic from a variety of perspectives, thus contributing to a number of scholarly debates linked to the history of manuscript reporting in general and parliamentary history in particular.

2

To start with the field of scribal news studies, this volume further confounds any lingering expectations of a premature death of manuscript around 1700, suggesting a much longer but also more complex chronology. For too long many scholars have taken the superior quality of print for granted, and afforded scribal news only a right of existence as a clandestine medium that disappeared once censorship was lifted.

To be sure, this latter assumption is not entirely unfounded. It holds true for certain periods and territories and also for certain genres of scribal news. In the British case, newsletters and scribal poetry disappeared temporarily during the 1640s and 1650s, as the chapters by Jason Peacey and Edward Taylor demonstrate. Taylor also points out that handwritten political verse did indeed lose currency from the 1690s at the latest, an observation that given the oppositional character of much political verse can be attributed most likely to the relaxing of restrictions on freedom of speech.[19] Historians of *ancien régime* France have likewise shown to what extent *nouvelles à la main* provided a vital means of communication in a monopolised and heavily policed news market.[20]

---

[18] This was true of the author of the *London News-Letter*, who had previously distributed a scribal newspaper. It is also true of William Wye, though he appears to have continued to produce both print and manuscript in parallel.

[19] For more on the subject see David Como, 'The Origin of the Concept of Freedom of the Press', in *Freedom of Speech, 1500–1850*, ed. R.G. Ingram, Jason Peacey and A.W. Barber (Manchester, 2020), 98–118.

[20] See, e.g., *Répertoire des Nouvelles à la Main: Dictionnaire de la Presse Manuscrite Clandestine XVIe–XVIIIe Siècle*, ed. François Moureau (Oxford, 1999); *La Plume et le Plomb: Espaces de l'imprimé et du Manuscrit au Siècle des Lumières*, ed. François Moureau (Paris, 2006).

More fundamentally, however, scribal news showed a remarkable resilience in the face of the new print medium. As Heiko Droste and others have argued recently, for parts of central and northern Europe, scribal news on the whole flourished throughout the 17th century despite the existence of a far greater number of newspapers than the British Isles ever witnessed during the same period.[21] In Britain too, newsletters, whether official or commercial, appear to have proliferated from the later 17th century onwards. This trend continued well into the 18th century, and certainly beyond the year 1715 that older research on newsletters has often described as the end point for the significance of scribal news,[22] as the chapters by Leith Davis, Robin Eagles and Markman Ellis amply indicate. It seems more appropriate to date the decline of newsletters to the period after the middle of the 18th century when the capacity of print to convey more voluminous information finally undermined the business model on which commercial newsletters had relied.[23] Even this statement, however, has to be treated with circumspection as other forms of scribal news still continued to serve a purpose. The enduring pre-eminence of diplomatic despatches and the continuing demand for political and (in particular) parliamentary information in private correspondence are cases in point.[24] The essays in this volume thus give a more nuanced answer to the perennial question of the survival or decline of scribal news: an answer that pays attention to the various forms of handwritten news and acknowledges that not all manuscript genres followed the same chronology.

What then attracted recipients to scribal news? Why did they seek out information that in some cases at least was available in print too? There is probably no single answer to these questions. First of all, it should be noted that scribal news was the older medium while print's credibility as the newcomer on the scene was in doubt for much of the 17th century. By contrast scribal news enjoyed its 'established authority', to borrow Davis's phrase, well into the 18th century.[25] Besides aspects of trust, manuscript had clear advantages in terms of speed of reporting and building a special relationship with readers. As has often been stated, newsletter writers could add information that came in late much more easily than printers. Readers obviously cherished the sense of receiving something that felt more personal, even if it was largely generic, a point made explicitly by Eagles. Although newsletters were never personalised in any meaningful way, the simple fact of receiving a handwritten sheet of news moved them closer to more private forms of communication than print could ever aspire to. Salutations, even if they were restricted to a simple 'Sir', further corroborated this impression. Women's easier access to manuscript than print, an argument that is explored in more detail by King in this volume, also points in the same direction.

[21] Heiko Droste, 'How Public was the News in Early Modern Times?', in *Handwritten Newspapers: An Alternative Medium during the Early Modern and Modern Periods*, ed. Droste and Kirsti Salmi-Niklander (Finish Lit. Soc. 2019), 38; Droste, *Das Geschäft mit Nachrichten: Ein barocker Markt für soziale Ressourcen* (Bremen, 2018). See also Holger Böning, ' "Gewiss ist es/ dass alle gedruckten Zeitungen erst geschrieben werden müssen": Handgeschriebene und gedruckte Zeitungen im Spannungsfeld von Abhängigkeit, Koexistenz und Konkurrenz', *Daphnis*, xxvii (2008), 203–42 and Johannes Arndt and Esther-Beate Körber, *Periodische Presse in der Frühaufklärung (1700–1750): Ein Vergleich zwischen Deutschland, Frankreich und den Niederlanden* (2 vols., Bremen 2020), i, 231–9.

[22] H.L. Snyder, 'Newsletters in England', 3; Atherton, ' "The Itch Grown a Disease"', 55.

[23] Similarly, King, ' "All the News That's fit to Write"', 115.

[24] Reid, 'Reporting by Letter' and the chapter by Markman Ellis in this volume.

[25] Atherton, ' "The Itch Grown a Disease"', 40; King, 'Manuscript Newsletter', 418, 436.

Finally, scribal news promised and, in some cases, provided access to information that was not easily forthcoming otherwise. This does not mean to say that manuscript forms of reporting were viable only as means of clandestine or scandalous communication as was discussed above. Rather the claim is more modest. Contemporaries ascribed to scribal news the capacity to report at closer range and sometimes in more detail than newspapers. This could be the proverbial 'bigoted Tory country parsons and fox-hunting squires' caricatured by Joseph Addison,[26] who paid for a correspondent to send first-hand reports of events in the capital, or foreign princely courts who employed a man on the spot to give a running commentary on day-to-day politics in London. In addition, under certain circumstances scribal news did indeed deliver privileged knowledge. As will be illustrated below, scribal news penetrated the sphere of privacy surrounding parliament more effectively than any print medium during the period under investigation and supplied recipients with insights into the goings-on in both Houses that were rarely to be read in print. In the end, readers were never guaranteed that what they were getting was exclusive information. What mattered was the promise of access, however precarious, to a world of news that may not have been protected by censorship but for whatever reason was difficult to enter. It gave armchair politicians and statesmen alike the comforting feeling of being well informed.

Who these readers were is difficult to establish precisely, though the articles in this volume give some indications that could be followed up by future research. Diplomats eager to amass any information that they could lay their hands on were one obvious set, and examples of foreign agents at various levels are considered by Brendan Dooley and Davide Boerio, Michael Schaich, Charles Littleton and Ugo Bruschi. However, as some of the other chapters make clear, many other types of people were eager to remain abreast of topical events. Alasdair Raffe draws our attention to Scottish landowners, burgh magistrates and clergymen, while King highlights female readership as a blatant lacuna in the history of scribal news. Women were important as news factors (in the case of one example mentioned by King) as well as the eventual recipients of commercial newsletters. Ellis also mentions female aristocrats as readers of letters of news, an observation that could be extended to diplomatic despatches circulating among courtiers of both sexes. Davis and Eagles, finally, both suggest ways in which those out of step with the Whig regime remained informed through subscription to manuscript news services.

In more general terms, it is beyond doubt that the readership of commercial newsletters was broad and went far beyond those who took it upon themselves to subscribe to a particular service. It is well documented that newsletters could be accessed in coffeehouses, a phenomenon that was not confined to London.[27] Provincial coffeehouses were entrepôts for London news: both Mrs Davies' and Fogg's in Oxford stocked copies of scribal news from London providers, including Thomas Guy and Francis 'Elephant' Smith. We might also point to the experience of Roger Whitley, a visitor to Chester in 1684, where one of his activities was catching up on the latest newsletters.[28]

[26] Mark Knights, *Representation and Misrepresentation in Later Stuart Britain: Partisanship and Political Culture* (Oxford, 2005), 227n.

[27] Brian Cowan, *The Social Life of Coffee: The Emergence of the British Coffeehouse* (New Haven, CT, 2005), 172–3.

[28] *Roger Whitley's Diary 1684–1697 Bodleian Library, Ms Eng Hist C 711*, ed. Michael Stevens and Honor Lewington (2004): https://www.british-history.ac.uk/no-series/roger-whitley-diary/1684-97/june-1684.

One of the collections highlighted in this volume, a set of newsletters now in the Bodleian Library produced by the under-researched William Wye, also demonstrates that it was not only within Britain that such scribal products were distributed. It comprises letters sent between 1722 and 1725, the first two directed to the exiled Lord Lansdown, living in the Faubourg St Germain in Paris, with the remainder going to a merchant named Dorvall, also in Paris.[29] It is possible that Dorvall was acting as an agent for Lansdown, but only the first two of the set were specifically endorsed 'My Lord' rather than the more usual generic 'Sir', so Dorvall was perhaps the intended recipient of the main cache. Littleton's chapter cites further evidence of a British newsletter being sent abroad, this time by the notorious Abel Boyer to Thomas Wentworth, earl of Strafford, Britain's ambassador to the United Provinces. In turn, Philip Yorke subscribed to a French *nouvelle à la main* as late as the 1750s although he was less than satisfied with the result, as Ellis explains. National borders, therefore, clearly set no limits to the dissemination of newsletters and there appears to have been an international market that deserves more scholarly attention.

The essays in this volume also raise interesting questions about the geographies of news within Britain, and especially about the relationship between centre and periphery. It has repeatedly been said that official as well as commercial newsletters were an important channel of communication binding recipients in the provinces, among them country squires, members of parliament spending the parliamentary recess in the countryside or the provincial women described by King, to metropolitan actors and political events. Elsewhere, Barber has also shown how newsletter writers such as John Dyer exerted (or were perceived to exert) considerable political and electoral influence in the provinces, simply by giving a selective view of developments in London.[30] What is less well understood, though, is the relevance of provincial or regional news in scribal media as such. The centrality of London to political life on the one hand, and the often-mentioned preponderance of foreign news in newsletters and newspapers on the other, have resulted in a disregard for the topical coverage of events in parts of the British Isles outside the capital.

As yet we don't even know what share of reports in scribal media was reserved for provincial news. Isolated figures in previous studies seem to suggest a low proportion of between 8 and 16 % during the 1690s,[31] although there are tantalising glimpses of detailed coverage of electoral contests in various constituencies in John Dyer's newsletter.[32] The diplomatic despatches analysed in this volume give an equally inconclusive picture. Whereas the Italian diplomats explored by Bruschi were blissfully unaware of events outside London in the early 18th century, the German residents investigated by Schaich reported regularly about Scottish and Irish developments and occasionally also about the goings-on in some of England's provincial towns, even if London claimed the lion's share of domestic news. Meetings of the Edinburgh (before 1707) and Dublin parliaments, or of Scottish church assemblies, routinely caught their eye, as did rumours about Jacobite activities. The wider interest of provincial news, however, is not restricted to numbers but bears on fundamental

---

[29] Bodl., MS Rawl. C. 151.

[30] Barber, ' "It Is Not Easy What to Say of our Condition, Much Less to Write It" ', 299–300, 306–7.

[31] King, ' "All the News That's fit to Write" ', 112. However, the analysis of newsletters written by Muddiman between 1699–1700 indicates a higher share, see King, 'Manuscript Newsletter', 421.

[32] Barber, ' "It Is Not Easy What to Say of our Condition, Much Less to Write It" ', 311.

questions about the quality of scribal reporting, as Davis makes clear in her chapter on the 1715 rebellion. The plethora of localised uprisings and conspiracies secured provincial news a high degree of prominence in newsletters, but the diffuse nature of the incidents made it almost impossible for newsmongers to keep up with the rapidity of developments on the periphery and to convey a coherent and full picture of a disjointed sequence of events. In this respect newspapers, according to Davis, had an advantage. They provided their readers with a more comprehensive coverage, not least through eyewitness reports that would never have fitted into the format of a newssheet. It would be worthwhile to apply Davis's findings to other major political events. Regional or provincial news, sandwiched as it was between foreign and metropolitan reports, clearly warrants closer scrutiny.

It might also help our understanding of the inner workings of scribal news to explore in more detail what could be called regional news cultures. The focus on London as the centre of scribal news production has perhaps hindered us appreciating fully to what extent parts of the British Isles relied on the circulation of news and information within more narrowly defined areas. The contributions by Raffe and Eagles provide ample evidence for how closely Scottish aristocrats and clergymen were tied into the networks radiating out of London, although in both cases the link wasn't as straightforward as might be expected. In the instance of Robert Wodrow, a meagrely paid minister in a rural parish, access had to be established rather indirectly by reports from Scottish members of parliament in Westminster passed on by friends and relatives based more centrally in Glasgow, while the newsletter sent to John Fleming, 6th earl of Wigtown, was a somewhat atypical manuscript newsletter, not in keeping with the usual bifolium as produced by Dyer or Wye. At the same time, Raffe's chapter points to the existence of a separate, regionally confined news system that covered Scottish politics and, in the absence of an 'inner-Scottish' commercial newsletter on the scale of Dyer's outfit, relied in particular on the exchange of private letters of news between interested parties: that is, semi-official reports to supporters and friends by representatives in parliament, church courts and synods about the latest developments in their sphere of activity. As a consequence this news system seems to have been based not primarily on commercial considerations but on the reciprocity of social relationships of friendship and patronage, aspects that have been highlighted recently by scholars working both on epistolary cultures and commercial newsletters.[33] Rather than narrowing our field of vision to London as the centre of scribal news production, we should perhaps cast the net wider to explore the production of scribal news within certain parts of the British Isles that operated internal systems of information but were linked up with national networks.

At the other end of the geographical spectrum covered by this volume is of course the international dimension of information gathering and news provision that has attracted considerable scholarly interest in recent years in the context of the so called 'new diplomatic history'.[34] For the purposes of this volume it suffices to say that historians have gone

---

[33]S.E. Whyman, *The Pen and the People: English Letter Writers 1660–1800* (Oxford, 2009); Atherton, ' "The Itch Grown a Disease" ', 50–6; Droste, *Geschäft mit Nachrichten*.

[34]From the burgeoning literature see only T.A. Sowerby, 'Early Modern Diplomatic History', *History Compass*, xiv (2016), 441–56. For the wider context of diplomats' relationship with the public sphere see also Helmer Helmers, 'Public Diplomacy in Early Modern Europe: Towards a New History of News', *Media History*, xxii (2016), 401–20.

beyond a traditional interest in both clandestine spying operations and the interception of posts as practised by intelligence history, and the fixation on states as crucial players in international relations. They have rediscovered a variety of official or informal actors of both sexes who engaged in diplomatic activity in the widest sense and dabbled in the amassing of information. Applying these new trends to the field of scribal news studies, several contributions to this collection bring a variety of aspects to the fore that help us to reorient the narrative further away from traditional assumptions.

First, they shine a spotlight on a group of minor diplomats and semi-diplomatic actors who are only slowly being recognised as important figures in the Europe-wide system of news.[35] From the chapters by Peacey, Dooley and Boerio, Schaich and Littleton emerge individuals in often subservient positions who formed the core of international information gathering. Among them were some better-known editors of newspapers such as Abraham Casteleyn who supplied foreign governments with intelligence in return for cash, obscure newsmongers who were only too happy to sell one of their newsletters meant for a domestic audience to a newly arrived envoy or ambassador and, most interestingly of all, a wide variety of subordinate diplomats invariably called agents, correspondents and residents. They were hired in significant numbers by early modern states in the late 17th century and occupied a liminal position between diplomacy and news writing.[36] Awarded some sort of diplomatic status that gave them privileged access to certain types of information, they retained their journalistic outlook and churned out regular reports about everyday politics and commercial developments in the various capitals in which they were employed. As part of a wider effort of information gathering, they added another layer of reporting to the official diplomatic despatches written by the envoys with their focus on high-level politics and negotiations.

Intriguingly, one of the main tasks of this peculiar group of information professionals was to cover the political assemblies in their countries of residence. Whether we talk about the States General in The Hague, or the estates of individual Dutch provinces as in Jason Peacey's article, the Swiss Tagsatzung, the target of Habsburg diplomacy,[37] the Imperial Diet,[38] the Polish Sejm,[39] or, closer to the usual remit of this journal, the English (later British) parliament, representative assemblies appear to have been the natural habitat of most scribal newsmongers in foreign service. With their multitude of different actors, their intricate procedures and particular provisions to shield debates from public view, assemblies were more difficult to comprehend for high ranking and mostly aristocratic diplomats than other political venues such as princely courts. This was a lesson the Austrian envoy, Count Thun, had to learn the hard way when in 1680 on a special embassy to London to establish

---

[35] For the growing interest in diplomatic personnel below the rank of ambassadors and envoys see *Zwischen Domestik und Staatsdiener: Botschaftssekretäre in den frühneuzeitlichen Außenbeziehungen*, ed. Florian Kühnel and Christiane Vogel (Cologne, 2021), especially 13–15 for references to earlier studies.

[36] For a case study on the Swedish network of official or semi-official newsmongers see Droste, *Geschäft mit Nachrichten*, 145–243; for English diplomatic information gathering after 1700, see Matthias Pohlig, *Marlborough's Geheimnis: Strukturen und Funktionen der Informationsgewinnung im Spanischen Erbfolgekrieg* (Cologne, 2016), 186–203.

[37] Klaus Müller, *Das kaiserliche Gesandtschaftswesen im Jahrhundert nach dem Westfälischen Frieden (1658–1740)* (Bonn, 1976), 257–8.

[38] Susanne Friedrich, *Drehscheibe Regensburg: Das Informations- und Kommunikationssytem des Immerwährenden Reichstags um 1700* (Berlin, 2007), 407–19.

[39] Droste, *Geschäft mit Nachrichten*, 148, 187.

an alliance with Charles II, he failed to make any headway in obtaining information about the political sentiments in parliament and instead had to pay a local source to provide him with the necessary insights.[40]

Many foreign diplomats in London appear to have shared this experience. They quickly realised that specialists were needed who had a good knowledge of parliamentary procedure, were well versed in the ins and outs of debates as well as being fluent in English, and in addition were either able to access the two Houses or had built up a network of contacts on which to draw for their reports. An exact timeline of when various European states started to install their own correspondents in London is difficult to come by. But the articles by Dooley and Boerio, Schaich and Littleton as well as a preliminary survey of the secondary literature seem to suggest that (as usual in this respect) some Italian states such as the grand duchy of Florence were equipped with regular news supplies earlier than Northern European powers, which received irregular and mostly short-lived reports for much of the 17th century and mainly from the 1680s onwards built up a permanent capacity for routine coverage of English affairs.[41] Once they had appeared on the scene, however, diplomatic newsmongers lasted for a long time. Most of them continued reporting well into the 1710s and 1720s, invariably specialising in parliamentary proceedings although they all betrayed peculiar predilections. In some cases (as Littleton suggests), residents prided themselves on providing detailed information about the minutiae of parliamentary arithmetic; for others, a concise analysis of the key features of political manoeuvring and the principal players involved was the greater point of focus. The motivation behind the arrival of these foreign parliamentary reporters, their sources, journalistic practices and – in particular – the uses the reports were put to by their patrons, need further elucidation. But it is beyond doubt that parliament provided the focal point for foreign scribal news. The ebbs and flows in reporting according to when parliament was sitting or in recess, and the difficulties many of the foreign correspondents faced to fill the pages of their missives during periods of parliamentary inactivity, underline to what degree the two Houses dictated the streams of scribal information that bound England to the continent.

If the articles in this collection prove the significance of parliament for the intensification of a European network of scribal news, they also shed light on the workings of parliament and its relationship with the public sphere. For example, they throw into sharper relief issues of access to the parliamentary chambers that have occupied scholars for a while. Recent scholarship has emphasised the relative openness of the Westminster estate. Jason Peacey and Chris Kyle have commented on this for the first half of the 17th century, while Robin Eagles has demonstrated that the old palace remained an open environment right through to the end of the 18th century (and beyond).[42] The classic example of someone making regular

<hr />

[40] Müller, *Gesandtschaftswesen*, 257.

[41] *Repertorium der diplomatischen Vertreter aller Länder seit dem Westfälischen Frieden* (3 vols., Oldenburg, 1936–65), i, 36, 93, 99, 253, 276, 293–4, 400, 460; Müller, *Gesandtschaftswesen*, 95, 153, 214; Judith Matzke, *Gesandtschaftswesen und diplomatischer Dienst Sachsens 1694–1763* (Leipzig, 2011), 192–3.

[42] Chris Kyle, 'Parliament and the Palace of Westminster: An Exploration of Public Space in the Early Seventeenth Century', in *Housing Parliament: Dublin, Edinburgh and Westminster*, ed. C. Jones and S. Kelsey (Edinburgh, 2002), 85–98; Jason Peacey, 'To Every Individual Member: The Palace of Westminster and Participatory Politics in the Seventeenth Century', *The Court Historian*, xiii (2008), 127–47; Robin Eagles, ' "Got Together in a Riotous and Tumultous Manner": Crowds and the Palace of Westminster, c.1700-1800', *Journal for Eighteenth-Century Studies*, xliii (2020), 349–66.

visits to Westminster Hall in search of news, of all sorts, was Samuel Pepys, but it seems fair to conclude that he was far from alone. In 1661 the Dutch traveller William Schellinks was able to visit Westminster Hall and both the Lords and Commons, as well as other parts of the palace 'too many to describe'.[43] Schellinks was clearly offered a tour when parliament was not sitting, but his experience underscores what Peacey has observed: 'the Palace of Westminster in the 17th century was anything but stately and serene. It was not heavily guarded, and indeed could not be, because it was intrinsically public'.[44] With its numerous stalls selling prints and pamphlets, and the law courts in its corners, Westminster Hall was an obvious location for people to seek news and information, but it also demonstrated how easy it was for news to filter out. Yet, the evidence of newsletters in the period suggests that access to even the more privileged parts of the palace – the chambers of the Lords and Commons – was far from impossible, and that purveyors of scribal news were able to capitalise on this in securing up-to-date accounts of the latest transactions in parliament.

There was some variety in accessing the Lords and Commons. From the end of the 17th century, the Commons had galleries, which were used by non-Members, while the Lords was generally resistant to the innovation. Galleries were installed on two occasions (and planned on a third) but never popular – one reason for the members' dislike being the ability of non-privileged spectators to observe the Lords in session.[45] Every so often both Houses attempted to clamp down on non-authorised access. In 1674 the Lords considered a report from the committee for privileges relating to keeping good order in the chamber, which resulted in an order for their officials to ensure that no one without specific business be permitted any closer than the Painted Chamber.[46] Nevertheless, it is clear from mostly anecdotal reportage, but also from the evidence of the *Lords Journal*, that non-members were able to make their way into the chamber and some of these were no doubt able to relay information to purveyors of news.

Perhaps more importantly, members of both Houses were on occasion the source of information which found its way into the papers (both printed and scribal). From the late 17th century onwards, the Lords made use of their privilege of entering formal written protests to indicate their objections to resolutions carried, and these were circulated across a variety of news media, including in scribal news. Both the Wye and Wigtown collections as well as reports by the Prussian resident Frédéric Bonnet included the full texts of protests, sometimes reproducing possibly earlier drafts of what was eventually entered formally in the *Lords Journal*. It may be that these newsmongers' coverage of protests offers a glimpse of the process by which the texts were written, edited and honed down. They also – along with other examples of parliamentary reportage – suggest that producers of scribal news appear to have been reliant on a common source, or that one newsmonger made use of the other in compiling their pieces (see Eagles and Littleton). This might point to an informal exchange in a venue such as Westminster Hall, or one of many Westminster or City coffeeshops. It was much less usual to find the texts of protests reproduced in printed newspapers, though there were occasional exceptions.

[43] *The Journal of William Schellinks' Travels in England 1661–1663*, ed. Maurice Exwood and H.L. Lehmann (Camden Soc. ser. 5, 1993), 59–60.

[44] Peacey, 'To Every Individual Member', 128.

[45] An order for the Lords' galleries to be removed in 1711 was directly linked to Abel Boyer's activities reporting their proceedings. We are grateful to Charles Littleton for this information.

[46] *LJ*, xii, 612.

As well as the members themselves, it also seems clear that lower functionaries such as doorkeepers played an important role in feeding news or facilitating access for news gatherers. That the Lords were aware of this is hinted at in an episode in February 1704 when the Lords ordered the doorkeepers out of the chamber when the House was sitting, no doubt eager to maintain the secrecy of their deliberations.[47] On other occasions, the Journals make reference to doorkeepers being at fault in allowing non-members to access privileged parts of the palace.[48]

Questions of access also raise the broader issue of government/state control of scribal news. It is important to consider the changing historical context in which parliamentary news was purveyed. Susan Whyman has pointed out for the late 17th century that imparting news was not without danger, citing one example from 1686 when Sir Ralph Verney's nephew, John Stewkeley, advised, ''Tis dangerous writing news… but… you shall certainly have all I may safely write'.[49] Between the lapsing of the licensing laws and the early 1740s there was some lifting of restrictions, though newsmongers like Dyer and Wye still found themselves occasionally summoned before parliament to explain themselves.[50] After 1740, parliament appears to have made a concerted effort to reimpose restrictions on reporting its business, and it was not until the late 1760s and ultimately the success of John Wilkes and his associates in the 1770s pushing the limits to which parliament was prepared to go to suppress reporting of debates that effective freedom of reporting was secured.

To what extent did manuscript news contain 'privileged' parliamentary information, not so easily entrusted to print? In 1660 the House of Commons promulgated an order restricting the ability of printed papers to report on parliamentary proceedings. This has been seen by some as offering an opening to providers of manuscript news to offer information within their publications which was off-limits to their print rivals. Brian Cowan has argued that one of the foremost retailers of manuscript news, John Dyer, himself a coffeehouse-man, 'established a tradition of clandestine and opposition newsletter writing that survived his own death as well as the Hanoverian accession'.[51] How far this is true is one theme considered in the volume. As several of the papers indicate, newsletters were not immune from investigation, and their authors were occasionally summoned before parliament or subject to other forms of control. But as the career of William Wye demonstrates, this did not deter promoters of scribal news from persisting in their trade and their copy was widely reused in the provincial press. Cowan has previously suggested that the coffee-men who kept their clients refreshed and informed, as well as sometimes publishing their own papers, also provided 'copies of manuscript newsletters of material too sensitive to commit to a press'.[52] What was this information? There were certainly times when newsmongers were

---

[47] *LJ*, xvii, 435. This order confirmed one of 1661 which spelled out that none of the officers except Black Rod was permitted to remain in the chamber during debates: *LJ*, xi, 255.

[48] For example, in March 1725 one doorkeeper was suspended for allowing a crowd to make its way into the chamber when the king was present. *LJ*, xxii, 476.

[49] S.E. Whyman, *Sociability and Power in Late-Stuart England: The Cultural Worlds of the Verneys 1660–1720* (Oxford, 1999), 7.

[50] In February 1697 Dyer was ordered into custody by the Commons for infringing their privilege by publishing details of their proceedings: *CJ*, xi, 710.

[51] Cowan, *Social Life of Coffee*, 215.

[52] Cowan, *Social Life of Coffee*, 172.

brought before parliament for publishing information considered by parliamentarians to be privileged, but this was true of both providers of print and manuscript news. It seems reasonable to suggest that even if scribal news writers were sometimes caught out, they were less likely to be so than their print counterparts.[53]

One issue with newsletters was the question of accuracy. It was a frequent taunt in the printed press that manuscript newsletters were less accurate than their own reports. But others seem to have seen things the other way around, and print newspapers were certainly not immune to accusations of inaccurate reporting.[54] This theme of accuracy was raised by Elizabeth Hervey writing to her husband John (the future earl of Bristol) while staying in London with her father in May 1702:

> … there is a great deal talked of in town; but I believe there is so little ground for it, I won't tell it you, having given you so many wrong informations already. what is true Papa will send you with the Newsletter.[55]

Certainly, some newsletter writers offered what appeared to be close and precise reporting, including the results of divisions in both Houses (covered by Littleton). These were not always entirely accurate, but were usually sufficiently so to be of genuine value to those wishing to understand how particular measures were faring in parliament. Besides, it is clear that some newsletter writers were more concerned with supplying their readers with the latest accounts than in establishing their accuracy, offering caveats that they were themselves not sure of the validity of what they relayed.[56]

Although many scribal reports avoided reproducing speeches in parliament in full, most did attempt to provide in-depth accounts of the direction of debates and the results of divisions. As Dooley and Boerio as well as Bruschi have suggested, in some cases one can detect an attempt to support the government in the way news was reported; in others, particularly true of newsletters conveyed to known Jacobites like those mentioned by Davis and Eagles, accounts might be much more hostile to the regime or the state of the nation. Members of both Houses were frequently named in relation to their actions in the chamber, normally in full without the tell-tale attempt to obfuscate by missing out the occasional letter. Business ranged from matters of national crisis, such as the South Sea Bubble, to apparently more marginal matters of privilege. For example, in January 1720 the Wye newsletter recounted that Earl Cowper 'and others' moved the Lords to consider the case of the duke of Dover, who claimed a seat in the Lords, only for the motion to fail. In this case,

---

[53] Atherton, ' "The Itch Grown a Disease" ', 40, 42, 55 also suggests that 'Restrictions on manuscript news were lighter than those on the printed', 40, but still maintains that 'censorship of manuscripts was real enough for much of the seventeenth century', 72.

[54] *The Grub-Street Journal* was one print newspaper that enjoyed pointing out the inadequacies of other newspapers. In March 1734, for example, it repeated the *Daily Posts'* announcement 'We hear that the Right Hon. the Earl of Scarborough will be sent Lord Lieutenant of Ireland', followed by the caustic 'I hear not'. *Grub-Street Journal*, 7 Mar. 1734.

[55] *Letter-books of John Hervey, First Earl of Bristol: With Sir Thomas Hervey's Letters during Courtship & Poems during Widowhood. 1651 to 1750* (3 vols., Wells, 1894), i, 169–70.

[56] This is true of one of the many newsletters conveyed to members of the Harley family, which reported news of numbers of men being in arms in the Highlands in September 1715 but was at pains to explain 'we can not learn there is any truth in it': *HMC Portland*, v, 519–20.

the arguments were not reported, though the numbers involved in the division were.[57] Others reported snippets of speeches, or the sense conveyed in speeches. When reporting the beginnings of the enquiry into the South Sea disaster, for example, the Wigtown newsletter reported:

> In the debates yesday in the house of Commons a Certain Gentleman Speaking In particular of some yt had lessned yr honor by associateing with Stock Jobbers Instanced yt 2 Knights of the Garter were seen to have helped [Grigsby] Accomptant to the So Sea Company and formerly a Coffee Man into his [Chariot]…[58]

In this case the name of the member was not given, and the two Garter knights were carefully anonymised. But enough information was offered both to indicate the sense of debate, and to enable identification of those involved with minimal further research. In a subsequent issue the same provider recounted a sense of Earl Stanhope's oration (making no effort to disguise the subject), offering a sense of phrasing but again without reproducing his speech in full. The effect, overall, is one of variety. Sometimes news writers appeared sufficiently confident to provide substantial detail, the names of those engaged in debate and parts of their addresses; at other times they were at pains to be far less overt. As this might alter from one issue to the next, the motivation remains slightly unclear and would benefit from further research.

Lastly, the articles in this volume offer a number of pointers for the evolving image of the two Houses and a history of styles of parliamentary reporting that is sensitive to genre and time. While some newsletters adhered to the older 'avvisi' mode of dry, factual reporting that concentrated on decisions and results without providing much linkage between them, others began to follow debates over a longer time and to trace the progress of bills through the two Houses. In both cases, a narrative was constructed that could be read not just for political enlightenment and information but, as King argues, for entertainment. In the long run this laid down a blueprint for parliamentary reporting that print media could adopt once they finally took over from newsletters towards the latter part of the 18th century. Scribal verse, in turn, left out the nitty-gritty of everyday politics and portrayed parliament as a unitary voice opposed to court and government. Some authors did not even shy away from fictionalising certain episodes. Diplomatic circulars, by contrast, claimed to be more objective but in their own way painted a range of highly stylised images of parliament. They vacillated between portraying the Lords as a stage for the basically harmonious interaction of monarch and aristocracy, and the Commons as either an arena of political in-fighting or a dangerously tumultuous place that threatened the stability and agency of the British government. Diverse as these notions of parliament may have been, they mattered not only because they forged contemporary perceptions of Britain and its political system but for the long shadow they cast. These depictions resurfaced in the 19th and 20th centuries in highly influential works by political historians like Leopold von Ranke, who in their narratives depended to a large extent on 17th and 18th-century diplomatic correspondence. It is not entirely off the mark, then, to stress the long after-life of scribal news.

[57] Bodl., MS Eng. hist. c. 1040, f. 4.
[58] Bodl., MS Eng. hist. c. 1040, f. 39.

3

The present volume is organised broadly along chronological lines. It begins in the Restoration period with an in-depth analysis by Jason Peacey of the mechanisms and methods by which the English state procured and managed information domestically as well as from abroad, in particular from the Dutch Provinces. Peacey locates his story in the wider context of shifting attitudes towards the credibility and character of manuscript news during the 17th century, tracing the changes back to the early Stuart period that is also the starting point for Edward Taylor's article on scribal verse's portrayal of parliament. Taylor investigates the wide variety of political poems circulating in manuscript that provided an outlet for commentary on parliamentary politics and rather uniformly, albeit from differing political vantage points, described the two Houses as an oppositional force against courtly corruption, at the same time highlighting and exacerbating the partisan nature of English politics.

The next three articles reverse the perspective and examine the information gleaned by foreign diplomats in London about English politics in the later 17th and early 18th centuries. Brendan Dooley and Davide Boerio concentrate on reports about the Great Fire of London (1666) sent to the Tuscan court in Florence, while Michael Schaich and Charles Littleton investigate the extensive coverage of parliament in the despatches by German and Dutch diplomatic representatives. All three articles put the second rank diplomats discussed above centre stage and flesh out the practices of information gathering and reportage that characterised the work of these early foreign correspondents.

With Rachael King's essay, the volume returns to the dissemination of scribal news within Britain primarily at the beginning of the 18th century. While King challenges facile assumptions about gender roles in the consumption of parliamentary news and draws our attention to female readers, at the same time elucidating processes of professionalisation and standardisation in the news industry, Alasdair Raffe carefully reconstructs Scottish networks of information. At the centre of his paper is Robert Wodrow, a Presbyterian minister in a small village near Glasgow, whose example throws much needed light on the circulation of handwritten political information outside the metropolitan context. The other two articles in this section, by Leith Davis and Robin Eagles, turn to the early years of George I's reign and examine moments of political crisis. Davis explores the coverage of the 1715 Jacobite rebellion, highlighting the disjointed picture of events that emerged from both newsletters and newspapers that was only reintegrated into a coherent narrative in printed histories *post festum*. Eagles in turn discusses the coverage of the high-profile impeachment processes of 1715 and 1723 in different media, and builds an argument why recipients continued to subscribe to scribal news well beyond what many historians would regard as the sell-by-date of manuscript reporting.

The last two chapters trace the fortunes of scribal news further into the 18th century. Ugo Bruschi uses diplomatic despatches by a variety of Italian diplomats and purveyors of news to delineate perceptions of the British political system by foreign observers before, during and after the Robinocracy. Markman Ellis pursues the manifold interests in scribal news by a prominent mid-18th century figure, Philip Yorke, 2nd earl of Hardwicke, who in his insatiable appetite for topical information engaged in his own exchange of letters of news with Thomas Birch and subscribed to French *nouvelles à la main*. In her Afterword Kate Loveman reflects upon some of the themes that emanate from this volume, touching upon issues of materiality, terminology and readership in particular. She also draws our attention to the difficulties in writing about this topic due to the ephemeral, and sometimes perilous, nature of the newsmonger's craft.

With this in mind, the contributions to this volume also point future research towards sources that allow us to probe deeper into the realm of scribal news. Analysing some of the major holdings such as the Newdigate newsletters and reports by the Dutch resident L'Hermitage and the Prussian Bonnet brothers, at the same time they direct our attention to lesser-known collections, among them the Wye newsletters and reports by junior diplomats from various European states. Taking note of these more hidden archives of scribal news broadens our picture of manuscript reporting of parliament and politics in the period and gives an idea of the enormous amount of material that has survived from the 17th and 18th centuries.

Several articles also experiment with methodologies that may fruitfully be applied in future studies on scribal news. Some authors pay particular attention to the materiality of manuscript and print, trying to elucidate the effects of layout and design on the recipient's consumption of news or to develop a typology of scribal news. Others adopt a comparative approach in their articles, setting print against manuscript or weighing different forms of scribal news in an attempt to throw into sharper relief the specificities of various media and the conventions governing topical reporting during the period under investigation.

In his chapter, Markman Ellis describes some of the first attempts at collecting and re-searching scribal news by two aficionados of the medium, Philip Yorke and Thomas Birch, in the middle of the 18th century. This volume continues this interest by highlighting the potential of different methodological approaches, by pointing out under-researched hold-ings and themes, and by contributing to a number of ongoing debates. It aims to stimulate further interest into a long neglected but fascinating topic.

'A Knowing but a Discrete Man': Scribal News and Information Management in Restoration England

JASON PEACEY

This article builds upon recent interest in scribal news by analysing official uses of manuscript newsletters during the Restoration, in domestic contexts as well as in relation to Anglo-Dutch affairs. It uses official correspondence and diplomatic archives to trace official attitudes to scribal news, as well as the processes devised for utilising newsletters. In part, this is a study of 'information management', and it explores the methods used for acquiring and analysing intelligence, as well as the personnel involved. But it also emphasises that officials were conscious of the shifting landscape of news across the 17th century, and of popular demand for both printed and scribal news. As such, intelligence strategies involved more than just spies and intercepts, in terms of the need to both 'consume' and produce scribal news, to develop relationships with intelligencers and journalists, and to exchange information. Mapping this complex news ecosystem enhances our appreciation of the ongoing relevance of scribal newsletters, but it also highlights some intractable challenges faced by the government, in terms of the tensions between disseminating information to friendly correspondents and imperilling some of its most valued intelligencers.

Keywords: Scribal news; newsletters; newsbooks; Restoration; intelligence; diplomacy

This article explores official attitudes to 'scribal' news in Restoration England, building upon recent interest in handwritten newsletters to examine the challenges of 'information management'. This involves a 'processual' approach, which analyses the practices associated with the acquisition and use of intelligence, but it also involves situating such strategies within the wider landscape of news culture, recognising that newsletter genres evolved over time, and appreciating that such changes were profoundly influenced by developments in print culture. In other words, analysing how the Restoration state coped with the threat of 'information overload' – a particularly acute problem in the context of international conflict – requires the perspectives of both the 'parachutist' and the 'truffle-hunter', understanding decades of experimentation regarding censorship and propaganda, and appreciating audience responses to the 'news revolution'.

In many ways, the importance of scribal texts has been recognised in a body of scholarship produced in response to claims about the print revolution. Thus, while historians have rightly devoted considerable attention to print genres to gain a better understanding of contemporary political culture, meaningful analysis of the 'communications revolution' also involves appreciating the persistence of scribal modes for circulating information and ideas.[1] Accordingly, historians and literary scholars have devoted considerable attention to a

---

[1] Richard Cust, 'News and Politics in Early Seventeenth-Century England', *P&P*, cxii (1986), 60–90.

variety of handwritten genres, from letters to manuscript 'separates'.[2] Particularly important have been studies of early modern news, as historians have complemented investigations into printed corantos, gazettes, and newsbooks with scrutiny of manuscript news, either in terms of private correspondence or commercial newsletters, or some mixture of the two. Scholars are now familiar with men like John Pory and John Chamberlain, Edmund Rossingham and Joseph Mead, and with the networks to which they belonged, as well as with the post-Restoration newsletters of Henry Muddiman, Joseph Williamson, and John Dyer.[3] Indeed, while the existence of scribal newsletters is hardly a new discovery, recent interest has heightened awareness regarding the ongoing importance of such material into the 18th century. In other words, since scribal genres were not displaced by developments in print culture, it has proved necessary to reflect upon contemporary attitudes towards newsletters and separates, and to understand the utility of such material in relation to printed genres.

Nevertheless, there remain important gaps in our understanding of both scribal culture and the early modern 'communications revolution'. Attention sometimes focuses too narrowly upon technological developments, upon the speed with which information and ideas circulated, and upon how a 'communications infrastructure' facilitated the *transmission* of information and ideas, not least in terms of the inclusivity and accessibility of texts and their social and geographical 'reach'.[4] Beyond this, analysing the textual dimensions of politics and governance has often revolved around the emergence of new modes of communication between regimes and various 'publics', in terms of propaganda, censorship and the 'public sphere', and what Daniel Bellingradt calls 'public dynamics'.[5] In the context of the

---

[2] Harold Love, *Scribal Publication in Seventeenth-Century England* (Oxford, 1993); A.F. Marotti, *Manuscript, Print and the English Renaissance Lyric* (Ithaca, NY, 1995); Peter Beal, *In Praise of Scribes: Manuscripts and their Makers in Seventeenth-Century England* (Oxford, 1998); *The Uses of Script and Print, 1300–1700*, ed. Julia Crick and Alexandra Walsham (Cambridge, 2004); Gary Schneider, *The Culture of Epistolarity: Vernacular Letters and Letter Writing in Early Modern England, 1500–1700* (Cranbury, NJ, 2005); H.R. Woudhuysen, *Sir Philip Sidney and the Circulation of Manuscripts, 1558–1640* (Oxford, 1996); Noah Millstone, *Manuscript Circulation and the Invention of Politics in Early Stuart England* (Cambridge, 2017).

[3] Ian Atherton, '"The Itch Grown a Disease": Manuscript Transmission of News in the Seventeenth Century', in *News, Newspapers and Society in Early Modern Britain*, ed. Joad Raymond (1999), 39–65; F.J. Levy, 'How Information Spread among the Gentry, 1550-1640', *Journal of British Studies*, xxi (1982), 11-34; S.A. Baron, 'The Guises of Dissemination in Early Seventeenth-Century England: News in Manuscript and Print', in *The Politics of Information in Early Modern Europe*, ed. Brendan Dooley and S.A. Baron (2001), 41–56; David Randall, 'Joseph Mead, Nouvellante: News, Sociability and Credibility in Early Stuart England', *Journal of British Studies*, xlv (2006), 293–312; H.L. Snyder, 'Newsletters in England, 1689–1715, with Special Reference to John Dyer', in *Newsletters to Newspapers: Eighteenth-Century Journalism*, ed. D.H. Bond and W. Reynolds McLeod (Morgantown, 1977), 3–19; J.G. Muddiman, *The King's Journalist, 1659–1689* (1923); J.B. Williams, 'The Newsbooks and Letters of News in the Restoration', *E.H.R*, xxiii (1908), 252–76; R.S. King, 'The Manuscript Newsletter and the Rise of the Newspaper, 1665–1715', *HLQ*, lxxix (2016), 411–37; Lindsay O'Neill, 'News and the Personal Letter, or the News Education of Theophilus Hastings, 7th Earl of Huntingdon, 1660–71', in *Connecting Centre and Locality: Political Communication in Early Modern England*, ed. C.R. Kyle and Jason Peacey (Manchester, 2020), 193–208.

[4] Wolfgang Behringer, 'Communications Revolutions: A Historiographical Concept', *German History*, xxiv (2006), 333–74; Heiko Droste, 'How Public Was the News in Early Modern Times', in *Handwritten Newspapers: An Alternative Medium During the Early Modern and Modern Periods*, ed. Heiko Droste and Kirsti Salmi-Niklander (Helsinki, 2019), 29–44.

[5] Jason Peacey, *Politicians and Pamphleteers: Propaganda During the English Civil Wars and Interregnum* (Farnham, 2004); Jason Peacey, *Print and Public Politics in the English Revolution* (Cambridge, 2013); David Zaret, *Origins of Democratic Culture: Printing, Petitions, and the Public Sphere in Early Modern England* (Princeton, 2000); Peter Lake, *Bad Queen Bess? Libels, Secret Histories, and the Politics of Publicity in the Reign of Queen Elizabeth I*

Restoration this has involved focusing upon journalists and polemicists like Henry Muddiman and Sir Roger L'Estrange, the suppression of Whig and nonconformist literature, and the lapse of licensing in 1679, as well as the circulation and finances of the *London Gazette*.[6] These are all vital issues, but they are not the only ways of exploring communications revolutions, and the aim here is to focus instead upon how information was *processed*. In the context of newsletters this means being attentive to issues of genre, in terms of the relationship between different kinds of scribal text and how these related to changes in the landscape of print news, and in terms of how texts were perceived and received. In ways that were long true of printed newsbooks, scribal newsletters have often been exploited as repositories of evidence, rather than as phenomena requiring careful scrutiny, regarding how they were produced, by whom and for what reasons.[7] In terms of how contemporaries engaged with scribal material, attention has more obviously been paid to 'sociable' authorship and the circulation of texts than to their 'reception', an issue where analysis has largely been confined to reading practices associated with print culture, and to readers' tactics for coping with 'information overload'.[8] Assessing how contemporaries responded to news has proved particularly challenging, although David Randall has highlighted the possibilities for exploring the consumption of scribal texts. Crucially, Randall highlights the need to consider not just the relationship between authority and credibility, but also how perceptions of scribal news were affected by the emergence of printed newsbooks.[9] Nevertheless, more needs to be done to supplement evidence about the government's attempts to disseminate news with evidence about how officials acquired and processed reliable intelligence, and how attitudes to scribal news were coloured by the landscape of print and by consumer demand for print and manuscript genres.

This article uses scribal news to address these neglected aspects of the early modern communications revolution, focusing upon official practices of information management, and

---

[5] *(continued)* (Oxford, 2016); Daniel Bellingradt, 'The Early Modern City as a Resonating Box: Media, Public Opinion, and the Urban Space of the Holy Roman Empire, Cologne and Hamburg ca. 1700', *Journal of Early Modern History*, xvi (2012), 201–40.

[6] Muddiman, *King's Journalist; Roger L'Estrange and the Making of Restoration Culture*, ed. Anne Dunan-Page and Beth Lynch (2008); Peter Hinds, '*The Horrid Popish Plot': Roger L'Estrange and the Circulation of Political Discourse in Late Seventeenth-Century London* (Oxford, 2009); Mark Knights, *Politics and Opinion in Crisis, 1678–1681* (Cambridge, 1994); Phyllis Handover, *A History of the London Gazette, 1665–1965* (1965); John Childs, 'The Sales of Government Gazettes During the Exclusion Crisis, 1678–81', *E.H.R.*, cii (1987), 103–6; Thomas O'Malley, 'Religion and the Newspaper Press, 1660–1685: A Study of the London Gazette', in *The Press in English Society from the Seventeenth to Nineteenth Centuries*, ed. Michael Harris and A.J. Lee (1986), 25–46.

[7] A good example involves the 'Newdigate' newsletters, named after their recipient, rather than analysed in terms of their origins: Folger, L.c.1-3950. For a key exception, see Peter Fraser, *The Intelligence of the Secretaries of State and their Monopoly of Licensed News, 1660–1688* (Cambridge, 1956).

[8] Margaret Ezell, *Social Authorship and the Advent of Print* (Baltimore, MD, 1999); David Hall, *Ways of Writing: The Practice and Politics of Text-Making in Seventeenth-Century New England* (Philadelphia, PA, 2008); S.E. Whyman, *Sociability and Power in Late-Stuart England: The Cultural World of the Verneys, 1660–1720* (Oxford, 1999); Kevin Sharpe, *Reading Revolutions: The Politics of Reading in Early Modern England* (New Haven, CT, 2000); *Reading, Society and Politics in Early Modern England*, ed. Kevin Sharpe and S.N. Zwicker (Cambridge, 2003); W.H. Sherman, *John Dee: The Politics of Reading and Writing in the English Renaissance* (Amherst, MA, 1995); W.H. Sherman, *Used Books: Marking Readers in Renaissance England* (Philadelphia, PA, 2007); Ann Blair, *Too Much to Know: Managing Scholarly Information before the Modern Age* (New Haven, CT, 2010).

[9] Joad Raymond, 'Irrational, Impractical and Unprofitable: Reading the News in Seventeenth-Century Britain', in *Reading, Society and Politics*, ed. Sharpe and Zwicker, 185–212; Randall, 'Mead'; David Randall, *Credibility in Elizabethan and Early Stuart Military News* (2008).

arguing that these were predicated upon awareness of the evolving landscape of early modern news culture, in terms of its genres and its audience. It explores the *kinds* of information that the government procured, in terms of the relationship between intelligence, scribal news and printed newsbooks, and it studies the *methods* used for acquiring and processing information. Officials grappled with the possibility that there was 'too much to know'; while a small state needed to gather information, it also ran the risk of being overwhelmed by the available evidence, and of struggling with the complex task of managing sizeable volumes of intelligence. As such, the article relates to Nicholas Popper's argument about the emergence of an 'information state': a government increasingly preoccupied by the business of collecting, interpreting and disseminating information to exercise and maintain power; and a government that needed to develop new strategies and processes.[10] The aim is to build upon the existing historiography on 'intelligence', focusing less on motivations involved – including the need to undermine Whig 'fanatics' – than the processes used, and less on the world of 'spies' and intercepts than the practices devised to collate evidence from trusted sources.[11] The article highlights contemporary concerns regarding the credibility of news sources, the relationships that developed between officials and intelligencers, and the ways in which scribal and printed news informed rather than just represented government perspectives, as well as the ways in which official attitudes acknowledged broader changes in news culture.

1

Processes of information management in Restoration England were predicated upon a culture of scribal news, rather than simply one of spies and intercepts, and appreciation of scribal news was inseparable from developments in news culture during the English revolution. This may seem perverse, given that scribal news all but disappeared during the 1640s, but this period is crucial for developing Ian Atherton's argument that newsletter genres adapted to the rise of print news, and that these changes affected public trust in the media. As such, there is scope to map – somewhat schematically – the shifting landscape of news in the period before 1660, and to suggest that, while scribal news survived the civil wars and Interregnum, it did so in radically altered ways.[12]

As scholars have shown, pre-civil war scribal news involved both sociable and commercial genres. The former involved letters by news-gatherers like Joseph Mead and John Chamberlain, whose efforts were undertaken as part of private networks, and as extensions of the kind of private correspondence that blended public news with personal affairs. Commercial news, meanwhile, involved professional reporters – 'decayed gentlemen' – like John Pory and Edmund Rossingham providing services for wealthy clients like the earl of Northumberland and Viscount Scudamore, who paid as much as £20 p.a. for weekly letters. One contemporary noted that Rossingham 'sets so high a rate upon his news 'tis scarce

[10]Nicholas Popper, 'An Information State for Elizabethan England', *Journal of Modern History*, xc (2018), 503–35.

[11]For these approaches, see Alan Marshall, *Intelligence and Espionage in the Reign of Charles II, 1660–1685* (Cambridge, 1994); Fraser, *Intelligence*.

[12]This section draws heavily upon: Atherton, ' "The Itch Grown a Disease" '; Peacey, *Politicians*; Peacey, *Print and Public Politics*.

credible to report'.[13] Of course, the distinction between commercial and sociable genres was fuzzy, since commercial newsletters could be personalised, while sociable newsletters sometimes included material drawn from commercial sources.[14] The examples of John Castle and John Beaulieu, meanwhile, suggest a third genre, involving news-gatherers working exclusively for specific patrons, rather than in an entrepreneurial fashion.[15] Whatever the differences between these subgenres of scribal news, the result was a heavily circumscribed news community.

Crucially, scribal genres raised complex issues regarding the 'authority' and 'credibility' of news. Men like Mead monitored from whence news came, to minimise the number of links in the chain of contacts separating them from a story's source, and they were careful to comment upon the reliability of their reports. However, their trustworthiness was also affected by the emergence of commercial news, and to the extent that they became reliant upon 'professional' newsmongers it became harder to trace stories back to identifiable individuals. As such, readers were prompted to read texts more intensively, and to engage in 'extensive' reading, and the use of multiple competing accounts can certainly be observed in Mead's letters, as well as in the diaries of William Whiteway and John Rous, both of whom endeavoured to cross-check – and revisit – specific stories.[16] For readers of commercial newsletters, meanwhile, credibility was premised upon the proximity of individual reporters to centres of power. Such men probably observed comings and goings in Whitehall, as well as in parliament, at first hand. Indeed, the cost of Rossingham's letters may have been regarded as a proxy for their reliability, the latter of which was certainly commented upon.[17] In other words, the 'authority' of pre-civil war scribal news was predicated upon exclusivity, and upon the proximity of those involved to credible sources of information, but not on the idea that they worked for the authorities. Apart from hints regarding Georg Weckherlin's digests of continental news, there is scant evidence that early Stuart regimes participated actively in the circulation of news.[18]

One striking effect of the print revolution was an undermining of exclusivity, as newsbooks achieved greater social and geographical reach, as sociable news-gathering was eclipsed, and as the link between commercial news and privileged information became less clear. The period after 1641 witnessed the disappearance of both sociable and commercial news writers ('Rossingham's undone and lost'), and a dramatic decline in news reporting within familial letters.[19] As even Mead began to do, it became increasingly common for correspondents to enclose printed newsbooks as a substitute for personal commentary, not least amid fears that letters might be intercepted. Rossingham's trade was 'engrossed' by a

[13] Bodl., MS Tanner 65, f. 78; BL, M390 (Alnwick Castle, U.I.5). See Baron, 'Guises of Dissemination', 48; Randall, 'Mead', 301. For Rossingham newsletters, see Henry E. Huntington Library, San Marino [hereafter cited as HL], HA 9597-8; Staffordshire RO, D603/K/2/1; BL, Add. MS 11045; TNA, C 115/106/8426-54; Bodl., MS Carte 77, ff. 346–428. For Pory, see TNA, C 115/106/8317-8425; William Stevens Powell, *John Pory, 1572–1636* (Chapel Hill, 1977).

[14] For Mead's use of Rossingham, see Northamptonshire RO, IC210.

[15] For Castle, see HL, EL7807-7863; BL, Add. MS 72275. For Beaulieu, see BL, Add. MS 7010.

[16] Randall, 'Mead'; *William Whiteway of Dorchester: His Diary, 1618 to 1635* (Dorset Record Society, 12, 1991); *Diary of John Rous*, ed. M.A.E. Green (Camden Society, 1856).

[17] Bodl., MS Tanner 65, f. 78.

[18] For Weckherlin, see Atherton, '"The Itch Grown a Disease"', 41–2; TNA, C 115/106/8455-83.

[19] *The Great Assizes Holden in Parnassus* (1645), 2.

new breed of journalist, initially in the form of scribal texts ('Diurnall occurrences') and then in the form of printed newsbooks. The new breed was epitomised not just by Marchamont Nedham, John Berkenhead, and Henry Walker, but also by John Dillingham and Daniel Border, who previously wrote newsletters for specific patrons.[20]

However, while such developments clearly influenced the perceived authority of news, contemporaries adapted to, rather than rejected, printed news. Mead was troubled by the credibility of corantos, but did not ignore them; Pory described them as 'toys', but shared an address with Nathaniel Butter, one of the genre's pioneers.[21] While some contemporaries consumed newsbooks less than seriously – listing them among 'idle expenses', and calling them 'factious' or 'frivolous' – other readers grappled with their credibility.[22] Henry Oxinden admitted that 'I can write you no news but what the diurnalls have', and that 'for news I know none but what is in this diurnall'. This did not imply trust, and it is noticeable how frequently contemporaries used phrases like 'you *see* by the London print', 'I *see* by the Gazette', and 'you will *find* in the London prints'. This was distancing language, which suggests that readers were critical and sceptical but not necessarily dismissive, and contemporaries clearly reflected upon what they read: '*if* the print say true', '*if* one may guess by the books', and 'it *seems* by the books'. Some referred to 'the hard digestion of the prints', picked holes in particular reports, and wondered about what was not being reported. Some argued that newspapers were 'empty', that old news was being recycled, and that 'the omissions are more observable than the relations'. Scepticism sometimes morphed into cynicism, as evidence emerged about journalists whose work reflected the agendas of patrons, factions and the government, reaching a peak with Marchamont Nedham in the 1650s. One commentator claimed that 'the news… is very uncertain, being represented through *Politicus* his spectacles', and it was said that Nedham 'hath his orders', and that Cromwellian newspapers would 'hardly be worth reading nor the money for postage'.[23]

Nevertheless, doubts about the credibility of print journalism fostered new practices – more intensive and extensive reading – rather than despair.[24] Individuals can be observed acquiring two or more newspapers each week, reading across the political divide, and even privileging perspectives other than their own, or seeking a blend of serious and racy titles, and works that were 'mischievous'. Readers can also be observed comparing different accounts of the same event, and gathering further evidence with which to revisit, amend and correct texts with annotations and comments. Newsbooks could thus be read even though their accounts were considered questionable, and contemporaries were certainly capable of distinguishing between evidence and interpretations. In 1647, Sir Arthur Hopton explained that 'for matters of fact you will have it in the *Diurnall*, which is the best intelligencer', even

---

[20] For 'Diurnall occurrences' (1640–1), see Durham UL, Mickleton and Spearman MS 30. For Border, see BL, Add. MS 70122, unfol. For Dillingham, see Warwickshire RO, CR 1886, vol. 1, unfol.; E.S. Cope, *The Life of a Public Man: Edward, First Baron Montagu of Boughton, 1562–1644* (Philadelphia, PA, 1981), 157–8, 168–9, 184–5, 197. For fears that the circulation of newsletters would result in punishment, see BL, Add. MS 78303, f. 45.

[21] Randall, 'Mead', 302, 305–7; Levy, 'Information', 23.

[22] Longleat House, Thynne Papers 66, f. 77; BL, Add. MS 78220, f. 14.

[23] *The Oxinden and Peyton Letters, 1642–1670*, ed. Dorothy Gardiner (1937), 96; BL, Add. MS 28002, f. 174; BL, Add. MS 78194, f. 99; BL, Add. MS 78195, ff. 75, 103, 110; BL, Eg. MS 2535, ff. 88, 118, 214, 284v, 301, 478; BL, Eg. MS 2534, f. 236; Bodl., MS Clarendon 67, f. 246v.

[24] Randall, 'Mead', 307.

though it was hard to make 'a judgment upon matter of fact'.[25] Newsbooks, in other words, were problematic, but better than nothing, and they might even be considered useful, providing an interpretative tool, and a guide to 'the variety of opinions'. Edward Hyde, earl of Clarendon, professed to 'learn much by them' because they 'prove somewhat as they do not think of'. However, any sense that they might be useful for understanding popular politics, on the basis that they 'might take with the people of ordinary capacity', was qualified by concerns that ordinary readers might be 'poisoned', 'dazzled' and 'captivated', and that newsbooks would not be handled with the requisite care. For political elites, the popular appetite for printed news provided the impetus for producing an 'antidote' to the 'poison' promulgated by political opponents.[26]

In other words, while pre-civil war scribal news was predicated upon exclusivity and proximity to reliable sources, printed news fostered accessibility, raised questions about credibility, and provoked politicians to wonder whether audiences would be sceptical or gullible. This conjuncture helps to explain increasingly proactive approaches to news management, and it also provides the context for a resurgence in scribal journalism, and a remodelling of manuscript newsletters. Outside elite royalist circles, this first became evident during the republic, in terms of the revival of sociable newsletters of the kind provided by agents and employees in London, as well as attempts to create new subscription services.[27] Nedham at least contemplated quitting newsbooks to 'imprison his pen within the narrow confines of private correspondence', having apparently 'settled with a considerable number of honour and quality' who would pay £10 p.a. Another royalist – styled 'Pragmaticus' after a leading newsbook – offered to write 'pretty correspondence' for 18*d.* per letter, boasting that recipients would no longer need to purchase 'corrantos, gazettes… [and] mercuries… from noddy-land'.[28] Such initiatives suggested that readers would willingly pay a premium for credible and privileged information, but while this was acknowledged by Charles II's government, officials were reluctant to allow a return to Rossingham's world. One adviser argued that pre-civil war scribal news 'did as much hurt' as printed news, 'if not more', because journalists could be 'bolder' in script than 'they durst in print'. Banning older kinds of scribal news would thus 'cool the nation'.[29] At the same time, it was no longer deemed feasible to suppress printed newsbooks, and L'Estrange famously responded to concerns that print made ordinary subjects into 'statesmen' by arguing that 'tis the press that has made 'em mad, and the press that must set 'em right again'.[30]

As such, the Restoration regime accepted the demand for both newsbooks and scribal newsletters, and sought to achieve a blend of exclusivity, accessibility and political control. This involved combining strict censorship with the publication of official news for a

[25] *Sydney Papers, Consisting of a Journal of the Earl of Leicester, and Original Letters by Algernon Sidney*, ed. R.W. Blencowe (1825), 68; BL, Add. MS 78191, f. 133.

[26] BL, Add. MS 78198, f. 21; Bodl., MS Clarendon 29, f. 183; BL, Eg. MS 2535, f. 557; Edward, Earl of Clarendon, *The History of the Rebellion*, ed. W. Dunn Macray (6 vols, Oxford, 1888), ii, 64, 69, 71, 74, 84, 134, 226, 309, 376, 389, 394, 405, 424.

[27] Staffordshire RO, D593/P/8/2/2. See Jason Peacey, 'Marchamont Nedham and the Lawrans Letters', *Bodleian Library Record*, xvii (2000), 24–35.

[28] *Oxinden and Peyton Letters*, ed. Gardiner, 149; BL, Add. MS 78298, f. 41v.

[29] *Ideology and Politics on the Eve of the Restoration: Newcastle's Advice to Charles II*, ed. T.P. Slaughter (Philadelphia, PA, 1984), 56.

[30] *The Observator*, 13 Apr. 1681, p. 1.

general audience, and officials like George Downing were pleased that the *London Gazette* 'takes infinitely, particularly because of its being so portable, which makes it every man's money'.[31] However, the government also experimented with a new kind of subscription newsletter, produced officially by the editor of the *Gazette*, Henry Muddiman, such that the distinction between printed and scribal news became more hazy than ever.[32] Muddiman quickly became a controversial figure, and his service was supplemented by another official newsletter, from the office of Joseph Williamson. In both cases, however, the strategy involved appealing to public demand for credible sources of information, of a kind that was not made available in print, not least parliamentary news. News from Westminster had certainly been supplied by Rossingham, and it remained a feature of scribal news after 1660.[33] Moreover, while some officials became concerned when readers grew frustrated by the *Gazette* – because it was 'wanting domestic intelligence', and because 'they have nothing in them as to the proceedings of Parliament' – they also recognised that many readers acquired both newsletters and newsbooks.[34]

The Restoration thus witnessed a conscious attempt to synthesise previous experiments, based upon a symbiotic relationship between printed and scribal genres. It is noteworthy, therefore, that the *Gazette* and official newsletters both drew upon printed sources of news, not least European newsbooks.[35] More importantly, the newsletter was not only meant to be authoritative, but also to be less exclusive than its predecessors. Individual newsletters may have sold for as little as 6*d.*, and annual subscriptions appear to have cost between £1 10s. and £7 10s.; while Rossingham had perhaps 25 customers, the circulation of Muddiman's newsletter was as high as 150. The readership was also more mixed, including clerics, booksellers, mayors and town clerks, as well as postmasters and postmistresses. Eventually newsletters may have been distributed even more widely, and made available in coffeehouses, even if this made Williamson rather nervous.[36] Moreover, while the readership of Williamson's newsletter may have been slightly more limited, it was no less socially diverse. It included noblemen (and noblewomen) as well as senior clerics and officials, but it also included the mayors of Bristol, Preston and York, and customs officials and postmasters from across the country, and Williamson's correspondence with men like James Hickes indicates that many such recipients also received copies of the *Gazette*, and that they paid as little as £2 for weekly intelligence.[37]

The final point to note about the informational landscape with which officials grappled is that it eventually became more diverse, in terms of the challenge of

---

[31] *CSP Dom 1670*, p. 704.

[32] For Muddiman newsletters, see HL, HA 9600-9631. For overlaps see *CSP Dom 1680–1*, pp. 375, 477.

[33] Baron, 'Guises of Dissemination', 53–4; *CSP Dom 1670*, p. 88; Fraser, *Intelligence*, 54; Knights, *Politics and Opinion*, 175. Dyer's parliamentary reporting sometimes landed him in trouble. See Snyder, 'Newsletters', 5. Francis Benson, one of the clerks who worked with Williamson, sent scribal newsletters to Leoline Jenkins during the Treaty of Nijmegen (1676–9): HL, HM 30314-15.

[34] *CSP Dom 1666–7*, pp. 16, 282; *CSP Dom 1667–8*, p. 102; TNA, SP 29/225, f. 211. Other readers complained when gazettes were late and out of date: *CSP Dom 1666–7*, pp. 20, 35–6; *CSP Dom 1667*, p. 476.

[35] *CSP Dom 1670*, p. 392; *CSP Dom 1679–80*, p. 569; *CSP Dom 1680–1*, pp. 447, 457, 460, 526; *CSP Dom 1682*, p. 193. See Fraser, *Intelligence*, 52; King, 'Manuscript Newsletter', 415.

[36] *CSP Dom 1666–7*, pp. 167, 209, 386; TNA, SP 29/183, f. 125; *CSP Dom 1670*, p. 188; TNA, SP 29/275, ff. 47–8; *CSP Dom 1672–3*, p. 585; *CSP Dom 1676–7*, p. 368; Atherton, '"The Itch Grown a Disease"', 52–4, 58.

[37] *CSP Dom 1667*, pp. 311, 499; TNA, SP 29/218, ff. 128–234; Fraser, *Intelligence*, 140–4; *CSP Dom 1666–7*, p. 459; TNA, SP 29/188, f. 214.

maintaining press censorship, and in terms of an increasingly vibrant scribal culture. This partly involved the proliferation of unofficial commercial newsletters, which provided outlets for Whig perspectives, and which also became cheaper and less easy to distinguish from printed newsbooks. However, it also involved fuzzy boundaries between other kinds of newsletters, on a spectrum from ambassadorial reports to unsolicited accounts by informers, and including letters that were more or less sociable, formal and regular. The key conclusion for the authorities was that, whether or not news was susceptible to governmental control, official policies and processes needed to acknowledge the appetite for both scribal and printed news, and to capitalise upon the possibilities offered by newsletter genres.[38]

2

It is this shifting landscape of scribal and printed news that provides the context for analysing government processes for managing flows of information. Like ordinary readers, government officials grappled with the task of securing reliable supplies of credible information, and in both domestic and European contexts this involved not just spies, informers and intercepts, but also scribal and printed news.

First, the intelligence-gathering machinery of men like Joseph Williamson involved a serious engagement with printed news, as well as a dependence on the appetite for scribal newsletters. Officials went to considerable lengths to secure reliable supplies of foreign gazettes, and in doing so they built upon changing attitudes towards such material within diplomatic and official circles. Over time, newsbooks ceased to be treated as mere 'entertainment', and greater effort was devoted to the business of obtaining, circulating and discussing a diverse range of titles. Such practices are evident not just from official correspondence but also from financial accounts, which record that after 1660 considerable sums were spent upon 'gazettes... from all parts'. Williamson certainly amassed a large library of newsbooks, and his own accounts for 1660–2 reveal an outlay of over £16 on such material.[39] As has occasionally been noted, official accommodation of the news landscape also involved capitalising upon the audience for newsletters in order to secure supplies of domestic intelligence.[40] Government newsletters were not only sold by subscription, but also traded for local intelligence, which probably explains the eagerness with which postmasters and customs officials were added to the list of Williamson's correspondents. One such recipient was Captain Silas Taylor, storekeeper at Harwich, who frequently forwarded information gleaned from Dutch ships, as well as copies of Dutch gazettes, and who clearly

---

[38] For the variety of newsletters during the Exclusion Crisis, see Knights, *Politics and Opinion*, 175. During the Exclusion Crisis, and towards the end of the 17th century, the story of government-backed newsletters is more difficult to reconstruct: Knights, *Politics and Opinion*, 176. For examples, see HL, HA 9622-57 (1691–2). Eventually, there emerged hybrid genres, in which scribal news was appended to copies of printed newspapers, and in which printed newsbooks were given the appearance of scribal newsletters. See King, 'Manuscript Newsletter'; Atherton, '"The Itch Grown a Disease"', 55. Dyer's newsletter cost perhaps £4 p.a.: Snyder, 'Newsletters', 8.

[39] TNA, SP 84/86, ff. 107–8; SP 84/216, f. 162; BL, Eg. MS 2543, ff. 115–16; Fraser, *Intelligence*, 138. See Jason Peacey, '"My Friend the Gazetier": Diplomacy and News in Seventeenth-Century Europe', in *News Networks in Early Modern Europe*, ed. Joad Raymond and Noah Moxham (Leiden, 2016), 420–42.

[40] Atherton, '"The Itch Grown a Disease"', 54; Fraser, *Intelligence*, 30, 33, 140.

expected to receive news in return.[41] Another was Daniel Fleming, a prominent gentry figure in Westmorland, who had a close personal relationship with Williamson, but who also provides evidence about the appetite for official newsletters, which he was anxious to acquire, and which he preserved in large quantities. Like Taylor, Fleming reciprocated with well-received intelligence reports, and although he sent money to Williamson's office, this merely involved a voluntary 'reward' – of 50s. p.a. – to the clerks, rather than payment for the letters themselves.[42] For Williamson, the process of gathering credible intelligence involved transactional relationships grounded in the popular appetite for news.

Williamson's reliance upon the contemporary news ecosystem – with its symbiosis of print and scribal genres – is also apparent in the acquisition of intelligence from the Dutch Republic. Here, the logic was explained by the English ambassador Sir William Temple, who was frustrated to discover – 'by the gazettes' – that the man who 'furnishes… intelligence from hence is but at random', but who was also determined that 'the constant occurrents should come from any hand than mine'. Since supplies of intelligence might be erratic, and his own reports needed to concentrate upon high-level diplomacy, it made sense to hire 'pensioners' to secure regular supplies of scribal news.[43] The process of finding a suitable intelligencer may not have been easy. While reference was made in October 1668 to someone who offered to furnish news 'every Tuesday', Temple subsequently complained about being 'much out of heart with my correspondent here', adding that he was endeavouring to 'search after another'. Another report referred to 'a new offer made me of an intelligencer here of the same kind with what I had at first, which I have promised to try next week and shall treat accordingly as I find, for the last I discarded wholly some time since'. Eventually, in January 1670, he reported to Williamson that, 'after much search and industry', he had 'found… a correspondent here who will I hope abundantly supply the loss I had of our old man soon after my arrival here'. Although Temple professed to 'know nothing of the person myself, being helped to him by a third hand', he 'judged him by this his last week's paper', and concluded that he was 'not only a knowing but a discrete man'. The following week, William Blathwayt (Temple's secretary) reported that he had received 'the first fruits of our new intelligencer, which I shall always continue to do though but once a week', and Temple described the weekly 'paper of intelligence' as being 'so exact that I can add little to it'.[44] Recruiting intelligencers in this way did mean that supplies of news were imperilled when ambassadors returned to England, and one reason for keeping Blathwayt in The Hague in July 1671 was that the 'ordinary intelligence… failed since Sir William Temple's revocation'. Blathwayt explained that, unless Temple could persuade his intelligencer to resume work, new orders would be needed 'for the procuring some new intelligence', and subsequent ambassadors evidently needed to find their own way. In 1680, for example, Henry Sidney (later earl of Romney) reported that 'there is a man here that makes it his business to furnish everybody with news, and sometimes he does it very

---

[41] Fraser, *Intelligence*, 143; *CSP Dom 1668–9*, p. 588; *CSP Dom 1671–2*, p. 536; *CSP Dom 1672*, p. 113; *CSP Dom 1672–3*, p. 35; *CSP Dom 1675–6*, pp. 243–4, 255, 260, 282, 357; *CSP Dom 1676–7*, p. 238.

[42] HMC, *Le Fleming*, 35–168.

[43] TNA, SP 84/185, f. 51.

[44] TNA, SP 84/184, f. 50; SP 84/185, ff. 51, 78, 210, 211; SP 84/186, f. 62v.

well'.[45] Nevertheless, it is striking that ambassadors went to such lengths to acquire regular intelligence.

In dealing with 'intelligencers', moreover, English officials tapped into a community of established newsletter writers, some of whom also edited printed gazettes.[46] When he arrived in The Hague in 1681, the envoy Thomas Plott not only referred to one intelligencer – who quickly became 'my friend' – as someone who had been 'pensionary' to Henry Sidney, but also described him as the French 'gazetteer', who supplied both printed and scribal news. Plott also referred to having 'another intelligencer here who is paid for it, that gives me twice a week what comes to his hands, whose original papers and likewise those of the French gazetier [sic] I shall hereafter send you'. Of course, using established journalists did not solve every problem. Plott was acutely aware of the problems involved in securing steady supplies, adding that, 'when I return for England I shall settle a correspondence between you and them, that you may have a continuance of their news'.[47] Others were conscious that newsmen might prove unreliable. In May 1682, Thomas Chudleigh apologised to Lord Conway 'that after all my endeavours and the hopes I had of settling a private correspondence, I find myself at last disappointed by the person I had made account of for it'. Nevertheless, he promised to 'endeavour some other way to bring it about, and your lordship may be assured that if I cannot do it to good purpose, at leastwise His Majesty's money shall be saved, in the well disposing whereof I shall be more careful than I would be of my own'.[48]

Such evidence reveals the effort involved in securing reliable supplies of credible intelligence, and the frequency with which officials paid for a newsletter service. Here too a revealing picture emerges about the reliance upon contemporary news culture. In July 1671, when Blathwayt referred to 'the intelligence which I have hitherto transmitted you from these parts', he also explained the need for 'procuring an allowance for some other which may be equivalent with the former'. The accounts of George Downing for 1671/2 indicate that his 'extraordinary charges for letters, expresses and intelligence at the Hague' came to 168 guilders, while Temple's accounts between May 1675 and May 1676 included £364 for 'intelligence and expresses'.[49] Such evidence also confirms that the government relied upon professional newsmen. Between June and December 1682, Chudleigh's 'extraordinary' disbursements included 50 guilders to a Leiden man for the *gazette a la main*, or scribal newsletter. In November 1668, Temple explained to Williamson that 'I continue to send you the papers which come weekly to my hands, both here and from France, as I receive likewise your weekly accounts', and he asked to know 'whether you desire these French *gazettes a la main*, which cost £15 a year'.[50]

In other words, while the government and its agents sought to secure steady supplies of reliable intelligence, the relationships involved were transactional, and officials were

[45] TNA, SP 84/187, f. 84; SP 84/216, f. 54.

[46] For Muddiman's use of informers for his newsletters, see *CSP Dom 1665–6*, p. 15.

[47] *The Dispatches of Thomas Plott (1681–1682), and Thomas Chudleigh (1682–1685), English Envoys at the Hague*, ed. F.A. Middlebush (The Hague, 1926), 1.

[48] BL, Add. MS 37980, f. 119.

[49] TNA, SP 84/187, f. 89; SP 84/188, f. 148; SP 84/201, f. 222. L'Estrange paid spies £500: *CSP Dom 1665–6*, p. 17.

[50] BL, Add. MS 37980, f. 269; TNA, SP 84/184, f. 77.

somewhat reliant upon prominent figures from the world of commercial news, whose work involved scribal news services or printed gazettes, or both. For men like Williamson intelligence-gathering mirrored the structures of news production with which they were involved in England.

In identifying their suppliers little precise evidence survives, and it also seems likely that intelligence networks extended far beyond such trusted specialists. More work is needed to analyse the mass of loose and mostly unsigned newsletters in the State Papers, which perhaps involved unsolicited information from numerous correspondents.[51] Likewise, it is difficult to establish the nature of Williamson's relationship with Thomas Gwynne, who offered to supply news in 1668, or indeed with Joseph Bampfield, many of whose intelligence letters survive from 1663 onwards, but who was evidently treated with a degree of suspicion.[52] It would be naïve to discount the possibility that Williamson's intelligence network was large and complex, and that different suppliers raised different challenges in terms of their credibility and trustworthiness.

Nevertheless, it seems reasonable to conclude that Williamson became somewhat reliant upon a limited number of intelligencers, one of whom – Abraham Casteleyn – reinforces the link between intelligence, scribal news and printed gazettes. Casteleyn is well known as the pre-eminent Dutch journalist of the age, but his business model also involved scribal newsletters, based upon his ability to provide intelligence beyond what appeared in the *Haarlem Courant*. It was by virtue of being unusually well informed that Casteleyn became an intelligencer for the English government, and his letters occupy a prominent place within Williamson's extensive collection of Dutch newsletters. A volume covering 1667–8, for example, contains no fewer than 119 of Casteleyn's letters. Although these were unsigned, they were written in a distinctive hand and invariably endorsed as having been sent from Haarlem. Occasionally, it was explicitly noted that they came from Casteleyn.[53] What set Casteleyn apart was that his letters, while often brief, contained high-grade intelligence and commentary. He provided evidence about debates and resolutions within the States General, not least regarding diplomatic manoeuvres and disputes between the provinces, and he conveyed the mood of 'most men' within the Dutch political elite, as well as prevailing sentiments regarding the English king and his ambassadors, not to mention expectations about how they would behave. All of this was based upon 'talk' within elite political circles, to which Casteleyn clearly had privileged access.[54] Naturally Casteleyn was not the only person who could provide such intelligence, and in 1672 a deal was struck with Heinrich Hildebrand – Dutch agent of the duke of Saxony – for 'punctual advice of all affairs'. Here, explicit reference was made to the fact that Williamson did not need 'the common news

---

[51]TNA, SP 101. The correspondence that is preserved is particularly dense for certain periods, and successive boxes cover 1594–1622, 1623–6, 1627–65, Jan. to Apr. 1666, and May to July 1666, after which there are normally 1–2 boxes per year until the late 1680s.

[52]TNA, SP 84/184, f. 3; SP 84/167, ff. 105–290.

[53]TNA, SP 101/51; SP 101/54. See Jason Peacey, 'Managing Dutch Advices: Abraham Casteleyn and the English Government, 1660–1681', *Media History*, xxii (2016), 421–37. References were also made to sending copies of the *Haarlem Courant*: SP 101/51: Casteleyn to Williamson, 9/19 Aug. 1667. Casteleyn appeared in Williamson's address book, but stopped sending letters during the third Anglo-Dutch war: TNA, SP 9/32, ff. 211–30; See Fraser, *Intelligence*, 44, 102–3; SP 101/55: 22 Mar., 26 Mar., 2 Apr., 30 Apr. 1673. Other archives also reveal that similar newsletters were sent to men like William Blathwayt, at least during 1669: BL, RP 3189.

[54]TNA, SP 101/51, unfol. See Fraser, *Intelligence*, 5, 44–6, 91–2. Later, Casteleyn helped Williamson by providing his letters in French rather than the more difficult Dutch.

of the gazettes', but 'what secretly is consulted and concluded in the States General'.[55] Nevertheless, it is revealing that the best documented of Williamson's relationships with his intelligencers involved a professional newsman.

3

What also emerges from Williamson's archive, and from his correspondence with Casteleyn, are the processes devised for analysing the intelligence that poured in from across Britain and the Continent. These can be explored by re-evaluating contemporary evidence about the government's control of the Post Office and its production of propaganda, and by focusing less upon the urge to 'intercept' the mail and manipulate the public sphere than upon the practices associated with information management.

Official reading practices can be observed in different ways and in relation to different kinds of information. Sometimes this involved European newsbooks. These might be considered irrelevant to this discussion, not least because official analysis was often predicated upon concerns about how English news was reported on the Continent, and about such gazettes being read in England. Nevertheless, surviving evidence is revealing, because it provides an unusual indication of the care with which news could be read, and because of the central role played by officials like Hickes and Sir Philip Frowde.[56] It was such men who made extracts from the Rotterdam gazette in July 1667, which provided a nonconformist and old Cromwellian perspective on English affairs, and an unflattering account of a political situation that was 'growing every day worse and worse'.[57] It was careful reading of other newsbooks that indicated how far Muddiman not only drew upon European newspapers and 'Dutch letters', but also did so by exchanging information. More than once in the early 1660s, Downing noted that the Haarlem gazette repeated 'word for word' the Whitehall newsletters, and in 1666 Hickes identified passages in Casteleyn's newsbook 'that could never have come there if not from Mr Muddiman'. Hickes's fear was that Muddiman had set up a private and unauthorised channel of communication with a foreign journalist. This not only sheds further light upon the tensions between Williamson and Muddiman, but also upon the centrality of Casteleyn to English news culture, and the complex interdependence of different kinds of news, and of newsletters that were read and produced by English officials.[58]

Another tangential issue that sheds valuable light upon information management involves official attempts to supply information to the *London Gazette*. Here, evidence can be used less to think about the propaganda impulse, and about print, than about the processes by which intelligence was analysed, not least through documents and notes annotated to

---

[55] Fraser, *Intelligence*, 103–4.

[56] *CSP Dom 1667*, p. 16. This concern with European publics led to tactics for intervening in the continental public sphere: Peacey, 'My Friend the Gazetier'.

[57] *CSP Dom 1667*, pp. 294, 312; TNA, SP 29/209, f. 126.

[58] *CSP Dom 1665–6*, p. 246; TNA, SP 29/148, ff. 8; Fraser, *Intelligence*, 44. This was used as part of an unsuccessful attempt to dismiss Muddiman. For links between the translator of the *London Gazette*, Monsieur Morainville, and the editor of the *Amsterdam gazette*, see *CSP Dom 1671–2*, 269.

indicate that they were destined 'for the Gazette'.[59] These involved suggestions, or indeed instructions, about stories that might usefully be covered. Whether these came from the Privy Council, from individual courtiers or from correspondents across the country they were based on the idea that the intelligence system was collaborative, and that Williamson was responsive to those who read the *Gazette* and who supplied him with news. They also reveal awareness that Williamson was helped to finalise the text of the *Gazette*.[60] On one occasion Williamson was sent papers about Anglo-Dutch issues that were thought suitable for publication because they would 'enflame all England against the Dutch'.[61] More importantly, such documents reveal the processes involved in selecting and analysing intelligence, for reasons beyond propaganda. These processes not only involved the much-discussed interception of letters at the Post Office, but also correspondence from established contacts, perhaps including those with whom intelligence was traded for copies of the *Gazette* and official newsletters.[62] It is certainly possible to observe how letters were copied by Robert Yard (under-secretary of state) or edited by Williamson before being directed to the *Gazette*, and how intelligence directed to Hickes was extracted for publication. In the spring of 1669, for example, it is possible to compare a series of letters that Hickes received from ports on the south coast with the edited highlights that were prepared for officials. Only one extract – news from Lyme Regis dated 3 April – appeared in print, which perhaps suggests that the synopsis was primarily intended for the secretary of state, rather than for the editor of the *Gazette*.[63]

With European letters, meanwhile, Frowde, Hickes, and Yard, as well as Robert Francis, were employed in 'extracting, copying, translating… all matters of correspondence'. This too involved the *Gazette*, but the process was more complicated, and in 1669 Williamson insisted that Francis should 'watch the letters when they come in, and as well to extract them, as to frame out of them, what is fit for the gazette'. This suggests that the extracts were made for Williamson's use, rather than simply for the *Gazette*, and that they were forwarded to Whitehall as well as to the newsbook.[64] Beyond this, Williamson also received bundles of letters, presumably after they had been extracted, and although this was occasionally done so that he could 'view and judge the fitness of communicating some part of the same', it also seems clear that this process was used to inform official thinking.[65] What can be observed is a process in which intelligence, from various kinds of scribal news, was fed to, and analysed by, Williamson and his clerks. This certainly included Temple's ambassadorial reports, which were systematically annotated with marginalia, and occasionally

---

[59] *CSP Dom 1666–7*, p. 16; *CSP Dom 1672*, pp. 270, 370; TNA, SP 29/311, f. 319; SP 29/313, f. 30; *CSP Dom 1678*, p. 575; TNA, SP 29/366, f. 333.

[60] *CSP Dom 1666–7*, p. 120; *CSP Dom 1673*, p. 312; *CSP Dom 1673–5*, p. 304. For other correspondence, see *CSP Dom 1666–7*, pp. 125, 160, 359; *CSP Dom 1667*, pp. 89, 427. For Williamson, see *CSP Dom 1671*, p. 318.

[61] *CSP Dom 1671–2*, p. 388; TNA, SP 29/306, f. 135.

[62] Fraser, *Intelligence*, 33, 59.

[63] *CSP Dom 1672*, p. 84; TNA, SP 29/310, f. 12a; *CSP Dom 1673*, p. 338. For the synopsis of south coast news, see TNA, SP 29/258, f. 160. For the original letter, see *CSP Dom 1668–9*, pp. 254–65. For the printed extract, see *The London Gazette*, 5–8 Apr. 1669, 354.

[64] *CSP Dom 1668–9*, pp. 452, 494, 544; *CSP Dom 1671*, p. 314; TNA, SP 29/264, f. 83; SP 29/290, f. 247; *CSP Dom 1660–85*, p. 403; TNA, SP 29/441, ff. 305–6; Fraser, *Intelligence*, 59.

[65] *CSP Dom 1668–9*, p. 474; *CSP Dom 1665–6*, p. 246; TNA, SP 29/148, f. 8.

extracted.[66] That Williamson was keen to utilise such material seems clear. His correspondence demonstrates an acute sense of the need for such material to be processed rapidly, even as he recognised the need for caution. Henry Oldenburg once described how he raced to make extracts from foreign letters, not least for the *Gazette*, and Williamson's eagerness to receive the latest supplies was also driven in part by his determination to get supplies to his news editors. More generally, however, Williamson's associates were habitually poised to act as soon as letters arrived, forwarding letters 'immediately… by an express', generally on a daily basis.[67] At the same time, the decision to delay the publication of certain stories indicates that attempts were occasionally made to reconcile different versions of events from different sources.[68]

Other evidence indicates how Williamson analysed the news he received, by preparing an index of his Dutch papers, and by compiling notebooks on Dutch affairs. The latter offer intriguing insights into his methods, in terms of his sources and the speed with which he worked. He referred to 'yesterday's letters from Holland' and 'letters just now arrived', as well as to 'Holland letters of Friday last arrived this morning', and 'Dutch letters arrived this morning', not to mention domestic suppliers like Silas Taylor. It also seems clear that he and Muddiman both collected information from Dutch 'letters' as well as from the *Haarlem Courant*, and that with Dutch correspondence both men worked from the same source, presumably the extracts prepared by Williamson's team.[69] This is evident from the occasions when Muddiman's newsletters and Williamson's notebooks contained precisely the same reports in exactly the same words. Both men cited the report that 'De Witt talks big, tells the people all our offers are but arts and tricks, and so prepares vigorously for the war', and both men added that De Witt had 'lost a great point in the business of the treaty, the provinces having declared they will each send one or two apiece as their plenipotentiaries to Breda'. Both men also noted that 'Zeeland and Gelderland continue extremely zealous for the peace, and Zeeland desires much that our ambassadors may in their way to Breda pass by Middleburg'.[70] Similarly, both men picked up the story that 'De Witt is now become a great Spaniard, and having occasion in the assembly to speak of the great design France discovers to have upon Flanders, he replied they should now see who was furthest from being a Frenchman, he or they that accused him all along to be so'.[71] Finally, both men noted the letter from May 1667 in which it was claimed that 'De Witt's faction hath prevailed upon false suggestions that we and France understand one another and will force them to a disadvantageous peace at Breda'. According to this report, De Witt had been 'tampering with the Prince of Orange's friends to have him disown forever

---

[66] TNA, SP 84/196, ff. 219–72; SP 84/197, ff. 1–131; SP 84/198, ff. 5–203.

[67] *CSP Dom 1672–3*, p. 569; TNA, SP 29/333, f. 182; *CSP Dom 1666–7*, p. 193; *CSP Dom 1668–9*, p. 488; *CSP Dom 1671*, p. 314; TNA, SP 29/290, f. 247.

[68] *CSP Dom 1672–3*, p. 530.

[69] TNA, SP 9/164; SP 29/231, ff. 4, 6v, 7v–8v, 10–11, 16, 17v–18, 20v, 21v–22, 23v–24v, 26, 31v, 33, 39, 43v, 45, 46v, 51, 56–9, 63–4, 67, 82v; SP 29/319a. Muddiman sometimes referred to the *Haarlem Courant*, but sometimes to 'the Dutch print', and he also referred to Dutch letters, and like Williamson he had access to high-grade intelligence. See HL, HA 9611; Longleat House, Thynne Papers 41, ff. 10, 23, 28, 34v, 43, 45, 75, 156v, 161, 440. There is scope to work on his Longleat notebook, which contains the notes from which he selected material for the newsletter: Knights, *Politics and Opinion*, 175–6; HMC, *Third Report*, 184.

[70] Longleat House, Thynne Papers 41, ff. 52v, 55, 56; TNA, SP 29/231, ff. 7v, 10–11.

[71] Longleat House, Thynne Papers 41, ff. 63; TNA, SP 29/231, f. 17v.

all his pretensions or claims to the office of stadtholder or governor of the province of Holland, and upon this condition De Witt offers to make him admiral and general at land immediately'. Both men also noted the suggestion that 'this trick will not take'.[72] Although it is possible that Williamson was taking notes from Muddiman's newsletters – and attempts were certainly made to monitor the latter's reports – a more likely explanation is that both men were drawing their intelligence from the same pool of translated and extracted Dutch newsletters.[73]

It also seems clear that this process involved correspondence intended for Williamson, rather than intercepts. When Yard sent Williamson letters from the Post Office in May 1673, he explained the absence of material from the 'French packet' by noting that the latter contained no material intended for Williamson, barring a copy of the French gazette.[74] As such, it seems likely that at least some of the material that Williamson received from the Post Office involved scribal news rather than private correspondence, and material that arrived as part of arrangements with a range of suppliers, each of whom received official newsletters in return. In addition to its many domestic recipients, therefore, Williamson's newsletter was also sent to diplomats like Essais Pufendorf, the Swedish resident in Paris, as well as to professional news writers, including the Brussels-based journalist, Francois(?) Foppen, and Casteleyn himself.[75] Casteleyn's letters also reveal evidence of careful scrutiny, in terms of passages translated and highlighted by different hands. In 1668 the following passage from Casteleyn's letter of 31 July (new style) was translated and then highlighted by Williamson's clerks:

> We have very bad news for the French out of the Indies, that they being arrived at Madagascar had engaged themselves in the war that was between the kings there, where they had lost abundance of men, and that they were grown to that height of pride, that they would not bear their arms themselves but forced the inhabitants to bring them after them, who taking that opportunity had fallen upon the French and destroyed them, those that remained alive suffering hunger and many other hardships there resolved to go to Suratte where they arrived in December last, but they having no great desire to stay there had gotten a French ship which arrived the 6 of April at the Cape of Good Hope, desiring that they might return home in the company of our ships, but our commander in chief, having no orders so to do, did excuse it, in the meantime, we have yet no news of the arrival of the said ships in France.[76]

That this story subsequently appeared – almost word for word – in the *Gazette* is clearly significant, although given the importance that Williamson attached to his relationship with Casteleyn, and his wider obsession with 'Dutch letters', it also seems likely that this process of translation and extraction served other purposes in terms of information management.[77] The same presumably applies to other stories that were culled from Casteleyn's letters and

[72]Longleat House, Thynne Papers 41, f. 70; TNA, SP 29/231, f. 24v.
[73]*CSP Dom 1665–6*, p. 246; TNA, SP 29/148, f. 8; Fraser, *Intelligence*, 44; Williams, 'Newsbooks', 275.
[74]*CSP Dom 1673*, p. 251.
[75]Fraser, *Intelligence*, 64, 70, 73, 153–5.
[76]TNA, SP 101/51: Casteleyn to Williamson, 31 July 1668.
[77]*London Gazette*, 23–27 July 1668, 281.

then appeared in the *Gazette*, such as the report about a decision in the States General to enhance De Witt's salary, and to provide 60,000 guilders 'by way of present', in acknowledgement of his 'good service'.[78]

4

Pivoting away from discussions of intercepts, censorship and propaganda makes it possible to highlight the central role of scribal news in the government's intelligence operations, and to probe the processes used to secure and sift credible and reliable supplies of information, as well as the personnel involved. It highlights the importance of information management and suggests ways in which this task could be made feasible. This is not to deny that it could also be fraught with difficulties, in cross-border contexts and in situations where the gathering and analysis of intelligence was intimately connected with the popular appetite for news and the need to produce various kinds of 'propaganda'. In short, the imperatives to publicise information sometimes came into conflict with the processes by which it was acquired. Thus, among the many complaints that surfaced about stories in the *Gazette*, worries were expressed that the incorporation of sensitive Dutch intelligence might put supplies in jeopardy.[79] In 1670, for example, Temple urged Williamson to treat the weekly 'advices' with care. He was nervous about the possibility that they would 'fall into the hands of the ordinary intelligencer', suggesting that 'discretion' should be used 'in drawing what he will out of them for furnishing his gazette', and he was worried 'least the publishing of them… may occasion an inquiry here into their source'. Indeed, Temple explained that specific stories in the *Gazette* 'had very near broke off my intelligence, and I should be very sorry to lose it, because he gives me what passes in the States of Holland as well as General, which is not usual'. Blathwayt also recommended 'secrecy', because newsletter writers were concerned about the 'severity' with which the Dutch government might treat those peddling intelligence, a reference to what Temple described as 'the late rout among the clerks'. In July 1671, Blathwayt explained that his Dutch intelligencer 'dares not venture any further', because the States General was 'offended' by passages in the *Gazette* culled from his letters. The story in question came from a Casteleyn newsletter, and Blathwayt indicated that maintaining supplies of intelligence would require not just the payment of a healthy 'allowance', but also 'better management for the future'.[80]

However, such challenges merely provide further evidence that the task of information management provides a useful way of addressing the ongoing relevance of scribal news. Here, this has involved reflecting upon the fuzzy boundaries between intelligence and scribal news, examining how scribal news was constructed, deployed and read, and analysing complex relationships involving producers and consumers. With respect to the latter, the article has demonstrated that officials recognised and responded to the changing

---

[78] *London Gazette*, 30 July to 3 Aug. 1668, 283; TNA, SP 101/51: Casteleyn to Williamson, 7 Aug. 1668. For the possibility of newsletters that were sent to Williamson making their way into the *Gazette*, see Fraser, *Intelligence*, 90.

[79] *CSP Dom 1666–7*, p. 359; *CSP Dom 1672*, p. 156.

[80] TNA, SP 84/187, f. 79; *London Gazette*, 18 to 22 May 1671, 575; TNA, SP 101/54: Casteleyn to Williamson, 26 May 1671. For other concerns about the need for secrecy, in response to the tendency for evidence about the Privy Council to appear in print within hours, see *CSP Dom 1680–1*, p. 532.

landscape of news across the 17th century. Before the civil wars, when news culture was exclusive, expensive and authoritative, texts were generally unofficial but could be regarded as credible by virtue of proximity of their authors to reliable sources. During the civil wars, meanwhile, news became commonplace and cheap, but also problematic in terms of its reliability and truthfulness, thereby incentivising reading practices that were more intensive and extensive. It became harder to claim that news was authoritative by virtue of journalists being close to credible witnesses, and more obvious that it was being manipulated by political authorities. Moreover, if civil war news culture represented the antithesis of early Stuart news culture – a contrast symbolised by the disappearance of scribal newsletters and the dramatic arrival of printed newspapers – then a synthesis seems to have been achieved after 1660. This involved newsletters and newspapers operating in tandem rather than as competitors; a commitment to the idea of news being commonplace, even to the extent that scribal news was dramatically reduced in price; the relative absence of the opportunities for extensive reading (at least initially); and a much more obvious sense that news was 'authoritative' in terms of being officially controlled.

This story matters because government policies needed to acknowledge the demand for, and availability of, different kinds of scribal and printed news, and because officials needed to secure and produce scribal newsletters rather than just to read and print gazettes. This means recognising that newsletters had become entangled with newsbooks and gazettes, and successful information management required obtaining large quantities of information, establishing relationships with credible suppliers of high-grade reports and processing incoming evidence. To the extent that intelligence-gathering became a more pressing issue, officials not only grappled with the potential for 'information overload' but also with the need to diversify supply lines, beyond diplomats and envoys, and beyond letters intercepted at the Post Office. It seems plausible to suggest that this involved a 'core and periphery' model, in which the government amassed evidence from a wide variety of sources while also relying heavily upon a small group of intelligencers, among whom professional journalists and newsletter writers were prominent. However, to the extent that officials co-opted commercial newsletter services, strategies for obtaining intelligence – and different kinds of scribal news – were also predicated upon popular demand for news (both in scribal and printed forms), and upon the need to establish processes for exchanging information. Indeed, in a situation where the government was both a consumer and a producer of scribal news, officials encountered complex and perhaps incompatible imperatives. For those involved in information management, the dissemination of authoritative news in the *Gazette* and scribal newsletters could be central to the process of securing regular intelligence, from readers and officials at home, as well as from agents and journalists abroad. But it could also be inimical to the task of obtaining reliable scribal news, by imperilling the very channels of communication upon which the government relied. Such challenges were made particularly acute by European entanglements and diplomatic imperatives, and they indicate how complex issues of information management became in terms of tensions between secrecy, publicity and the gathering of intelligence, and in terms of the need to navigate a shifting news ecosystem.

'Our Masters the Commons Begin Now to Roar': Parliament in Scribal Verse, 1621–81[*]

EDWARD TAYLOR

Scribal verse was an important source of news and comment about parliament in 17th-century Britain, especially in the 1620s and 1660s–80s. Unlike other forms of scribal news, poems that circulated in manuscript did not report on parliamentary proceedings as such, but either sum-marised parliamentary news or provided comment on parliament's actions, nature or wider pur-pose, and typically presented parliament as a unitary agent that expressed a single voice. Scribal verse overwhelmingly disseminated a view of parliament as an agent of oppositional/'country' politics in a polarised, partisan political landscape. In the 1620s, poems represented parliament in conflict with court figures such as Francis Bacon, Viscount St Alban, and George Villiers, duke of Buckingham. Most took an oppositional perspective, praising parliament as a virtu-ous, corruption-fighting body, while some loyalist/'court' poems depicted it as the multitude's dangerous tool. Under Charles II, oppositional poems tended to emphasise that parliament was thwarted from its rightful oppositional role by threatened prorogation and corruption by the court, while loyalist poems discredited parliament with the memory of its revolutionary mid-century predecessors. Evidence about readers, such as the clergyman John Rous in the 1620s and the student Peter Le Neve in the 1670s, indicates that poems were consumed as part of wider bundles of news media. Some poems were themselves embedded within parliamentary culture, being written by members of parliament such as Andrew Marvell and read by others such as Sir William Haward.

Keywords: news; satire; poetry; partisanship; Court and country; Exclusion Crisis

1

One of the more distinctive sources of scribal news and comment about parliament in early modern Britain was scribal verse. Poems about current affairs that circulated in manuscript – often known as 'libels' – were an important outlet for political expression in the 17th century. Their dominant mode was satire.[1] Building on medieval and Tudor roots, scribal political verse developed into a national phenomenon from around 1600, with its first,

---

[*] I would like to thank the editors for commenting on an early draft of this article, and Victoria Moul for discussions about the Latin poems used in the article.

[1] This does not mean that they all adopted the same genre – there were epigrams, epitaphs, ballads, dream nar-ratives, dialogues and so on – but a satirical 'mode', characterised broadly by elements of censure and wit/humour, was in most of these poems. For satire as a 'mode' rather than a 'genre', see Ashley Marshall, *The Practice of Satire in England, 1658–1770* (Baltimore, MD, 2013), 5–8.

early Stuart wave peaking during the politically tempestuous 1620s.[2] Political verse shifted towards print during the civil wars,[3] but experienced a second, post-Restoration wave of manuscript transmission between the 1660s and 1690s, increasingly alongside print, before the medium declined.[4] At their height, scribal political poems circulated widely, both within and beyond a social and political elite: handed between individuals, or copied into or enclosed with letters, or placed publicly or semi-publicly in alehouses, taverns or coffeehouses, at court or in the streets, or transmitted orally through speech or song. They were prominent in the early Stuart and Restoration periods partly because of legal restrictions on print, especially pre-publication print licensing regimes before 1641, 1662–79 and 1685–95, and partly because manuscript was a 'freer' medium for political expression than print, being more easily transmitted anonymously and clandestinely.[5] In addition, and most fundamentally, manuscript remained a natural, default medium for 17th-century writers despite the growth of print.

Scribal poems often included discussion of parliament, ranging from brief mentions to longer treatments. This article examines parliament's place in scribal verse in the latter's two most prominent periods: during James I's and Charles I's parliaments in 1621–9, and during Charles II's parliaments in 1666–81.[6] Scribal poems discussed parliament differently from other media such as newspapers, newsletters and manuscript separates.[7] Being verse,

---

[2] For early Stuart scribal political verse, see esp. Andrew McRae, *Literature, Satire and the Early Stuart State* (Cambridge, 2004). See also Pauline Croft, 'The Reputation of Robert Cecil: Libels, Political Opinion and Popular Awareness in the Early Seventeenth Century', *TRHS*, 6th ser., i (1991), 43–69; Alastair Bellany, ' "Rayling Rymes and Vaunting Verse": Libellous Politics in Early Stuart England, 1603–1628', in *Culture and Politics in Early Stuart England*, ed. Kevin Sharpe and Peter Lake (Houndmills, 1994), 285–310; A.F. Marotti, *Manuscript, Print, and the English Renaissance Lyric* (Ithaca, NY, 1995), ch. 2; Thomas Cogswell, 'Underground Verse and the Transformation of Early Stuart Political Culture', in *Political Culture and Cultural Politics in Early Modern England: Essays Presented to David Underdown*, ed. S.D. Amussen and M.A. Kishlansky (Manchester, 1995), 277–300; Alastair Bellany, *The Politics of Court Scandal in Early Modern England: News Culture and the Overbury Affair, 1603–1660* (Cambridge, 2002), ch. 2; Andrew McRae, 'Political Satire in Early Stuart England: New Voices, New Narratives', *Literature Compass*, i (2003), 1–23; Alastair Bellany, 'Railing Rhymes Revisited: Libels, Scandals, and Early Stuart Politics', *History Compass*, v (2007), 1136–79; James Doelman, *The Epigram in England, 1590–1640* (Manchester, 2016), ch. 10. ESL is an invaluable online edition of political libels, 1590–1640.

[3] Timothy Raylor, *Cavaliers, Clubs, and Literary Culture: Sir John Mennes, James Smith, and the Order of the Fancy* (Newark, 1994), and Marotti, *Manuscript*, ch. 2, contain some discussion of civil war manuscript verse, esp. among royalists.

[4] For Restoration scribal political verse, see esp. Harold Love, *English Clandestine Satire, 1660–1702* (Oxford, 2004). See also R.D. Hume, ' "Satire" in the Reign of Charles II', *Modern Philology*, cii (2005), 332–71; Marshall, *Practice*; and scholarship about Andrew Marvell's post-Restoration satire, e.g., W.L. Chernaik, *The Poet's Time: Politics and Religion in the Work of Andrew Marvell* (Cambridge, 1983); Nigel Smith, *Andrew Marvell: The Chameleon* (New Haven, CT, 2010). POASY is a seven-volume edition of political verse in manuscript and print, 1660–1714, but is not comprehensive. See L.H. McLaughlin, ' "Poetick Rage" to Rage of Party: English Political Verse, 1678–1685', University of California PhD, 2018, pp. 21–4. For the decline of scribal political verse, see Love, *Satire*, 145–6.

[5] Harold Love, *Scribal Publication in Seventeenth-Century England* (Oxford, 1993), 177–95. There *were* legal restrictions on manuscript libels, although authorities were unwilling or unable to enforce them. See Bellany, 'Rhymes Revisited', 1151.

[6] The main limitation of this approach is that it omits the civil wars. Much 1640s–50s verse did, of course, discuss parliament, but it was usually printed, and in the absence of editions like ESL (pre-1640) or POASY (post-1660), the extent of mid-century scribal political verse is unclear.

[7] Parliament appeared in a few scribal poems before 1621. For some Elizabethan poems, see *Verse Libel in Renaissance England and Scotland*, ed. S.W. May and Alan Bryson (Oxford, 2016), poems 47 (1566) and 48–48A (1589). The most important example, however, was the 'Parliament Fart' (after 1607), which humorously catalogued the

they did not report parliamentary proceedings as such. Some provided semi-fictionalised narratives of events in parliament, such as 'Upon the Nameinge of the Duke of Buckingham the Remonstrance' (1628) and Andrew Marvell's 'Last Instructions to a Painter' (1667), but they conflated and distorted events and gave them a literary guise.[8] More often, poems either summarised parliamentary news or provided comment on parliament's actions, nature or wider purpose. Moreover, they typically presented parliament as a unitary agent: simply as 'Parliament' or the 'Senate', or specifically the 'Commons', or collectively the 'Houses', depicted as expressing a single voice. Strikingly, poets rarely mentioned or distinguished the Lords: they were most interested in activity in the Commons, or in how far the Commons represented the multitude or was corrupted by the court.

Overwhelmingly, manuscript poems associated parliament with *oppositional* politics. In both periods, parliaments witnessed tensions between loyalist/'court' and oppositional/'country' forces of one sort or another that were also reflected beyond parliament, including in scribal verse.[9] Parliament usually appeared in manuscript poems as an oppositional agent in a polarised political landscape, defined against the court. In the 1620s, they represented parliament in conflict with court figures such as George Villiers, duke of Buckingham; most poems themselves took an oppositional perspective, praising parliament as a virtuous, corruption-fighting body, while some loyalist poems depicted parliament as the multitude's dangerous tool. Under Charles II, oppositional poems tended to emphasise that parliament was thwarted from its rightful oppositional role by threatened prorogation and corruption by the court, while loyalist poems discredited parliament with the memory of its revolutionary mid-century predecessors. Partisanship – a political culture selfconsciously characterised by internal divisions rather than unity, which developed in Britain during the 17th century – was therefore the key force that shaped parliament's treatment in manuscript

---

[7] *(continued)* supposed responses of individual members of parliament to a fart issued by a member during a Commons debate. Despite its convivial tone, scholars have suggested political readings of the fart as an expression of Commons defiance, reflecting growing institutional self-confidence and the assertion of the right to freedom of speech. See esp. Michelle O'Callaghan, 'Performing Politics: The Circulation of the "Parliament Fart"', *HLQ*, lxix (2006), 121–38; Michelle O'Callaghan, *The English Wits: Literature and Sociability in Early Modern England* (Cambridge, 2007), ch. 4; Andrew McRae, 'Farting in the House of Commons: Popular Humour and Political Discourse in Early Modern England', in *The Power of Laughter and Satire in Early Modern Britain: Political and Religious Culture, 1500–1820*, ed. Mark Knights and Adam Morton (Martlesham, 2017), 67–83.

[8] Both are discussed below.

[9] There are long-standing debates about the structure of politics in the 1620s and 1660s to 1670s, as periods that preceded, respectively, royalist–parliamentarian splits in the civil wars and Tory–Whig splits in the Exclusion Crisis. In general, 'revisionist' scepticism about overstating political divisions has been superseded by 'post-revisionist' acceptance that divisions were real, if shifting and episodic, and were found in parliament and, especially political language. For the 1620s, see Richard Cust, 'News and Politics in Early Seventeenth-Century England', *P&P*, cxii (1986), 60–90; Linda Levy Peck, *Court Patronage and Corruption in Early Stuart England* (1993), ch. 8; Richard Cust, '"Patriots" and "Popular" Spirits: Narratives of Conflict in Early Stuart Politics', in *The English Revolution, c.1590–1720: Politics, Religion and Communities*, ed. Nicholas Tyacke (Manchester, 2007), 43–61. For the 1660s to 1670s, see Tim Harris, *Politics under the Later Stuarts: Party Conflict in a Divided Society, 1660–1715* (1993), ch. 2; Mark Knights, *Politics and Opinion in Crisis, 1678–1681* (Cambridge, 1994), esp. ch. 5. The terminology for describing these divisions is not wholly adequate: using 'country' as a shorthand for those concerned about 'court' corruption oversimplifies political realities, and 'oppositional' and 'loyalist' could imply a more fundamental constitutional division than actually existed. However, if we allow for the shifting and occasional character of divisions and avoid overinterpreting these terms' connotations, both pairs of labels are good general descriptors for how divisions tended to crystallise during both periods.

poems.[10] From a literary perspective, this also reflected a tendency to praise and censure that was inherent to verse, and especially the satiric mode that dominated scribal verse, as satire operates by discriminating between a satirical target and a positive standard.[11] Scribal poems indicate that parliament contributed to partisanship not just as a location of partisan activity, but because news and comment *about* parliament stimulated partisan politics.

The discussion below is divided into three sections. The first two examine how parliament was represented in scribal verse in the two periods, and the last addresses how the poems were consumed. In total, over 60 poems from across the two periods are considered.[12] They range from two lines to several hundred lines in length.[13] Most are in English, with a few in Latin.[14] Most are anonymous, reflecting their semi-clandestine nature.[15] Many have multiple variants, and they survive in various disparate manuscripts, including separates, personal miscellanies and professional anthologies.[16]

2

During the 1620s, parliament appeared in dozens of manuscript poems, in two main clusters: poems about the 1621 parliament, which represented parliament in opposition to the monopolists, Sir Francis Michell and Sir Giles Mompesson, and Francis Bacon, Viscount St Alban, the lord chancellor; and poems about the 1626 and 1628 parliaments, which represented parliament in opposition to the duke of Buckingham, the controversial royal favourite.[17] In both cases, a larger number of oppositional poems that praised parliament's

---

[10] On partisanship, see esp. Mark Knights, *Representation and Misrepresentation in Later Stuart Britain: Partisanship and Political Culture* (Oxford, 2005).

[11] See esp. McRae, *Satire*, ch. 4.

[12] Verse is usually taken from ESL and POASY, supplemented by other manuscript and printed sources where necessary. Quotations and dating follow ESL and POASY where possible, with some adjustments. Poems are included if they appeared in print as well as manuscript, but excluded if they appeared exclusively or overwhelmingly in print.

[13] The longest is Marvell's 'Last Instructions', at nearly 1000 lines, but this is exceptional. Most are well under 100 lines.

[14] There was a substantial tradition of Latin manuscript verse during the 17th century whose full dimensions are only now becoming visible to scholars, and which has yet to be integrated properly with English-language verse. ESL and POASY both contain exclusively English verse, although sometimes allude to Latin. The breadth and nature of Latin manuscript verse in England is currently being examined by Victoria Moul's Leverhulme-funded project, 'Neo-Latin Poetry in English Manuscript Verse Miscellanies, c.1550–1700'; as part of this, I am publishing on Latin political verse elsewhere. See Edward Taylor, '*Poemata* on Affairs of State: Political Satire in Latin in Later Stuart Britain, 1658–1714', *The Seventeenth Century* (2021).

[15] Authors are identified where known or plausibly attributed.

[16] Information about manuscript survivals is found in ESL; POASY; the Folger 'First Line Index' (https://firstlines.folger.edu/); the 'Catalogue of English Literary Manuscripts 1450–1700' (CELM: https://celm-ms.org.uk/); and Love, *Satire*, appendix. Where a poem survives in only one manuscript, this is indicated (for early Stuart poems, ESL gives details). A single survival does not itself indicate lack of circulation, as manuscript survival is generally poor. Variants of poems are usually not considered. Dates given are sometimes uncertain, and some poems circulated in relation to multiple events, or accrued extra content over time. Many poems are also preserved in the original printed *Poems on Affairs of State* (1689–1716), which explicitly brought manuscript poems into print: see POASY, i, p. xxvi.

[17] Early Stuart poems are cited by ESL number; further bibliography and information about individual poems is in ESL. Scribal verse did not engage much with parliament in 1624, 1625 or 1629, although see ESL Oi1 for a depiction of parliament in 1624 supporting a pro-Protestant foreign policy, and ESL Oiii14 for a poem that

actions were countered by a few loyalist poems that accused parliament of exceeding its proper role.

To begin with the 1621 parliament (which had two sessions, January to June and November to December): a conflict between a virtuous parliament and vicious Michell and Mompesson was a theme in oppositional poems circulating at this time. The two monopolists had incurred enemies for harsh execution of their patents for licensing inns and alehouses and manufacturing gold and silver thread, and were impeached by parliament for corruption; Michell was sent to the Tower and Mompesson escaped to France.[18] One 'lamentable newe Ballade' purported to be Michell's 'Complaynte', although it was clearly written by an adversary.[19] 'Michell' describes his 'sudden overthrowe' after his corrupt actions had been thwarted, and indicates parliament's responsibility for his downfall, warning other corrupt individuals that they risked the same fate:

> And then by mee Example make
> How you get goods, how bribes you take…
> Before this Parlamente I myghte
> Have done all this…
> But they are nowe so busy growne
> Alas [our] Faults must all be knowne…
> and this my storey may asseuer yee
> If you bee badde theyle not endeuer yee[.]

After narrating his humiliating removal to the Tower, jeered at by passers-by, 'Michell' concludes by acknowledging that parliament deserved praise for its actions, despite his own suffering:

> and ene on the howses highe & lowe
> I pray to God his grace bestowe
> For they are like if they goe on
> to leave noe faulte unthaught uppon
> and then Ime suer howere I bee
> I shall have still more companey.

At a similar time, another libel praised 'our thrice noble, happy Parliament' for impeaching Mompesson, punning on his surname: 'The earth growes happy & the heaven smiles / Theres no respect of Persons. Mum Sir Giles'.[20] Parliament also appeared as Mompesson's nemesis in a long, widely-circulating poem of 1621/2 that satirised a catalogue of Jacobean corruption: 'Sir Gyles is much displeased with king / that he a parlament doth call'.[21]

---

[17] (*continued*) may relate to the dissolution of 1629. The lack of verse about 1624 may reflect this parliament's not being a site of conflict like earlier and later parliaments; that about 1629 perhaps reflects the centrality of Buckingham, now removed from the scene after his assassination, to late 1620s verse.

[18] For a recent discussion of the 1621 parliament, see Andrew Thrush, 'The Fall of Thomas Howard, 1st Earl of Suffolk and the Revival of Impeachment in the Parliament of 1621', *Parl. Hist.*, xxxvii (2018), 197–211. In addition to general literature about early Stuart libels referenced above, see Tom Lockwood '"Empericks of State": Manuscript Verse and the Impeachment of Francis Bacon', *Philological Quarterly*, xci (2012), 23–47.

[19] ESL Mi1. Only in one manuscript.

[20] ESL Mi3. Only in one manuscript.

[21] ESL Miii2.

Other oppositional poems praised parliament's actions against St Alban, who was impeached for corruption and lost office in May 1621. In one libel, 'The greate assemblie of the parliamente' is said (with an inevitable pun on his surname, 'Bacon') to have sought 'a dantie bitt of bacon', which transpired to be rank: 'But when it came it greatly did distast / Theire palletts & disliked much theire minde'.[22] The bacon was physically 'corrupte & putrified', perhaps because ''twas hunge so high' – his having been over promoted. The 'Cooke' – Sir Edward Coke, who orchestrated the impeachment – concluded that 'how to remedy this rustie bacon / I doe not know unless it be downe taken'. A second poem also used a bacon motif:

> The Parliament with one consent
>   I oft have heard it spoke
> Hath made a law to singe it with straw
>   And hange it up in smoake.[23]

Taking a more sophisticated line, another poem placed parliament's clash with St Alban in a historical context, claiming the 'Sennate' was like virtuous republican institutions of past and present:

> [It] verry hardly parraleld may bee
> for wisedome Courage & Integrety[;]
> Athens Rome Vennice yeild preheminence
> to theyr farr more admired excellence[.][24]

The 'Comons' were the 'brave Heroes of the state' because it was 'theyr power / that curbed & crusht your famous Chancellour'. Therefore, 'this fayre act' of impeaching St Alban 'shall add renoune to theyr thrice honoured name'.

The 1621 parliament continued to attract the attention of oppositional poets after its dissolution in January 1622, indicating that the perception of an oppositional parliament fighting court corruption persisted. A widely-circulating poem of 1623, which took the form of a petition to a departed Elizabeth I that lamented the people's sufferings under corrupt Jacobean rule, observed wistfully that, in 1621, 'Wee had a Parliament a salve for soares'.[25] A long satiric poem of a similar time also commended this parliament as a moment when popular grievances were aired:

> … when the Prince perceiv'de this discontente
> he cheeres them upp with name of parliamente,
> wich giveth warmth unto their frozen joyntes
> as if, our God the remedie appointes.[26]

---

[22]ESL Mii5. Only in one manuscript.

[23]ESL Mii2.

[24]ESL Mii9. Only in one manuscript. This answered ESL Mii8, discussed below.

[25]ESL Niv1.

[26]ESL K1. Only in one manuscript.

The parliament had positive results:

> For Monoples are rent in sunder quite,
> and Francis Mitchell is noe more a knight
> Mompesson flyes, and manie Pattents fall
> and true complaints are heard amongst them all.
> A manie foule enormities are righted
> and blinded Justice is made nowe quickesighted.
> For Englands loftie Chancellor is founde
> a foule delinquent, and on speciall grounde
> Is to the Tower as a prisoner sente[.][27]

However, as 'the busines of the Parliamente / doth his greate majestie much discontente', the king 'resolves / to Crosse them all; and soe the same disolves'. From this sceptical perspective of 1623, the 1621 parliament was a brief moment of 'country' success before a reversion to corrupt norms.

Although the spirit of satire is critical and censorious, it was never solely the preserve of the opposition minded in 17th-century England; loyalists also directed satire against the Court's opponents. A prominent 1621 poem by William Lewis, provost at Oriel College, Oxford, defended St Alban against parliament's actions, which were the expression of a populace – 'Oh, that the monster multitude should sit / In place of justice, reason, conscience, witte' – that had gone too far.[28] In 1623, a widely-circulating poem that purported to be the king's own response to libellers argued that parliament should know its place:

> The parliament I will appoint
> When I see thyngs more out of joynt
> Then will I sett all wry things straight
> And not upon your pleasure waite[.][29]

Instead, he insisted that 'When kings should aske their subjects ayd / Kings cannot soe be made affraid', in contrast with his difficult experience of 1621. These poets shared with the oppositional poets the depiction of a political divide between the 1621 parliament and court figures, but instead mounted a loyalist condemnation of parliament. Where oppositional poems focused on Michell, Mompesson and St Alban as symbols of corruption, these loyalist poems tended to be non-specific, expressing a generalised objection to parliament acting out of place.

After 1621, the next parliaments to attract significant attention from scribal poets were those of 1626 and 1628, at the height of the ascendancy of the controversial royal favourite, George Villiers, duke of Buckingham.[30] The poets drew attention to these parliaments'

---

[27] The 'Chancellor' is St Alban.

[28] ESL Mii8. This was answered by ESL Mii9.

[29] ESL Nvi1.

[30] Buckingham was the most common subject of early Stuart libels. In addition to general literature on early Stuart libels referenced above, see Gerald Hammond, *Fleeting Things: English Poets and Poems, 1616–1660* (Cambridge, 1990), ch. 2; James Holstun, ' "God Bless Thee, Little David!": John Felton and His Allies', *English Literary History*, lix (1992), 513–52.

conflict with Buckingham, and especially to the attempted impeachment of the duke in 1626 and the debates over whether to name him as the source of the nation's ills in a re- monstrance in 1628, shortly before his assassination. These poems adopted similar patterns to those of 1621. Oppositional poems now took Buckingham as a symbol of court corrup- tion against which a virtuous parliament was attempting to act, while loyalist poems again criticised parliament for constitutional overreach.

First, oppositional poems praised the stormy 1626 parliament (which ran February to June) for attempting to impeach Buckingham.[31] An anti-Buckingham song, which was publicly performed in 1627 but also circulated in manuscript, commended the impeach- ment while hinting presciently at the possible need for stronger action:

> [The] Lower House they did thunder itt
> the upper house they did grumble itt,
> his necke from his shoulders they could not sunder itt,
> which made the people much to wonder itt[.][32]

Another poem about this parliament, beginning 'The Kinge and his wyfe the Parliament / are parted both in discontent', presented parliament's defiance against Buckingham in sexualised language.[33] It claimed that Buckingham 'did stryve with all his might, / To robbe her of her antient right' through 'rape committed on her' – an effort that failed when parliament jeeringly 'turned up her tayle [i.e., bottom], / to him… to kisse: / As shee will do to all his faction, / Who were the cause of this distraction, / That hindred once our blisse'. The question of what to do about Buckingham also caused conflict between the king- husband and parliament-wife. While 'parliaments are bent / to purge that putrifaction', by impeaching Buckingham, the king was reluctant 'to urge the house for's people' to take action against his 'minion'. Instead, he ordered that three leading anti-Buckingham members of parliament, 'Turner, Eliot, and Digges / Shall scourged be like whirlegigges / and suffer for their dinns'.[34]

After parliament was dissolved in June 1626, not to meet again for nearly two years, po- ems circulated that claimed that Buckingham despised parliament and sought to prevent its reassembling. When Buckingham left England for the continent in December for a mili- tary campaign in France, one poem observed that the 'Parliament benches [were] brusht' in the expectation that parliament would now be free to sit.[35] Another asked if Buckingham 'hasten[ed]' back to England in 1627, after the French campaign had ended in disaster at the Isle of Rhé, 'to prevent / A fruitlesse hop'd-for needfull Parliament', and reminded Buckingham that his anti-parliament position had not won him victory: 'Nor could thy Parliamento-Mastix Vowes / Prevaile t'impose the Garland on thy browes?'[36] A third li- bel, 'Upon the Duke Buckingham [sic] His Opposition to the Parliament', lamented that

---

[31] For a recent discussion of the 1626 parliament, see David Coast, ' "Reformation" or "Ruin"? The Impeach- ment of the Duke of Buckingham and Early Stuart Politics', *Historical Research*, xc (2017), 704–25.

[32] ESL Oi17.

[33] ESL Oi10.

[34] Samuel Turner, Sir John Eliot and Sir Dudley Digges. See *HPC, 1604–1629*, s.v. 'John Eliot', 'Sir Dudley Digges' and 'Samuel Turner'. Eliot and Digges were imprisoned after this parliament's dissolution.

[35] ESL Oi11.

[36] ESL Oii12. 'Parliamento-Mastix' is parliament whipping.

Buckingham had survived his foreign adventures only to threaten parliament again: 'Since thou hast guilt of all the bloud Rhee spent / must thou still live to breake a Parliament!'[37]

The debates over the remonstrance in the following parliament, of March to June 1628, were the subject of further oppositional poems.[38] One purportedly gave Buckingham's 'answere to the Lower house of Parliament', although was actually a satirical impersonation.[39] Attacking the Commons for trying to 'ruin mee', 'Buckingham' gives a parody 'court' view of the house as the voice of the 'giddie-headed Multitude'. He arrogantly claims that he could have prevented the 'brabling confus'd parliament' from meeting, 'For in my power it was… / To say it should, or it should not be soe'. The same parliament was represented in a different way in 'Upon the Nameinge of the Duke of Buckingham the Remonstrance', a poem of around 100 lines that provided a more detailed account of parliamentary events than any other early Stuart scribal poem.[40] Unusually, it depicted divisions *within* parliament, rather than treating parliament as a unitary oppositional agent. It described the contributions of individual members of parliament on both sides, such as the pro-Buckingham Sir Humphrey May ('but May makes mouthes, and tells you as a freind / to name the man were not to woorke your end') and anti-Buckingham Sir Edward Giles (who 'as angry said that hee / would have him named, as it was fitt to bee'); these can often be matched with actual Commons speeches, albeit not from a single day, as presented in the poem.[41] The thrust of the poem, however, was oppositional. Referring to Sir John Eliot, who orchestrated the remonstrance, it began, 'Excuse me Eliott if I heare name thee / the tyme requires itt since fewe honest bee' – a satirical swipe against Buckingham's defenders, who were dishonestly trying to keep Buckingham unnamed in the remonstrance.

Buckingham's assassination on 23 August 1628 by John Felton, a disgruntled lieutenant who had served in the 1627 French campaign, provoked an outpouring of scribal verse that took the public debates around Buckingham to new levels. Parliament continued to feature prominently in these discussions, as the 1626 and 1628 parliaments were remembered for their attempts to curtail the duke's powers. One poem used medical imagery to recall that the two 'senates' of 1626 and 1628 had at least tried to resist Buckingham:

> England was sick, a plewresey possest her
> a raging greife did long molest her
> Two senates to fynde out this sore long sought
> & found a member neare the head[.][42]

Taking an optimistic reading of the infrequency of recent parliaments as a sign of Buckingham's fear of their power, an anti-Buckingham satirical epitaph suggested that his inability to manage the 'lower house' would now be superseded by his having to face the 'lowest house' – Hell:

---

[37] ESL Oiii1. Only in one manuscript.

[38] For the 1628 parliament, see Paul Christianson, 'Politics, Patronage, and Conceptions of Governance: The Duke of Buckingham and His Supporters in the Parliament of 1628', *HLQ*, lx (1998), 289–302.

[39] ESL Oiii5.

[40] ESL Oiii4. Only the 'Parliament Fart' is longer, but this does not represent real events (apart from the fart itself).

[41] *HPC, 1604–1629*, s.v. 'Humphrey May' and 'Sir Edward Giles'.

[42] ESL Pi8. Only in one manuscript.

Thou daily stood'st in feare of Parliaments
the lower house thou never could'st endure
which caus'd them broken upp in discontents
but now the lowest house will keepe thee sure[.][43]

Satirical epitaphs of Buckingham were common at this time. In a second, the duke was described simply as 'Fortunes darling, Kings Content, / Vexation of the Parliament'.[44] Another poem explicitly defended the assassination on the grounds that the legal means to stop Buckingham – impeachment – had been blocked by his closure of parliament:

For when the Commons did, with just intent
Pursue his Faults in open Parliament…
There might his Grace have had a legall triall,
Had hee not it oppos'd with strong deniall.
But hee then scorn'd, and proudly sett at nought
The howse, and those that him in question brought.
Therefore when Law nor Justice takes noe place,
Some desperate course must serve in such a case…
For what the Parliament did faile to doe,
God did both purpose and performe it too.[45]

The same idea circulated in an epitaph for Felton (who was executed in November 1628), which claimed the assassin achieved justice with his 'Arm' where parliament failed: 'Loe, heere he lies, that with one Arm could more / Than all the Nerves of Parliament before'.[46] Another pro-Felton epitaph asserted that he 'did endeavour by one stroke to make / The King and Commons (by him [i.e., Buckingham] put asunder) Joyne all in one'.[47] Again and again, parliament and Buckingham were presented as political rivals.

As with 1621, there were also poems that expressed this conflict from a loyalist perspective. One widely-circulating poem by Richard Corbett, bishop of Oxford, rejected the 1628 Parliament's attacks on Buckingham as:

A sadd presage of daunger to this land,
When lower strive to gett the upper hand;
When Prince and Peares to Peysants must obey,
When lay-men must their Teachers teach the way[.][48]

---

[43] ESL Pi24. Only in one manuscript.

[44] ESL Pi17.

[45] ESL Pii6. Only in one manuscript.

[46] ESL Pii12.

[47] ESL Pii18. Only in one manuscript.

[48] ESL Oiii2. This may have circulated in relation to parliament in 1629, but V.L. Pearl and M.L. Pearl, 'Richard Corbett's "Against the Opposing of the Duke in Parliament, 1628" and the Anonymous Rejoinder, "An Answere to the Same, Lyne for Lyne": The Earliest Dated Manuscript Copies', *Review of English Studies*, xlii (1991), 32–9, argues that it was originally composed in 1628.

Another poem implicitly blamed parliament for laying the path to Felton: 'Whereon if Princes but reflect, they will / … blame those maisters, who / Inspire th'Assassines such foule deeds to doe'. It also attacked parliament for constitutional overreach:

> Doth it with Monarchie in sequence fall,
> The comons thus should doe? and undoe all
> Give lawes unto theire kings, they may not smyle
> Without an Act of parliament the while[.][49]

Finally, a pro-Buckingham epitaph described the duke as 'A Soule inricht with soe much good / As kings (not Commons) understood'.[50] Although loyalist poems were less common than oppositional ones, together they indicate that the image of parliament disseminated through scribal verse in the 1620s was overwhelmingly inflected by a partisan understanding of parliament as a unitary agent of political opposition against the court. This feeds into the wider post-revisionist view of politics in the 1620s being increasingly characterised by division rather than harmony.

3

Between the revival of manuscript political verse in 1666 and the dissolution of Charles II's final parliament in 1681, poems again depicted parliament standing up against the court, and adopted partisan positions praising or condemning parliament; again, too, oppositional poems outweighed loyalist ones. In these poems, parliament – the long Cavalier Parliament (1661–79), and the three short Exclusion Parliaments of 1679–81 – was defined successively against the ministries of Edward Hyde, earl of Clarendon (1660–7), the 'Cabal' (1667–73/4) and Thomas Osborne, earl of Danby (1673/4–9), and then against loyalists during the Exclusion Crisis (1678–82). However, compared with the 1620s, oppositional poems more often emphasised parliament's failure to fulfil this role in practice due to ongoing threats of prorogation and dissolution, and of corruption through being packed with court supporters. Even the most optimistic oppositional poems, in 1666–7 and 1678–9, ultimately depicted parliamentary weakness. Loyalist poets, meanwhile, compared the current parliament with revolutionary mid-century parliaments to discredit oppositional politics, both by scaring readers with memories of the bloody consequences of overmighty parliaments and by mocking the relative impotence of Restoration parliaments.

Parliament's first, and most extensive, appearance in post-Restoration scribal verse was in a group of oppositional satires in 1666–7, which blamed court corruption for failures and mismanagements during the Second Anglo–Dutch War (1664–7). These satires were centred on the well-known series of 'advice to a painter' poems. Following Edmund Waller's printed panegyric 'Instructions to a Painter' (1665), which adopted the conceit of directing a painter how to depict the times as a mechanism for praising the regime, a satiric 'Second Advice to a Painter' (1666) circulated in manuscript that parodied Waller's poem to attack the court, as did subsequent 'Third', 'Fourth' and 'Fifth' advices and 'Last Instructions

---

[49] ESL Piii5. Only in one manuscript.
[50] ESL Piii14.

to a Painter'.[51] These poems discussed parliamentary events, especially in the sessions of September 1666 to February 1667, July 1667 and October to December 1667.[52] Unlike most of the other poems discussed, they can also be attested as having been themselves embedded in parliamentary culture: several were written by Andrew Marvell, a member of parliament,[53] and they were partly aimed at parliamentary readers, designed to corral oppositional forces.[54]

Parliament appeared in the 1666–7 satires as an oppositional agent of mixed success: moderate achievements in scrutiny, legislation and influencing office holding, but at risk of prorogation and corruption. The widely-circulating 'Fourth Advice to a Painter' (June/July 1667) described the stormy 1666–7 session in terms of a conflict between a public-minded but weak parliament and a corrupt court.[55] The poem began with the Commons lamenting the corrupt misuse of previous supply, being reluctant to grant fresh supply, and seeking a committee to examine spending:

> Draw England ruin'd by what was giv'n before,
> And draw the Commons slow in giving more.
> Too late grown wiser, they their treasure see
> Consum'd by fraud or lost by treachery,
> And vainly now would some account receive
> Of those vast sums which they so idly gave[.]

However, parliamentarians were coaxed into granting fresh supply for the war following the king's appearance before them in January 1667, after granting only a minor royal concession about importing Irish cattle:

> And then the King to Westminster is brought…
> He tells the Parliament he cannot brook
> Whate'er in them like jealousy doth look…
> Thus pass'd the Irish with the Money Bill,
> The first not half so good as th'other ill.

Supply having been granted, the king could now dispense with parliament. Courtiers sought a dishonourable peace that would enable them to pocket the funds:

[51] On the painter poems, see esp. Smith, *Marvell*; Warren Chernaik, 'Harsh Remedies: Satire and Politics in "Last Instructions to a Painter" ', in *The Oxford Handbook of Andrew Marvell*, ed. Martin Dzelzainis and Edward Holberton (Oxford, 2019), 443–62. Their circulation was exceptional, as they survive in many manuscripts (esp. the 'Second', 'Third' and 'Fourth' advices) and were also illicitly printed as pamphlets.

[52] The session that began in October 1667 in fact only ended with prorogation in March 1669, but I am calling this first period, after which there was an adjournment (not a prorogation) until February 1668, a 'session' for convenience.

[53] Marvell definitely wrote the 'Last Instructions', probably wrote the 'Second' and 'Third' advices, and did not write the 'Fourth' or 'Fifth' advices. Identifying the extent of Marvell's authorship of post-Restoration satires is notoriously difficult. I follow Chernaik, *Poet's Time*, and Smith, *Marvell*. For Marvell as a member of parliament, see Edward Holberton, 'Representing the Sea in Andrew Marvell's "Advice to a Painter" Satires', *Review of English Studies,* new ser. lxvi (2014), 71–86; Paul Seaward, 'Marvell and Parliament', in *Handbook of Marvell*, ed. Dzelzainis and Holberton, 79–95.

[54] Love, *Satire*, 112; Holberton, 'Representing the Sea'; Chernaik, 'Harsh Remedies'; Seaward, 'Marvell'.

[55] POASY, i, 141–6. The 'Second' and 'Third' advices do not cover parliamentary proceedings.

After two millions more laid on the nation,
The Parliament grows ripe for prorogation:
They rise, and now a treaty is confess'd…
All that was given for the state's defense
These think too little for their own expense[.][56]

Despite a final suggestion that courtiers feared parliament ('But, Painter, end here till it doth appear / Which most, the Dutch or Parliament, they fear'), the overall impression is of parliament being unable to stand up to the court.

The 1666–7 session also featured in Marvell's satiric epic 'Last Instructions to a Painter' (September 1667). At over 200 lines, this was the longest account of a 17th-century parliament in scribal verse.[57] Marvell depicted the session differently from the 'Fourth Advice', using a careful selection of events to present oppositional figures as courageous, if ultimately unsuccessful. Marvell used an oppositional victory against a court proposal to raise supply via an excise – not mentioned in the 'Fourth Advice' – as a set-piece event. He explicitly constructed this as a conflict between 'Court' and 'Country', with country members of parliament concerned that an excise might be misappropriated to 'dissolve the vain / Commons, and ever such a court maintain'. Marvell initially represented this as a backgammon-like game called 'trick-track', with the pro-court Speaker, Sir Edward Turnor – 'the cheat Turnor' – unfairly rolling the dice for both sides:

Draw next a pair of tables op'ning, then
The House of Commons clatt'ring like the men.
Describe the Court and Country, both set right
On opposite points, the black against the white.
Those having lost the nation at trick-track,
These now advent'ring how to win it back.
The dice betwixt them must the fate divide
(As chance doth still in multitudes decide).
But here the Court does its advantage know,
For the cheat Turnor for them both must throw.

The narrative then develops into a mock-heroic battle, with a catalogue given of each side's forces. On the court side, an array of troops, mired in corruption, arrived on the battlefield: 'Of early wittals first the troop march'd in';[58] 'Of the old courtiers next a squadron came, / That sold their master'; 'Then march'd the troop of Clarendon, all full… / Gross bodies, grosser minds, and grossest cheats'. This formidable army almost succeeded in passing the excise by arriving early in the morning, when 'the House was thin'. Then, the 'other side' arrived – a smaller, 'scatter'd body', but individually virtuous – which fought bravely, although 'strength at last still under number bows'. Only when reinforcements arrived for the country army did 'the excise receiv[e] a total rout'. Significantly, unlike the 'Fourth

---

[56] 'These' refers to courtiers.

[57] POASY, i, 99–139.

[58] 'Wittals' are cuckolds.

Advice', the 'Last Instructions' emphasises the strength of court forces *within* the Commons. The literary context here is critical – the Commons battle parallels battles in the Anglo–Dutch war – but its effect is nonetheless to present a divided Commons, which was otherwise unusual in scribal poems. This division foreshadowed 1670s poems that would present parliament as containing, and therefore corrupted by, court figures.

Marvell continued to magnify oppositional success in the poem's coverage of the rest of the 1666–7 session. Courtiers' attempts to persuade parliament to grant supply by running down England's defences and bringing the king to address them directly are presented as a failure. They ultimately only succeeded by reverting from an excise to a land tax. 'Thus, like fair thieves,' Marvell comments, 'the Commons' purse they share'. After parliament was prorogued, Clarendon barely escaped: 'Blither than hare that hath escap'd the hounds, / The House prorogu'd, the Chancellor rebounds'. Despite Clarendon's survival, it is claimed triumphantly that 'What frosts to fruit, what ars'nic to the rat... / A Parliament is to the Chancellor'. A similar emphasis on oppositional pluck featured in the poem's depiction of the short session of July 1667 that met after the humiliating Dutch Medway raid. Oppositional members 'threaten Hyde to raise a greater dust' and one member of parliament, Sir Thomas Tomkyns, dramatically called a motion – which passed – that the newly raised standing army be disbanded after the war's end.[59] Soon, however, court control over parliament was reasserted; the Speaker led the Commons to the Lords for the prorogation, 'like his pris'ners to the bar... / Where mute they stand to hear their sentence read'. This 'petty session' appeared similarly in the 'Fifth Advice to a Painter' (late 1667?):

> But 'twas abortive, born before its day;
> No wonder then it di'd so soon away.
> Yet breath'd it once, and that with such a force,
> It blasted thirty-thousand foot and horse.[60]

The 'Fifth Advice' also took the narrative beyond the 'Last Instructions', into the autumn 1667 session. When parliament met in October, it was as a ghost sent to terrify the court by scrutinising corruption: 'Now draw the shadow of a Parliament, / As if to scare the upper World 'twere sent'.

Another poem directed at members of parliament in the autumn 1667 session was '*Vox et Lachrimae Anglorum*' (summer 1667; 'The Voice and Tears of the English'), perhaps by Edward Raddon.[61] This also attacked court corruption and Clarendon, although was more explicit about parliament's role as guardian. It addressed parliamentarians thus:

> Renowned Patriots, open your Eyes,
> And lend an Ear to th' Justice of our Cries...
> On you, next God, our Confidence relies,

---

[59] *HPC, 1660–1690*, s.v. 'Thomas Tomkyns'.

[60] POASY, i, 146–52.

[61] Not in POASY. Quoted from a 1668 pamphlet (Wing W3208A, one of three versions on ESTC). The printed version was directed at parliament in February 1668, but the dedication indicates that the poem was originally written for members of parliament in October 1667. See S.K. Roberts, 'A Poet, a Plotter and a Postmaster: A Disputed Polemic of 1668', *BIHR*, liii (1980), 258–65; David Norbrook, 'Some Notes on the Canon of George Wither', *Notes & Queries*, ccxli (1996), 276–81.

You are the Bulwarks of our Liberties.
… make us happy by your gentle Rayes,
And You shall be the tenour of our Praise;
And our posterities with joynt consent,
Shall call you *Englands healing Parliament.*

However, this panegyric is mixed with a warning:

But if you still will make our Bands the stronger…
If you mens Lusts and Av'rice gratifie…
… shall it on your Doors and Tombs be writ,
This was that Parliament so long did sit,
Whilst Conscience, Liberty, our Purse and Trade,
The Country, City, Ships, and All's betray'd?…
Since now you have an opportunity,
Redeem yourselves and us from Slavery[.]

Raddon, like Marvell, was concerned that parliamentarians could be corrupted into not being proper 'Bulwarks of our Liberties'.

A final example from 1666–7 is a widely-circulating Latin epigram of late 1667 that presented parliament as a cause of Clarendon's eventual downfall. Clarendon was dismissed in August and, after an attempted impeachment, fled to France in November. With a tightly constructed format, the poem lists Clarendon's foreign policy decisions that destroyed England ('1') and personal corruption that enabled him to build the opulent Clarendon House ('2'), before claiming that parliament – here a romanised '*Senatus*' – contributed to his downfall ('3').

1 *Pacto Vno, Binis Thalamis, Belloque Triformi,*
2 *Lege emptâ, Gallis repetundis, Fraude Telonum,*
3 *Principis edicto, Populi prece, voce Senatûs*
1 1 *Regnum perdidit, 2 Ædes condidit, 3 Exuit ostrum.*[62]

(1. By one agreement, two marriages, threefold war;[63]
2. By legal corruption, extortion of the French, customs' fraud
3. By prince's order, people's prayer, Senate's vote;
1. He destroyed the kingdom; 2. He built a palace; 3. He cast off the purple.)

The king's dismissal of Clarendon ('*principis edicto*'), public opinion ('*populi prece*') and actions in parliament ('*voce senatus*') – presumably the impeachment attempt – are presented as joint causes of his departure ('*exuit ostrum*').

[62] Not in POASY. Quoted from Society of Antiquaries, MS 330, f. 48v. This survives in many manuscripts, in variant forms. For more on this epigram, see Taylor, 'Political Satire'.

[63] The 'one agreement' is the sale of Dunkirk to France in 1662; the 'two marriages' are those between Charles II and Catherine of Braganza, and James, duke of York, and Anne Hyde (Clarendon's daughter); the 'threefold war' is the Second Anglo–Dutch War, against the Dutch, French and Danes. See BL, Add. MS 18220, ff. 7–8, for an English paraphrase explaining these references, and Harold Love, 'Sir William Petty, the London Coffee Houses, and the Restoration "Leonine"', *Seventeenth Century*, xxii (2007), 383.

Oppositional poems in the 1670s, under both the Cabal and Danby, even more strongly emphasised the limitations on parliament than the 1666–7 satires. One prominent theme was of parliament risking dismissal if it became too troublesome – an unsurprising fear given that there were lengthy prorogations in 1671–3, 1674–5 and 1675–7. A long satire, 'The Dream of the Cabal' (1672), depicted a scheming Cabal seeking to expunge parliaments altogether.[64] The poet dreams of a meeting between the five members of the Cabal, plus the duke of Ormond and the king. The Cabal all support action against parliament. The duke of Buckingham (son of the 1620s favourite) argues that there is 'too great mixture of democracy / Within this government', and this must be 'allay'd' by 'nulling parliaments', which are:

> O'th' people's pride and arrogance the vents,
> Factious and saucy, disputing royal pleasure,
> Who your commands by their own humors measure.
> For king in barnacles and to th'rack-staves ti'd
> You must remain, if these you will abide.

The duke of Lauderdale adds, in mock-Scots, 'De'il hoop his lugs that loves a parliament!';[65] the earl of Arlington concedes that 'this House the best is you can call, / But, in my judgment, best is none at all'; the earl of Shaftesbury argues that 'parliaments, nor new, nor old, nor none, / Can well be trusted longer'; Sir Thomas Clifford contends that, as financial help from France had been secured, 'thus without tumultuous noise or huff / Of parliaments, you may have money enough'.[66] '"Well mov'd!" the whole Cabal cri'd, "Parliaments / Are clogs to princes and their brave intents"'. Only Ormond dissents, arguing that parliament should remain because 'very vain would be the plea of crown, / When statute laws and parliaments are down'. However, he fails to convince the king, and the poem ends with the threat of dismissal looming. During Danby's ministry, another poem, 'The Royall Buss' (1675), represented the king proroguing parliament after it refused to fund Charles's mistress, attacked the royal prerogative and defended Protestantism:

> But when the Parliament would no more
> Raise taxes to maintain the whore,
> When they would not abide the awe
> Of standing force instead of law,
> When law, religion, property
> They'd fence 'gainst will and Popery,
> When they'd provide that all shall be
> From slav'ry and oppression free…
> … so, red hot with wine and whore,
> He kick'd the Parliament out of door.[67]

---

[64] POASY, i, 192–203.

[65] I.e., 'May the devil box his ears'.

[66] It is unclear whether the poem was written before or after Clifford became Baron Clifford of Chudleigh in Apr. 1672.

[67] POASY, i, 263–5.

Similar perspectives were expressed in more minor references in other 1670s poems, including 'The King's Vows' (c.1668–70), possibly by Marvell, where a satirical impersonation of the king says, 'I will have a fine Parliament always to friend / That shall furnish me treasure as fast as I spend, / But when they will not, they shall be at an end'; and John Freke's 'History of Insipids' (1676), which observed that 'When to give money he can't collogue them / He doth with scorn prorogue, prorogue them'.[68]

A second major theme in 1670s oppositional verse was of parliament being itself corrupted by the court, especially through bribes and pensions for members of parliament (as were indeed administered by Clifford, then Danby). A 'Further Advice to a Painter' (1671), possibly by Marvell, condemned the court interest's advance within this 'motley Parliament'.[69] The poet instructs his painter to depict court members of parliament 'All looking this way how to give their votes, / Their new-made band of pensioners… / And of his dear reward let none despair'. He expressed particular concern about five opposition-minded members, the 'recanters of the House', who had defected to the court in November 1670. These five parliamentarians were also attacked in another poem, 'On the Prorogation' (1671):

> These patriots malcontent did plot
> Their country's good, till they had places got,
> Bluster'd and huff'd till they were officer'd,
> But then o'th'country more the Devil a Word[.][70]

This poem assumed the voice of a court member of parliament expressing satirical outrage that parliament had been prorogued despite court members' best efforts to ruin the country:

> Have we our country plagu'd, our trust betray'd,
> Giv'n polls, loans, subsidies, and royal aid…
> Crush'd poor Fanatics and broke through all laws
> Of Magna Charta and the Good Old Cause,
>   to be thus fobb'd at last?

In Danby's time, 'The Chequer Inn' (1675) described 'A Supper given by the Treasurer to the Parliament Men': Danby's imaginary banquet to bribe members of parliament.[71] Answering this poem, an honest countryman angrily responds that members of parliament 'are but engines to raise tax, / And the whole business of their acts / Is to undo the nation'. Other 1670s poems that disseminated similar views include 'A Dialogue Between the Two Horses' (1675/6), in which a statue of Charles I's horse condemns the fact 'That traitors to their country in a brib'd House of Commons / Should give away millions at every

---

[68] POASY, i, 159–62; 243–51. Others include John Ayloffe's 'Britannia and Raleigh' (1674/5) ('Present to [the king's] thought his long-scorn'd Parliament, / The basis of his throne and government'), at POASY, i, 228–36; and 'The Dissolution' (1679), which claims that the king's search for 'new Supplyes' enabled him to 'Prorogue & then Dissolve their heats', not in POASY but found at BL, Add. MS 34362, ff. 48–9.

[69] POASY, i, 164–7.

[70] POASY, i, 179–84.

[71] POASY, i, 253–62.

summons'; and 'Sir Edmund Berry Godfrey's Ghost' (1678/9), which depicted Danby as 'that man who had for divers years / Paid the brib'd Commons pensions and arrears'.[72]

There were also a few loyalist poems about parliament in the 1670s. Two related to the 1673–4 sessions, when Charles II reversed his anti-Dutch and pro-toleration policies after extensive criticism. 'The Banished Priests' Farewell to the House of Commons' (1673) mocked country members of parliament for 'huffing' in vain about religion and liberty:

> Go! sots, home to your gammons, go! and boast
> The speeches you have made to every host…
> Crack how you sweat to set the people free,
> Secure religion and their liberty;
> Tell…
> How Country huff'd, and how the Court did quake…
> But also tell, it was not worth a fart.[73]

The poem also compared parliament with a revolutionary predecessor: 'If wit and courage 'mongst you had been seen, / You sure enough had Rump the Second been'. This was a double satiric blow, both suggesting that parliament shared the radical aims of the Rump Parliament (1648–53) and scoffing that it was too ineffective to realise them. 'A Charge to the Grand Inquest of England' (1674) condemned 'Bedlam Commons' for encroaching on the royal prerogative by inventing 'rights and privileges' and inverting the constitutional order: 'The very arse is hoisted o'er the head'.[74] Again, it recalled the civil wars, telling parliament to 'Ransack your writers, Milton, Needham, Prynne' to justify 'Vot[ing that] your own privilege is what you please'.

In a different way, a pair of Latin epigrams by Sir William Petty, dated 1 February 1676, also criticised parliament for going too far, in this case in the sessions of 1675, thereby provoking the 'long prorogation' of 1675–7.[75] They express a moderate loyalism, blaming parliament for overreach while hoping to prevent an excessive monarchical response. The first takes the voice of 'Democraticus', who criticises the 'quarrelling houses of Parliament' ('*discordes Domos Parlamenti*'). Parliament is like a pair of lungs that becomes enflamed after too much activity, and risks killing the body (politic).

> *Anglia sit corpus, Londinum Cor, sit aorta*
> *Et Thamesis; quid ni Pulmo Senatus erit?*

---

[72] POASY, i, 275–83; ii, 7–11. Others include 'Nostradamus' Prophecy' (1672), ('When legislators shall their trust betray, / Hir'd for their share, to give the rest away'); 'A Litany' (1672), whose speaker sought freedom 'From Parliament-sellers elected for ale, / Who sell the weal public to get themselves bail'; 'On the Statue Erected by Sir Robert Viner' (1674/5), perhaps by Marvell, which claimed that a statue of Charles II erected at 'Stocks Market' was appropriate, because 'a market, they say, does suit the King well, / Who the Parliament buys and revenues does sell'; 'Hodge' (1679), which claims a pliant parliament 'in a brib'd committee… contrive[d] / To give our birthrights to prerogative'; and 'An Historical Poem' (1680), which asserts that parliament had 'give[n] the realm away… / And annual stipends for their guilt receive[d] / Corrupt with gold'. POASY, i, 186–9; 190; 267–9; ii, 146–53; 155–63.

[73] POASY, i, 204–10.

[74] POASY, i, 221–7.

[75] Not in POASY. Quoted from BL, Add. MS 72899, f. 46. Only in this manuscript. Alternatively, the epigrams may date from 1 Feb. 1675, in which case they would refer to the sessions of 1673–4.

Spiritibus varijs inflatur Pulmo, Senatus
  Spiritibus totidem, turget & Ipse suis;
Pulmo inflammatus mortem minitatur; Utroque
  Nunc flammate […], Quantula Vita? […]

(Let England be the body, London the heart, and the Thames the aorta. What else will be the Senate but the lungs? Lungs are inflated by many breaths, and the Senate swells with just as many breaths of its own. Lungs that are inflamed threaten death. For each, now burning […], how short is life? […])

A second epigram provides Monarchy's uncompromising answer: parliament should be abandoned to the flames because these lungs are less necessary to the body politic than are lungs to a fish.

Quem dixti sit Pulmo; sed Infans Ventre materno
  Non pulmone caret, sic neque Piscis eget,
Leviathem fœtus minus his pulmone carebit
  In flammas igitur Pulmo Senatus eat.

(Let the lungs be what you have said. But an infant in its mother's belly does not want lungs, like a fish does not need them; the offspring of a leviathan will want lungs less than these. Therefore, let the lungs, the Senate, go into the flames.)

Rather than being a wholesale attack on parliament, this heavy-handed response is a warning to parliament to behave reasonably or risk this strong reaction.

In August 1678, allegations about the existence of a 'popish plot' to bring down Charles II and Protestantism in England caused a public sensation. By appearing to confirm oppositional concerns about 'popery and arbitrary government', these revelations catalysed a series of cycles of oppositional action and loyalist reaction (increasingly labelled 'Whig' and 'Tory' respectively by 1681), in parliament, the courts, the streets and the media, that came to form a period of national political turbulence known as the Exclusion Crisis. In parliament, a turbulent session in autumn 1678, including the attempted impeachment of Danby, led Charles finally to dissolve the Cavalier Parliament in January 1679. He then summoned a new parliament, the First Exclusion Parliament of March to May 1679, which proved even more troublesome, by attempting to impeach and then attaint Danby, to impose limitations on a future Catholic monarch – Charles's heir being his Catholic brother James, duke of York – and then to exclude York from the succession altogether. The king angrily prorogued, and later dissolved, this parliament too, although he accepted Danby's downfall.

Several oppositional poems circulated in 1678–9 that depicted parliament in a more active light than at any time since 1667. One poem, variously called 'Queries' and 'Upon the Lord Chancellor's Speech' (1679), parodied a rousing speech by the lord chancellor, Heneage Finch, on 6 March 1679, which exhorted parliament to defend Protestantism using a series of rhetorical questions that all ended with the refrain, 'This is the time'.[76] The satiric response used the same formula to urge parliament to take bolder action:

---

[76]POASY, ii, 293–7. Finch subsequently became earl of Nottingham in 1681.

Would you turn Danby out of doors,
Banish Italian and French whores,
The worser sort of common shores,
    This is the time…
Would you our sov'reign disabuse,
And make his Parliaments of use,
Not to be chang'd like dirty shoes,
    This is the time.

A widely-circulating anti-Danby ballad of 1678/9, 'What a Devil Ails the Parliament', also defiantly advocated parliamentary action against Danby:

But our new Parliament we hope
    As Thou deservst will brand thee
And with Saint Colemans holy Rope
    Hang Thomas Earle of Danbye.[77]

In 'The King's Farewell to Danby' (1678/9), which satirically impersonates the king, 'Charles' tells Danby that 'Our masters the Commons begin now to roar, / And swear they will have both thee and my whore'.[78] Although he initially accepts that he must 'leave thee to hang like a traitor forlorn', he subsequently changes his mind, realising that 'should I now leave thee… / Next follows in course my brother'. Hence, 'I'll once more prorogue 'em, and if this won't do, / I'll break up their House, then imprison 'em too'.

Loyalist poems of the same period criticised parliament, again drawing on the memory of civil war parliaments. 'The Character' (1679) attacked the autumn 1678 session for constitutional overreach by 'Contending with the King, his laws and pow'r, / Entrenching on's prerogative each hour', thereby forcing a dissolution that left the popish plot uninvestigated; this cleverly appropriated anti-Catholic feeling for a loyalist position.[79] Moreover, recalling the revolutionary Long Parliament (1640–60), the poem claimed that 'Great Hell's Long Parliament is rais'd from's den / To teach young colt his black rebellion', but the 'young' long parliament – the Cavalier Parliament – was even worse because it sought to 'assume at once, and at one hour, / The royal office and the supreme pow'r'. The poem concluded:

In short, your venom'd character is this:
A curse you're to the nation, not a bliss.
The House of Commons is the rabble's god,
The courtiers' scourge, the bishops' iron rod,
The Lords' vexation, and the King's, by God!

Another poem was a parody 'Commons Petition to the King'. This depicted a revolutionary Commons seeking to subject monarchy to its will:

---

[77] Not in POASY. Quoted in Love, *Satire*, 122. See also McLaughlin, 'Poetick Rage', 74–7. 'Coleman' is Edward Colman, who was implicated in the popish plot and executed in Dec. 1678.

[78] POASY, ii, 111–13. The 'whore' is Charles's mistress, Louise de Kéroualle, duchess of Portsmouth.

[79] POASY, ii, 135–9.

In all humility we crave
Our Soverain to be *our* slave:
Beseeching him that he may be
Betrayd by us most loyally[.][80]

This also recalled the civil wars: it was originally printed in 1642, but was here reapplied to Charles II, and circulated widely in 1679.

As the Exclusion Crisis developed, printed political verse became more common, especially after print licensing laws lapsed in May 1679. Print is beyond the scope of this discussion. However, verse also circulated in manuscript between mid 1679 and March 1681, when Charles II's final parliament was dissolved, and a few examples will be surveyed briefly to conclude this section.[81] Indeed, even these examples did not circulate wholly in manuscript; many also appeared as printed broadsides. From both oppositional/Whig and loyalist/Tory perspectives, scribal poems were now more negative about parliament's prospects than in 1678–9. Several oppositional poems lamented the repeated prorogation of a new parliament that was summoned for October 1679 but only met a year later (the Second Exclusion Parliament of October 1680 to January 1681).[82] These included one that was supposedly posted on the Commons' door, and a Latin epigram on 'the still born Parliament':

> *Nata mori Vetus & Justum est sed iniqua Deorum*
> *Sævitia est Nondum Nata jubere mori.*[83]

(What is born must die – this is ancient and just. But it is a harsh cruelty of the gods to command the not-yet-born to die.)

In 'The Fancy' (1680), York satirically counsels his brother to continue proroguing parliaments, because dismissing them or allowing them to meet would each undermine royal authority: 'To shake off Parliaments will be too great… / To baffle therefore, but not cast them off, / To hold them still, but hold them still in scoff / Must be your work'.[84] An oppositional ballad offered a defiant, frustrated account of the Lords' defeat of an exclusion bill in November 1680, which it blamed on the bishops.[85] Among loyalist poems, Wentworth Dillon, earl of Roscommon's 'The Ghost of the Old House of Commons' (1681) presented a personified Second Exclusion Parliament informing the coming Third Exclusion Parliament (March 1681) that it had 'limits to the King prescribe[d]', but ultimately 'undid all I had done before' because its exclusion bill challenged the 'one only tree' that

---

[80] Not in POASY. Quoted from BL, Add. MS 18220, f. 125.

[81] The examples given represent all of those found in the sources consulted for this research. For the suggestion that more manuscript poems remain to be uncovered for this period, see Love, *Satire*, 123; McLaughlin, 'Poetick Rage', 24–6.

[82] POASY, ii, 344–7.

[83] The Latin epigram is not in POASY. Quoted from BL, Add. MS 34362, f. 107. This is repurposed from an epigram of Christiaan Huygens.

[84] POASY, ii, 381–90, is a printed version called 'Popish Politics Unmasked'; ii, 540, discusses a version called 'The Fancy' that is also found in manuscripts.

[85] POASY, ii, 375–9.

the king had deemed sacrosanct, the law of succession.[86] 'The Parliament Dissolved at Oxford' (1681) depicted this brief final parliament as a moment when 'Under 500 kings three kingdoms groan[ed]'.[87] Finally, referring to one of these last two parliaments, 'A Caution to King Charles the Second from Forty One' (1681) urged defiance on the king after 'The murm'ring of thy Senate House / Smells rank of Forty One', as 'When Kings are call'd to give account... / It is a Sign we all are kings, / Or that no King shall be'.[88] These examples were comparatively sparse; by 1681, the dominant medium of political verse was print, not manuscript.[89] However, the manuscript verse of the previous 15 years had been an important source of news and comment about parliament, which overwhelmingly presented parliament as an oppositional agent, like its 1620s equivalent, but now with a greater sense of impotence that was variously a source of delight or frustration to the poets.

4

How were scribal poems about parliament consumed? Evidence is limited, but some general impressions can be formed by examining surviving manuscripts.[90] A first important observation is that the poems were not always read for their political content at all. Many consumers of 1620s poems, in particular, were simply collectors of verse. Many poems survive in manuscript miscellanies or anthologies that wholly contain verse, not principally on political themes.[91] For example, Margaret Bellasys' notebook, compiled in around 1630, contains three poems that reference parliament – the poem narrating parliamentary debates in 1628 about naming Buckingham in the remonstrance, an anti-Buckingham poem that presents parliament as Buckingham's nemesis, and William Lewis's attack on St Alban's impeachment – mingled with verse by Donne, Shakespeare and others.[92] Collectors often gathered verse for non-political reasons, including its aesthetic value or simply the desire to preserve.[93] Some miscellanies and anthologies, however, had a greater concentration of political verse, so can more reasonably be judged to have had political interest to readers. A few of these more political collections survive from the early Stuart period, but they became especially common after the Restoration.[94] For instance, a 1680s verse anthology

[86] POASY, ii, 407–10.

[87] POASY, ii, 411–13.

[88] Not in POASY. Quoted from *Poems on Affairs of State, From 1640. to This Present Year 1704*, iii (1704, ESTC T144915), 189.

[89] Most famously John Dryden's 'Absalom and Achitophel' (Nov. 1681), which depicted parliament, allegorised as the 'Sanhedrin', as a dangerous force.

[90] Manuscript survivals are a tiny and skewed sample of the manuscripts through which poems must have originally circulated – they are weighted towards personal and professional miscellanies and anthologies, into which poems might have been transcribed after initially circulating as separates – but they nevertheless provide useful evidence about consumption.

[91] For miscellanies and anthologies, see Marotti, *Manuscript*; Love, *Scribal Publication*, ch. 6; Love, *Satire*, ch. 8; David Colclough, *Freedom of Speech in Early Stuart England* (Cambridge, 2005), ch. 4.

[92] BL, Add. MS 10309, f. 40 (ESL Oiii4); f. 42 (ESL Oii12); f. 128v (ESL Mii8). Other examples include BL, Add. MS 22118; Harley MS 6383; Bodl., MS Ashmole 38; MS Rawl. poet. 160; MS Eng. poet. c. 50; MS Eng. poet. f. 10; Leeds UL, Brotherton Collection MS Lt q 44.

[93] Colclough, *Freedom*, 201–4.

[94] Early Stuart examples: BL, Sloane MS 826; Bodl., MS Malone 23; Bodl., MS Rawl. poet. 26. Other Restoration examples include BL, Add. MS 23722; Add. MS 73540; Burney MS 390;

owned by Sir Samuel Danvers contains 14 of the poems that included discussion of parliament mentioned above, among a mass of other political verse.[95] However, it is difficult to judge how these manuscripts were consumed. It cannot be assumed that readers agreed with the politics of the poems they contained; indeed, this was usually impossible, as the poems gathered in manuscripts took different political perspectives. Another complexity is that the poems could remain 'topical' for a long period: although they sometimes circulated during or immediately after the parliaments they described, sometimes they reflected on parliamentary activity over several years, and sometimes they circulated for decades. In this way, despite the apparent ephemerality of manuscript poems, they could in fact be among the most lasting forms of media, disseminating news and comment well beyond their original political context.

These issues can be explored further by considering a few manuscripts – two early Stuart, three Restoration – that provide glimpses of individual readers. All contain manuscript verse about parliament alongside other sources of parliamentary news and comment, indicating that these readers consumed poems for their political content as part of a wider bundling of news media. Even in this small selection, a range of reading patterns can be detected: sometimes in line with their partisan sympathies, sometimes against; sometimes immediate, sometimes longer-term. One early Stuart reader was John Rous, a Suffolk clergyman, who kept a news diary between 1625 and 1643 that recorded various sources of parliamentary news, including oral reports from a member of parliament, manuscript separates of parliamentary speeches, and scribal verse. Rous was critical of the latter, commenting that 'Light scoffing wittes not apte to deeper reache, can rime upon any the most vulgar surmises', but this did not prevent his reading libels and copying them into his diary. In June or July 1628, Rous transcribed one of the anti-Buckingham poems discussed above with a sceptical comment: 'whether anymore be sette downe then vulgar rumor, which is often lying, I knowe not; but this I knowe, that those which are in esteeme and greatest favour with princes are most subjecte to slander of tongues, the vulgar delighting herein, who judge of all things by events, not by discretion'. He also transcribed a poem that took the opposite political perspective, Corbett's poetic defence of Buckingham, which was 'delivered' to him on 6 August 1629, over a year after its original composition.[96] Rous had complex political sympathies – he appears to have had an instinctive loyalism that was challenged by the regime's actions in the late 1620s – but these two poems alone indicate that he read scribal verse that took different points of view.[97]

A second, anonymous observer of 1620s parliaments compiled a manuscript that included two poems that referenced parliament. One was William Lewis's 1621 defence of St Alban. The transcriber was not fully cognisant of events in 1621 but was aware that parliament had been St Alban's opponent, writing that St Alban had been 'put off by the Parlement howese for some occasions to me unknowen'. In the margin, the transcriber commented that Lewis was 'too bould in his censure, & partiall in his loue, as maye appeere by the

[94] (continued) Harley MS 7315; Harley MS 7317; Harley MS 7319; Bodl., MS Add. A. 48; MS Firth c. 15; Leeds UL, Brotherton Collection, MS Lt 55; MS Lt 87; All Souls College, Oxford, MS 116; Lincolnshire Archives Office, ANC 15/B/4; Chetham's Library, Manchester, Mun. A.4.14; Nottingham UL, Pw V 40.

[95] BL, Add. MS 34362.

[96] BL, Add. MS 22959, f. 27; f. 22 (ESL Oii12); f. 35 (ESL Oiii2).

[97] Cust, 'News', 84–6.

sequell' (i.e., the fact that St Alban had fallen from power). This poem is followed by a transcription of another loyalist poem, James I's 1623 verse response to libellers. Both poems are included among other documents, including several relating to the 1624 parliament: a list of 'Articles propounded by the parlement', an address by Buckingham, a royal response to a parliamentary address, and a Commons petition. The manuscript must therefore date from 1624 or later, indicating that these poems were transcribed long after their composition. The transcriber's political leanings are unclear; although the two poems he included were both loyalist, his interest in the triumphally Protestant parliament of 1624 and his comment on the Lewis poem suggest that he may have had oppositional leanings.[98] Certainly, however, he read them for their political, parliamentary interest.

After the Restoration, another Suffolk clergyman, John Watson, compiled a miscellany between 1667 and 1673 that included a parliamentary speech and three scribal poems relating to parliament: the Latin epigram on Clarendon (apparently entered into the miscellany in February/March 1668), 'The King's Vows' (received by Watson on 20 May 1670) and 'On the Prorogation' (received on 5 August 1672).[99] All are oppositional poems, but Watson titled the second 'A Libellous Poem' and the third 'A Scurrilous Libel', so these transcriptions clearly did not reflect his political sympathies. They also appeared in the miscellany at least a few months after their composition: the Clarendon epigram was probably written in late 1667, 'The King's Vows' in several versions from c.1668 onwards, and 'On the Prorogation' was a response to a prorogation decision of September 1671. A higher concentration of parliament-related poems can be found in the miscellany of Sir William Haward, compiled between the 1660s and 1682: 27 of the poems discussed above, alongside many prose parliamentary separates, including transcriptions of speeches, petitions and proceedings. Haward was also a member of parliament, which provides another hint that the poems were read by parliamentarians as well as written about them. However, although Haward was active as a pro-court member of parliament, the range and scale of his collecting suggests that he gathered this verse as a chronicler rather than as a partisan.[100]

In contrast, a final example of a reader does indicate a partisan approach to consumption: Peter Le Neve, a student at Cambridge and the Middle Temple, who kept a news diary between 1678 and 1681.[101] Like Rous's diary, it was interspersed with parliamentary speeches and documents, and included some scribal verse, which reflected his political sympathies with oppositional/Whig forces during the Exclusion Crisis. Three poems referenced parliament: the 1679 'Queries' poem (entered in his diary on 19 March 1679), the anti-Danby poem, 'What a Devil Ails the Parliament' (entered 20 March 1679), and the 'Dialogue Between the Two Horses' (entered in early 1680). The first two were immediately topical, having reached Le Neve during the 1679 parliament to which they referred, as perhaps befitted a Londoner's superior access to news; the third was transcribed around four years after its composition, its striking equine-voiced condemnation of Restoration corruption

---

[98] BL, Add. MS 29303, f. 3 (ESL Mii8); f. 5 (ESL Nvi1).

[99] BL, Add. MS 18220, f. 7; f. 44; f. 101. The 1679 parody Commons 'petition' at f. 125, discussed above, was added by a later hand. See Love, *Satire*, 269–73.

[100] Bodl., MS Don. b. 8. See Love, *Scribal Publication*, 211–17; Love, *Satire*, 267–9; *HPC, 1660–1690*, s.v. 'Sir William Hawarde, (Hayward)'.

[101] BL, Add. MS 61903, f. 30; f. 33; f. 65. The diary's last entry is in 1685, but all but the last two pages cover 1678–81.

remaining relevant for the opposition-minded Le Neve during the Exclusion Crisis. Despite the varied patterns of consumption suggested by these readers, together they affirm the primary wider observation: that scribal verse was an acknowledged and accepted part of the mix of news media available to 17th-century observers of parliament.

5

Scribal verse was an important source of news and comment about parliament in 17th-century England. Poems that circulated in manuscript disseminated a view of parliament as an agent of oppositional politics in a polarised political landscape, praised in oppositional/'country' poems for acting as a bulwark against court corruption and criticised in loyalist/'court' poems for exceeding its proper subordinate role within the constitution, in relation to both the turbulent parliaments of the 1620s and the more chequered parliaments of the 1660s–80s. Collectively, these poems achieved a wide circulation. Rare glimpses of individual readers, such as the clergyman John Rous in the 1620s and the student Peter Le Neve in the 1670s, reveal that they were consumed as part of a bundle of news media about parliament. Some poems were even embedded within parliamentary culture themselves, being written by members of parliament such as Andrew Marvell and read by members such as Sir William Haward. The consistency of parliament's representation in scribal verse, however, indicates that all readers would have encountered a partisan depiction of parliament's role on the political stage. The primary significance of these poems is, therefore, for their contribution to a key theme that unites 17th-century political culture before, during and after the civil wars: the emergence of partisanship.

Hot News: The Florence Resident Reports on the Great Fire of London

BRENDAN DOOLEY AND DAVIDE BOERIO

This paper analyses the European impact and circulation of news concerning the Great Fire of London in 1666. The study dwells on the diplomatic correspondence and manuscript newsletters of Italian diplomats residing in England, on the testimonies of contemporary observers, and on the production of printed news publications. In particular, it analyses the role played by the Tuscan resident in London, Giovanni Salvetti Antelminelli, while investigating the functioning of the information-gathering process as well as the material and cultural resources put in place in the effort to report news about a disaster. In this regard, the event has been contextualised within a much larger period comprising the pandemic crisis of 1665 and the military campaign carried out by the English Crown during the Second Anglo–Dutch War. The analysis of the European media landscape during this period illuminates the mechanisms related to circulation and transmission of news and the relationship between internal political propaganda, as well as the response and the positioning of external observers in regard to an unexpected occurrence. Finally, comparison of sources allows us to stress the essentially dialectical nature between manuscript newsletters and printed news publications during the early modern period.

Keywords: disaster; *avvisi*; newsletters; diplomacy; Great Fire of London of 1666; plague; Anglo–Dutch Wars; Restoration

In September 1666, a newsletter from London destined for the Tuscan court described the scene in the most extreme language: 'After that horrible and stupendous fire that burned the whole city of London last week except for four or five streets, there has been nothing to talk about apart from the terrible effects of that deplorable incident', it began, in somewhat stilted Italian.[1] As the story was already five days old, the reporting focused on the few elements of closure, of resolution, of return to normality that could be discerned as things unfolded, perhaps with some indication of the role played by public authorities who might be worthy of respect back in Italy, where the newsletter's idiom and circulation guaranteed a ready audience.

---

[1] 'Dapoi quel horribile et stupendo fuoco che abbruciò la settimana passata tutta la Città di Londra fuori di quattro o cinque strade, non si ha hauto altro discorso qui che delli funesti effetti di quel deplorabile accidente. La confusione non è però tanto grande come si temeva tra il Popolazzo che haveva perso le lor habitazioni; infinite famiglie essendosi già ritirate in altre Città dove sono per commando espresso di Sua Maestà riceuto, et logiati. Alli più poveri che rimanevono alla campagna sul coperto del tiglo, si è concesso tutte le chiese per hospidalle et altri luoghi publici non abruggiati nelli fuburgi per habitarvi sin che si possi fabricarli qualche picole cabanne', ASFi, Mediceo del Principato [hereafter cited as MdP], 4206, f. 605v: 14/24 Sept. 1666.

Normally in a handwritten newsletter from this period, stories follow one another in quick succession, briefly recounted from available sources. But in this case one story dominates:

> the confusion among the lower people who lost their houses however is not as much as was feared, and uncountable families having already left for other cities where they have to be allowed entry and lodging by His Majesty's command, the poorest who were staying under linden trees in the countryside, have been offered, as hospitals, all the churches and other public places in the suburbs that were not burned, and there they can go and live while little shelters are being constructed for them.

While the promised hovels were still on the drawing board, 'the worst disorder currently seems to be robbery by the poor from each other, which at times causes great outcries immediately silenced by the prudence of His Majesty'.[2] One of the earliest royal proclamations in the wake of the disaster had sought to tackle petty theft, especially of foodstuffs, taking place in the London suburbs, for which unspecified severe penalties were threatened, while laying the groundwork for a mass distribution of necessaries to the destitute. Later the interests of those worried about their surviving silver and furnishings would be taken up and accommodated by orders for the sheltering and protection of goods.[3]

The newsletter's report was dated 24 September new style (that is, 14 September old style), and regarded events that concluded a week before. As the Great Fire is customarily said, within British historiography, to have occurred between Sunday 2 September and Thursday 6 September 1666, we will adopt the conventional expression of 2/12 September through to 6/16 September in order to co-ordinate both styles of dating. But timing is only one of many problems of perspective that occur in handling the news regarding such an event, given the types of sources at our disposal. Another problem has to do with point of view.

Hindsight, to some degree, has robbed the historian of the means for re-experiencing what is already so deeply etched in the British consciousness, and not only for reasons connected with the temptations of anachronism. More pertinently, how were words and deeds perceived from day to day as yesterday's assumptions received verification or contradiction, in an ongoing process of discovery?[4] The linear unfolding of events absent of any foreknowledge as to outcome can only be apprehended by analogy, by imagination, and by a close reading, such as we will be attempting here, of sources that are still relatively untapped in spite of the documents' availability at least since the 19th century: in the State Archives in Florence where the originals are kept (Mediceo del Principato, 4206), and in the British Library where copies were made in view of a possible publication (Add. MSS.,

---

[2] 'Il maggiore disordine che aparisce presentemente è nel rubare (tra li poveri) le robbe li una dell'altro, che causa alle volte grand rumori che sono subito pacificati dalla prudenza di Sua Maestà', ASFi, MdP, 4206, f. 605v: 14/24 Sept. 1666.

[3] Charles II, king of England, *His Majesty, in his Princely compassion…*, 5/15 Sept. 1666, https://ota.bodleian. ox.ac.uk/repository/xmlui/handle/20.500.12024/A32288 (accessed 29 Jan. 2021); as well as Charles II, king of England, *A proclamation for restoring goods imbezzell'd* … 19/29 Sept. 1666, https://quod.lib.umich.edu/e/eebo2/ B19760.0001.001?rgn=main;view=fulltext (accessed 29 Jan. 2021).

[4] Consider reflections about these processes in Michael Schudson, 'The Anarchy of Events and the Anxiety of Story Telling', *Political Communication*, xxiv (2007), 253–7.

27962 A–W), as Stefano Villani explained in an article laying the groundwork for a modern edition.[5]

Giovanni Salvetti Antelminelli, author of the despatches and handwritten newsletters on which we will chiefly rely in this detailed anatomy of a single case study, served as the Medici resident in London for 13 years before, during and after the grim events that are the focus here.[6] As a writer of a newsletter in addition to his official despatch he followed the procedure of his father and predecessor Amerigo Salvetti, in-line with the strategy of bringing major events to the attention of a range of readers, within the limits placed on another former resident to Venice, Ippolito Buondelmonti, 30 years before. Did he risk getting into the same trouble as Buondelmonti, who was told in no uncertain terms that sending such newsletters to anyone outside the Tuscan diplomatic circle was out of bounds, only to hint in response that such was the only way to receive in exchange, from many sources, the precious information his employers so craved?[7] In both types of communication he follows the rules of the genre; standard letter form for the despatch, and for the newsletter, giving only place of publication and date, with no indication of the author, although the similarity of handwriting, and the references in the official signed despatch, allow no mistake about who is writing. Between the two forms, newsletters are of course the upstart: having been invented in Italy as early as the 15th century and subsequently adopted for divulging news across a vast network of Europe-wide distribution.[8]

As a paradigm for successful information delivery, Salvetti (the younger) could rely on an example close at hand: the memory of his father, who after resorting to political exile in London having fled from Lucca as a young man, had for 40 years held the same diplomatic position in grand ducal officialdom until his death in 1657.[9] Giovanni, born in England in 1636, would have been a toddler when Amerigo was conveying news of the English Civil War to correspondents in newsletters and despatches with a precision and comprehensiveness that Villani claims as a model of the genre. The father's warm recommendation, added perhaps to the usual dynastic logic of 'like father like son' guaranteed his succession to the role. And as the Protectorate crumbled and the Restoration loomed, he had no shortage of drama to relate.

For his Tuscan audience, and especially Grand Duke Ferdinando II, it was a particularly important moment in British history, as the monarchical regime once more resumed contacts with the princely courts of Europe, presumably guaranteeing access and reliability. Just 40 years before, in regard to another republican government, the Florentine ambassador to

[5] Stefano Villani, 'Per la progettata edizione della corrispondenza dei rappresentanti toscani a Londra: Amerigo Salvetti e Giovanni Salvetti Antelminelli durante il Commonwealth e il Protettorato (1649–1660)', *Archivio Storico Italiano*, clxii (2004), 109–25.

[6] Stefano Villani, 'Giovanni Salvetti Antelminelli', *Dizionario Biografico degli Italiani,* xc (2017), http://www.treccani.it/enciclopedia/giovanni-salvetti-antelminelli_res-995b3240-9654-11e8-a7cb-00271042e8d9_(Dizionario-Biografico)/ (accessed 8 Apr. 2021).

[7] ASFi, MdP, 3016, f. 457v. Concerning Buondelmonti's activity as a news writer, Brendan Dooley, 'A Plague of News: Florence, 1629–33', *Tales of Two Cities: Urban News/Legends between Print and Archive*, ed. Pasquale Palmieri (forthcoming).

[8] On the phenomenon of early newsletters, Mario Infelise, *Prima dei giornali: Alle origini della pubblica informazione* (Bari, 2002).

[9] Davide Boerio 'La trasmissione delle notizie tra modelli teorici, contaminazioni linguistiche e scambi informativi tra la penisola italiana e l'Inghilterra nella prima metà del XVII secolo', *Rivista di Letteratura Storiografica Italiana*, iv (2020), 61–76.

Venice had complained, 'Here we are not in Tuscany or in any other state ruled by a single prince'. Instead, 'two hundred brains, all different', discuss and endlessly deliberate, and 'on things not of public urgency, they all have to agree; so they must be won over one by one', making persuasion agonisingly slow, and bribery prohibitively expensive. Much easier to approach, he added, were those places where 'the will of a single prince determines and executes in the same moment'.[10] The Tuscan court could not agree more, and in case of any doubt, could brandish Scipione Ammirato's treatise on princely absolutism, a locally-based handbook of sanitised Machiavellianism published in the last years of the 16th century.[11] In the new English regime, the possible role parliament might eventually play was anybody's guess, and if the eyes of Europe were fixed on the outcome, so especially were those of Ferdinando and the court, as they engaged in a long-term strategy to understand and navigate the power shifts that inevitably impinged on their small state's chances of survival in the emerging world of gunpowder empires.[12]

The features of late Stuart rule that concern us here, are those which have proven most durable while setting the stage for the eventual regime change that would occur in 1689. An often contentious scholarship has constructed powerful theses out of the evidence for a highly agitated spiritual consciousness needing to be sedated, a dynasty to be preserved or combatted, a political world to be restructured.[13] These and other elements of Restoration society and culture have fascinated and challenged historians, one might even say, since Clarendon. Rather than revisionism and post-revisionism, the opposing schools include those who would hold that the developing situation emerged due to political manoeuvring, power grabbing and short-term planning, contrasted with others who pay more attention to deeper forces at work in the modernisation process.

Giovanni Salvetti, an attentive observer of the human as well as political ramifications, is concerned in the documents we are examining, to convey the operation and effects of governing forces. At the same time he shows a certain fascination for local institutions, no

[10] ASFi, MdP, 3007, f. 449: from Sacchetti, 12 Oct. 1621: 'In somma, in Pregadi entrano 200 cervelli, et tutti diversi, se bene in questo particolare devono esser pur troppo d'accordo'. ASFi, MdP, 3007, f. 435: from Sacchetti, 9 Oct. 1621: 'Questo governo come ho detto è dissimilissimo, come ella sa, da quel degli altri stati d'Italia, nei quali la volontà di un sol Principe determina et esseguisce in un subito, ma qui nelle cose che on premono al pubblico, bisogna guadagnarseli a uno a uno con una estrema patienza, et poi anche si corre risico, che rizzandosi su qualcheduno a dir quattro parole in contrario, si rivolti quanto si è fatto, et si habbi a ricominciar da capo'.

[11] Scipione Ammirato, *Discorsi sopra Cornelio Tacito* (Florence, 1594).

[12] On parliament and political culture, B.D. Henning, 'Introductory Survey', *HPC 1660–1690*, ed. B.D. Henning (3 vols, 1983), i, 1–84, and other sources mentioned below. Ferdinando II's reign in the Grand Duchy has been less well studied; although here we take into account Luca Mannori, *Il sovrano tutore: Pluralismo istituzionale e accentramento amministrativo nel principato dei Medici (sec. XVI–XVIII)* (Milan, 1994); L. Mannori, 'Lo Stato di Firenze e i suoi storici', *Società e Storia*, xx, 1997, 401–15; Marcello Fantoni, 'The Grand Duchy of Tuscany: The Courts of the Medici 1532–1737', in *The Princely Courts of Europe: Ritual, Politics and Culture under the Ancien Régime 1500–1750*, ed. John Adamson, (1999), 255–74; Niccolò Capponi , 'Le Palle di Marte: Military Strategy and Diplomacy in the Grand Duchy of Tuscany under Ferdinand II de'Medici', *Journal of Military History*, lxviii (2004), 1105–41; as well as *Florence et la Toscane XIVe–XIXe siècles, les dynamiques d'un état italien*, ed. Jean Boutier, Sandro Landi and Olivier Rouchon (Rennes, 2004), ch. iv by Boutier, Landi, Hélène Chauvineau and Caroline Callard; and Caroline Callard, *Le Prince et la République: Histoire, pouvoir et société dans la Florence des Médicis, au XVIIe siècle* (Paris, 2007).

[13] The major bibliographical questions are covered in ch. 1, 2 and 7 of George Southcombe and Grant Tapsell, *Restoration Politics, Religion, and Culture: Britain and Ireland, 1660–1714* (Basingstoke, 2011). Also consider the contextualisation in Tim Harris, *Restoration: Charles II and His Kingdoms, 1660–1685* (2005), ch. 1. In addition, Alan Houston and Steven Pincus, 'Introduction: Modernity and Later Seventeenth-Century England', in *A Nation Transformed: England After the Restoration*, ed. Alan Houston and Steven Pincus (Cambridge, 2001), 1–19.

doubt nurtured by having lived most of his life in England. He pays particular attention to the activities of the Cavalier Parliament, whose modus operandi would have been an object of considerable curiosity among his Florentine correspondents. Explaining the activities of parliament in terms of the passing of bills and laws, he attempts to domesticate English political vocabulary in a way that still preserves what may be presumed to be the basic extraneousness of the experience from the Tuscan point of view. Bills, as debated by the members, are called 'biglietti', bearing connotations unrelated to parliamentary matters. 'Committee' requires a fresh neologism, namely, 'committi'.

Salvetti was not yet 30 years old when the Restoration's high hopes encountered a major setback as plague broke out in London in 1665.[14] Setting aside the terror and evident danger to himself, for the young diplomatic communicator it was an extraordinary opportunity. Since 1663, there had been sporadic outbreaks even in the city. By April 1665, fears were mounting about what might occur; and by June, weekly deaths from the disease had doubled. Salvetti continued reporting on matters of state, gaining the expressed admiration of his audience, at least according to the court secretary Persio Falconcini, who responded, 'You will be. . . pleased to hear that the contents of [the despatch] and the insert [i.e., the newsletter] were benignly heard by the Most Serene Patron, as befits the curiosity of the information transmitted with your usual diligence and comprehensiveness'.[15] He held out in London until the end of July, at which point he moved his operations to Tonbridge, Kent, a few miles away from Tunbridge Wells, which in pre-plague times had begun to establish a reputation as a spa resort. At a safe distance from the metropolis Salvetti continued to report, until finally returning in the following January, dating his intervening newsletters from Tonbridge.

For reporting the dramatic events transpiring in London to his Tuscan audience, he had an important source at hand: namely, the 'bills of mortality', published weekly by the Worshipful Company of Parish Clerks and consisting of a single sheet with the city's mortality figures accompanied by the various causes of death.[16] First appearing at the end of the 16th century, these innovative printed publications informed readers about the spread of plague and other diseases, allowing assessment of the early signs of a possible contagion. A plausible estimate holds that during the 17th century some 5,000 to 6,000 copies of each number were printed by an official printer with the approval of the city authorities and then sold for a penny in the book stalls of St Paul's Churchyard and other places in London.

Not surprisingly, Salvetti's accounts of the plague assume a rather quantitative tone. In a newsletter of mid October 1665, he reported:

> The contagious evil continues this week to diminish in the city and suburbs of London, where not less than 5,720 have died in the current week of all diseases and of the plague

---

[14] The event recounted long after the fact by Daniel Defoe in his fictional work *A Journal of the Plague Year* (1722), has been more particularly studied by J.F.D. Shrewsbury, *A History of Bubonic Plague in the British Isles* (Cambridge, 1970); and Patrick Wallis, 'Plagues, Morality and the Place of Medicine in Early Modern England', *E.H.R.*, cxxi (2006), 1–24.

[15] 'Si contenterà ella. . . di sentire che dal Padrone Serenissimo il contenuto di essa [lettera] e dell'inserto è stato benignamente udito, come hà ben meritata la curiosità degli avvisi da Lei trasmessi con la consueta sua diligenza et pienezza', ASFi, MdP, 4209, c. 777: Falconcini to Salvetti, 30 Apr./9 May 1665.

[16] N.G. Brett-James, 'The London Bills of Mortality in the 17th Century', *Transactions of the London and Middlesex Archaeological Society*, vi (1927–31), 284–309.

4,929, but we flatter ourselves with all that after the destruction of 73,194 people, who died during the present contagion, That the Lord God will eventually have compassion on this poor city, and deliver it in a short time from this scourge, and for this end (we observe for the whole Kingdom) the first Tuesday of every month as a day of humiliation to implore from God a cessation of the present pestilence.[17]

Despite invocations of divine mercy and the acts of contrition, the contagion abated only slowly; and in the last newsletter from Tonbridge, Salvetti reported the figures from the past year: 'The general note of this year reports that in the city and suburbs of London 97,306 people died of all diseases together, and of the pestilence alone 68,596, and that this year in the said city 79,009 more people died than in the previous year'.[18] The precision lent a note of verisimilitude, while conveying the frightful results so far.

The importance of events was not lost on the Tuscan court. In keeping with prevailing biological theories at the time, Florentine authorities had the pages of Salvetti's correspondence sanitised to avoid contagion, using a fumigation process that has left still-visible traces on our documents. Memories were still fresh of the plague that hit much of northern Italy in 1629–31.[19] As far as the contents were concerned, the competition for Ferdinando II's attention was considerable, in view of the wide distribution of qualified Tuscan representatives around Europe, as might befit a prince described without irony by Gaston d'Orleans, offspring of Ferdinando's great-aunt Maria de' Medici, as 'the most judicious prince in Europe, the best informed of foreign affairs, the most political in retaining the favour and respect of all the potentates and the most compliant there is'.[20] The Tuscan Court's foreign correspondents drew upon and competed with unofficial agents of all kinds: priests, monks, astrologers and singers. In every case, the choice of the right people in the key nodes of the information network assumed a strategic importance for Medici policy.[21] Experience as an agent, resident, secretary or ambassador in another European court was often an indispensable precondition for holding important government positions at home.

News reached Florence from every destination, sometimes to the dismay of foreign agents in the city, who worried that unauthorised intelligence distributed to unauthorised persons might convey an impression of their country at odds with the carefully-wrought image

---

[17] 'Il male contagioso continua anche questa settimana a deminuirsi nella Città, et fuburbi di Londra, dove non di meno sono morti nella corrente settimana di tutte le malatie insieme 5720 et della peste 4929; ma ci aduliamo con tutto ciò che doppo la distruzzione di 73194 persone morti durante la presente Contagione, che il Signor Dio haverà alla fine compassione di quella povera città, et che la liberarà tra poco da questo flagello, et per questo fine si osserva (per tutto il Regno) il primo Mercredì d'ogni Mese, come giorno d'umiliazione per implorare da Dio una cessazione della presente Pestilenza', ASFi, MdP, 4206, f. 398: 6/16 Oct. 1665.

[18] 'Il Biglietto generale di questo Anno [dice] esser morti nella Città et fuburbi di Londra 97306 di tutte Malatie insieme; et della Pestilenza sola 68596; et che siano morti questo Anno in detta Città 79009 più che nell'Anno precendente', ASFi, MdP, 4206, f. 442v: 30 Dec./8 Jan. 1665/6.

[19] Concerning this event, the Florentine side is explored in Giulia Calvi, *Histories of a Plague Year: The Social and the Imaginary in Baroque Florence*, tr. Dario Biocca (Berkeley, CA, 1989), and Giovani Baldinucci, *Quaderno: Peste, guerra e carestia nell'Italia del Seicento*, ed. Brendan Dooley (Florence, 2001).

[20] H. Acton, *The Last Medici* (New York, 1958), 55.

[21] The pattern was set by the grand duke's predecessors, on which, S. Dall'Aglio, ' "Qui capitano tutte l'importantie delle cose": Spie, informatori e ambasciatori medicei a Venezia nei primi anni del principato cosimiano', in *Varchi e altro Rinascimento. Studi offerti a Vanni Bramanti*, ed. S. Lo Re and F. Tomasi (Manziana, 2013), 313–26. Also note *Istruzioni agli ambasciatori e inviati medicei in Spagna e nell'Italia spagnola (1536–1648)*, 2: 1587–1648, ed. Francesco Martelli and Cristina Galasso (Rome, 2007), vii–l.

they were trying to convey. When a sporadically printed Florentine gazette struck up publication in these years, the English resident John Finch was irate. In May 1666 he recalled to the grand duke that 'many months ago, as an official of my Sovereign, I complained to Your Most Serene Highness about the great disorders appearing daily in the gazette printed in this city, highly damaging to His Majesty and His armies'.[22] The grand duke had accordingly assured him that subsequent copies would be thoroughly censored by a courtier. Yet now, in spite of this timely action, 'pasquinades against His Majesty [Charles II] and inflammatory words against his arms and state affairs are nonetheless being seen'. Accordingly, he demanded, in the name of King Charles, 'a remedy for this injury'. Every envoy engaged in a delicate balancing act between creating (or correcting) news and receiving it.

A month before the London fire began, an event known as 'Holmes' bonfire' had given rise to another example of Salvetti's reporting. A raid conducted by Admiral Robert Holmes on the estuary of Vlie in the Netherlands destroyed between 150 and 170 Dutch merchant ships and burned a village called Bandaris (present-day West-Terschelling) to the ground, one of the episodes of the Second Anglo–Dutch War.[23] In a newsletter dated 17/27 August 1666, Salvetti recounted the episode, basing his account on the bi-weekly *London Gazette*,[24] which incorporated a letter said to have been written by Holmes. In Appendix 1 we compare the two accounts. Places where the texts are related but differently worded are in bold, whereas parts that are unique to one or the other document are underlined.

At 429 words, Salvetti's manuscript text is scarcely half the length of the English gazette's printed one, at 956 words. Names of fleet commanders Prince Rupert and the duke of Albemarle are not featured with appropriate honorifics in the first paragraph. In addition, while the news sheet relates the destruction of 150 ships, describing them as 'vasselli olandesi' (Dutch vessels), the *Gazette* prefers 'enemy ships'. Such seemingly insignificant variations may reveal something of an effort to contrive an appearance of neutrality, while remaining clearly on the English side. Details of vessel types are rendered in more general terms than in the source, such that 'man-of-war', 'Hoy', and 'Ketches' become 'vasselli di guerra, barche e fregate' (warships, boats and frigates);[25] whereas emphasis is placed on the great value of the cargoes 'bound for Constantinople, Scanderoon, Muscovy, Guinea, [the] Indies and other long trips'.[26] Entirely omitted in Salvetti's narrative is the part of the *Gazette* account devoted to the naval minutiae of what Holmes, in his letter, calls his 'happy expedition,' in

---

[22] 'Molti mesi già sono che io come ministro del re mio signore ne feci lamenti appresso V.A.S. delli disordini grandi che nella stampata gazetta di questa città, giornalmente si vedevano in pregiudizio di S. Maestà e delli suoi armi. Et V.A.S. m'havendo assicurato che se ne compiacerebbe di commandar al Sig. Senator Federighi di guardar la gazetta avanti che ne fosse pubblicata, a finche non si ritrovasse nell'avvenire simile male creanze. [...] Ma accorgendomi che non solante così savio e riguardevole Senator ne habbia la revisione delle gazette, si lascia pur veder in esse pasquinate contra S.M. e parole infamatorii delli suoi armi e negozii di stato. [...] Non posso si non dolermi appo V.A.S. di così insolente parole e false stampate nella città capitale di V.A.S. [...] Ed al nome di S. Maestà ne dimando il riparo di questa ingiuria', ASFi, MdP, 1824, ff. nn.: John Finch, English Resident in Florence, to Grand Duke Ferdinand II, 29 May, 1666. In regard to the first Italian gazettes, Giuseppe Farinelli, 'Le origini del giornalismo', in Giuseppe Farinelli et al., *Storia del giornalismo italiano dalle origini ai giorni nostri* (Turin, 1997), 10–12.

[23] Gjis Rommelse and Roger Downing, '"Holmes's Bonfire", an Interpretation on the Basis of National Identities', *It Beaken Jiergong*, lxxix (2017), 201–14.

[24] *London Gazette*, 79: 13–16/23–26 Aug. 1666.

[25] ASFi, MdP, 4207, f. 594: *avvisi* from London, 17/27 Aug. 1666.

[26] 'la più parte di grand Valuta, essendo caricati per Constantiniopoli, Scanderone, Moscovia, Guinea, Indie et altri longhi viaggi', ASFi, MdP, 4207, f. 595.

terms of captains, ships' names and locations, and the like – features that would have fed the English audience's well-documented hunger for current war news.[27]

In contrast to his approach in the newsletter, in his despatches Salvetti adopted a less seemingly neutral viewpoint about the torching of a Dutch village. Rejecting the breezy enthusiasm of the *Gazette* account based on Holmes's report, he draws on sources originating among the victims to paint a dramatic picture of fear and suffering:

> I have seen at this moment letters from Holland that depict the great confusion of that People, who go like madmen through the streets banging their heads like desperate men against the wall or against each other, so stunned are they by this unspeakable Loss, which the same letter says would be too incredible to relate; it will suffice to say that this population has never experienced such a thing.[28]

The passage throws light on the variety of testimonies, ranging in geographical breadth and viewpoint, typical of the Tuscan diplomat's trade. Soon enough the pathos injected into his writing would serve him in an event occurring much closer to home.

The basic episodes of the Great Fire of London are well enough known not to require detailed recounting here. A conflagration began in a Pudding Lane baker's shop and spread to neighbouring buildings, quickly involving other neighbourhoods and eventually the whole city. Causes were as elusive as the final tally of destruction. In spite of relatively low mortality, 13,200 houses were reported to have been destroyed, leaving a homeless population estimated by the contemporary observer John Evelyn to have amounted to some 200,000 people, later thought to be closer to 70,000 to 80,000.[29] An emergency survival project to meet the most urgent demands soon developed into a plan for a model city, with effects that largely characterised the urban environment in the following centuries. A new concept of the 'city of London' was in the making, Erik Bond has pointed out, where practically none had been before.[30]

A new planning committee included the aspiring architect Christopher Wren, whose basic blueprint on the model of newly replanned Paris and Rome would have turned a congeries of medieval alleyways into a monumental showpiece with wide straight streets laid out in the geometrical contours of a baroque city.[31] The working group for carrying out the construction took such guidelines into account, while paying heed to practical necessities in terms of resources, housing demands, the resumption of commerce and time available.

---

[27] In this regard, Steven Pincus, *Protestantism and Patriotism: Ideologies and the Making of English Foreign Policy, 1650–1688* (Cambridge, 1996), 276–7.

[28] 'Ho visto in questo momento lettere d'Olanda, che depingono la grand confusione di quel Popolo, che vanno come Matti distrettamente per le Strade buttando le teste come desperati contra le muraglie, o, l'un l'altri, tanto storditi sono di questa indicible Perdita, la quale dice la medesima lettera sarebbe troppo incredibile a raguagliare; basterà a dire che quel Popolo non habbia mai sostentato un tale…', ASFi, MdP, 4206, f. 593: Despatch from Giovanni Salvetti Antelminelli to Persio Falconcini, 17/27 Aug. 1666.

[29] Adrian Tinniswood, *By Permission of Heaven: The Story of the Great Fire of London* (2003), 4, 101; T. F. Reddaway, *The Rebuilding of London After the Great Fire* (1951), 270; Hazel Forsyth, *Butcher, Baker, Candlestick Maker: Surviving the Great Fire of London* (2016).

[30] Erik Bond, 'Historicizing the "New Normal": London's Great Fire and the Genres of Urban Destruction', *Restoration: Studies in English Literary Culture, 1660–1700*, xxxi (2007), 43–64.

[31] Episodes analysed by Lisa Jardine, *On a Grander Scale: The Outstanding Career of Sir Christopher Wren* (New York, 2002), ch. 4; as well as Paul Rabbitts, *Sir Christopher Wren* (2019).

A city with representational spaces highlighting administrative power was still the object, with longing glances to the continental exemplars of absolutism. But as Michael Hebbert has emphasised, the plan as put into practice also reflected the realities of a monarchy in which parliament had a more and more established role in making decisions and setting the agenda.[32]

Charles II, having already gained public admiration for his apparent attention to emergency measures during the fire, took to the press to reinforce the message of tragedy turned into triumph. In his published *Declaration* he claimed that:

> no particular man hath sustained any loss or damage by the late terrible and deplorable fire in his fortune or estate, in any degree to be compared with the loss and damage we ourself have sustained, so it is not possible for any man to take the same more to heart, and to be more concerned and solicitous for the rebuilding this famous city with as much expedition as is possible.[33]

The purposes of divine providence must be taken into account:

> since it hath pleased God to lay this heavy judgment upon us all in this time, as an evidence of his displeasure for our sins, we do comfort ourself with some hope, that he will, upon our due humiliation before him, as a new instance of his signal blessing upon us, give us life, not only to see the foundations laid, but the buildings finished, of a much more beautiful city than is at this time consumed.

The king insisted that practical needs should be fully integrated with aesthetic ones, according to the architectural ideals of the day, taking account of the city's intrinsic geographical characteristics. 'As the seat and situation of it is the most convenient and noble for the advancement of trade of any city in Europe', the king went on:

> such care will be taken for the re-edification of it, both for use and beauty, and such provision made for the future against the ordinary and casual accidents by fire, as may, as far as human wisdom can provide, upon the sad experience we have had, reasonably secure the same, and make it rather appear to the world, as purged with the fire (in how lamentable a manner soever) to a wonderful beauty and comeliness, than consumed by it.

Efforts must be made to prevent the current shock from becoming desperation, especially where there were no other available options except to aid in the common effort. Thus,

> we receive no small encouragement in this our hope, by the alacrity and chearfulness [sic] we observe in those who have undergone the greatest loss, and seem the most undone; who, with undaunted courage, appear to desire the same as we do, and resolve to contribute their utmost assistance thereunto.[34]

[32]Michael Hebbert, 'The Long After-life of Christopher Wren's Short-lived London Plan of 1666', *Planning Perspectives*, xxxv (2020), 231–52.

[33]Charles II, king of England, *His Majestie's Declaration to His City of London upon Occasion of the Late Calamity by the Lamentable Fire* (1666), dated 13/23 Sept. the same year.

[34]*His Majestie's Declaration*, 4.

Eyewitness accounts of the events and the aftermath were many and varied. Among the best articulated is the diary of Samuel Pepys, originally penned not for publication but rather (so Claire Tomalin has surmised) for a kind of personal self-affirmation. His writing process is thought to have involved a daily entry, perhaps first inscribed in a now lost notebook, and then copied in the volumes that have been preserved at Magdalene College, Cambridge.[35] As a rising star in public administration Pepys was in a good position to observe the role of parliament in fire-related business, though he would not become a member of parliament until 1673. In his account he expressed his initial curiosity, followed by dismay as the gravity of the situation dawned on him during the course of the first day.[36] Within a matter of hours of his first being alerted to what was transpiring, he definitively set aside his initial impressions of a closely circumscribed and distant conflagration. He went on to show how he and his acquaintances shared the impact and general reactions, conveying excitement in terms that practically leap off the page in numerous run-on sentences constituting a narrative that comprises the recollections of the entire day, laying out events consecutively with little commentary apart from elucidations regarding emotional states.

Much more synthetic was the notice that appeared in the *London Gazette* on Monday 3/13 September, the day following the event, with the following coda, seemingly inserted at the last moment before publication, after two pages of reporting on all that had occurred in every other matter since Thursday 30 August: 'London, Sept. 2. About two a clock this morning a sudden and lamentable Fire broke out in this City, beginning not far from Thames Street near London Bridge, which continues still with great violence, and hath already burnt down to the ground many houses thereabouts...' The position taken by the crown, including public displays by the king and James duke of York, were given special relief, along with assurances concerning some of the measures being put in place:

> ...which sad accident affected His Majesty with that tenderness and compassion, that he was pleased to go himself in Person with his Royal Highness, to give order that all possible means should be used for quenching the fire, or stopping its further spreading. In which case the Right Honorable [sic] the Earl of Craven was sent by His Majesty to be more particularly assisting to the Lord Mayor and Magistrates; and several Companies of His Guards sent into the City, to be helpful by what ways they could in so great a calamity.[37]

Efforts were being made to provide reassuring demonstrations of solidarity, according to this writing probably by Charles Perrot, successor to the founding editor and newsletter writer, Henry Muddiman. The earliest numbers of the paper were specifically addressed, presumably by the putative publisher, undersecretary of state Joseph Williamson, 'for the use of some Merchants and Gentlemen, who desire them'.

In the ensuing chaos the paper suspended publication for a week, coming out again on 10/20 September with a report dated 8/18 September from Whitehall, to wit:

---

[35] Claire Tomalin, *Samuel Pepys: The Unequalled Self* (2002), ch. 6.

[36] *The Diary of Samuel Pepys*, ed. Robert Latham and William Matthews (11 vols, 1970–83), vii, 267–72.

[37] *London Gazette*, 30 Aug.–3 Sept. [10–13 Sept.], https://www.thegazette.co.uk/London/issue/86/page/1 (accessed 1 Feb. 2021).

The ordinary course of this Paper having been interrupted by a sad and lamentable accident of Fire lately hapned in the City of London: It hath been thought fit for satisfying the minds of so many of His Majesties good Subjects who must needs be concerned for the issue of so great an accident to give this short, but true Account of it.

Indeed, we are given two versions of events, as the main account [version A] was followed by a 'Farther Account of this Lamentable Fire' [version B], covering some of the same ground as the account on 3/13 September as well as version A in this issue.

Taking advantage of print's superiority for delivering voluminous content on a single page, the writer of version A elaborated on the more colourful aspects. For instance, a free provisioning of sea-biscuit was met with singular lack of enthusiasm by palates used to more tasty stuff:

> when his Majesty, fearing lest other Orders might not yet have been sufficient, had commanded the Victualler of his Navy to send bread into Moore-fields for the relief of the poor, which for the more speedy supply he sent in Bisket out of the Sea Stores; it was found that the Markets had been already so well supplyd that the people, being un-accustomed to that kind of Bread declined it, and so it was returned in greater part to his Majestys Stores again without any use made of it.

Salvetti, in reporting the sequence of events on the streets and behind the scenes, does not appear to have drawn exclusively from the *Gazette* for his coverage, despite his later reputation as a flagrant text re-user. One passage stands out, however, for its similarity to the *Gazette*, which we show next to its near identical counterpart:

London Gazette[38]	Salvetti[39]
Whitehall Friday September the 21[/1 October]. His Majesty according to his Message to both houses of the 18[/28], went to the Parliament, where being set in His Royal Throne, having on his Robes of Estate, the Crown upon his Head, and the Regal Ensigns carried after the usual manner before him, the Sword by the Earl of Oxford and the Cap of Estate by the Lord Bellasise; the House of Commons being called up, His Majesty was pleased in a Gracious Speech to both Houses, to express the satisfaction He had to see them happily met again; and so leaving them to their several Consultations, the House of Commons immediately returned to their House, where the	His Majesty, according to his message on the [18/]28th of September, Friday went personally to Parliament where, sitting on his Royal Throne, with the crown upon his head and the Royal insignia as usual borne before him, the Sword by the Signor Count of Oxford and the Cap of State by My Lord Bellassis, and the Lower House having been called, His Majesty was pleased to express his satisfaction at seeing them so happily met together; then leaving them to their separate consultations, the Lower House returned to the room where the address of His Majesty (consigned to the Speaker) having been read, they resolved unanimously: *that the humble*

[38] *London Gazette*, 20–24 Sept./[30 Sept.–4 Oct.], https://www.thegazette.co.uk/London/issue/89/page/1 (accessed 1 Feb. 2021).

[39] ASFi, MdP, 4206, f. 614 [29 Sept.]/8 Oct.

Coppy of His Majesties Speech delivered to the Speaker, being read, they unanimously Resolved, *That the humble and hearty Thanks of that House be returned to His Majesty for His great Care in the Management of the present Warr; and that the House will supply His Majesty proportionally to His present Occasions. And that the Lords concurrence herein be desired by Mr. Solicitor, and Mr. Garraway.*	*thanks of that House would be conveyed to His Majesty, for his great care in managing the present War, and that the House wished to furnish His Majesty with money proportionally to the present occasions [crossed out: past], and that the Signor Solicitor and Signor Garaway desired the concurrence of the Upper House in this.*

So far, this is the closest resemblance we have found between the two families of texts, at least in the period in question, suggesting that for the most part both Salvetti and the *Gazette* writer may have been drawing upon another yet unknown original, possibly Muddiman's newsletter. Both accounts make reference to a speech by the king dated 21 September, which was duly printed in London by John Bill and Christopher Barker and immediately reprinted in Edinburgh by Evan Tyler, warning that 'we have two very great and powerful Enemies', i.e., the Dutch and the French, 'who use all the means they can, fair and foul, to make all the World to concur with them, and the War is more chargeable (by that Conjunction) then anybody thought it would have been'.[40] The direct translation Salvetti claimed to have supplied of this text to accompany his newsletter appears to be lost.[41]

Concerning the role of parliament, Salvetti preferred terse summaries to extensive narratives. For instance, on 5/15 October we are told:

> Parliament has many great matters on the agenda, the main one being the decision about the rights of private persons in the burned city, as also the price to be paid to proprietors to facilitate rebuilding the city with wider streets and squares and other aspects creating uniformity, and it is said that this matter has been submitted to the prudence and will of the king, with the aim of then writing it up and ratifying it by Act of Parliament; meanwhile, referring to the challenge faced by the city of London, they have ordered the Parliament's humble thanks to be conveyed to His Majesty for his attention and efforts to avoid the burning of the city.[42]

[40] *His Majesties Gracious Speech to Both Houses of Parliament* (1666).

[41] 'Per conto di novità trasmetto a Vostra Signoria Illustrissima il mio solito foglio insieme con l'Haranga di Sua Maestà, tradutta il meglio ch'io potessi, alle due camere di Parlamento, onde mi resta solamente di aggiugnere che la flotta del che dicevano passò per le Dunnes alli 5 di questo mese circa li quatro hore di mattina, et che alli sei, tutta la flotta inglese vi fusse scoperta, velando verso l'oriente in ricerca della flotta Olandese', ASFi, MdP, 4206, f. 613.

[42] 'Il Parlamento ha molte et grandi affari sul tapeto, il pincipale delle quali è la decisione de diritti de Perticolari nella Città abruciata, come anche di apuntare a qual prezzo si comrarà il terreno dalli Interessati per potere fabricare la città con strade più larghe et piazze et altre convenienze di uniformità, et si dice che habbino rimesso questo affare alla Prudenza et volontà del Rè; dissegnando di rattificarlo poi per Atto di Parlamento. Hanno nel mentre ordinato (nel reassumere il contrasto toccante la Città di Londra) che li umili ringraziamenti del Parlamento siano resi alla Maestà Sua della di lei cura et grand briga presa per prevenire l'abrucciamento della Città', ASFi, MdP, 4206, f. 618.

Three weeks of negotiations, occasionally featured in the *Gazette*, are epitomised here in a single paragraph. Whether the extreme succinctness owes more to a particular style of Salvetti than to considerations of space, seems somewhat unlikely.

To protect the reputation of the city authorities as information circulated and a narrative took shape, blame was shifted away from the inadequate preventive measures and insufficient means of containment, despite widespread knowledge of potential risk. Likely arsonists were quickly rounded up, in a typical exercise of pragmatic scapegoating supported by long-standing public prejudices, fears and preoccupations. Enemies of the regime, Catholics, foreigners, especially those from among the antagonist countries in current disputes, were obviously at fault. Doubts lingered in isolated quarters.[43] A certain Frenchman named Robert Hubert seemed such a perfect match for the necessary criteria of a miscreant, confirmed by a voluntary confession inculpating numerous co-conspirators at home and abroad, and articulated in rather too many changing versions, that there was some suspicion, then and now, that the man was psychologically unwell: 'Almost certainly deranged', according to Tim Harris.[44]

Salvetti counted 18 prisoners taken by authorities and 11 murdered by crowds, as he followed the various persecutions in his news accounts:

> This week eleven persons [have been] freed who were imprisoned on suspicion of having fomented the fire with artificial bales and seven French and Dutchmen detained in order to deal with their trials against whom we have stronger evidence that they were instrumental in setting the aforementioned fire. For this fault eleven people were killed by the fury of the people during that confusion.[45]

He reported the Hubert episode on 19/29 October, with an abundance of details regarding the suspect's movements and declarations:

> This past Monday a trial was held of a certain Frenchman named Hubert for having started the fire that burned (as has already been written) almost the entire City of London, and after a short examination Hubert confessed that he had been brought expressly to England by a certain Monsignor Pettloc to burn the City of London, and because he could not come directly from France without danger he was first taken to Hamburg, and from there transported to this Kingdom, where he had been several weeks before implementing the diabolical plan…[46]

---

[43] CSP Ven., xxxv (1666–7), 77, n14 citing BL, Add. MS 27962 R, f. 478, quotes Salvetti as saying that some of these were tried on 22 Oct., 'piu tosto per sodisfare il popolo che per altro'. In this regard, F. Dolan 'Ashes and "the Archive": The London Fire of 1666, Partisanship, and Proof', *The Journal of Medieval and Early Modern Studies*, xxxi (2001), 379–408. Also, taking a European perspective on the Catholic danger and fears, J. F. Bosher, 'The Franco-Catholic Danger, 1660–1715', *History*, lxxix (1994), 5–30; as well as P. D. A. Harvey (ed.), 'A Foreign Visitor's Account of the Great Fire, 1666', *London & Middlesex Archaeological Society* (New Series xx, 1961), 84.

[44] Harris, *Restoration*, 79.

[45] 'Ha questa settimana liberato undici Persone che furono incarcerate sopra suspizione di havere fomentato il fuoco con balle artificiali, et ritenuti sette altri francesi et olandesi in ordine a fare il loro processo contra de' quali hanno prove più forti ch'erono instrumentale nell'aggrandire il predetto fuoco. Per la quale colpa undici persone furono durante quella conusione ammazzati dalla furio del Popolo', ASFi, MdP, 4206, ff. 606v–607: *Avvisi* from London, 14/24 Sept. 1666.

[46] 'Lunedì passato si fece il processo di un tale Hubert francese per havere dato principio a quel fuoco che abruciò (come si è già scritto) quasi tutta la Città di Londra, et doppo poco essaminazione confessò detto Humbert

Next came a plausible narrative situating Hubert at the place where the developing intelligence regarding events had located the origins of the blaze.

> …but that on the twelfth of September the wind, being very great and capable of carrying the fire from the east to the west of the City (which space comprises the whole length of London) [Hubert] set fire in the early morning to the house of a baker in Pudinge Lane near the Bridge, and from there gaining by the wind other houses and streets could not be extinguished before it had impetuously consumed almost the entire City.[47]

In closing, Salvetti added his answer to the question about motivation:

> He confessed moreover that he had been solicited by the aforesaid Frenchman several times before he was willing to put his plan into execution, but that in the end he had been gained as much by threats as by promises; not having had in his hand but a single shilling (that is to say about two Giulii) but that he was to receive in France a great reward.[48]

A soupçon of perplexity pervaded the rest of Salvetti's account, regarding this personage and the rush to convict:

> This was the sum of his Confession, which he made so voluntarily that the Judges suspected that he was ill in the Brain, and to test this they made him drive along several streets with his eyes shut, both in a carriage and on foot, and he always recognized not only the street but also the location where the house had been which he had set fire to, and when they showed him other burned streets similar to that one, and other houses, he always affirmed that those were not the streets or the houses.[49]

---

[46] *(continued)* che fusse condotto espressamente in Inghilterra per un tale Monsignor Pettloc per abrucciare la Città di Londra, et perché non poteva venire senza pericolo direttamente da Francia fu primo menato ad Hamburgo, et di là transportato in questo Regno, dove era stato più settimane dinanzi di mettere in essecuzione quello diabolico dissegno', ASFi, MdP, 4206, f. 626: *Avvisi* from London, 19/29 Oct. 1666.

[47] '[…] ma che alli dodieci di Settembre il Vento essendo assai grande et proprio per portare il fuoco dal oriente sin all'occidente della Città (nel quale consisteva la longhezza di Londra) messe fuoco di grand mattina alla casa di un fornaro in Pudinge Lane vicino della Ponte, et di là guadagnando per il Vento, altre case et strade non poteva estinguersi prima che havesse impetuosamente consumato quasi tutta la Città', ASFi, MdP, 4206, f. 626: *Avvisi* from London, 19/29 Oct. 1666.

[48] 'Confessò di più che fusse sollecitato dal predetto francese più volte prima che volse consentire di mettere il suo dissegno in essecuzione, ma che alla fine fusse guadagnato tanto per minaccie quanto per promesse; non havendo hauto in mano che un solo shilino (cioè circa dui Giulii) ma ˆcheˆ doveva ricevere in Francia grand ricompensa', ASFi, MdP, 4206, f. 626v: *Avvisi* from London, 19/29 Oct. 1666.

[49] 'Questa era la somma della sua Confessione, la quale faceva tanto volontariamente che li Giudici sospettavono che era male sano nel Cervello, et per fare la prova lo fecero condurre in più strade con li occhi serrati tanto in Carozza quanto a Piede, et riconosceva sempre non solamente la strada ma anche il luogo dove stava la casa nella quale messe il fuoco, et quando lo mostrorono altre strade abrucciate simili a quella, et altre case, affirmava sempre che quelle non erano le strade, le case', ASFi, MdP, 4206, f. 626v: *Avvisi* from London, 19/29 Oct. 1666.

The sanity tests proved the man to be responsible for his actions and for the fire, and appropriate action was taken: 'they passed sentence of death on him and on Wednesday he was hanged, showing great penitence for that terrible deed'.[50]

If Salvetti appeared most of the time to convey the positive outlook evinced by the official communications, other diplomats kept their distance. There was currently no Venetian colleague in London at the time, Pietro Mocenigo having been nominated in 1660 but not yet arrived. The Venetians instead received some intelligence of what was going on through their ambassador in France, Marc Antonio Giustinian, who wrote back to the Doge and Senate on 18/28 September concerning what he had heard, from a point of view distinctly different from that of Salvetti. Here, instead of the hopeful tone, we get a sense of abject desperation:

> The confusion, the terror and the death of those who were overwhelmed by the fall of roofs, by the ruin of the houses and by the press of those who were fleeing to save themselves and their goods is indescribable. The letters from London speak of the terrible sights of persons burned to death and calcified limbs, making it easy to believe the terror though it cannot be exactly described. The old, tender children and many sick and helpless persons were all burned in their beds and served as fuel for the flames. Suffice it to say, as the final word on an unspeakable calamity that a city of ninety-nine parishes, save only ten and these also in great part consumed, has been converted into innumerable heaps of ashes, and that a population of citizens has been obliged to take to the fields.

Prospects were not good, and further miseries might be on the way: 'The king's palace is not touched, but is possibly reserved to be the theatre of some dire spectacle, as cries are now heard on every hand, that since the House of Stuart came to the throne England has never enjoyed felicity but has suffered from incessant miseries'.[51] Giustinian was ready to prepare for the worst.

In his speculation about the cause of the Great Fire Giustinian did not refrain from lending some credence to even the more extravagant rumours. Hence after an account of the usual suspects, Frenchmen and Dutch, there followed another hypothesis, namely divine retribution in the context of anti-Catholic prejudice:

> I must not pass over another cause of this chastisement which from being in contumely of the first cause may also be the most adequate. It is talked about among the most pious and it would be a great impiety to keep silence about it. Two fathers of the Order of St Bernard, which is most austere here, of an exemplary and holy life, who were going to fulfil their obligations either to preach the gospel in the Indies or the Christian life in other parts, while they were travelling on a French ship, were taken prisoners by the English.[52]

[50] 'Il Mercordì fu impiccato, mostrando molta penitenza di quella horribile azione', ASFi, MdP, 4206, f. 627: *Avvisi* from London, 19/29 Oct. 1666.

[51] *CSP Ven.*, xxxv (1666–7), 77: Marc Antonio Giustinian, Venetian ambassador in France, to the doge and senate, 18/28 Sept. 1666.

[52] *CSP Ven.*, xxxv (1666–7), 77.

The arbitrary seizure of two Cistercians, in the view of the Venetian ambassador, exemplified deeply rooted prejudices, just as the account itself, from another standpoint, exemplified deeply rooted animosities against Protestant efforts to eliminate a Catholic threat:

> Being brought in triumph through the city as if they had made a great acquisition, having satisfied their barbarity by abuse and insults, they cut them into quarters and distributed their members to the four quarters of the city, amid the lamentation and tears of the Catholics who saw this cruelty.

The next events served as censure to the real culprits, in the ambassador's account: 'It was on the very day that their quarters were affixed that the fire began, and it may be considered the just punishment of Heaven for such a crime'.[53] Indeed, the worst was yet to come:

> But whatever the cause may be, whether the malignity of men, blind chance or the justice of Heaven, the result is the most lamentable and the most hurtful for England, worse than any defeat of her fleets, worse than the plague and than any other disaster, capable of making them change their government and principles.[54]

Would the current debacle lead to revolt and rebellion? The successful restoration of the monarchy appeared to have been checked, in the view of the ambassador, as was likely to be demonstrated by a further reorganisation of power.

By the time Giustinian reported the story of the monks, malign speculation was already rife in Venice, at least according to correspondence received in the English parliament. As expected, the Dutch were once again largely responsible for circulation of the worst reports. Members of parliament heard that:

> Dr. Harper… sends a scandalous relation of the fire in London, printed and sold in Padua. The Dutch are busy with their calumnies, and make the people believe that the fire is a judgment, because four friars of S. Bernard were taken by an English man-of-war, hanged and their quarters set on the four gates of the city some few days before. The Dutch print the news in Italian weekly, and send copies all over Italy, speaking of their great success and power, and representing England as ruined, not only by their victories, but by dissensions at home.[55]

A foreign conspiracy to spread negative opinion about a rival, using a domestic disaster as a focus, had more audience potential than any efforts to salvage a damaged city. With dangerous propaganda being circulated by commercial rivals and military enemies, no wonder the English court and parliament sought to give out a message of cheerful resilience, abundant resources and endless industry.

The Catholic conspiracy theory also made its way into Salvetti's newsletters, by way of a clamorous story about the discovery of a large number of weapons in the ruins of a house believed to belong to a person of that faith. The sheet from 2/12 November reported:

---

[53] *CSP Ven.*, xxxv (1666–7), 77.
[54] *CSP Ven.*, xxxv (1666–7), 77.
[55] *CSP Dom.*, 1666–7, 214.

Having been brought on the 5th day of the current month about 500 Stilettos found in
the ruins of the burnt City to the Commons Chamber of Parliament, and having been
proved on examination that the place where they were found was, before the fire, the
home of a Roman Catholic, gave great suspicion to the Parliament that these Catholics
had not only conspired to burn the city, but also had always had some design tending to
the destruction of His Majesty, of His government, and of the Protestant religion, and
this impression became in a moment prevalent, that the Catholics were held guilty and
damned in the speeches of every one.[56]

Proceedings were begun in order to punish Catholics as a group:

The Parliament began to pass votes against them, and the People more disposed to
censure them, and the Catholics themselves did not know what to think, fearing perhaps
that some bigots, or, too zealous in their Religion, might be engaged with the fanatics
in some conspiracy, knowing too well that it would be enough for a single Catholic
to be interested in them to ruin the interest and the liberties of the Catholics in this
country.[57]

In the event, the evidence was found to be a set of items for sale. As Salvetti intoned, 'By
the grace of God that apprehension has already vanished, since the said Stilettos have been
found to be the stuff of commerce, and that the Guinea Company often traffics with the
Barbarians with similar daggers'. However, such discoveries were to no avail:

This is not enough to satisfy the jealousy of the People, who do not want to be persuaded
that the Catholics are innocent of the Burning of the City of London, or, that they had
not really planned with the said daggers to murder all Protestants, and the Parliament did
not want to omit such an opportunity to revive the execution of the penal laws against
the said Catholics, and in accordance with this these following votes against them were
passed by both Houses of Parliament: 1st that all Jesuits and Priests be banished by royal
proclamation and to leave within thirty days, and if after that time they are found in the
territories of His Majesty they must be condemned as guilty of Lese Majesty; 2nd that
all those who refuse to take the oath of supremacy will be incapable of exercising any
office in this Kingdom, whether military or civil, and 3rd that all the laws already made
against Catholics be severely enforced.[58]

---

[56]'Essendosi portati alli 5 del corrente circa 500 Stiletti trovati tra le ruine dell'abbrucciata Città alla Camera
Comune di Parlmaneto, et provato sopra essaminiazione che quel luogo dove erano trovati fusse dinanzi l'incendio,
l'habitazione d'un Cattolico Romano, diede grand suspizione al Parlamento che detti Cattolici havessero non
solamente congiurato l'incendio della città, ma anche havessero sempre qualche diseggno tendente alla distruzione
di Sua Maestà del Suo governo, et della Religione Protestante, et questa impressione divenne in un momento
prevallente, che li Cattolici erano tenuti colpevoli et dannati nelli discorsi d'ogni uno', ASFi, MdP, 4206, f. 634:
Avvisi from London, 12 Nov. 1666.

[57]'Il Parlamento comminciò a passare voti contra di essi et le Persone meno pationati a censurarli, et li Cattolci
medesimi non sapevano che pensare, temendo forse che alcuni bizotti, ò, troppo zellosi nella lor Religione, si
potrebbe essere impegnato con li fanatici in qualche congiura, sapendo troppo bene che basterebbe ad un solo
cattolico ci fusse interessato per ruinare affato l'interesse et le libertà delli Cattolici in questo Paese', ASFi, MdP,
4206, f. 634v: *Avvisi* from London, 12 Nov. 1666.

[58]'Ma tutto questo non basta per soddisfare alle giallosie del Popolo, che non voglia essere persuaso, che gli
Cattolici siano innocenti dell'Incendio della Città di Londra, ò, che non havessero realmente dissegnato con detti

Emotions ran high, and material evidence had little influence on public opinion. Taking the bait, parliament pushed to revive and exacerbate already repressive measures, in the context of diverting attention away from other more intricate operations currently under way.

But material causes and human authors of destruction were rarely thought to operate on their own. If recent epochs in history seemed to offer few parallels for such an accumulation of ills, a larger plan needed to be put in operation, exceeding the potential of even the most malign human reason. The timing alone begged reflection, such that a year containing the three digits representing the 'beast' in the Book of Revelation surely called to mind the theme of good versus evil.[59] Such efforts to join the omens on a cosmic scale received unlikely support from many elements of the expert community. In spite of an emerging trend toward empirical natural science, enshrined in the recently formed Accademia del Cimento in Florence and the Royal Society in London, much remained of the prior philosophical and theological approach oriented toward the enigmatic signs and portents purportedly left on nature to be interpreted and deployed for greater mastery by the careful researcher attuned to analogies and similarities.[60] Rushing to interpret events in terms of a vast providential scheme were not only naturalists and divines but also poets, notably John Milton, whose *Paradise Lost* was only a year away from publication at the time of the events analysed here, with its reflection on lost innocence, lost freedom, lost safety, amid thinly veiled allusions to contemporary culture, society and politics.[61]

Reflecting the monarchy's official air of cheerful buoyancy, on the other hand, was John Dryden. His *Annus Mirabilis*, written in 1666, drew plague, fire and war together in a celebration of the power of mind over matter. Dedicated to the city itself, the work set out to promote a show of 'true Loyalty, invincible Courage and unshaken Constancy'. Indeed, 'Other Cities have been prais'd for the same Virtues, but I am much deceiv'd if any have so dearly purchas'd their reputation; their fame has been won them by cheaper trials then an expensive, though necessary, War, a consuming Pestilence, and a more consuming Fire'.[62] Surely Providence, he went on, could not have:

---

[58] *(continued)* pugnali assassinar di tutti li Protestanti, et il Parlamento non ha voluto omettere una tale opportunità di ravviare l'esecuzione delle leggi penali contra detti Cattolici, et in conformità questi seguenti voti contra di loro furono passati da Ambe le Camere di Parlamento P° che tutti Gesuiti et Preti siano banditi per la Proclamazione del Re di partire tra trenta giorni, et se dopo quel tempo saranno trovati nelli territori di Sua Maestà devono essere processati come colpevoli di Lestà Maestà 2° che tutti quelli che negaranno di prendere il giuramento di supremazia saranno incapaci di esercitare carica alcuna in questo Regno, sia Militare, o civile, et 3°che tutte le leggi già fatte contra li Cattolici siano serveramente in essecuzione', ASFi, MdP, 4206, f. 634: *Avvisi* from London, 12 Nov. 1666.

[59] In this regard, interesting reflections in David Brady, '1666: The Year of the Beast', *Bulletin of the John Rylands Library*, lxi (1979), 314–36.

[60] On this and kindred matters, *Physico-theology: Religion and Science in Europe 1650–1750*, ed. Ann Blair and Kaspar von Greyerz (Baltimore, MD, 2020), ch. by Brendan Dooley and Simona Boscani Leoni.

[61] Still relevant concerning Milton's politics, Christopher Hill, *The Experience of Defeat: Milton and Some Contemporaries* (1984), introduction and ch. 10; now, David Loewenstein, 'The Radical Religious Politics of Paradise Lost', *A Companion to Milton*, ed. T.N. Corns (Oxford, 2003), 348–62.

[62] *The Works of John Dryden*, ed. H.T. Swedenberg Jr. et al. (20 vols, Berkeley, CA, 1956–2002), i, 48. See the analysis of the power of the royalist version of events, including Dryden's, in Christoph Heyl, 'A Miserable Sight: The Great Fire of London (1666)', *Fiasko – Scheitern in der Frühen Neuzeit: Beiträge zur Kulturgeschichte des Misserfolgs*, ed. Stefan Brakensiek and Claudia Claridge (Bielefeld, 2015), 111–32.

resolv'd the ruine of that people at home, which it has blessed abroad with such successes. I am therefore to conclude, that your sufferings are at an end; and that one part of my Poem has not been more an History of your destruction, then the other a Prophecy of your restoration. The accomplishment of which happiness, as it is the wish of all true English-men.

Nature had clearly set no limits on the possible progress of the country.

Salvetti stopped talking about fire as soon as London life appeared to be returning to some sort of new normality, and in the next issues of his newsletter he resumed the discussion about commerce and warfare, especially about the ongoing Dutch War, recently compounded by an engagement with the French.[63] Over the next months the tide of monarchical enthusiasm in the country began to ebb, in part replaced by disenchantment at the regime's perceived scandals and misdeeds, whose raucous reverberations through Restoration art and culture Salvetti prudently overlooked.

Although the fire would not linger in European consciousness in the way the Lisbon earthquake would a century later, nonetheless the importance from a planning perspective, as Salvetti implied in his communications, could hardly be ignored; and the current system for collectively organising public works showed its potential in difficult times. Meanwhile, a widespread population boom was under way, in England and elsewhere, and crowding into predominantly wooden medieval constructions was no longer a viable means of handling growth. A capital city emerged from the ashes, commensurate with the expanding role the country wished to play. Meanwhile a complex and variegated media landscape deeply involved in the cultural, social and political life of the country became further integrated within the European context, an aspect which Salvetti and his Florentine connection did much to advance.

APPENDIX

COMPARISON OF REPORTING ON 'HOLMES' BONFIRE'

ASFi, MdP, 4207, *Avvisi* from London, [17/]27 August 1666, f. 594	*The London Gazette*, 13-16[23-26] August 1666, n°79.
Di Londra [17/]27 Agosto 1666	Whitehal, Aug. 15[/25]
1. Il cavaliere Horuandi arrivò ieri sera su le Poste a Whyt Hall essendo stato spedito dalla flotta inglese, uscito del Vly, con una piena narrativa del successo felicissimo del Cavaliere Holmes tanto nel distruggere et abbruciare più di 150 **Vasselli olandesi,** quanto nell'abbruciare la città di Brandati (consistendo più di mille case) nell'isola di Schelling, come sperisse la seguente lettera scritta dal medesimo Holmes	[1.] Last Night arrived here in Post Sir Philip Howard, dispatched Express from His Majesties Fleet off the Vlie, with a full account from his Highness Prince Rupert, and his Grace the Duke of Albemarle, of the late happy success of Sir Robert Holmes his Expedition in the burning and destroying more than 150 of **Enemies ships** in the Vlie, as also of the Town of Bandaris, on the Island of Schelling, consisting of about 1000

[63] Steven Pincus, 'Popery, Trade and Universal Monarchy: The Ideological Context of the Outbreak of the Second Anglo–Dutch War', *E.H.R.*, cvii (1992), 1–29.

La lettera di Holmes

2. Essendo ordenato martedì dal Principe Roberto et il Generale Monke di andare nel Vly per bbruciare quel Isola, il Giovedi seuente entrai il Canale, et essendo nella rada di Schelling scopri una grossa flotta di circa 170 vele ad anchora nella Rada di Vly,

3. concepivo che sarebbe un buon servizio a distugerle, et sentendo che non ci erano molti Vaselli da Guerra tra di loro, et vedendo che stavano vicinissimi l'uni dall'altri, saposi che sarebbe facile a distrugerli,

4. entrai però con cinque vesselli di fuoco et alcune Barche fregate et si bene lasciando delle altre nella rada di Schelling.

5. Li Vasselli di fuoco abrucciorno subito due navi di Guenea et altri legni che defecero la loro flotta, il che fatto mandai tutti li miei schifi et barche per abbruciar tutti li altri Vaselli, il che fecero con tanto buon successo che in poco tempo la maggior parte di quella grossa flotta era in una fiamma; eccetto un vasello di Guinea con alcuni Privatieri che radunandosi nel stretto del cannale protessero cinque altri legni ch'erano a capo di loro, si che era impossibile per mancamento di acqua; il quale impedi anche lo sbarcamento delli nostri huomini sopra di Vly,

6. Andai nulladimeno con undieci compagnie a terra sopra il Schellling, dove incontrammo qualche pochi huomini armati, che ci fecero pochissima resistenza, abburciai la principale città di quell'Isola, quale era ricchissima, havrei anche abrucciato tutti li altri Villaggi di quell'isola se la marea non fusse allora quasi piena, et che non potessi però perdere quella opportunità di Guadagnare il Mare, il quale stimai più considerabile [...] di aspettare venti quattro hore al manco per abruggiare due ò tre Villaggi.

7. Non posso dare un ragguaglio perfetto del danno che gli Olandesi habbiano sostentato da noi, ma deve per certo essere molto grande; Sapungo che tra poco haveranno la

houses, of which you will see elsewhere a Particular. In the mean time, you have the Sum of this glorious Success in the following Letter from Sir Robert Holmes his own hand.

[2.] Being ordered on Tuesday night last, by his Highness, and his Grace, to go into the Vlie, to burn that Island; in order thereunto, on Thursday morning I got into the Channel, and being in Schelling Road, could espie a great Fleet, consisting of about 170 Sail, small and great, at Anchor in Vlie Road:

[3.] I conceived it might be very good service to destroy them, and understanding there were not many men of war amongst them, and seeing that they rid very thick, I supposed it might be the sooner performed;

[4.] I went therefore in with Five Fireships, some Ketches, and one Fifth-rate Fregat, leaving some other Fregats in Schelling Road.

[5.] I sent the Fireships ahead, who soon burned two men of War, and other ships that stood defending the whole Fleet, and immediately sent all my Boats to burn the rest of the ships, which they did with so good success, that in a short time the most of that great Fleet was in a flame, except a *Guinny* man of 24 Guns, and three small Privateers, that getting together in the Narrow of the Channel, protected five Sail more that were got a head of them, so that our Boats could not possibly come at them; and the most of our Ketches being on ground, which hindered also the landing of our men upon the Vilie; which notwithstanding we resolved to do the next morning, and had accordingly proceeded in it, had not in the Night a Gust happened with so much Rain, that spoiled a great many of our men's Arms and Ammunition on board the Hoyes, Ketches and Boats:

[6.] However, I went with Eleven Companies on shore upon the Shelling, where we saw some scattering Fellows, but met with no great opposition; I burned the chief Town upon that Island, which, by all

piena narrativa da Amsterdam, la nostra perdita era poco considerabile circa dodici tra morti et ferite. Il numero delli Vasselli abbruciati supongo essere tra 150 et 160 vele <u>la più parte di grand Valuta, essendo caricati per Constantiniopoli, Scanderone, Moscovia, Guinea, Indie et altri longhi viaggi.</u>

<u>the Relation I could get</u>, was very Rich, I had burnt all the Villages there, but that it was almost High-water; and could not lose that opportunity of getting out again to Sea, which I thought to be more considerable, than to stay 24 hours at least, to demolish one or two small **inconsiderable** Villages, <u>and the Channel between the Buoyes very narrow, and not bold without a frank wind.</u> [7.] I cannot give an exact Account of what damage the Dutch might sustain by us, but certainly it must be great. I suppose we may hereafter have a more full Account of that from *Amsterdam*, Our own loss was not very considerable, having not about 12 men killed and wounded. The number of the ships burnt, I suppose to be between 150, and 160 Sails.

(Extra)ordinary News: Foreign Reporting on English Politics under William III

MICHAEL SCHAICH

During the late 17th and early 18th centuries a number of German governments received regular updates on English politics from London-based intelligencers. This article examines and compares two sets of these reports from the year 1694, composed by Guillaume Beyrie and Frédéric Bonnet for the Guelph courts in Celle and Hanover and the Prussian court in Berlin respectively. It describes the distinctive character of the reports and situates them within a typology of scribal news ranging from commercial newsletters to the classic diplomatic despatch. In addition, it analyses the detailed political coverage of the accounts which was centred mainly on the royal court and parliament and uncovers some of the sources from which the information originated.

Keywords: diplomatic correspondence; commercial newsletters; parliamentary reporting; foreign perceptions of English politics; Gulliaume Beyrie; Frédéric Bonnet

From the 1680s through to the 1710s roughly a dozen purveyors of scribal news based in London supplied a select number of German courts with up-to-date intelligence on English politics.[1] Most prominent among them are the two brothers Frédéric and Louis-Frédéric Bonnet, who catered for the needs of the Prussian rulers, and Guillaume Beyrie who acted for the courts of the Guelph dynasty in Celle and Hanover. Their reports are well known to historians of the period. The Bonnets' despatches, in particular, have attracted attention since the 19th century. Starting with Leopold von Ranke, who used them to great effect in his *History of England Principally in the Seventeenth Century*, American and British scholars like Henry Horwitz, Geoffrey Holmes and the contributors to the relevant volumes in *The History of Parliament* series have mined the accounts for information on what happened in Westminster and Whitehall during the reigns of William III, Queen Anne and the first years of George I, especially since the original despatches, then housed in the central archives of the GDR, became available as microfilms during the Cold War.[2] The reports by Beyrie

---

[1]Michael Schaich, 'Information Professionals: Huguenot Diplomats in Later Stuart London and Their European Context', in *Huguenot Networks, 1560–1870: The Interactions and Impact of a Protestant Minority in Europe*, ed. Vivienne Larminie (New York, 2018), 75–91.

[2]Leopold von Ranke, *A History of England Principally in the Seventeenth Century* (6 vols, Oxford, 1875), vi (hereafter cited as Ranke); Wolfgang Michael, *Englische Geschichte im achtzehnten Jahrhundert* (5 vols, Leipzig, 1896–1955), i; *The Divided Society: Parties and Politics in England, 1694–1716*, ed. Geoffrey Holmes and W.A. Speck (1967); Henry Horwitz, *Parliament, Policy and Politics in the Reign of William III* (Manchester, 1977); Geoffrey Holmes, *British Politics in the Age of Anne* (1987); B.W. Hill, *The Growth of Parliamentary Parties 1689–1742* (1976) (indirectly via

---

have also been consulted in the past, although they received a less favourable reception from English and German historians alike, who found them wanting of the unique insights into high-level politics that they were looking for.[3]

In contrast to these earlier scholars, this article will not appraise the value of the reports for political history but examine them from the perspective of a history of news and information. The despatches allow us to probe into the role scribal news played in (foreign) reporting about the political scenery in London, and parliament in particular. They reveal the predilections and mental maps that refracted their authors' view of English politics and, at least to a certain extent, also the sources on which they relied. Taking the reports from one year during the middle part of William III's reign, 1694, as an example this article aims to analyse how two foreign observers described the peculiarities of the post-revolutionary set-up, the fractious equilibrium between the court and other centres of political power, and the sometimes cumbersome workings but remarkably efficient outcomes of the parliamentary process. By comparing the two sets of reports it will also become clear how much coverage of the early stages of the 'Age of Party' could diverge. The reports provide snapshots of two distinct ways of portraying England's post-revolutionary transition to a foreign audience. In addition, the two collections of manuscript reports help us refine our understanding of the various types of scribal news. Belonging neither to the category of the commercial newsletter nor to the classic diplomatic despatch, they occupy a middle ground between the two, hinting at the wide variety of forms of manuscript reporting that was prevalent in the late 17th and early 18th centuries.

The article will start with a discussion of the latter point, situating the two sets of reports and their authors within the wider context of scribal news as well as against each other. Questions of materiality and scribal conventions will prove crucial in this regard. It will then discuss the content of the two streams of reporting in more detail, giving particular emphasis to their coverage of parliamentary affairs before finally trying to cast some light on the ways purveyors of news in 1690s London could get hold of valuable political information.[4]

1

Both Beyrie and the Bonnet brothers are rather shadowy figures whose lives disappear behind the masses of reports that survive in the archives.[5] The limited knowledge we have about them shows a remarkable degree of homogeneity. All three belonged to the Huguenot

2 (*continued*) Ranke); *HPC 1690–1715*, ed. Eveline Cruickshanks, Stuart Handley and D.W. Hayton (5 vols, Cambridge, 2002), i, 859. Henry Snyder secured microfilms of Bonnet's reports from the Deutsches Zentralarchiv in Merseburg in the former GDR for the University of Kansas and seems to have made them available to other American historians, see Horwitz, *Parliament, Policy and Politics*, x. The History of Parliament Trust, London, also holds a set of microfilms.

[3] Georg Schnath, *Geschichte Hannovers im Zeitalter der neunten Kur und der englischen Sukzession 1674–1714*, (5 vols, Hildesheim, 1976–82), ii, 240–1; B.W. Hill, *Robert Harley: Speaker, Secretary of State and Premier Minister* (New Haven, CT, 1988), 241–4.

[4] In the following, reference is made to the original reports in the Niedersächsisches Landesarchiv, Hanover, and the Geheimes Staatsarchiv Preußischer Kulturbesitz, Berlin. Extracts from some of Bonnet's despatches were edited by Ranke in his *History of England*, vi, 230–64 (for 1694). In those cases, I have added a reference to Ranke's edition in brackets for ease of access.

[5] Biographical information on all three is to be found in Ranke, vi, 144–7; Schnath, *Geschichte Hannovers*, i, 333, 494, 750–4, ii, 240–1, iv, 54–5 as well as Schaich, 'Information Professionals'.

diaspora that was scattered throughout parts of Europe in the course of the 17th century. While the Bonnets' family had already left France during the French wars of religion and settled in Geneva where it joined the ranks of the professional classes and produced a number of highly regarded physicians, Beyrie was part of the more recent wave of exiles after the revocation of the Edict of Nantes in 1685 ending up in London shortly afterwards. All three also pursued scholarly interests: numismatics in the older Bonnet's case, historical and genealogical studies in Beyrie's who also corresponded with the polymath Gottfried Wilhelm Leibniz.[6] The younger Bonnet in turn was elected a fellow of the Royal Society and the Berlin Academy of Sciences. Most importantly, all three made their careers on the back of the massive expansion in intelligence gathering that the politically ambitious German princes pursued in the wake of the Peace of Westphalia. Keen on projecting their status on the international stage and participating in great power politics, the princes began to establish permanent embassies in a number of European countries that towards the end of the century expanded their personnel. In addition to their envoys some German courts recruited so-called agents, correspondents or residents whose main task it was to open up an extra channel of information. They were entrusted with keeping ministers and courtiers in the Holy Roman Empire abreast of current developments at their postings and thus became, in the unflattering words of one German historian, 'mere news writers without any diplomatic role'.[7]

Frédéric Bonnet (1652–96), the older of the two brothers, was not the first such correspondent to be employed in the English capital by the court of Brandenburg-Prussia. Earlier examples go back to the days of the Interregnum,[8] but in contrast to his predecessors who reported for shorter periods of time and often had no immediate successor, leaving large gaps in the coverage of English affairs, Frédéric held on to his job for almost 12 years from 1685 to his death in 1696 only to be followed by his younger sibling Louis-Frédéric Bonnet (1670–1761). The latter remained in London for more than 20 years, rising to the rank of de facto envoy during the last decade of his long stay, a period that is explored in more detail by Charles Littleton in his contribution to this volume. Promotion to the position of official Prussian representative was rather exceptional for a former purveyor of news. His rise is partly to be explained by the stinginess of the Prussian King Frederick I, who recoiled at the expense of sending a new envoy to London on the death of the old one, and partly by the close family ties that bound the Bonnets to Ezechiel von Spanheim, one of the most prominent diplomats of his time and a highly respected figure at the court in Berlin. It had also been Spanheim who secured his nephew, the older Bonnet, the post in London in 1685 in the first place. Beyrie, by contrast, had to do without relatives in high places. His route to permanent employment was paved by his ability to write scribal news. From 1687 he had provided Count Bernstorff, a leading minister at the court of Celle, with regular updates on political developments in London. On the recommendation of Bernstorff and probably also on the merits of a manuscript pamphlet that he had written in early 1689 to set out Electress Sophia's claim to the English throne and circulated among members of the

---

[6]See the list of extant letters in the database accompanying the edition of Leibniz's correspondence: https://leibniz.uni-goettingen.de/persons/vie (accessed 22 Mar. 2021).

[7]'reine Zeitungsschreiber ohne diplomatische Funktion', Schnath, *Geschichte Hannovers*, i, 333.

[8]*Repertorium der diplomatischen Vertreter aller Länder seit dem Westfälischen Frieden* (3 vols, Oldenburg, 1936–65), i, 35.

© *2022 The Author(s). Parliamentary History published by John Wiley & Sons Ltd. on behalf of Parliamentary History Yearbook Trust.*

English political elite, Beyrie was taken on as correspondent for the court of Celle in the same year. In 1693 he added an assignment by the second branch of the Guelph dynasty, the court of Hanover, to his portfolio and stayed in his post until 1711.[9] Officially Beyrie was given the title of agent and only elevated to the rank of resident in 1706, whereas Bonnet appears in the records as 'resident' from the beginning.

Although Beyrie, and probably also Bonnet, ran errands for other persons in the wider orbit of the Guelph and Hohenzollern dynasties (Leibniz for example used Beyrie as an intermediary to access English scholarly networks),[10] their main duty consisted of composing bi-weekly newssheets to their patrons in Celle, Hanover and Berlin. Written in French, they were commonly referred to by both authors as 'ordinaires', a standard term used at the time for all sorts of reports whose periodicity was dictated by the delivery slots of the postal service.[11] In drafting their correspondence, both men had to bear in mind that they worked alongside officially accredited envoys who wrote despatches of their own. English high-level politics, the discussions going on between and the decisions taken by the monarch and his ministers, were beyond the scope of Beyrie, Bonnet and their like. Conversely, none of their reports dealt with the immediate political concerns of the courts that employed them.[12] Despite the fact that since 1692 the princes of Celle and Hanover had been allied with William III in the fight against Louis XIV Beyrie, for example, remained silent about the Anglo-Hanoverian negotiations in the autumn and winter of 1693/4 to stop Elector Ernst August from withdrawing his troops from the Grand Alliance and to persuade him to fulfil his treaty obligations during the next campaigning season.[13] This diplomatic wrangling had to be left to the envoy proper. Strikingly, Beyrie and Bonnet also did not relay news stories that may have had any bearing on the politics of the Holy Roman Empire. Apart from the visit of Prince Louis of Baden to William III at the beginning of the year, which as a London-based event fell within their remit, only half a dozen reports between them alluded to topics that were even remotely linked to imperial affairs.[14] And if any further evidence were needed, the absence of passages in cipher, the tell-tale sign of confidential diplomatic correspondence, confirms that the content of Bonnet's and Beyrie's reports differed markedly from what envoys would cover in their missives.

As a consequence, Bonnet's and Beyrie's reports contain only 'events which any intelligent observer could notice independently',[15] even if gleaning information on political

---

[9] The history of the Guelph dynasty in the 17th century is convoluted and marked by divisions and the exchange of territories between different branches of the family. For the purposes of this article, it suffices to say that until 1705 when the future George I united the two principalities under his rule, the duchy of Celle and (from 1692) the electorate of Hanover were ruled by two brothers, George I's uncle, Georg Wilhelm, and his father, Ernst August, respectively. For a succinct summary, see Andrew Thompson, *George II: King and Elector* (New Haven, CT, 2011), 10–15, 19.

[10] See, e.g., Nicolas Fatio de Duillier to Guillaume de Beyrie, London 30 Mar. 1694: http://ckcc.huygenknaw. nl/epistolarium/letter.html?id=huyg003/2853 (accessed 30 Jan. 2021).

[11] Wolfgang Behringer, ' "Von der Gutenberg-Galaxis zur Taxis-Galaxis": Die Kommunikationsrevolution. Ein Konzept zum besseren Verständnis der Frühen Neuzeit', *Kommunikation und Medien in der Frühen Neuzeit*, ed. Johannes Burkhardt and Christine Werkstetter (Munich, 2005), 44.

[12] NLA, Cal.Br. 24, no. 42, f. 79v contains one line on the arrival of merchant ships from Hamburg and Bremen in London.

[13] Schnath, *Geschichte Hannovers*, ii, 244–6.

[14] GStA PK, I. HA GR, Rep. 11, no. 1807, ff. 3v, 67, 74, 78v; NLA, Cal.Br. 24, no. 42, ff. 8v, 100, 108v–9.

[15] Ranke, vi, 145.

developments not shrouded by state secrecy was more difficult than this aside by Ranke makes us believe. Still, the accounts abound with news about proceedings at the English court and in parliament, Jacobite plotting, the arrival of merchant fleets, the fighting between English and French forces in various maritime theatres of war, the preparations for the next round of fighting in Flanders, and every now and then the latest gossip from London's aristocratic society. Sent out twice a week on post days, Bonnet's and Beyrie's newssheets gave their recipients a broad overview of the main political events occurring in London and other locations of the British Isles.

If this sets the reports apart from diplomatic despatches, they don't exactly conform to the traditional model of the 17th-century commercial newsletter either. We don't come across the staccato rhythm of rather short news items arranged in individual paragraphs and in the order in which they arrived that is characteristic of the world of the *avvisi*. Although Beyrie in particular set store by covering an array of different topics, as a rule both he and Bonnet offered their readers a more limited number of news items than conventional newssheets. Instead they provided more extensive information on each story, often adding their own comments and assessments – something that is unusual in other scribal news of the commercial variety, let alone printed newspapers. Theirs was a more specialised service that shied away from the matter-of-fact style of reporting to be found in other news outlets, although both men expected their readers to have a thorough grounding in English political affairs. Background information on, for instance, parliamentary procedures, constitutional rules and the geography of the British Isles was rarely forthcoming.[16] The emphasis clearly was on an extended digest of topical news.

The peculiar nature of the reports, falling as they do between the established categories of the traditional manuscript newsletter and the diplomatic despatch, is also reflected in their outward appearance and materiality. Laid out in neat handwriting and composed with little or no space for marginalia they were obviously meant for quick consumption. In contrast to the habit of some English newsletter writers trying to establish a formal relationship with their readers and addressing them with a formal 'Sir', neither Beyrie nor Bonnet used any form of address. Their reports just bear a heading of London and the date at the top of the page and then start without any introduction with the first news item. Both reporters also did without the elaborate closing salutations familiar from diplomatic despatches and refrained from signing their reports, which brought them more into line with the conventions of the manuscript newssheet.

In terms of length they comprised on average four pages. But while Beyrie adhered to the standard quarto format of many commercial newsletters, Bonnet wrote his reports on folio pages giving him almost double the space his counterpart had at his disposal: 510 to 520 words in Beyrie's case compared with roughly 950 words in Bonnet's.[17] In contrast to newsletters, though, the length of the reports could vary considerably. During William III's sojourns on the continent when topical news was harder to come by the number of pages repeatedly dropped to three and, in Bonnet's case, sometimes even to two or just one. The nadir was reached in the second half of October when, in the expectation of the imminent return of the king, political life in London came to a standstill and Beyrie had to admit that

---

[16] E.g., GStA PK, I. HA GR, Rep. 11, no. 1807, f. 68v; NLA, Cal.Br. 24, no. 42, ff. 270v–1, 103.

[17] Bonnet's reports from 1694 have not survived in their entirety, 20 out of a total of 103 are missing. Beyrie's despatches, with one exception (despatch dated 20/30 Oct.), are preserved complete.

© *2022 The Author(s). Parliamentary History published by John Wiley & Sons Ltd. on behalf of Parliamentary History Yearbook Trust.*

his reports had become 'stale' because there was nothing to report.[18] At the other end of the spectrum, moments of high political drama like important parliamentary debates or the final illness of Mary II in December resulted in much longer despatches of five or six and, in one instance, even eight pages.

Their affinity to both diplomatic despatches and manuscript news is also evident in the inclusion of further scribal documents and newspapers. The enmeshing of print and manuscript that has been identified by literary scholars and historians as a typical feature of the news production of the period also holds true for Bonnet's and Beyrie's reports.[19] Both men repeatedly added the French version of the *London Gazette*. Roughly a third of Bonnet's reports were accompanied by the latest issue of the court's semi-official mouthpiece and in one instance also by a Dutch newspaper. Beyrie's despatches must have sported a similar number of copies, but at least some of them were removed before archiving.[20] Unsurprisingly, both men enclosed more copies of the *Gazette* during the periods of William's absence to make up for the brevity of their reports. In addition to printed newspapers they also sent handwritten copies of documents circulating in parliament. Royal speeches, addresses by both Houses, protests by certain groups of peers, individual acts, a list of English warships, a pamphlet[21] and letters handed out to members of parliament, and even a *nouvelle à la main* from Versailles are among the enclosures to be found in Beyrie's and Bonnet's despatches, relayed either in full or as extracts but always faithfully translated into French.[22] So often did they send extra material that twice Beyrie added the same enclosures again within weeks without realising his mistake.

Despite these commonalities the two sets of reports also show some differences. Beyrie's accounts usually cover a greater variety of topics and venues from the royal court and parliament to developments in Scotland and Ireland, the fate of merchant shipping and the latest military news. This mode of reporting betrays some resemblance to the newsletter model, whereas Bonnet preferred to home in on a limited number of themes, sometimes just two or three, and cover them in a more detailed fashion as diplomats might have done. This applies in particular to his reports during parliamentary sessions, when he often focused almost exclusively on the debates in both chambers and dealt with other news items only very briefly at the end of his despatch or left them out entirely. Bonnet also ran a few stories about the activities of other diplomats at the court of St James's[23] while Beyrie never so much as touched upon the topic. Beyrie's reports, on the other hand, were repeatedly enlivened by what in modern parlance we might call feature stories. He wrote about a diver walking the width of the Thames from Whitehall to Lambeth, the winners of the main prize in a lottery draw, a man shot in a duel who had been bankrolled by a mysterious high

---

[18] 'sterile', NLA, Cal.Br. 24, no. 42, f. 225.

[19] See, e.g., R.S. King, ' "All the News That's fit to Write": The Eighteenth-Century Manuscript Newsletter', in *Travelling Chronicles: News and Newspapers from the Early Modern Period to the Eighteenth Century*, ed. S.G. Brandtzæg, Paul Goring, Christine Watson (Leiden, 2018), 95–118; R.S. King, 'The Manuscript Newsletter and the Rise of the Newspaper, 1665–1715', *HLQ*, lxxix (2016), 411–37; and the contributions by Rachael Scarborough King, Charles Littleton and others in this volume.

[20] E.g., NLA, Cal.Br. 24, no. 42, f. 116 refers to an issue of the London Gazette which has not survived.

[21] Samuel Johnson, *An Essay Concerning Parliaments at a Certainty, or, The Kalends of May* (1694).

[22] GStA PK, I. HA GR, Rep. 11, no. 1807, ff. 23–4v, 88–91, 118, 119–20v, 125–6, 130–v, 132–4v, 176–7, 193–4, 223, 225, 230–1v; NLA, Cal.Br. 24, no. 42, ff. 14–19, 32–3, 39–48v, 52, 110, 239–40.

[23] E.g., GStA PK, I. HA GR, Rep. 11, no. 1807, ff. 5, 19, 70v, 78, 199v, 204v, 217 (Ranke, vi, 261).

society lady for years, and the chivalrous behaviour of two officers who during a shipwreck let their wives take the last two remaining places in a rescue boat thereby sacrificing their own lives.[24] He also had a soft spot for crime and made a habit of covering sensational murder cases[25] as well as the misdeeds of English aristocrats such as Lord Mohun,[26] the earl of Warwick[27] and others who were prone to losing their temper and attacking or even killing their social inferiors and sometimes those of their own rank.[28] None of this would ever have found its way into Bonnet's despatches. They were too focused on politics, and parliamentary politics in particular, to regard human interest stories as newsworthy.

Both men, therefore, did not comply fully with the conventions of either of the two main genres, the manuscript newsletter and the diplomatic missive. Their reports have to be situated somewhere in between these two extremes, but on this spectrum Beyrie's accounts were certainly closer to newssheets while Bonnet's gravitated towards the diplomatic variant.

2

The substance of their reporting, by contrast, had much in common. It does not come as a surprise that in the middle of the Nine Years War English military preparations and naval warfare formed a major thread as did the state of overseas trade, gauged usually by the eagerly awaited arrival of fleets from the colonies and the success or failure of raids by French privateers on merchant shipping. Even in times of war, though, politics trumped any other topic. Most of the available room – in Bonnet's case even more so than in Beyrie's – was given over to the inner workings of Whitehall, Westminster and Kensington.

Remarkably, what was going on at court and in parliament dominated coverage to such an extent that other aspects of political culture were relegated to the margins. In recent years historians have pointed to the significance of popular politics and the role of print and public discourse for the analysis of the later Stuart period, but neither Beyrie nor Bonnet paid much attention to these aspects.[29] Beyrie referred a few times to the anti-French and anti-Catholic feelings of a seething populace and described the intimidation of witnesses by an angry mob during a political trial, but despite his Huguenot heritage his disdain for such outbursts of popular sentiment was unmistakeable.[30] Crowds were only allowed a walk-on part as backdrop to monarchical ritual, for example when they were cheering the king on his return to London from the continent.[31] Print publications did not fare much better. Between them Beyrie and Bonnet found just a handful of pamphlets worthy of mention

---

[24] NLA, Cal.Br. 24, no. 42, ff. 56v, 224v, 102, 254; for further examples, see ff. 226, 251v.

[25] NLA, Cal.Br. 24, no. 42, ff. 221v–2, 228v, 231v–2.

[26] Charles Mohun, 4th Baron Mohun of Okehampton; *HPL 1660–1715*, iii, 794–802.

[27] Edward Rich, 6th earl of Warwick; *HPL 1660–1715*, iv, 194–7.

[28] NLA, Cal.Br. 24, no. 42, ff. 57v–8, 74v, 113, 219v, 257v.

[29] See, among others, Andy Wood, *Riot, Rebellion and Popular Politics in Early Modern England* (Basingstoke, 2001); Mark Knights, *Representation and Misrepresentation in Later Stuart Britain: Partisanship and Political Culture* (Oxford, 2005); Tim Harris, *Revolution: The Great Crisis of the British Monarchy, 1685–1720* (2006).

[30] NLA, Cal.Br. 24, no. 42, ff. 86, 120v, 231v, 233.

[31] NLA, Cal.Br. 24, no. 42, f. 237v. William's entry is also one of the rare occasions when Bonnet talks of the 'people', GStA PK, I. HA GR, Rep. 11, no. 1807, f. 192 (Ranke, vi, 248).

© *2022 The Author(s). Parliamentary History published by John Wiley & Sons Ltd. on behalf of Parliamentary History Yearbook Trust.*

during the course of 1694, in one case mainly because it gave rise to diplomatic frictions between England and Denmark.[32] Coffeehouses are equally conspicuous by their absence. Only once, in the wake of William III's rejection of the Place Bill, did Beyrie note the anger virulent in London's coffeehouses, at the Exchange and in the City more widely.[33] At least London's merchant community had a certain presence in the accounts because of both men's strong interest in the financial benefits of English trade for the king's coffers[34] and their wonder at the riches that investors could make from the colonial enterprise.[35] City merchants or trading companies such as the East India Company petitioning parliament for more military protection of their ships and the prolongation of their monopoly appear in a number of reports, especially by Bonnet.[36] Political wrangling about the City lieutenancy was also the subject of a couple of despatches.[37] Yet the City as an independent political actor was an outlier in both men's perception of English politics, predicated as it was on the dominance of court and parliament.

Even Jacobitism did not fundamentally alter this view. Rather than portraying it as a movement with strong popular support, Beyrie – whose coverage in this respect was more extensive – represented it mainly as a nebulous threat emanating from individual (Scottish) conspirators.[38] When supporters of the exiled James II show up in his reports they have just been apprehended, are under guard pleading for better prison conditions or have escaped with amazing ease from their confinement. Sometimes one cannot avoid the impression that Beyrie's interest in Jacobitism came first and foremost from the colourful stories that it offered, which would also explain Bonnet's silence about some of the arrests and escapes. This rather impressionistic coverage of Jacobitism had, of course, also to do with the low level of plotting in 1694. Still, when in the late summer and autumn of that year the authorities uncovered an alleged plot in Lancashire and Cheshire, arrested numerous suspects and put them on trial, Beyrie wasn't unnecessarily concerned. Even before some of the prisoners were acquitted and a second trial collapsed due to a lack of evidence, he clearly regarded the official reaction as paranoid and heavy-handed and saw no danger to the king's regime.[39] From his point of view, and probably also Bonnet's whose reports are missing for parts of the period, there simply wasn't enough popular support for the Jacobite cause to pose a serious threat. For both men the real political impact unfolded only when in December the Commons began to investigate the handling of the affair by ministers and revived

---

[32]GStA PK, I. HA GR, Rep. 11, no. 1807, ff. 3v, 9, 12v (Robert Molesworth's *Account of Denmark*), 57 (an anonymous riposte to Molesworth), 214v (Ranke, vi, 259) (an unnamed tract by Charles Davenant on the king's finances); NLA, Cal.Br. 24, no. 42, ff. 78 (tract on Naturalisation Bill), 244 (an unnamed tract by Charles Davenant on the king's finances), 260v (Arthur Bury's *The Naked Gospel*).

[33]NLA, Cal.Br. 24, no. 42, ff. 35v–6v.

[34]NLA, Cal.Br. 24, no. 42, ff. 77, 105; GStA PK, I. HA GR, Rep. 11, no. 1807, ff. 55, 60, 199v.

[35]NLA, Cal.Br. 24, no. 42, ff. 88, 101, 103, 233v, 258v; GStA PK, I. HA GR, Rep. 11, no. 1807, ff. 71v, 68, 199v.

[36]NLA, Cal.Br. 24, no. 42, ff. 84, 102v; GStA PK, I. HA GR, Rep. 11, no. 1807, ff. 1, 7–8, 35, 48, 65, 70, 71v, 183, 189. For the convoy system, see Patrick Crowhurst, *The Defence of British Trade 1689–1815* (Chatham, 1977), 46–50.

[37]GStA PK, I. HA GR, Rep. 11, no. 1807, ff. 31v, 57.

[38]See, e.g., NLA, Cal.Br. 24, no. 42, ff. 12, 23, 69v, 78v, 104v, 228, 265; GStA PK, I. HA GR, Rep. 11, no. 1807, ff. 8v, 39, 83.

[39]NLA, Cal.Br. 24, no. 42, ff. 221, 227–8, 231v, 247, 249v; GStA PK, I. HA GR, Rep. 11, no. 1807, ff. 185, 187v.

the High Treason Bill that William III had already rejected earlier in the year. This was a more serious challenge to the monarch than secret Jacobite plotting and one that featured prominently in their reports.[40]

If court and parliament mattered most to Beyrie as well as Bonnet, there were still notable differences in the way they characterised the role of these institutions and their relationship to each other in the aftermath of the Glorious Revolution. Of the two Beyrie put more emphasis on the court. Throughout the year he assiduously chronicled the movements of king and queen, reporting their hunting excursions and visits to other royal palaces in and around London, their stays in town and country houses of the nobility and their attendance at court festivities or religious observances.[41] The state visit by Prince Louis of Baden, one of William III's German allies, at the beginning of 1694 afforded him a welcome opportunity to paint a detailed image of court life, from the prince's public entry and the official festivities laid on for his entertainment to the numerous sightseeing tours, invitations by members of the aristocracy, the odd ceremonial dispute and a rather salacious dinner spent in the company of celebrated court beauties.[42] Interestingly, Beyrie spilled so much ink on the visit despite the fact that Louis of Baden was detested in Hanover for his opposition to the recent elevation of Duke Ernst August to the rank of elector.[43] Other major events at court which Beyrie covered were less controversial such as the celebrations for the king's birthday and his return from Flanders in November.[44] Beyrie also faithfully conveyed the illnesses and miscarriages in the royal family and among the king's favourites,[45] culminating in a blow-by-blow account of the queen's final sickness and death at the end of 1694.[46]

Gossip about court intrigues and the rise and fall of ministers and courtiers was another feature in Beyrie's coverage.[47] He left his recipients in no doubt about the significance of the court as a place where careers and reputations were made (and destroyed).[48] Repeatedly he commented on the efforts of noble families to strike marriage alliances or secure office for one of their own or of individual courtiers, politicians and military men in search of employment to curry favour with the king.[49] Besides, reports about the deaths of the great and good and speculations about who was going to succeed them in their position,[50] the investment of noblemen with regiments,[51] and the creation of new peerages[52]

[40]NLA, Cal.Br. 24, no. 42, ff. 247v, 251v–2, 258, 259v, 266, 268v; GStA PK, I. HA GR, Rep. 11, no. 1807, ff. 200v–1 (Ranke, vi, 251–2), 204 (Ranke, vi, 253), 205v (Ranke, vi, 254), 208, 210v, 209 (Ranke, vi, 255 and 257), 216 (Ranke, vi, 259), 217v (Ranke, vi, 261), 221v–2.

[41]E.g., NLA, Cal.Br. 24, no. 42, ff. 67v, 81v, 83, 99, 101, 118, 119, 220, 224, 253v–4, 255, 257, 260v, 261, 264v.

[42]NLA, Cal.Br. 24, no. 42, ff. 2, 4v–5, 7–8v, 9v, 11, 21v, 24, 27v, 31, 34v–5, 54v, 59, 61, 62.

[43]Schnath, *Geschichte Hannovers*, ii, 244.

[44]NLA, Cal.Br. 24, no. 42, ff. 226, 231, 233, 237, 241, 255.

[45]NLA, Cal.Br. 24, no. 42, ff. 27, 71v, 86, 119, 231, 243v, 247v, 251, 253v, 255, 257.

[46]NLA, Cal.Br. 24, no. 42, ff. 265v–6, 267–8, 270–2v.

[47]NLA, Cal.Br. 24, no. 42, ff. 12, 24v, 53v–4v, 67, 75.

[48]Tellingly, Beyrie also speculated about the rise of a reversionary interest after the death of Mary II (NLA, Cal.Br. 24, no. 42, ff. 272v–3) while Bonnet said nothing of this sort.

[49]NLA, Cal.Br. 24, no. 42, ff. 51, 60v–1, 63v–4, 69, 71, 81, 83, 106, 238, 257.

[50]NLA, Cal.Br. 24, no. 42, ff. 1v, 9, 90, 112.

[51]NLA, Cal.Br. 24, no. 42, ff. 12, 59, 113.

[52]NLA, Cal.Br. 24, no. 42, ff. 117, 118, 122.

provided a running commentary on aristocratic society. In sum, Beyrie conveyed to his readers the image of a princely court like any other in Europe, keen on splendour and ceremonial, riven by personal ambition and functioning according to the rules of rank, honour and clientelism. They would instantly have recognised in Beyrie's account the world they themselves inhabited in Celle and Hanover.

Court news was not absent from Bonnet's despatches either.[53] By and large they followed the same pattern as Beyrie's, but the Prussian resident was less fascinated by the subject matter. He reported unevenly, ignored certain stories when other topics seemed more important,[54] and in addition kept his account often very brief, sometimes adding just one short sentence at the end of his despatch, where Beyrie had been more comprehensive.[55] Bonnet's coverage rarely surpassed that of his counterpart, and when it did it was mainly because parliament did not generate enough newsworthy material.[56] At least once Bonnet had to pay a heavy journalistic price for his reserve. Wary of reporting sickness in the royal family,[57] he failed to inform his readers in Berlin of the first signs of Mary's fatal disease and had to rectify the omission in his next despatch while the courts of Hanover and Celle knew about the grave news that reverberated throughout Europe days earlier.[58]

Strikingly, Bonnet also put a different spin on court affairs. He often presented them in contexts that suggested a wider relevance beyond princely spectacle and aristocratic socializing. While Beyrie, for example, devoted a whole paragraph to the dismantling of James II's Chapel Royal in Whitehall Palace and noted the reuse of the marble stone for the decoration of Hampton Court Palace, Bonnet passed over William's attempt at monarchical representation and took the opportunity that the rededication of the space as the king's library gave him to talk about Richard Bentley, the new librarian, whom he regarded as the greatest living scholar in England.[59] In a similar vein he used William's review of troops which Beyrie mentioned as part of his routine coverage of public royal engagements as an excuse to discuss the preparations for embarking English regiments bound for the continent.[60]

Bonnet's slant emerges most clearly in his treatment of changes in court and government positions. Where Beyrie had stressed family connections, patronage and royal favour to explain the rationale behind individual decisions Bonnet drew on party politics and considerations of parliamentary expediency. The appointment of a new vice chamberlain was thus reported as a scant success for a group of Tory politicians around Sir Edward Seymour,

[53] See, e.g., the following run of reports: GStA PK, I. HA GR, Rep. 11, no. 1807, ff. 74, 78v, 81, 87v, 192 (Ranke, vi, 248).

[54] E.g., Bonnet doesn't mention William's and Mary's visit to the Chapel Royal at Easter (GStA PK, I. HA GR, Rep. 11, no. 1807, f. 66) nor does he pass on information about the preparations in October for the great ball in honour of William's birthday.

[55] GStA PK, I. HA GR, Rep. 11, no. 1807, ff. 37v, 44, 207, 213v. For the rare example of a despatch opening with (albeit very brief) court news f. 46.

[56] GStA PK, I. HA GR, Rep. 11, no. 1807, ff. 4–5, 6, 61, 77, 184, 195, 197v.

[57] For an instance where Bonnet stayed silent about Mary II's illnesses, see GStA PK, I. HA GR, Rep. 11, no. 1807, ff. 49–52. For a few examples where Bonnet did mention illnesses, see ff. 199v, 201v, 204v, 219v.

[58] GStA PK, I. HA GR, Rep. 11, no. 1807, ff. 220–1v.

[59] NLA, Cal.Br. 24, no. 42, f. 88; GStA PK, I. HA GR, Rep. 11, no. 1807, f. 57v.

[60] GStA PK, I. HA GR, Rep. 11, no. 1807, f. 70v; NLA, Cal.Br. 24, no. 42, f. 101.

which was losing its political clout but could still cling on to a minor court office that had previously been held by one of their allies.[61] The award of the second regiment of guards to John, Lord Cutts, in turn, was presented as a ruling by the king in favour of an able courtier but also a 'grand Whig' and strong supporter of the government in the Commons.[62] And when at the end of April 1694, after the parliamentary session had come to a close, William III enacted a major reshuffle Beyrie mentioned just the names of a few newly appointed figures without giving much background information, while Bonnet provided an extensive analysis of the raft of new appointments and honours detailing in each case the political reason why someone was dismissed (punishment for voting against the ministry, Jacobite leanings) or given a job (usefulness in parliament, pertinent knowledge).[63] This pattern repeated itself on other occasions when posts in central government or at county level had to be filled.[64]

On reflection, then, Bonnet's was in many ways a more 'modern' view of political decision making that accentuated structural and (party) political considerations. He saw the court as an important, but ultimately secondary arena and interpreted developments there within the wider framework of ministry and parliament. Beyrie, on the other hand, subscribed to a vision of English politics with the court at the centre and one which as a consequence still pivoted around personal relationships and the interests of kinship networks.

3

Accordingly, both men's treatment of parliament diverged as well. Each of them allocated the two chambers a central place in their reporting; even Beyrie spent more time writing on parliament than the court. But their assessment of parliamentary proceedings and parliament's place in the political landscape digressed again in characteristic ways. To start with, the breadth of their coverage was slightly at odds. For pragmatic reasons both covered only what could be deemed salient to ministers and courtiers in the Holy Roman Empire. Topics 'concerning only domestic politics', as Beyrie put it, were to be excluded.[65] In theory, this meant private bills and discussions below the level of national or international politics. In practice, however, things were never as clear cut. Beyrie, for example, excused himself in some despatches from reporting about the debates in the Lords with the argument that only private bills had been discussed but in others was more than happy to deal in some detail with the frequent disputes in the English nobility about succession to a title, inheritance of the family fortune and the claims of wives to their dowry.[66] This clearly reflected his obsession with the traditional pillars of society, but Bonnet had preoccupations of his own. He was alone, for example, in reporting about the delayed compensation of some victims of

---

[61] GStA PK, I. HA GR, Rep. 11, no. 1807, ff. 35v, 39.

[62] GStA PK, I. HA GR, Rep. 11, no. 1807, f. 184; for a similar case f. 81.

[63] NLA, Cal.Br. 24, no. 42, f. 117v; GStA PK, I. HA GR, Rep. 11, no. 1807, ff. 78v, 80. For the context, see Horwitz, *Parliament, Policy and Politics*, 132.

[64] GStA PK, I. HA GR, Rep. 11, no. 1807, ff. 80, 84v, 86, 209 (Ranke, vi, 257); NLA, Cal.Br. 24, no. 42, f. 121.

[65] 'qui ne regardent que le dedans', NLA, Cal.Br. 24, no. 42, f. 70.

[66] NLA, Cal.Br. 24, no. 42, ff. 35v, 50v, 53, 55v, 59, 63, 71, 73, 74v, 77v, 257v.

Charles II's Stop of the Exchequer, the debates about the coinage and counterfeit money, and Irish forfeitures, topics that probably appealed to his abiding interest in issues of money and finance.[67] In other respects, too, Bonnet's coverage of parliamentary affairs differed from Beyrie's. Regular readers of his despatches were also acquainted with a draft bill to encourage British privateering,[68] the Naturalisation Bill,[69] an attempt to reform the legal basis for the treatment of crimes committed at sea,[70] and the possible introduction of capital punishment in certain cases of perjury.[71] All of these topics Beyrie treated marginally at best and in most cases not at all.[72]

There was, however, agreement about what parliamentary business could not be left unreported. At the top of the agenda were the finances of the monarchy. Here parliament's central concern in the first half of William's reign, supply legislation,[73] converged with the wider strategic interests of the German courts reliant on English subsidies for the continuation of the war against France. Both sets of despatches are awash with more or less detailed summaries of endless debates over which one of the many alternative finance proposals and tax schemes put forward by different groups in the Commons should be adopted to fund the fledgling fiscal-military state. This was on the one hand, as Bonnet put it, 'the most curious [topic] for those abroad',[74] but on the other could bore even the 'Curious' who had to trawl through a mass of financial detail as Beyrie recognised.[75] Debating these issues was also a long-drawn-out process. During the spring of 1694 both correspondents complained about the 'great slowness' of the deliberations and a lack of decisive action.[76] Only from the beginning of April, parliamentary proceedings appeared to gain momentum when William III's desire to leave for the continent and the inordinate length of the session put pressure on Members to finalise their deliberations.[77] It was with a sigh of relief that Beyrie at long last could report the end of the waiting game in the closing days of April.[78] Needless to say, the same story repeated itself in December when the Commons started to ponder the various means of supply for the following year.[79]

[67] Compensation: GStA PK, I. HA GR, Rep. 11, no. 1807, ff. 46v, 49v, 56v–7 (Ranke, vi, 245); a brief reference to this subject in NLA, Cal.Br. 24, no. 42, f. 91v; coinage: GStA PK, I. HA GR, Rep. 11, no. 1807, ff. 76v–7 (Ranke, vi, 248); Irish forfeitures: GStA PK, I. HA GR, Rep. 11, no. 1807, ff. 10v, 31, 53v, 55 (Ranke, vi, 244), 204 (Ranke, vi, 253).

[68] GStA PK, I. HA GR, Rep. 11, no. 1807, ff. 65, 71v–2, 75v (Ranke, vi, 247), 76v (Ranke, vi, 248), 219 (Ranke, vi, 261), 219 (Ranke, vi, 261).

[69] GStA PK, I. HA GR, Rep. 11, no. 1807, ff. 42 (Ranke, vi, 241–2), 55 (Ranke, vi, 244).

[70] GStA PK, I. HA GR, Rep. 11, no. 1807, f. 76v (Ranke, vi, 248).

[71] GStA PK, I. HA GR, Rep. 11, no. 1807, ff. 216v (Ranke, vi, 260), 217v, 219 (Ranke, vi, 261).

[72] Perjury: NLA, Cal.Br. 24, no. 42, f. 266r.

[73] *HPC 1690–1715*, I, 393–4.

[74] 'le plus curieux pour le dehors', GStA PK, I. HA GR, Rep. 11, no. 1807, f. 217 (Ranke, vi, 261).

[75] 'Curieux', NLA, Cal.Br. 24, no. 42, f. 2; similarly ff. 81v–2.

[76] 'beaucoup de lenteur', GStA PK, I. HA GR, Rep. 11, no. 1807, ff. 7, 36 (quotation); NLA, Cal.Br. 24, no. 42, ff. 4, 8v, 26.

[77] GStA PK, I. HA GR, Rep. 11, no. 1807, ff. 64, 66, 71, 73, 76v (Ranke, vi, 248); NLA, Cal.Br. 24, no. 42, ff. 98, 99–100, 104v, 105v, 113.

[78] NLA, Cal.Br. 24, no. 42, f. 116.

[79] NLA, Cal.Br. 24, no. 42, ff. 243v, 247, 252, 254v, 256, 258, 262; GStA PK, I. HA GR, Rep. 11, no. 1807, ff. 198 (Ranke, vi, 249–50), 200v–1 (Ranke, vi, 251–2), 205 (Ranke, vi, 253–4), 210 (Ranke, vi, 256).

Despite all of this, admiration for the financial might of the English monarchy is widespread in the reports and outweighed any reservations that Beyrie and Bonnet might have had against the slowness of the process. The apparent eagerness with which the Commons agreed to vast sums of money for the war effort at the beginning of December, for example, excited Bonnet more than any other event during this year. In an emphatic tone he told his readers that there never had been a parliament that gave the king more money in a shorter time span and with more grace than the current one, almost £5,000,000 in just one week.[80] Beyrie's reports also conveyed the image of a parliament that despite the odd squabble was compliant most of the time and mainly argued about the best way to find the funds that it had gladly promised to the monarch. This positive assessment came on the back of a more general appreciation of the wealth that England as a nation acquired. Both men were in awe of the 'great riches' that had been accumulated through trade and that formed the basis of her political power.[81]

For this reason, they were also prepared to go into intricate detail about the various finance schemes that were discussed in the Commons despite the tiresome effect this might have had on their readers. Bonnet, for example, had no qualms about rehearsing not only the stratagems of the various groupings in the Commons to push through their specific proposals, but gave free rein to the technicalities of financing the war against France.[82] The newly created Bank of England caught his attention in particular.[83] He covered the debates in both Houses setting out the arguments for and against a national bank, analysed its governance structure and funding and wrote about the scramble of the wealthy to invest their money once the subscriptions had opened. He confidently predicted that in financial terms it would become the most profitable venture of its kind in the world. Early on he also recognised the political dividend that William III earned from the new institution. By putting their money into the bank, the social elites literally bought into the government agenda.

Although there is no suggestion in the sources that Bonnet had been prompted by the court in Berlin to supply intelligence on this novel form of deficit financing, he clearly was acutely aware of the implications and the exemplary character of many of the debates in the Commons for other states seeking to exploit new financial resources. This applies in some measure also to Beyrie, who informed ministers in Celle and Hanover of the progress of the various finance bills going through parliament. Yet his reports often lacked the technical detail that distinguished Bonnet's despatches.[84] He remained focused on politics, and when he went into the finer points of the various schemes it was mainly the proposals for a new lottery that caught his attention.[85] Conversely, the new national bank received a more

---

[80]GStA PK, I. HA GR, Rep. 11, no. 1807, ff. 202, 204 (Ranke, vi, 252–3). Bonnet was similarly upbeat at the end of the parliamentary session in April, f. 75v (Ranke, vi, 247).

[81]'grandes richesses', NLA, Cal.Br. 24, no. 42, f. 105; GStA PK, I. HA GR, Rep. 11, no. 1807, f. 71.

[82]A good example of both is his coverage of the debates on 15 and 18 Dec., see GStA PK, I. HA GR, Rep. 11, no. 1807, f. 214 (Ranke, vi, 258–9). See also ff. 40, 63, 61, 66, 73, 75, 202, 204 (Ranke, vi, 252–3), 205 (Ranke, vi, 253–4), 217 (Ranke, vi, 260–1).

[83]GStA PK, I. HA GR, Rep. 11, no. 1807, ff. 68, 72, 73, 75 (partly in Ranke, vi, 246), 88–91, 93, 183v–4, 187, 189v–90.

[84]Compare, e.g., NLA, Cal.Br. 24, no. 42, ff. 81, 85v–6, 101 with GStA PK, I. HA GR, Rep. 11, no. 1807, ff. 43, 49, 68.

[85]See, e.g., NLA, Cal.Br. 24, no. 42, ff. 91v–2, 99v, 224, 263v–4, 266. Bonnet, by contrast, regarded lotteries as rather unreliable means of raising money, see GStA PK, I. HA GR, Rep. 11, no. 1807, f. 67v.

guarded reception.[86] He did not come down on either side of the argument, but his coverage of the debates was certainly more cautious and ambiguous than Bonnet's. Rather than promoting new ways of tapping the national wealth he appears to have been in favour of more conventional forms of government funding.

If in their coverage of state finance Beyrie and Bonnet wrote with one eye on their patron's putative interests, the remainder of the space devoted to the two Houses was taken up by the set pieces of parliamentary oratory as they occurred during the year. In this respect the two correspondents stayed true to their journalistic ethos and were solely guided by the saliency of debates in Westminster. As a result, alongside a few smaller debates,[87] the inquiries into naval mismanagement and crown payments to Members[88] and the aborted Place Bill[89] in the first half of the year, and the Triennial Act,[90] the revival of the Place Bill[91] and the High Treason Bill[92] in the second, were at the forefront of what ministers and courtiers in Berlin, Celle and Hanover came to know about English affairs in 1694. Both men thus covered what most historians nowadays would regard as the political high points of the year.[93]

Thematic coherence notwithstanding, there were differences, in the way they reported parliamentary business. Not least among them was the depth of analysis. Beyrie's journalistic style did not lend itself to detail in the same way as Bonnet's more targeted 'diplomatic' approach. Since Beyrie prized a greater variety of topics over focusing on a smaller number of core themes he had to deal with parliamentary proceedings in a more generic manner. This difficulty was compounded by the more restricted space that he had at his disposal due to the smaller paper format he used. In those rare cases when he concentrated mainly on one major debate in the Commons at the expense of other news items Beyrie wrote 40% less than Bonnet in his parallel despatch.[94] If we take one of Beyrie's average reports with its mixture of subject matter the proportions become even more skewed. Then Bonnet's coverage of parliament could be more than four times that of

---

[86] NLA, Cal.Br. 24, no. 42, ff. 102v, 105v–6, 113v–15 where, in an unusually detailed analysis of the Bank of England's structure, he pointed out the liability risks that investors excluded from the board of the Bank faced. A rather ambiguous report about the Bank also f. 222v.

[87] E.g., on a bill for the punishment of deserters and mutineers: GStA PK, I. HA GR, Rep. 11, no. 1807, ff. 38 (Ranke, vi, 241), 43, 45v (Ranke, vi, 242–3), 49v, 46v, 48, 216v (Ranke, vi, 260), 219 (Ranke, vi, 261); NLA, Cal.Br. 24, no. 42, ff. 70, 84, 105.

[88] NLA, Cal.Br. 24, no. 42, ff. 4, 11v–12, 20–1, 24, 26v–7, 31v, 55v–6, 60v, 64; GStA PK, I. HA GR, Rep. 11, no. 1807, ff. 1v, 5, 12, 13v–14 (Ranke, vi, 233), 17 (Ranke, vi, 235), 20v, 27, 32, 33, 35, 36–7, 40v, 42 (Ranke, vi, 241).

[89] NLA, Cal.Br. 24, no. 42, ff. 4, 29v–31, 34, 64; GStA PK, I. HA GR, Rep. 11, no. 1807, ff. 18, 20 (partly in Ranke, vi, 236), 21, 23–5v (Ranke, vi, 236–8), 36–7.

[90] NLA, Cal.Br. 24, no. 42, ff. 244v, 247, 256v, 260, 261v–2, 264, 268; GStA PK, I. HA GR, Rep. 11, no. 1807, ff. 198 (Ranke, vi, 249–50), 202v, 204 (Ranke, vi, 253), 208v, 210 (Ranke, vi, 255–6), 211 (Ranke, vi, 257–8), 216 (Ranke, vi, 260), 217 (Ranke, vi, 260–1), 221v (Ranke, vi, 262), 223.

[91] NLA, Cal.Br. 24, no. 42, ff. 244v, 247, 264; GStA PK, I. HA GR, Rep. 11, no. 1807, ff. 198v (Ranke, vi, 250), 204 (Ranke, vi, 253), 216 (Ranke, vi, 259–60).

[92] GStA PK, I. HA GR, Rep. 11, no. 1807, ff. 204 (Ranke, vi, 253), 208, 201v, 209 (Ranke, vi, 255 and 257), 216 (Ranke, vi, 259), 221v–2, 217v (Ranke, vi, 261); NLA, Cal.Br. 24, no. 42, ff. 259v, 266, 268v.

[93] Horwitz, *Parliament, Policy and Politics*, 132–9; *HPC 1690–1715*, i, 447–8.

[94] Take for example the debate on 23 Nov.: Beyrie's 525 words fall way behind Bonnet's 740; NLA, Cal.Br. 24, no. 42, ff. 247–9v; GStA PK, I. HA GR, Rep. 11, no. 1807, ff. 200–1v.

Beyrie.[95] As a result Beyrie usually provided what can best be described as an executive summary of proceedings. He gave a rundown of the most important bills discussed on that day, briefly described some of the main arguments for or against them, assessed the way the debates were going from the point of view of the government and sometimes ventured a guess as to their likely outcome.[96] Only a few particularly heated debates in the two chambers merited a more specific treatment. On these occasions he recorded the names of a few speakers, usually of those regarded as 'the best heads'[97] of the House, conveyed the gist of what they were saying and sometimes also the numbers of divisions albeit not always correctly.[98]

Bonnet by contrast preferred the elaborate report to the executive summary and, in addition, prided himself on accuracy. None of the divisions he reported appears to have been wrong, and despatches that rehearsed individual debates in some detail are plentiful.[99] Naming the principal speakers, outlining their main points and reporting the majorities in the House had become second nature to him. He was also attuned to the manoeuvring and positioning going on in the Commons, and repeatedly informed his readers about strategic moves by one party or the other.[100] On some occasions Bonnet went even further than that and covered parliamentary business beyond the debates. He reported for example from committee meetings, relayed the punishment of a clergymen who had fallen foul of a Member and devoted a whole paragraph to the selection of commissioners for the public accounts, mentioning that in one case the Speaker had to cast a decisive vote between two candidates and that one of the merchants chosen did not hold a seat in the Commons.[101] Bonnet was not above assessing Members' performances on the floor of the House either. He described Cutts for example as 'one of the best speakers',[102] and called Seymour whom otherwise he portrayed with some irritation as a thorn in the side of the government as a 'great parliamentarian'.[103]

One of the most noticeable traits of Bonnet's style of reporting was his ability to capture the atmosphere in the two Houses. With obvious delight he described a withering attack launched by the earl of Montagu on Seymour's erratic behaviour since the Revolution, his constant changes of political positions and party loyalties that put private above public interests. For good measure he also added that many in the chamber secretly applauded this assault.[104] On another occasion, at the start of the new parliamentary session in

---

[95] Compare Bonnet's 664 words with Beyrie's 151 on 4 Dec.; GStA PK, I. HA GR, Rep. 11, no. 1807, ff. 202, 204; NLA, Cal.Br. 24, no. 42, f. 256. For further examples, see the parallel reports by both men in: NLA, Cal.Br. 24, no. 42, ff. 77v–8. 88, 107v–8, 112v–113, 259v–60v; and GStA PK, I. HA GR, Rep. 11, no. 1807, ff. 40, 53, 55 (partly in Ranke, vi, 243–4), 73, 75, 76 (Ranke, vi, 247–8), 208, 210 (Ranke, vi, 255–7).

[96] Good examples of his style of reporting are NLA, Cal.Br. 24, no. 42, ff. 35v–6, 69v–70.

[97] 'les meilleurs testes', NLA, Cal.Br. 24, no. 42, f. 268v, similar 'testes fortes', f. 74.

[98] NLA, Cal.Br. 24, no. 42, ff. 12, 14–15, 35v, 63, 112, 268v. For reports which give the numbers of divisions incorrectly, see ff. 70, 261v–2.

[99] See, e.g., GStA PK, I. HA GR, Rep. 11, no. 1807, ff. 38 (Ranke, vi, 240–1), 40, 42v (Ranke, vi, 241), 53, 55 (partly in Ranke, vi, 243–4), 56–7 (Ranke, vi, 244–5), 58v–9.

[100] GStA PK, I. HA GR, Rep. 11, no. 1807, ff. 56–7 (Ranke, vi, 244–5).

[101] GStA PK, I. HA GR, Rep. 11, no. 1807, ff. 10v, 49, 72.

[102] 'un des meilleurs parleurs', GStA PK, I. HA GR, Rep. 11, no. 1807, f. 42 (Ranke, vi, 241).

[103] 'grand Parlamentaire', GStA PK, I. HA GR, Rep. 11, no. 1807, f. 191.

[104] GStA PK, I. HA GR, Rep. 11, no. 1807, ff. 56–7 (Ranke, vi, 244–5).

November, Bonnet described in vivid terms over the course of several despatches the barrage of criticism aimed at the government and, remarkably, at William III personally, while the supporters of the court struggled to contain the onslaught and had to resort to ridiculing their opponents.[105] At his best Bonnet was capable of capturing the high drama of the oratorical contest in the Commons while at the same time dissecting the tactics of the various parties, providing pithy summaries of their main political points and reliably predicting the future course of events.

Yet Bonnet's penetrating analysis had wider implications for the image of parliament that was emerging from his pages. Unsurprisingly, given what we learned earlier about his treatment of the court, the Prussian resident created the impression that parliament and the Commons in particular had become the dominant arena in English post-revolutionary politics. By simply allocating so much space and detailed coverage to the two Houses and side-lining all other venues, the balance of power shifted perceptibly in Westminster's favour. Even more importantly, Bonnet's blow-by-blow account of debates and divisions impacted on perceptions of the nature of parliamentary politics. What his audience was taking away from his descriptions was the picture of a cut-and-thrust environment where coteries of politicians were vying for influence and power.

Bonnet's treatment of parties was at the bottom of this portrayal. Rather than depicting them as organisations united by common beliefs, he described parliamentary parties as loose groupings without much of a programmatic basis. Every now and then he marked out members as Whigs or Tories, supporters or enemies of the court, but what these terms stood for, which political loyalties they denoted remained unclear.[106] Only on a few occasions did Bonnet hint at certain principles underpinning party allegiances. They were primarily about religion, a subject that with few exceptions was otherwise curiously absent from both our reporters' missives. In the context of the appointment of the new archbishop of Canterbury in December 1694, for example, Bonnet pitted Whigs and their support for dissenters, or Presbyterians as he called them, against intransigent high church zealots and hotheads,[107] terms of abuse that appear a few more times in his and also Beyrie's accounts.[108] Apart from such instances, though, politics was mainly a mundane pursuit without ideological demarcations. Creating this perception may not have been intentional, since Bonnet was well aware of the origins of political parties in England and of the differences between them.[109] But his brand of journalism, concentrating as it did on the slow progress of day-to-day politics and a few high profile oratorial contests, certainly gave rise to such a reading. Even debates about constitutional issues such as the Triennial Act or the High Treason Bill were often

---

[105] GStA PK, I. HA GR, Rep. 11, no. 1807, ff. 196–7 (Ranke, vi, 248–9), 189 (Ranke, vi, 249), 200–1 (Ranke, vi, 250–2).

[106] Intriguingly, the term Country Party appears neither in Bonnet nor Beyrie. When Bonnet gave a brief overview of the various parties extant in England, he mentioned that there were 'des Whigs & des Torys' and then those 'pour la Cour & contre la Cour', GStA PK, I. HA GR, Rep. 11, no. 1807, f. 46.

[107] GStA PK, I. HA GR, Rep. 11, no. 1807, f. 209 (Ranke, vi, 257).

[108] E.g., NLA, Cal.Br. 24, no. 42, ff. 56, 69v, 248; GStA PK, I. HA GR, Rep. 11, no. 1807, f. 199 (Ranke, vi, 250).

[109] Once, when speaking about Irish affairs, Bonnet used the term Tory in its original derogatory meaning as 'Torys ou Raperies', GStA PK, I. HA GR, Rep. 11, no. 1807, f. 219.

broken down to the level of legal technicalities and thus lost their wider political significance.[110]

Bonnet's penchant for figures and numbers and all things financial did not help either. Much of his parliamentary coverage was about Members bogged down in discussions about the ins and outs of state finances. Such were the minutiae of examining supply bills that on occasion even Bonnet had to admit that an altercation centred round an 'obscurity', a minor clause in a bill, which did not stop him, though, from reporting it in extenso.[111] Strikingly, the wider arguments that he rehearsed, especially those put forward by supporters of the ministry, in some cases boiled down to stressing natural constraints such as time pressure, procedural restrictions or simply a lack of alternatives and refrained from giving a substantive reason for a certain course of action.[112] It may have been this focus on Realpolitik that appealed to Ranke when he discovered the despatches. It is also no coincidence that Bonnet grouped Members according to whether they voted with or against the government. They were either among the 'well-intentioned' who formed 'the party of the Court' or they were 'discontented', 'those who oppose the interests of the Court' whom Bonnet on one occasion denounced as 'Crieurs'.[113] The more ideologically loaded terms Whigs and Tories were seldom part of the equation and mainly used when Bonnet had to deal with politics outside parliament, for example the appointment of office holders or political pamphlets.[114]

In any case, reporting debates was as much about personal ambition as it was about party affiliation. In the gladiatorial contests between the main orators, arguments could play a lesser role than tactics or individual agendas. For example Bonnet wrote with some amazement about Members who, for no apparent reason, shifted allegiances and as a result contradicted views which they had held only a short while earlier or voted against the side to which they nominally belonged.[115] For some debates Bonnet clearly stated from the start that Members were not debating along party lines but according to their personal views and private interests.[116] Besides, Bonnet repeatedly referred to Members in government pay in order to explain the success of ministerial policies.[117] The prominence of debates about

---

[110]See, e.g., the debate in the Lords about the Triennial Act and the endless discussions whether as a consequence of the act the sitting parliament had to be dissolved in 1695, 1696 or 1697, GStA PK, I. HA GR, Rep. 11, no. 1807, f. 216 (Ranke, vi, 260). References to constitutional issues can be found in GStA PK, I. HA GR, Rep. 11, no. 1807, ff. 21v (Ranke, vi, 236–7), 208, 210 (Ranke, vi, 255–7).

[111]'obscurité', GStA PK, I. HA GR, Rep. 11, no. 1807, f. 66v.

[112]GStA PK, I. HA GR, Rep. 11, no. 1807, ff. 16 (Ranke, vi, 234), 40v, 49, 73, 75 (partly in Ranke, vi, 246), 76 (Ranke, vi, 247–8).

[113]'bien-intentionnez', GStA PK, I. HA GR, Rep. 11, no. 1807, f. 189v; 'le parti de la Cour', 'mécontens', ff. 200v and 201 (Ranke, vi, 251–2); 'ceux qui s'opposent aux intérêts de la Cour', f. 205v (Ranke, vi, 254). Other examples in Bonnet are: 'partie de la Cour', 'le parti, qu'on peut en general apeller le bien intentionné', ff. 58v–59; 'parti de la Cour', ff. 208 and 210 (Ranke, vi, 256); 'les Seigneurs affectionnez à la Cour', f. 76 (Ranke, vi, 247); 'Membres, qui avoient la direction des intérets de la cour', 'parti oppose', f. 202 (Ranke, vi, 252–3); 'le parti contraire à celuy de la cour', f. 220v. In some despatches Bonnet called those opposed to the court 'Jacobites', see e.g., f. 18.

[114]See, e.g., GStA PK, I. HA GR, Rep. 11, no. 1807, ff. 31v, 57, 80, 209 (Ranke, vi, 257). For rare examples of the use of 'Whig' and 'Tory' in parliamentary contexts, see ff. 18v, 52, 56v–57 (Ranke, vi, 245).

[115]See, e.g., GStA PK, I. HA GR, Rep. 11, no. 1807, ff. 36v, 40v, 45 (Ranke, vi, 242–3), 208 and 210 (Ranke, vi, 256), 211v (Ranke, vi, 258).

[116]See, e.g., GStA PK, I. HA GR, Rep. 11, no. 1807, ff. 13 (Ranke, vi, 232), 36v, 46, 65, 66v, 211v (Ranke, vi, 258), 216 (Ranke, vi, 260).

[117]E.g., GStA PK, I. HA GR, Rep. 11, no. 1807, ff. 36, 33v, 76v (Ranke, vi, 248), 209 (Ranke, vi, 257).

the Place Bill in 1694 also helped to reinforce the impression that private interests went a long way to explain the outcome of policy decisions. In the end, it was a rather Namierite vision of parliamentary politics that unfolded in Bonnet's despatches.[118]

Some of these observations also ring true for Beyrie's reports. In his account, too, ideological concerns played second fiddle to more pragmatic reasoning. Politics was at best about finding practical, short-term solutions to problems such as the funding of the war effort and at worst the outcome of erratic personal behaviour.[119] Members again fell into two categories, 'the party fond of the Court' and 'the party opposed to the Court'.[120] Still, Beyrie looked at parliament from a slightly different angle that was informed by older notions of what constituted parliament or assemblies of estates more generally. His parliament was a less adversarial and competitive place but one where the idea of an ultimately harmonious relationship with the monarch had not lost all its currency.

To be sure, Beyrie could not avoid dealing with the repeated conflicts between William and parliament. On the contrary, he repeatedly drew William as a strong figure that enforced his will on parliament. For example, early in 1694 Beyrie credited William's address to the Lords with ending a stalemate between the two Houses over the land tax.[121] When shortly afterwards a draft treason bill threatened to restrict the government's room for action, William appeared in the Lords, followed the debate for hours and by his sheer presence cowed the anti-court party into submission.[122] During the final stages of the controversy surrounding the establishment of the Bank of England the king once more made his views known to a number of lords in private and thus achieved the passing of the Tonnage Act.[123] And if all else failed Beyrie's William harboured no doubts about denying the royal assent, as was the case with the Place Bill. Beyrie justified this move that caused immense anger among Members by stating that 'nothing was capable of bending him [the king] to do something that was prejudicial to what he believed to be his authority' and added for good measure that William had exercised this right in his first few years as king twice as often as Charles II in the whole of his reign.[124] This depiction of events was slightly at odds with Bonnet's, who also reported the royal veto but didn't highlight William's agency during this controversy, shining the light instead on the supporters of the king in the Commons who after a raucous debate defused the situation.[125] Interestingly, Bonnet had also omitted to mention the king's intervention before the vote on the Tonnage Act and ascribed the success of the bill purely to parliamentary arithmetic.[126]

---

[118] A view shared by many contemporaries, see Julian Hoppit, *A Land of Liberty? England 1689–1727* (Oxford, 2000), 146.

[119] For an example of the latter, see NLA, Cal.Br. 24, no. 42, ff. 63, 74.

[120] 'le parti affectionné a la Cour', NLA, Cal.Br. 24, no. 42, f. 35v, similarly ff. 74, 92, 113; 'bien intentionné', f. 86; 'La partie opposé a la cour', f. 77v. The terms 'Whig' and 'Tory' occur hardly at all in Beyrie's parliamentary reporting, for the few references to 'Wiggs', see NLA, Cal.Br. 24, no. 42, ff. 56, 64, 244v–5v.

[121] NLA, Cal.Br. 24, no. 42, f. 29.

[122] NLA, Cal.Br. 24, no. 42, ff. 73–4. Bonnet's despatch for this debate is missing but see GStA PK, I. HA GR, Rep. 11, no. 1807, f. 38v (Ranke, vi, 241) where he mentions plans within government to use the king's presence to stifle opposition.

[123] NLA, Cal.Br. 24, no. 42, f. 112v–13.

[124] 'que rien n'étoit capable de le plier a rien faire au prejudice de ce qu'il croyoit estre de son authorité', NLA, Cal.Br. 24, no. 42, ff. 29v–31 (quotation at 29v), 34v, 35–7.

[125] GStA PK, I. HA GR, Rep. 11, no. 1807, ff. 18, 20 (partly in Ranke, vi, 236), 21, 23–5v (Ranke, vi, 236–8).

[126] NLA, Cal.Br. 24, no. 42, ff. 112v–13; GStA PK, I. HA GR, Rep. 11, no. 1807, f. 76v (Ranke, vi, 248).

In a way, the rendering of William as a strong king only confirmed the image of parliament's subservience to the monarch that was prevalent in many of Beyrie's reports. Especially in the coverage of supply legislation parliament appears as docile, with Members squabbling among themselves but giving the king what was his due.[127] William, on the other hand, is portrayed by Beyrie on many occasions as magnanimous, showing clemency to his Jacobite enemies[128] and 'prudence' in his dealings with parliament. He was prepared, for example, to compromise in the best interest of the country over bills[129] and to listen to the advice given by parliament. In an extraordinary report, Beyrie presented the heated debate in the Lords about the revamped High Treason Bill shortly before Christmas 1694 – a bill that fundamentally threatened to undermine the government – as a classic example of the peers of the realm giving counsel to their king, rather than a power struggle that William lost as Bonnet did.[130] Once again the king was present during the debate. This time he was not depicted as overawing the lords but as 'listening to their opinion', with opponents and supporters of the bill weighing arguments and giving their 'contrary opinion' on the matter in hand. Strikingly, Beyrie dispensed with all party-political labelling and drew the lords in their entirety as servants of the king who saw it as their duty to 'counsel' the monarch. The same concept pervaded other reports, for example, when he described how William invited Louis of Baden to watch him give his royal assent in front of the political nation assembled in parliament.[131]

Beyrie's more benign view of parliament can partly be explained by his more broadbrush style of reporting. Where Bonnet preferred the close up and dissected debates, Beyrie zoomed out and gave a summary of events that by necessity tended to gloss over frictions and tensions. In no small measure, however, it was also the upshot of his emphasis on debates in the Lords. Whereas Bonnet in his parliamentary coverage clearly prioritised the lower over the upper chamber relishing its confrontational style some of Beyrie's most detailed accounts dwelt on proceedings in the queen's chamber which with their ceremonial trappings and repeated presence of the monarch harked back to a more traditional understanding of parliament, and one that, for many of his German readers, was closer to how they envisaged the relationship between ruler and estates.

4

This, finally, begs the question how foreign residents and agents were able to gain access to the information that underlies these two diverging views of English politics. As with most providers of scribal news, be they commercial newsletter writers or diplomats, neither Bonnet nor Beyrie disclosed the sources from which they were drawing, especially when they were not generally available and thus only served to highlight the particular value of the newsmonger in question.

---

[127] See, e.g., NLA, Cal.Br. 24, no. 42, ff. 251v–2, 254v, 256.

[128] NLA, Cal.Br. 24, no. 42, ff. 12, 69v, 104v, 253v.

[129] 'prudence', NLA, Cal.Br. 24, no. 42, f. 20v; inquiry into naval mismanagement: f. 20v–1; Mining Bill: ff. 50v, 55v.

[130] 'd'entendre leur avis', 'avis contraire', 'conseille', NLA, Cal.Br. 24, no. 42, f. 268v; GStA PK, I. HA GR, Rep. 11, no. 1807, f. 218v (Ranke, vi, 262).

[131] NLA, Cal.Br. 24, no. 42, f. 29.

The only references as to the origins of news in both sets of reports are to unnamed 'letters' which contained intelligence about events outside London. Both men regularly drew on letters from various port cities along the English south coast as well as from Edinburgh, Dublin and other Irish ports. In addition, letters from the Netherlands and, in declining order of frequency, ports in Spain and Portugal as well as some colonies in the West Indies supplied information about events further afield.[132] In most cases these letters 'derived from people, usually merchants, who were commissioned to write regularly to London', but were not necessarily paid for their services.[133] Like most other Londoners, Bonnet and Beyrie probably did not subscribe to these letters but consulted them in places where they were readily available such as coffeehouses and the Royal Exchange. At any rate it is striking how frequently both men relied on a common source when they were covering the fate of merchant fleets, military engagements on sea, the English war preparations or the latest developments in Scotland and Ireland.[134] How much detail they fetched from the letters may have differed, but the specifics of a story, the mistakes they shared and sometimes even the wording make it abundantly clear that they had used the same template. In addition to these 'letters of public news'[135] Bonnet at least appears to have had access to government information that either was provided to all foreign diplomats (or those of allied powers) or came from sources within the various departments that he had befriended. This would explain why Bonnet could report about what was debated in the cabinet council, in one case even down to the particulars of a discussion.[136]

It is more difficult to find out where Bonnet and Beyrie gleaned their information about proceedings in the two Houses. As is well known, under parliamentary privilege debates were supposed to take place out of the public gaze. Recent research has shown, though, that 'the palace [of Westminster] was a remarkably permeable space open to far larger numbers of people than is often assumed' and that foreign diplomats especially could get access to the two chambers with the Commons installing a visitors' gallery in the 1690s.[137] This does not mean, however, that both men really availed themselves of the opportunities open to them as semi-diplomatic reporters or that they indeed qualified as foreigners to whom access was not denied. Although both Houses were at the centre of their reporting, Bonnet and Beyrie did not so much as hint at their sources or say whether they were present at debates or not. Still some circumstantial evidence may point us in the right direction.

Beyrie, in particular, does not appear to have been a frequent visitor to the Commons, if he was one at all. Many of his less detailed reports certainly could have been written on the basis of English newsletters that were circulating at the time,[138] and it has to be

---

[132] Sometimes called 'ordinaires', e.g., NLA, Cal.Br. 24, no. 42, f. 60.

[133] Mark Goldie, *The Entring Book of Roger Morrice 1677–1691* (7 vols, Woodbridge, 2007), i, 126–7.

[134] Compare, e.g., NLA, Cal.Br. 24, no. 42, ff. 261v, 78v–9, 93, 103, 107, 108, 112, 116v; and GStA PK, I. HA GR, Rep. 11, no. 1807, ff. 213, 42v, 60, 63, 71v, 75v, 74, 77, 80.

[135] Goldie, *Entring Book*, 126.

[136] GStA PK, I. HA GR, Rep. 11, no. 1807, f. 196. For a further instance where Bonnet seems to have received information from inside government, ff. 60 and 63.

[137] Robin Eagles, ' "Got Together in a Riotous and Tumultous Manner": Crowds and the Palace of Westminster, c. 1700–1800', *Journal for Eighteenth-Century Studies*, xliii (2020), 350.

[138] A.W. Barber, ' "It is Not Easy What to Say of our Condition, Much Less to Write It": The Continued Importance of Scribal News in the Early 18th Century', *Parl. Hist.*, xxxii (2013), 293–316.

left to future research to determine if his reports were dependent on what could be found there. But even some of his more detailed despatches don't have the air of being eye-witness accounts. As has been noted earlier they rarely managed to convey the heat of debates in the same way as Bonnet. It is also worth stating that Beyrie's reports about proceedings on post days on occasion did not contain developments that happened late in the afternoon or in the evening, presumably because he was not present in the chamber and had to wait for the latest news to come in from other sources.[139] For example, in one instance he had already finished his report by saying that one could not fathom what resolution the Commons had taken today when 'in that moment' he learned that they had been adjourned till tomorrow.[140] On another occasion he opened his despatch with a brief and rather convoluted outline of the king's speech from the same day based perhaps on hearsay and concluded it with a detailed and structured summary after he probably had got hold of a handwritten copy.[141] There are, though, a small number of debates where the intimate knowledge of particulars makes his presence in the House likely. One of them is the inheritance dispute fought out between the earls of Bath and Montagu in the Lords in February that he covered in great detail, analysing not only the various stratagems deployed by both parties but the confidence, or lack thereof, with which participants in the debate spoke.[142]

Tellingly, Bonnet did not attend the debate as his rather succinct account and the use of qualifying language like 'they say' indicate.[143] Instead he seems to have been in the Commons listening to a parallel discussion about corrupt Members taking bribes from the court that was conducted 'with Heat', as he noted in a report typical of his thorough résumé of parliamentary business.[144] This level of detail that regularly included observations on the mood in the house, technical detail of legislation, tactical ploys and Members' rhetorical style would have been difficult to achieve if Bonnet had had to rely on written sources, and most likely came from first-hand experience.[145] There are other indications that corroborate this conclusion. On one occasion he appears to report conversations between Members that he overheard before or after a Commons session, although the wording of the passage is not entirely clear.[146] In addition, Bonnet's reporting on post days rarely ever slacked. He mostly maintained the same exhaustive coverage[147] and repeatedly reported occurrences that Beyrie could not include because the information hadn't reached him in time. When Beyrie had problems laying his hands on what William had said in the Lords, Bonnet inserted the king's speech verbatim at the beginning of his despatch. On the day that Beyrie

---

[139] NLA, Cal.Br. 24, no. 42, ff. 67, 70v, 88v, 102v, 258, 259.

[140] 'dans ce moment', NLA, Cal.Br. 24, no. 42, f. 88v.

[141] NLA, Cal.Br. 24, no. 42, ff. 91, 92v.

[142] NLA, Cal.Br. 24, no. 42, ff. 63, 65–7. For another occasion where Beyrie may have been present, this time in the Commons, f. 249.

[143] 'on dit', GStA PK, I. HA GR, Rep. 11, no. 1807, f. 37.

[144] 'avec Chaleur', GStA PK, I. HA GR, Rep. 11, no. 1807, ff. 36–7, quotation at 36v.

[145] Particularly revealing GStA PK, I. HA GR, Rep. 11, no. 1807, ff. 202 and 204 (Ranke, vi, 252–3), 208 and 210 (Ranke, vi, 255–7). See also, ff. 66, 196–7 (Ranke, vi, 248–9), 200–1 (Ranke, vi, 250–2), 211 (Ranke, vi, 257–8).

[146] GStA PK, I. HA GR, Rep. 11, no. 1807, f. 192v.

[147] For three examples among many GStA PK, I. HA GR, Rep. 11, no. 1807, ff. 38 (Ranke, vi, 240), 48, 53 (Ranke, vi, 243–4).

heard of the adjournment of the Commons only the moment he was finishing, Bonnet covered the six-hour debate in his usual meticulous way.[148] None of this would have been possible had he not been in the chamber on these occasions. Although we lack incontrovertible evidence that links Bonnet to the houses of parliament it is highly likely that he spent many a day in the Commons in particular, closely following debates and later on conveying their content to his patrons. Bonnet certainly relied for some of his parliamentary reporting on commercial newsletters, but large parts must derive from his presence in the Palace of Westminster.

5

Despite some commonalities, then, Beyrie's and Bonnet's accounts of English politics betray telling differences. Bonnet can indeed be described as a parliamentary reporter *avant la lettre*. He seems to have observed debates from close range, put them at the centre of his coverage and prided himself on his knowledgeable and exhaustive analysis of proceedings. This has earned him the appreciation of modern historians, but it remains an open question why courtiers and ministers in Berlin wanted to be informed in such detail about what was going on in Westminster.[149] Beyrie, on the other hand, cast himself as a foreign correspondent who tried to give equal weight to a range of news stories that happened under his watch even to the inclusion of human interest stories, although parliament still claimed the lion's share of his coverage. More than his Prussian counterpart, he regurgitated information from other news outlets such as public letters and probably also commercial newsletters which suited the more elevated position from which he covered events. These differences in journalistic groundwork and style went hand in hand with a differently nuanced view of court and parliament that reflected the transitionary nature of post-revolutionary English politics. Whereas Beyrie still attributed considerable political weight to the machinations at court and described England in some respects as an *ancien régime* monarchy, Bonnet laid his emphasis on parliament describing it as a place where technocratic thinking, personal ambition and ministerial management converged.

These are preliminary findings given the source base of just one year of reporting, although samples from other reports by Beyrie and Bonnet appear to confirm the rough outlines of what has been said.[150] It is beyond doubt, however, that Bonnet's and Beyrie's despatches are further proof of the wide variety of scribal news in the later 17th century. Both men cultivated a particular type of scribal news that should be recognised by future research. Defying easy categorisation as either newsletters or diplomatic despatches the reports can best be described as diplomatic letters of news. Their example highlights how much attention we have to pay to the differences in social status and professional self-understanding of writers of scribal news as well as to the nuances of content, style and materiality.

Acknowledgement

Open Access funding enabled and organized by Projekt DEAL.

[148] GStA PK, I. HA GR, Rep. 11, no. 1807, f. 53 and 55 (partly in Ranke, vi, 243–4), 58; for further examples f. 37,68.

[149] For a general discussion of these issues Matthias Pohlig, *Marlboroughs Geheimnis: Strukturen und Funktionen der Informationsgewinnung im Spanischen Erbfolgekrieg* (Cologne, 2016), 302–72.

[150] See for Bonnet Ranke, vi, 148–274 (1690–95) and for Beyrie NLA, Cal.Br. 24, no. 62 (1701).

Diplomatic Residents in England and Approaches to Reporting Parliament in the First Years of George I[*]

CHARLES LITTLETON

This article seeks to enrich understanding of the conditions for news-gathering in the early 18th century by focusing on three of the most frequently referenced sources for reports on parliamentary proceedings: the diplomatic residents Louis-Frédéric Bonnet and René de Saunière de l'Hermitage, who compiled their despatches of political intelligence in manuscript, and the print journalist Abel Boyer. It will show that although frequently presented together as parallel, and equally reliable, observers of parliament, each one's interpretation and presentation of what he observed could vary according to his professional position, perception of his duties and the audience for which he was writing. In examining some of the characteristics that distinguish each one's work, this essay will raise questions about what constituted parliamentary reporting in this period and what standards of accuracy can be expected from such accounts.

Keywords: parliamentary reporting; journalism; diplomatic despatches; Abel Boyer; René Saunière de l'Hermitage; Louis-Frédéric Bonnet

Michael Schaich has drawn attention to the many Huguenots employed by German states as diplomatic residents, and 'information professionals', in England in the late 17th century.[1] This contribution will concentrate on the reporting of events in parliament in the manuscript despatches of two such Huguenot intelligence-gatherers: Louis-Frédéric Bonnet, resident for the king in Prussia, and René de Saunière de l'Hermitage, agent for the States General. It will compare their handwritten accounts, intended for their employers at Berlin and The Hague, to the public printed parliamentary reporting of another Huguenot exile in England, Abel Boyer.

Louis-Frédéric Bonnet and his elder brother Frédéric came from a Huguenot family which had fled to Geneva in the early 17th century. The brothers joined their illustrious uncle Ezechiel von Spanheim in the diplomatic service of the Elector of Brandenburg from about 1685, when they were posted to England. The elder brother served as resident and gatherer of news for Brandenburg-Prussia until his death in 1696, when his younger brother took over his duties. Spanheim himself was the kingdom of Prussia's ambassador in Britain

[*]I wish to thank the editors, Robin Eagles and Michael Schaich, for their constructive and useful comments on earlier drafts of this paper, and particularly to Michael Schaich for his insights on our mutual subject of interest, the Bonnet brothers. I would also like to thank the archivist at the Geheimes Staatsarchiv Preussischer Kulturbesitz (GStA PK) in Berlin who kindly provided me with information on the proper archival reference for Bonnet's letters, as given in note 5.

[1]Michael Schaich, 'Information Professionals: Huguenot Diplomats in Later Stuart London and Their European Context', in *Huguenot Networks, 1560–1780: The Interactions and Impact of a Protestant Minority in Europe*, ed. Vivienne Larminie (Abingdon, 2018), 75–91. See also Michael Schaich's contribution to this volume.

from 1702 until his death in November 1710. From that point Friedrich I, the king in Prussia, 'committed the management of his affairs in Great Britain' to Louis-Frédéric, who always retained the title of resident, even after his appointment was confirmed by Friedrich Wilhelm I in 1713.[2] Bonnet became one of George I's German confidantes, but by early 1720 felt it prudent to return to Geneva after he had become the target of attacks by British politicians suspicious of the king's reliance on foreign ministers.[3] Bonnet's contemporary René de Saunière, sieur de l'Hermitage, acted as resident in England for the States General of the United Provinces from about August 1693. He had already established a newsletter correspondence with the grand pensionary of Holland, Anthonie Heinsius, who in turn persuaded the States General to authorise l'Hermitage to send them information of events in England.[4] For the following 35 years, until his death in late 1729, l'Hermitage served both the States General and Heinsius by sending regular despatches to The Hague with news from London.

Both of these diplomatic residents prepared twice-weekly reports, written by hand in French, dated and despatched on the post-days of Tuesdays and Fridays. Their neatly transcribed despatches deposited in the British Library have been used extensively by scholars working on politics under William III and Anne because of their coverage of proceedings in both houses of parliament.[5] Both Louis-Frédéric Bonnet and his elder brother appear frequently, usually in tandem with l'Hermitage, in the notes to Henry Horwitz's detailed study of parliament under William III. So important are their accounts to this work that there are sections where both Bonnet and l'Hermitage appear in just about every endnote.[6] They are the most commonly paired parliamentary reporters for this period. The letters of both are presented as reliable parallel accounts to be set alongside the entries in the 1698–1702 parliamentary diary of the member Richard Cocks.[7] They were also relied on extensively by Geoffrey Holmes in his seminal work on politics in the age of Anne, and by Edward Gregg in his biography of that queen.[8] They have been less used to study the first years of George I's reign, and this article aims to show the richness they can add to knowledge of British politics in this latter part of their careers.

[2] *Repertorium der diplomatischen Vertreter aller Länder seit dem Westfälischen Frieden* (3 vols, Oldenburg, 1936–65), i, 36; Sven Externbrink, ' "Internationaler Calvinismus" als Familiengeschichte: Die Spanheims (ca. 1550–1710)', in *Grenzüberschreitende Familienbeziehungen: Akteure und Medien des Kulturtransfers in der Frühen Neuzeit*, ed. Cordula Nolte and Claudia Opitz (Cologne, 2008), 137–55; *London Gazette*, 21 Dec. 1710; *Post Boy*, 7 Mar. 1713.

[3] Schaich, 'Information Professionals', 82.

[4] BL, Add. MS 17677 NN, f. 207: l'Hermitage to States General, 3/13 Aug. 1693; *Repertorium der diplomatischen Vertreter*, ii, 24.

[5] Transcriptions of l'Hermitage's despatches are in BL, Add. MS 17677 NN (1693) – 17677 KKK.10 (1728). His letters to Heinsius are found throughout *De Briefwisseling van Anthonie Heinsius 1702–1720*, ed. A.J. Veenendaal (19 vols, Rijks Geschiedkundige Publicatiën. Grote Serie, 1976–95). Transcriptions of Bonnet's despatches for 1696–1701 are in BL, Add. MS 30000 A–E. His full corpus, 1697–1720, including the letters used in this paper, are in GStA PK, I. HA Geheimer Rat, Rep. 11 Auswärtige Beziehungen. Bonnet's letters for 1715 are in 'Akten no. 1891' from this larger collection. For this paper, these letters were consulted on microfilm and they will be referenced as GStA PK, Bonnet despatches 1715 (or otherwise if for another year), with the folio numbers derived from the microfilm image and the date of composition.

[6] Henry Horwitz, *Parliament, Policy and Politics in the Reign of William III* (Manchester, 1977), e.g., 194–7.

[7] *The Parliamentary Diary of Sir Richard Cocks: 1698–1702*, ed. D.W. Hayton (Oxford, 1996).

[8] Geoffrey Holmes, *British Politics in the Age of Anne* (rev. edn, 1987); Edward Gregg, *Queen Anne* (New Haven, CT, rev. edn, 2001).

In their concentration on parliament these two diplomatic residents were similar to Abel Boyer. After arriving in England from France, the Huguenot Boyer plied his trade as a reporter of contemporary events from the last years of William III's reign. From 1711 until his death in 1729 he produced a monthly print journal, *The Political State of Great Britain*, which featured some of the earliest printed reports of parliamentary debates intended for a public readership.[9] Boyer's printed work gained almost canonical status and was used in later compendia of parliamentary proceedings such as Chandler, Timberland and Cobbett.[10] All of these reporters, then, specialised in recording proceedings in the British parliament, and all have been used for their accounts by subsequent generations of historians studying that institution in the late Stuart period.[11] Yet historians have used their reports largely unquestioningly for the information they provide on events in the parliamentary chambers, with little attention devoted to their actual production or to important differences between the men who compiled them. What can a comparison of these familiar news writers, working in different media, in different languages and for different audiences, tell us about the limits of parliamentary news reporting in the early 18th century?

1

Abel Boyer presents another example of the overlapping of print and scribal forms of news presentation in the early modern period which is a common theme in the essays of this volume.[12] The monthly issues of the printed *The Political State* were set out in the form of a personal newsletter, with each month headed with the word 'Sir,' in large print. Boyer perhaps intended to enhance his periodical's authority by recreating it as if it were a manuscript newsletter individually addressed to the reader. Nor was this necessarily a subterfuge to give his printed productions an air of familiarity. Boyer produced scribal newsletters for subscribing patrons at the same time as he was compiling the material for his printed periodical. In the preface to his compendium of issues of *The Political State* from 1711–14, he explained 'That these papers are really the Abstracts of Letters to his Correspondents abroad... and written with all the Candor and Disinterestedness

[9] Charles Littleton, 'Abel Boyer and Other Huguenot Reporters of Parliament: Hansard *Avant la Lettre*?', in *Huguenot Networks, 1560–1780: The Interactions and Impact of a Protestant Minority in Europe*, ed. Vivienne Larminie (Abingdon, 2018), 61–74. The most comprehensive account of Boyer's career is a series of articles by Graham Gibbs published in the *Proceedings of the Huguenot Society of Great Britain and Ireland*. They are: xxiii (1977–82), 87–98; xxiv (1983–8), 46–59; xxvi (1994–7), 14–44; xxvii (1998–2002), 211–31; xxviii (2003–7), 388–400; xxix (2008–12), 51–61; xxix (2008–12), 364–84.

[10] *The History and Proceedings of the House of Commons from the Restoration to the Present Time*, ed. Richard Chandler (12 vols, 1742); *The History and Proceedings in the House of Lords from the Restoration in 1660 to the Present Time*, ed. Ebenezer Timberland (7 vols, 1742); *Cobbett's Parliamentary History of England from the Norman Conquest to the Year 1803* (36 vols, 1806–20).

[11] Boyer is also used frequently in the works mentioned above, and all three parliamentary reporters appear often in the notes to *HPC 1690–1715*.

[12] For the coexistence of both print and manuscript newsletters, see R.S. King, ' "All the News That's fit to Write": The Eighteenth-Century Manuscript Newsletter', in *Travelling Chronicles: News and Newspapers from the Early Modern Period to the Eighteenth Century*, ed. S.G. Brandtzaeg, Paul Goring and Christine Watson (Leiden, 2018), 95–118; R.S. King, 'The Manuscript Newsletter and the Rise of the Newspaper, 1665–1715', *HLQ*, lxxix (2016), 411–37; A.W. Barber, ' "It is Not Easy What to Say of our Condition, Much Less to Write It": The Continued Importance of Scribal News in the Early 18th Century', *Parl. Hist.* xxxii (2013), 293–316.

imaginable'.[13] From July 1714 Boyer was hired, at the rate of a guinea a month, to send a newsletter every post to Thomas Wentworth, earl of Strafford, Britain's ambassador to the United Provinces. Strafford's brother Peter Wentworth was impressed by Boyer's diligence as he never missed a post day. Strafford, a Tory, was intent on keeping his identity secret from Boyer, a known Whig, but the Frenchman's reputation as a reliable and regular gatherer of British news overcame any objections Strafford might have had concerning his partisan slant.[14]

All three of our subjects, then, produced manuscript newsletters. There are, however, important differences between Boyer and the two diplomatic personnel. Boyer had no special privileges for access to the parliamentary chambers or to report their proceedings and on more than one occasion was hauled before parliament for publishing accounts of debates. The most notorious incident was in 1711, just as Boyer began publishing *The Political State*, and it resulted in the house of lords dismantling the 'strangers' gallery' which had allowed Boyer and others to observe proceedings.[15] The Commons did not go this far with its own gallery, but it did frequently expel strangers from particularly sensitive debates. Representatives of a foreign power, even residents such as Bonnet and l'Hermitage, were generally among those allowed to observe and exempted from expulsion. Boyer showed his resentment of this dispensation extended to the diplomatic corps. In *The Political State* he wrote of a debate in the house of lords on 5 April 1714 when 'all the strangers were obliged to withdraw, except the Baron Schütz, Envoy Extraordinary from Hanover'.[16] Bonnet in at least one example noted explicitly his physical presence in the chamber, during the second reading in the Lords of the Septennial Bill in April 1716.[17] Even diplomatic agents could on occasion be excluded from proceedings. On 10 June 1715 Bonnet complained that the Commons, immediately before an important debate, 'closed the doors of their chamber, and they are currently debating without anybody being able to discover today what they will resolve'.[18]

Bonnet was nevertheless later able to find out from his many (unnamed) parliamentary contacts the general tenor of the resolutions in this secretive debate. Personal contacts with parliamentarians provided the other principal source for these reporters' political news. Bonnet frequently mentioned conversations he had had with individual figures in parliament, and emphasised that he spoke to peers of both parties.[19] He was keen to show his masters in Berlin that he had inside knowledge through his contacts, of the type not usually

---

[13] Abel Boyer, *Quadrennium Annae Postremum or The Political State of Great Britain During the Four last Years of the Late Queen's Reign* (8 vols, 1718–19), i, 1.

[14] *The Wentworth Papers, 1705–39: Selected from the Private and Family Correspondence of Thomas Wentworth… Created in 1711 Earl of Strafford*, ed. J.J. Cartwright (1883), 391–3, 400, 414, 415, 420. Some of Boyer's manuscript newsletters, written in French, are in the Strafford MSS, BL, Add. MS 22202, ff. 97–103, 106–7, 110–11, 120–2, 132–3, 148–54, 159–66, 170–7.

[15] Littleton, 'Huguenot Reporters of Parliament', 63–6; *London Diaries of William Nicolson, Bishop of Carlisle, 1702–18*, ed. Clyve Jones and Geoffrey Holmes (Oxford, 1985), 84–6. For some of Boyer's later run-ins with parliament, Bodl. MS Eng. hist. c. 1041, ff. 57v, 63v.

[16] Boyer, *Quadrennium Annae Postremum*, vii, 316–17.

[17] GStA PK, Bonnet despatches 1716, f. 80v: 17/28 Apr. despatch.

[18] 'fait fermer les portes de leur Chambre, et ils deliberent à présent sans qu'on puisse savoir aujourdhuy ce qu'ils resoudrent', GStA PK, Bonnet despatches 1715, f. 79v: 10/21 June despatch.

[19] 'J'ay conversé avec les pairs de l'un et de l'autre parti', GStA PK, Bonnet despatches 1715, f. 120: 15/26 July despatch.

relayed in the newspapers. Bonnet recounted how Charles Montagu, earl of Halifax, had contested the king's prerogative right to dispose of a lucrative patent, while himself seeking to direct the patent to a woman whom he wished to make his mistress. Bonnet emphasised that this scandalous story was kept secret from the general public, but as he was in the confidence of the British political elite, he could impart it.[20] L'Hermitage clearly relied on British political associations for his sources, but never named or even acknowledged them. Boyer also had a wide range of contacts among parliamentarians to supplement his reporting. In 1718 he admitted that in compiling his parliamentary reports he was 'befriended by some eminent Members, who are fully apprised of his honest Intentions to serve the Publick'.[21] Later, in a retrospective in the last year of his life, 1729, he asserted that 'Many Eminent and publick-spirited Members of that honourable Assembly, have, at divers times, furnished me with their own Speeches in Parliament, and other valuable Materials for my Historical Collections'.[22]

2

The following study will concentrate on the parallel accounts these three news-gatherers provided in the weeks surrounding the introduction of the impeachment articles against members of the Tory ministry of 1710–14 which had seen through the Treaty of Utrecht. The hearings and debates on these charges obviously preoccupied the two diplomatic residents employed by states which had often felt betrayed by Britain's actions in the negotiations. Boyer was also keenly aware of public interest in these proceedings against the previous ministry. Always adept at repackaging his products for commercial purposes, in 1716 he gathered his parliamentary accounts which had appeared in volumes of *The Political State* and linked them in a narrative to produce a larger stand-alone volume, which will be referred to here.[23]

We start on 8 July 1715, when the articles of impeachment against the former lord treasurer Robert Harley, earl of Oxford, were first read and debated in the Commons. These proceedings were well-covered by all the reporters. Boyer's printed account named individuals, and included speeches, some purportedly directly quoted, from prominent members such as Edward Harley, William Cadogan and Sir Joseph Jekyll.[24] There is much overlap in speakers and the progression of events between his journalism and the despatches sent by the residents. One common feature of all the reports, though, was notice of the divisions held in the Commons and their results, and these can be checked against the official record of the *Commons Journal*. According to the *Journal* the divisions were on the questions: whether the amended first article should stand as part of the impeachment charges (280 yeas against 125 noes); whether the words 'and traitorously' should stand as part of the 11th

---

[20] 'Cette historiette est tenüe forte secrete', GStA PK, Bonnet despatches 1715, f. 75: 20/31 May (postscript).

[21] Boyer, *Quadrennium Annae Postremum*, i, 3; Littleton, 'Huguenot Reporters in Parliament', 66–7, tries to reconstruct some of Boyer's British political sources.

[22] Boyer, *Political State*, xxxvii, pp. iv–viii.

[23] Abel Boyer, *A Full and Impartial History of the Impeachments of the Last Ministry: With the Whole Proceedings, Debates, and Speeches, in Both Houses of Parliament, Relating thereto, to the Close of the Last Sessions, Sept. 21 1715* (1716).

[24] Boyer, *History*, 125–7; *Political State*, x, 124–6.

article of the charges (247 yeas against 131 noes); and whether the amended 11th article should stand as part of the impeachment charges (247 yeas against 127 noes).[25] None of these reporters was consistent in relaying either the matter of the divisions or the numbers involved. Boyer was imprecise about the content of the question of the first division. He remarked that the first ten articles of impeachment were read a second time, 'and upon the Question severally put thereupon (with Amendments to some of them) there was a long debate from Two till Eight in the Evening, when they were agreed to, by a Majority of 280 Voices against 125'.[26] Bonnet also stated that the first division was called on the question whether the House approved 'articles' in the impeachment charges, without specifying which in particular were in question.[27] L'Hermitage's description of the division was the most specific: 'After long debates on the first [article], the chamber was divided on the question if it approved or not'.[28] Both Bonnet and l'Hermitage concurred with Boyer that the numbers in the first division were 280 to 125. After this initial agreement among the news-gatherers as to the general subject of the first division and its numbers, concurrence broke down. Boyer introduced the second division of that day as 'the question put, that the further consideration of the said report be adjourned till the next morning', which was very different from the question as recorded in the *Journal*, and he stated it was carried in the negative, 247 noes to 139 yeas. Boyer might have been thinking of the second division when he described the third division as 'whether the 11th article amounts to high treason', which he stated was agreed 247 to 127.[29] Bonnet did not even address the second and third divisions of that day. L'Hermitage omitted the second, but did in his final paragraphs treat the third, on which he agreed with Boyer's description, that the House divided on whether the 11th article amounted to treason, and that the yeas had the majority, 247 to 131.[30]

Measuring the reporters' accuracy in recording numbers in divisions can again be used when comparing the accounts of the proceedings on the impeachment articles in the house of lords on 9 July 1715.[31] In this instance all three news-gatherers agreed on the subject matter of the three divisions held in the Lords: whether consideration of the articles be adjourned to the following Monday (52 contents to 86 not contents); whether the judges be asked if articles 11 and 12 constituted treason (52 contents to 84 not contents); and whether Oxford be placed in the custody of Black Rod (81 contents to 52 not contents).[32] Both Bonnet and l'Hermitage were correct in the constant minority figure of 52 across the three divisions, while Boyer had the 52 correct in only one, with a minority vote of 54 and 50 in the other two. All three agreed in the size of the majority in the first division; Boyer and l'Hermitage were correct in the second, where Bonnet did not bother to give

[25] *CJ*, xviii, 219.

[26] Boyer, *History*, 125, 126; *Political State*, x, 124, 126.

[27] GStA PK, Bonnet despatches 1715, f. 104v: 8/19 July despatch.

[28] 'après de longs debats sur la premier [article] la chambre s'est divisée sur la proposition, si elle l'aprouvoit ou non', BL, Add. MS 17677 III, f. 298v: 8/19 July 1715 despatch.

[29] Boyer, *History*, 125; *Political State*, x, 124.

[30] BL, Add. MS 17677 III, ff. 298v–9: 8/19 July 1715 despatch.

[31] Boyer, *History*, 165–70; *Political State*, x, 165–70; BL, Add. MS 17677 III, ff. 301–7: 12/23 July 1715 despatch; GStA PK, Bonnet despatches 1715, ff. 116–19: 12/23 July despatch.

[32] John Sainty and David Dewar, *Divisions in the House of Lords: An Analytical List 1685 to 1857* (House of Lords Record Office Occasional Publications no. 2, 1976).

its size; in the last only l'Hermitage was accurate, while Boyer provided 82 and Bonnet 83. The only one to repeat precisely the official figures for all three divisions was l'Hermitage, while Boyer was correct in only one.

The three reporters were all by this time highly experienced and diligent parliamentary observers, and the inconsistencies noted here should be seen more as an indication of the difficulties they faced in recording proceedings than an imputation of carelessness. The discrepancies raise questions about the extent to which these reporters can be used as an early modern version of Hansard, as they so often have been by later historians. It is not clear that any of them saw themselves in that role. True, Boyer presented himself consistently as an impartial historian, and his work as a repository of matters of fact for future generations. As he claimed when introducing his volumes dealing with the last four years of Anne: 'I flatter myself that future Historians will be obliged to me, for furnishing them with proper materials, to set it in a true light'.[33] The diplomatic residents, however, had no eye to posterity. They were concerned with accuracy certainly, but only insofar as it fulfilled the requirements of their masters. The irony is that the demands for passing on useful intelligence about parliamentary affairs may have led the diplomatic residents, and l'Hermitage in particular, to be more precise and detailed in the accounts of events in parliament than the self-styled historian Boyer. For his part, Bonnet felt free to skip much of the blow-by-blow detail of proceedings to concentrate on the salient points, such as the fact that impeachment charges were passed by the Commons, and by majorities of over 100. Was he any less accurate in his assessment of the proceedings than his two colleagues? How, indeed, is accuracy to be defined and determined?

As the above examples suggest, the records produced by the clerical staff of parliament, the *Journals* and the committee minutes, are now seen as the official record of both Houses against which these reporters can be judged. The *Journals* were produced retrospectively; though they could be compiled with care, it is largely convention which has set them up as the standard. The element of time also needs to be considered when judging these accounts. The diplomatic representatives had strict deadlines to meet, the post days. The debate in the Commons, in which the residents occasionally left out divisions and the numbers involved, took place on a Friday, a post-day, and both their despatches were dated and sent that day. They would have been finishing their despatches in a rush and to a tight deadline after a long sitting in the Commons, and they would not have had time to double-check all their details. The debates in the Lords were the following day, 9 July, and Bonnet and l'Hermitage did not send their despatches until the following Tuesday, 12 July, giving them more time to fine-tune their accounts so that there is more agreement between them and the official numbers recorded by the clerks. In a sense the diplomatic despatches are among the closest there is to first-hand, immediate and rough accounts of parliamentary proceedings. Strangely, these manuscript newsletters are closer to newspaper copy, with its own strict daily deadlines, than the work of the early print journalist Boyer, who would have had more time to prepare his monthly *The Political State*.

---

[33] Boyer, *Quadrennium Annae Postremum*, i, 4.

3

The preceding section emphasised some discrepancies between the three parliamentary reporters. There are also, however, similarities between the diplomatic correspondents in particular which suggest that such agents of European states, even those with widely varying geopolitical interests as the States General and Prussia, did not work in isolation. Bonnet's despatch of 8/19 July 1715, in which he recounted the divisions in the Commons, also included a summary of the 16 articles of impeachment and, folded within this summary, another newsletter. This was written in French but in a different hand, one with a distinct orthography and which appears only occasionally in Bonnet's corpus, in enclosures to his despatches.[34] This enclosed newsletter featured exactly the same text as l'Hermitage's letter to the States General of the same date.[35] Nor was this the only example of duplication of text between Bonnet and l'Hermitage in this period. A newsletter headed 'Londres ce 9 juillet 1715', written in the same hand as that of the 8/19 July enclosure, is also inserted in the bound volume of Bonnet's diplomatic correspondence, and features text identical to much of l'Hermitage's despatch of 28 June/9 July, although l'Hermitage's has text additional to that in the Bonnet papers.[36] This suggests that these Francophone residents either shared their copy among themselves or subscribed to a separate French-language newsletter. This latter suggestion, however, raises questions of whether examples of these texts survive in other diplomatic collections, and what individual would have been relied on by both these experienced observers of parliament to provide them with more authoritative copy.

A further indication of the congruence in l'Hermitage's and Bonnet's work comes from their accounts of the proceedings in the Lords on 9 July 1715. There was little duplication of text between their individual despatches of 12/23 July, but there were similar emphases and, in some cases surprising overlap. Of the earl of Oxford's consistent core of 52 supporters, both Bonnet and l'Hermitage singled out the same three for specific mention by name, the earls of Anglesey, Rochester (whom Bonnet misidentified as 'earl Hyde') and Uxbridge. Similarly, both residents listed the same three peers who were absent from the vote, the earls of Grantham, Orrery and Carnarvon, although these were hardly the only peers not in the House that day.[37] The most that can be said at this stage is that these two diplomatic agents did not work in separate bubbles, and that they shared or had access to the same detailed information on which to build their despatches.

On the other hand, there were wide differences in the styles, emphases and agenda of these two news-gatherers. The duke of Shrewsbury's resignation as lord chamberlain on 4 July 1715 provides a good first case study to highlight these. On this event l'Hermitage merely wrote, as a separate paragraph all to itself as he was wrapping up his despatch of 5/16 July, 'Yesterday evening the duke of Shrewsbury returned to the king the lord chamberlain's staff'.[38] In his despatch of the same date, Bonnet connected the duke's resignation to the

---

[34] GStA PK, Bonnet despatches 1715, ff. 106–7: French newsletter headed 'Londres ce 19 juillet 1715'.

[35] BL, Add. MS 17677 III, ff. 297–9: 8/19 July 1715 despatch.

[36] GStA PK, Bonnet despatches 1715, f. 110: 28 June, French newsletter headed 'Londres ce 9 juillet 1715'; BL, Add. MS 17677 III, ff. 284–5: 28 June/9 July 1715 despatch.

[37] GStA PK, Bonnet despatches 1715, ff. 117v, 118v: 12/23 July despatch; BL, Add. MS 17677 III, f. 307v.

[38] 'Hier au soir le duc de Shrewsbury remit au Roy sa baguette de chambellan', BL, Add. MS 17677 III, f. 292: 5/16 July 1715 despatch.

incipient impeachments against Oxford and the other former ministers. Shrewsbury was as implicated in the secret negotiations for the Treaty of Utrecht as Oxford, but still remained popular at large and influential at court. The Whigs knew that his prosecution would be unpopular, but that leaving him alone in such a prominent position close to the king while his colleagues were impeached would smack of hypocrisy. The ministry, supported by the king, hinted strongly to Shrewsbury that he should resign to save face, otherwise they would publicly dismiss him. Bonnet noted that he was initially unwilling as it would be a tacit admission of guilt, but eventually, seeing that otherwise he would be dismissed humiliatingly, he returned the key and staff of his office.[39] Bonnet did not present this resignation in isolation, as l'Hermitage did, but ensured that it was put in its political context.

L'Hermitage in his despatches largely limited himself to a strict relaying of newsworthy items, without interposing himself or his informants. This was probably owing to his diplomatic status. L'Hermitage's initial commission as resident in 1693 assigned him to convey news to the States General in the absence of a formal ambassador.[40] In the period treated here, there were two ambassadors representing the States General at the court of St James's. Early in 1715, Arent van Wassenaer-Duivenvoorde and Philips Jacob van Borssele van der Hooghe were sent as ambassadors extraordinary to renew the Dutch alliance with Britain after the rancour caused by the Treaty of Utrecht.[41] During this period Wassenaer-Duivenvoorde acted as lead envoy with the British and sent regular despatches to both the clerk of the States General and to Anthonie Heinsius. Wassenaer-Duivenvoorde's despatches paralleled l'Hermitage's in time but were dissimilar in content.[42] They concerned the ambassadors' negotiations on Anglo–Dutch relations with British statesmen such as Townshend, Stanhope and Cadogan, and there is almost no mention of parliamentary proceedings. Wassenaer-Duivenvoorde conveyed his insights about British politics from the vantage point of the court and the ministry, but not necessarily from parliament. That was the remit of the resident. L'Hermitage was assigned to provide intelligence on developments in Britain, ranging from parliamentary affairs through ecclesiastical debates to shipping news and the price of shares in joint-stock companies, but without adding advice or commentary as he was not in contact with the ministers. Therefore, two separate streams of intelligence, with different emphases and range, flooded into the hands of the clerk ('greffier') of the States General, as well as of Heinsius himself.[43]

L'Hermitage's separate letters to Anthonie Heinsius by and large duplicated word for word those sent to the clerk of the States General and were equally impersonal. L'Hermitage's letters may not have been discursive, but Heinsius evidently valued the intelligence conveyed and used them in his dealings. For example, in April 1714 relations between Britain and the States General were at a low point, and the earl of Oxford's informal agent at The Hague, John Drummond, was anxious to smooth matters over. Heinsius

---

[39] GStA PK, Bonnet despatches 1715, f. 113: 5/16 July despatch. For Shrewsbury's resignation, see Dorothy Somerville, *King of Hearts: Charles Talbot, Duke of Shrewsbury* (1962), 343–4.

[40] BL, Add. MS 17677 NN, f. 207: 3/13 Aug. 1693 despatch.

[41] Ragnhild Hatton, *Diplomatic Relations between Great Britain and the Dutch Republic, 1714–21* (1950); *Nieuw Nederlandsch Biografisch Woordenboek*, ed. P.C. Molhuysen (10 vols, Leiden, 1911–37), ii, 1518–19.

[42] They are interspersed with l'Hermitage's correspondence in both the States General's papers on Britain (BL, Add. MS 17677 III) and the published collection of Heinsius's letters (*Briefwisseling*, xvii).

[43] Schaich, 'Information Professionals', 82–3.

encouraged Drummond to return to Britain to keep him informed of developments as Heinsius's 'letters from England' told him 'of great disputes in the House of Lords, and of great differences and jealousies amongst the first ministers and courtiers'. Heinsius also hesitated in sending Joost van Keppel, earl of Albemarle, to Britain as an envoy, because 'his letters said that there were great animosities at Court', and Heinsius felt that matters were too unsettled. Heinsius was most likely referring to his many long letters from l'Hermitage which throughout April 1714 concentrated on the debates in the house of lords on the motion that the Hanoverian succession was in danger.[44] Drummond was frustrated as his own intelligence was insufficient to negotiate adequately with the Dutch. Regarding the debates in the Lords, he professed himself 'entirely a stranger' and could only 'hope they are not so great as was reported at The Hague' by l'Hermitage.[45]

L'Hermitage's intelligence-gathering went beyond the letters he sent to the States General and Heinsius. With each despatch to Heinsius he usually, at least after 1715, sent an accompanying cover letter to Heinsius's secretary, Abel Tassin d'Alonne. These tended to be more personal and discursive than his newsletters. They also provide a further indication of the continuing enmeshment of print and scribal communications, for almost all of the letters to d'Alonne enclosed printed newspapers and pamphlets for his and Heinsius's perusal. L'Hermitage was not above sending contemporary printed products to his patron to supplement his own manuscript accounts of British affairs.[46]

While l'Hermitage's missives concentrated on matters that would concern the statesmen of the States General in their negotiations with Britain, Bonnet framed his accounts by showing how events in Britain mattered to Prussian interests. Friedrich Wilhelm I, king in Prussia from 1713, was closely aligned militarily, diplomatically and personally with the Hanoverian dynasty, as he was both George I's nephew and his son-in-law, and at this point Hanover's ally against Sweden in the Great Northern War.[47] Bonnet's despatches from 1715 revealed his great anxiety concerning the stability of the Hanoverian regime in Britain, and the continuing opposition to it. In early June Bonnet felt that, in the wake of demonstrations against the king, 'some bloodletting in the state is necessary to stop this contagion of Jacobitism which is gaining ground'.[48] He placed a great deal of importance on Oxford's impeachment, which he saw as a test for the survival of the regime. He thought that it would help determine once and for all 'who of the king or the Tory party will be master and sovereign'.[49]

Bonnet's concern was present in his parliamentary reporting. He did not just recount what he saw and heard in the chambers but commented also on the characters involved and the importance of the decisions taken. As noted above, Bonnet was more sparing than the other reporters considered here in his account of the debate on the articles of impeachment

[44] *Briefwisseling*, xv, 571–3, 578–9, 584–5, 593–4.

[45] HMC *Manuscripts of the Duke of Portland*, v, 427. On Drummond, see Ragnhild Hatton, 'John Drummond in the War of the Spanish Succession: A Merchant Turned Diplomatic Agent', in *Studies in Diplomatic History*, ed. R. Hatton and M.S. Anderson (1970), 69–96.

[46] *Briefwisseling*, xvii, 127–8, 135–6, 145, 213–14, 249, 259, 272, 386–7, 442, 595, 608, 647–8, 702, 823, 826–7.

[47] Ragnhild Hatton, *George I: Elector and King* (1978), 184–90.

[48] 'quelque saignée d'etat pour arreter cette contagion de Jacobitisme qui gagne du terrain', GStA PK, Bonnet despatches 1715, 76v–7: 31 May/11 June despatch.

[49] 'il s'agit de savoir qui du Roy ou du parti Tory sera Maître et Souverain'. GStA PK, Bonnet despatches 1715, ff. 91v–2: 17/28 June despatch.

of 8 July 1715. He only mentioned the first division of that sitting, which approved the articles (or so he interpreted it). Rather than detail the course of the other divisions, he summarised what he saw as the salient points of the debate and particularly what it revealed of the state of the Tories:

> All the Tory party, ready to contest this ground until the very end, ... wishes their [the former ministers'] impunity, in order to avoid censuring in them all of the previous Tory Parliament, ... so that this affair does not only concern the cause of the accused, but that of the entire party...[50]

The united front put up by the Tories, despite Oxford's personal unpopularity among them, became a frequent source of worry in Bonnet's next few despatches.

Bonnet's despatch of 22 July/2 August, however, emphasised that Tory efforts at whipping up popular opposition against the impeachments had backfired on the king's enemies. It was written in the wake of the king's address to parliament informing it that the government had received intelligence that France was planning to take advantage of popular unrest to launch an invasion in support of the Pretender. Bonnet devoted most of the despatch to demonstrate his superior analysis and knowledge of British society, and to warn his Prussian readers not to succumb to the frequent misjudgments of the country's people and politics, as the French so often did. Writing from his self-professed superior knowledge, he was sure that the French did not properly understand that all the disturbances that they were keen to exploit were like 'a wave raised by the wind, which shakes the ship, but which wakes all the sailors to save it from danger'.[51] As suggested by this nautical metaphor, the news of the threatened invasion had silenced all division in parliament and the parties had united to defend the king. He concluded his missive with a positive analysis and prediction, so different from his previous anxieties:

> From all this I conclude... that whatever the danger which threatens us, the power of the king is more established than it ever has been, and consequently that of his ministry, and that it will be able to prosecute more determinedly the trial against those accused, whose case is now worse because of this danger to which they have exposed the realm.[52]

Can this despatch, one of the longest among Bonnet's missives for 1715, stretching to fourteen closely written pages, be considered a 'newsletter' or even 'parliamentary reporting'? There was not any detailed account of proceedings in parliament concerning the king's address on the threatened invasion. Most of the letter was commentary on the present state of the nation, with lengthy sections looking back to the past to account for the present unrest and to find precedents for his contentions. L'Hermitage's despatch of the same day

---

[50]'Tout le parti Tori, étant disposé de disputer le terrain jusqu'à l'extremité, ... veut leur impunité, de peur de censurer en eux tout le dernier Parlement Tory... de sorte qu'il ne s'agit pas icy de la cause seule des accusés, mais de celle de tout ce Parti...', GStA PK, Bonnet despatches 1715, f. 104v: 8/19 July despatch.

[51]'une vague que le vent soulève, qui agite la vaisseau, mais qui reveille tous les matelots pour le garentir du péril', GStA PK, Bonnet despatches 1715, ff. 124v–5: 22 July/2 Aug. despatch.

[52]'Je conclus de tout cela ... que quel que soit le danger dont on étoit ménacé, le pouvoir du Roy est plus établi qu'il n'a jamais été, et par consequent celui de son ministère, et qu'il pourra poursuivre plus hardiment le procés contre les accusés, dont le cas est aggravé par ce danger où ils ont exposé le Royaume', GStA PK, Bonnet despatches 1715, f. 127v: 22 July/2 Aug. despatch.

conveyed the same development in British politics, but in a more conventional manner. He described the proceedings in both houses of parliament as they debated the text of the address pledging their support to the king. He noted those Tories in particular who stood to assert their new-found willingness to defend the regime. He listed the preparations undertaken hurriedly to prepare for the invasion.[53] Nowhere, though, did he indulge in metaphors, digress on the long history of Anglo–French animosity, or let his feelings of relief and exultation show.

A final example of the features of the reporters considered here is provided by the debates surrounding the passage of the Septennial Act in April 1716. The account of the debate on the second reading of the bill in the house of lords on 14 April 1716 stretched to 19 pages in that month's issue of *The Political State*. Boyer identified the speakers involved and provided detailed summaries of the content of their speeches. L'Hermitage's despatch of 17/28 April 1716 was remarkably close to Boyer in content and emphasis.[54] Bonnet, in his despatch of the same day emphasised that he was present at this important moment: 'As I was at this division…' However, he did not use this first-hand experience to give a detailed account of what transpired in the chamber. Instead he noted that as an eyewitness he was surprised to see that eight peers, each of whom had recently received tokens of favour from the king, were all nevertheless among those opposed to this court measure. The bulk of his despatch was devoted to conveying an idea of the positive long-term consequences of this legislation rather than actually recounting its laborious progress through both Houses.[55] That, for Bonnet, was the principal information that he felt impelled to convey concerning the progress of the Septennial Bill through the house of lords.

Bonnet's despatches differ from l'Hermitage's in tone and style because in 1715–16, indeed from 1710, he was both Prussia's envoy and resident in Britain. Bonnet was of a higher rank in the diplomatic world, and he does appear to have travelled in higher social circles than the journeyman l'Hermitage. He was often received at court, where he delivered messages from the king in Prussia, and the newspapers sometimes referred to him as that king's 'envoy' or 'minister'.[56] Thus his despatches were framed to convey the items of general news, found in the resident l'Hermitage's missives, as well as the analysis and policy advice that would be expected from a full ambassador's despatches. While on one hand Bonnet's different position in the diplomatic world may reduce his usefulness as a straightforward and detailed reporter of events in parliament, a task performed more single-mindedly by l'Hermitage, it can also make his thoughtful and informed letters more insightful about developments in British politics and wider society.

4

The manuscript despatches of l'Hermitage and Bonnet and the printed productions of Boyer prompt questions about what constitutes parliamentary reporting and the factors that

---

[53] BL, Add. MS 17677 III, ff. 329–33: 22 July/2 Aug. 1715 despatch.

[54] BL, Add. MS 17677 KKK.1, ff. 217–19: 17/28 Apr. 1716 despatch.

[55] 'Comme je me suis trouvé à cette division', GStA PK, Bonnet despatches 1716, f. 82: 17/28 Apr. despatch.

[56] *Post Man*, 26 Feb. 1717; *Daily Courant*, 9 May, 20 Dec. 1717; *Evening Post*, 9 May 1717; *Weekly Journal*, 6 Apr. 1717.

can influence its production. Hansard and televised broadcasts of proceedings in parliament make it too easy to conceive of parliamentary reporting in one form, as an account of what 'actually happened', motion by motion, speech by speech, in each chamber. However, the three subjects treated here were all equally experienced observers of parliament, yet each produced a different model of reportage, accurate and informative in its own way.

The most familiar are Boyer's accounts, with their emphasis on progression and identification – who said what and in what order. Such information was highly prized in the 18th century precisely because it was so difficult to procure through parliament's close watch over its privilege to keep its debates secret. Boyer presented himself as the period's historian, an impartial gatherer of matters of fact, that could be used in both the present and the future. The Preface to his *History of the Reign of Queen Anne*, published in 1722, was primarily a long essay on the nature of history and the criteria which make a creditable historian, in which group he wished to include himself.[57] His audience was 'discerning and unprejudiced readers', who would value 'a most faithful and impartial Account of Matters of Fact' as well as 'the most remarkable Debates and Speeches in both houses of parliament, which the Author takes care to collect, with indefatigable Labour and Industry'.[58] Boyer has justly acquired his reputation for his assiduous reporting of parliamentary proceedings in a time of tight restrictions on access to the parliamentary chambers.

Yet if there were to be a ranking of accuracy in recording correctly the numbers (and the contents of the questions) in parliamentary divisions, the Dutch resident l'Hermitage would probably be at the top of the table. Boyer and l'Hermitage could produce accounts of proceedings very similar in content and emphases, but the former wrote his as journalism for a general British readership, both in the present and the future, while the latter produced his as intelligence on British politics for the contemporary use of Dutch ministers and diplomats. Both sought to convey an impartial stance to the news/intelligence they were conveying. But for Boyer this was through his wish to portray himself as a proper historian for the ages, while for l'Hermitage it was because judgment or advice was not part of his remit as resident, and was left to the proper Dutch ambassadors. It is intriguing that parliamentary reporting so similar in tone and content could come from such different motives and agenda.

In this matter Bonnet stood apart from both Boyer and l'Hermitage. He was at the same time a resident, trained by long experience to observe and record parliamentary proceedings, and also Prussia's envoy in Britain from 1710 in the absence of a formal ambassador. He had to combine both roles. Thus, his despatches featured the frequent accounts of proceedings in parliament one finds in the other two, but he expressed his opinions and conveyed his commentary to his readers in Berlin. He often neglected the detail of parliamentary proceedings in order to explain the more general significance of what he witnessed in the chambers and express his opinions. The word 'je' appears frequently in Bonnet's despatches; almost never in l'Hermitage's. Bonnet more closely resembles an editorialist than an *annaliste* like l'Hermitage or Boyer.

The three parliamentary reporters discussed will, and should, continue to appear in the notes of works in late Stuart and early Hanoverian political history. They were some of the

---

[57] Abel Boyer, *The History of the Life and Reign of Queen Anne* (1722), i–xii.

[58] Boyer, *Quadrennium Annae Postremum*, i, 3.

most diligent observers of the parliament of the time. Yet their reports are inflected by their different perceptions of their own roles and duties: Boyer, the historian reliably putting into print otherwise inaccessible 'matters of fact' for the enlightenment of his own and future generations; l'Hermitage the assiduous diplomatic resident fulfilling his duty to provide his masters with reliable intelligence to be used alongside the despatches of the formal ambassadors; and Bonnet, the sole diplomatic representative of Prussia between 1710 and 1720, who had to provide Berlin with intelligence on developments in Britain, accompanied by his own analysis of that intelligence. The richness of what they have to reveal about the British parliament comes from the different directions from which they approached their mission, and goes well beyond seeing them largely as early modern replacements for Hansard.

'Si̶r̶ Madam': Female Consumers of Parliamentary News in Manuscript Newsletters

RACHAEL SCARBOROUGH KING

This article examines the manuscript newsletters received by two women in the late 17th and early 18th centuries, Anne Pole and Susannah Newey. Although women have often been excluded from discussion of manuscript news circulation, these women's newsletters, especially the parliamentary news they contained, reveal important information about the turn of the 18th-century news industry. Both women received and shared parliamentary news provided by paid news writers in London. Their roles as recipients and circulators of manuscript newsletters elucidate how the news industry was developing and professionalising at a moment that also saw the takeoff of the printed newspaper.

Keywords: women; newsletters; parliamentary news; manuscript; provincial

1

In 1755 Frances Capel, countess of Essex, wrote a letter to her sister-in-law Lady Anne Capel that opened with the latest gossip. 'I was at the play last night with Miss Hulse, who desir'd her best Comp[limen]ts to you; I go to the opera tonight w[it]h L[ad]y Coventry she is very fond of me this Winter,' she wrote. 'The Dss of Dorset was very agreeable all the World was there'. But after these preliminaries, Lady Essex turned to politics, and her writing became more detailed and evaluative:

> They had a long day in the House yesterday. Mr. Pitt, Mr. Legge & Charles Townshend after having spoke against the Treaties, were rather slow in moving out of the House & the Door was shut upon them, so in numbering the Division they were set down amongst those who were for it. They say Mr. Pitt kept scratching at the Door to get out, like a Dog but to no Purpose.[1]

Discussing negotiations at the outbreak of the Seven Years' War, Lady Essex (neé Hanbury Williams) displayed a close interest in parliamentary machinations and an expectation that her female correspondents would share this interest. Such shifting registers were frequent in her letters. In another letter to Anne Capel written before Lady Essex's marriage, the latter wrote, 'I hope Master Hyde continues well. My Sister & I had Miss Mansel with us all yesterday evening. The Appleby Election was carried by 83 Votes in Ld Thanets Side'. She

---

[1] Lewis Walpole Library, Yale University [hereafter cited as LWL], MSS 7 v. 78, ff. 139–40: countess of Essex to Anne Capel, no date [after 1754].

closed, 'forgive this scrawl I am now in the middle of Dressing. But I will not seal this till I get to Whitehall where I perhaps may hear some news'.[2] For Lady Essex, political activity was one of the many kinds of news she shared with her extensive female correspondence circle.

Such voices are often left out of parliamentary history, which tends to emphasise official sources and their male producers and consumers. Despite Elaine Chalus's influential argument that the 18th century displayed 'a political culture where the boundaries between the social and the political were blurred, and where some degree of female political involvement was often accepted and even expected,' it remains the case that men are presented as the primary actors in studies of the history of parliament.[3] Yet women such as Lady Essex are still more legible to us than those on whom I will focus in this article: female recipients of manuscript newsletters containing parliamentary information. Lady Essex was, after all, a countess, her husband William Capel, 4th earl of Essex, a member of the house of lords and lord of the bedchamber to George II, and her father, Sir Charles Hanbury Williams, a prominent diplomat and member of parliament. As Chalus has argued, it was primarily elite women who were able to engage in politics.[4] The women whose collections of newsletters I will analyse are much more anonymous, to the point that we must guess at their names: Madam Pole of Radbourne Hall in Derbyshire, likely Anne (Mundy) Pole (*d*.1732), and Susannah Newey/Mrs Hobson in Tamworth, Staffordshire, who is possibly the same person before and after marriage but may in fact be two people. Neither of these women leaves much trace in the historical record — the latter none whatsoever — but they both left behind extensive collections of manuscript newsletters which they received at their country homes for decades in the late 17th and early 18th centuries. Their news habits elucidate the circulation and consumption of parliamentary news for everyday men and women.

The Pole and Newey collections of newsletters — the former held in two groups at the William Andrews Clark Memorial Library at UCLA and the Beinecke Library at Yale, and the latter at the Huntington Library — upset assumptions about women, manuscript circulation, and news consumption in a number of ways. On the one hand, the field of news history, especially of parliamentary news, has focused on male producers, consumers, and subjects of news. Earlier studies of journalism in the 18th century, the period when newspapers proliferated and began to take on some of their modern characteristics, tended to emphasise printed news products; while some scholars have noted that women were active in the print trades, media history has tended to highlight male publishers of news.[5] And work on manuscript newsletters may even more thoroughly assume a masculine sphere, as scholars have described newsletters as 'gentlemanly forms of communication' or noted that the newsletter appealed to men by 'beginning politely with the word 'Sir', and giving the recipient the pleasant feeling that he was reading his own private correspondence'.[6]

---

[2] LWL, MSS 7 v. 78, f. 117: countess of Essex to Anne Capel, 18 May, no date [before 1755].

[3] Elaine Chalus, *Elite Women in English Political Life, c.1754–1790* (Oxford, 2005), 17.

[4] Chalus, 17 and passim.

[5] The definitive account of women's work as printers is Paula McDowell, *The Women of Grub Street: Press, Politics, and Gender in the London Literary Marketplace 1678–1730* (Oxford, 1998).

[6] Christopher Reid, 'Reporting by Letter: The 2nd Earl of Hardwicke and his Parliamentary Correspondents', *Parl. Hist.*, xxxix (2020), 253; James Sutherland, *The Restoration Newspaper and Its Development* (Cambridge, 1986), 8.

Manuscript newsletters are understood as produced and consumed by elite men with connections to political or mercantile activity.

On the other hand, this focus on men and manuscript circulation is counterintuitive given broader scholarship on handwritten texts in the 17th and 18th centuries, which has argued that one reason for the continued prominence of manuscript after the rise of print was the medium's accessibility to women. Arthur Marotti, for example, writes that 'both the relative privacy of manuscript transmission and the relative hostility of print culture to women's writing affected women's choice of the manuscript medium of communication,' while George Justice has explored 'the problems (and opportunities) confronting women writers in historical circumstances that made manuscript circulation a necessity, or an option, for the distribution of their works'.[7] Furthermore, the letter has been understood as a particularly feminine genre. As Dena Goodman writes, in the 17th and 18th centuries letter writing began to be presented as a feminine skill: 'Whereas all writing had previously been considered primarily a male occupation, letter writing now entered the repertoire of cultural practices that… elite women were expected to master, even as it was assumed to flow effortlessly from their nature'.[8] Focusing on how the period's epistolary and conduct manuals associated women with letter writing, manuscript studies and especially epistolary studies have been areas that emphasise women's literary participation.

In keeping with this scholarly interest in 17th and 18th-century manuscript studies, recent work in media history has highlighted the multimedia news environment that supported the takeoff of printed newspapers and pamphlets in the period. In particular, scholars have argued that letters and manuscript newsletters remained important sources long after the advent of printed news and even after the lapse of the Licensing Act in 1695. Andrew Pettegree writes, 'for at least a hundred years the newspaper struggled to find a place in what remained a multimedia business. The dawn of print did not suppress earlier forms of news transmission'.[9] Ian Atherton adds that 'manuscript and printed transmission of the news went hand-in-hand' as news suppliers would send out newsletters and newspapers folded up together.[10] Printed newspapers also relied upon personal correspondence, diplomatic circulars, and manuscript newsletters for their information, as they sourced their items from 'letters received'.[11] Newsletters, both the official ones produced by the secretary of state's office and commercial ones produced by paid news writers, continued to circulate widely well into the 18th century.[12] Newsletters typically employed the format of a four-page quarto or two-page bifolium and were issued on a set periodical schedule up to three times a week (see Fig. 1). News consumers moved fluidly between the media and treated

---

[7] A.F. Marotti, *Manuscript, Print, and the English Renaissance Lyric* (Ithaca, NY, 1995), 61; George Justice, 'Introduction', in *Women's Writing and the Circulation of Ideas: Manuscript Publication in England, 1550–1880*, ed. George Justice and Nathan Tinker (Cambridge, 2002), 6.

[8] Dena Goodman, *Becoming a Woman in the Age of Letters* (Ithaca, NY, 2009), 1–2.

[9] Andrew Pettegree, *The Invention of News: How the World Came to Know about Itself* (New Haven, CT, 2014), 10.

[10] Ian Atherton, '"The Itch Grown a Disease": Manuscript Transmission of News in the Seventeenth Century', in *News, Newspapers, and Society in Early Modern Britain*, ed. Joad Raymond (1999), 40.

[11] R.S. King, *Writing to the World: Letters and the Origins of Modern Print Genres* (Baltimore, MD, 2018), 42–3.

[12] R.S. King, 'The Manuscript Newsletter and the Rise of the Newspaper, 1665–1715', *HLQ*, lxxix (2016), 419.

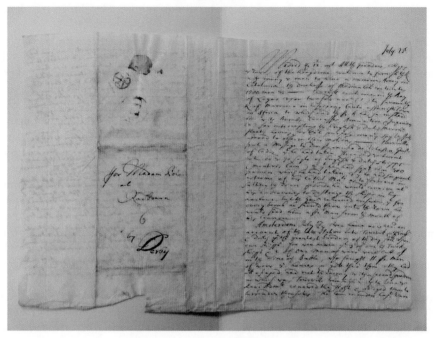

Figure 1: A newsletter addressed to 'Madam Pole at Radbourn by Derby', showing the manuscript newsletter's typical quarto format and layout dividing news items from separate locations ('Madrid', 'Amsterdam') into paragraphs, with a header featuring only the date and no personalised superscription. 25 July 1693. Pole Family News Collection, MS 1951.021, Box 1, Folder 61, William Andrews Clark Memorial Library, University of California, Los Angeles.

written and printed news as supplements to one another – not viewing manuscript as an outdated or superseded technology.

Manuscript news, that is, remained a central component of the media environment from the late Stuart through Hanoverian periods. Despite earlier assumptions that newsletters' purpose was to avoid censorship, scholars now tend to agree that legal restrictions were not the primary reason for their continuation after the rise of newspapers. Although there were a variety of prohibitions on the publication of domestic information, there was no specific ban on the printing of domestic news and both manuscript and printed productions were subject to oversight.[13] The content of newsletters also contradicts the assumption that they existed for the circulation of otherwise prohibited domestic news. Like newspapers they featured high proportions of foreign information, often adhering to the layout of the printed newspaper with two to three pages of foreign items followed by port news and local items (see Fig. 2). As Atherton writes, 'censorship alone does not account for the slanting

[13]S.A. Baron, 'The Guises of Dissemination in Early Seventeenth-century England: News in Manuscript and Print', in *The Politics of Information in Early Modern Europe*, ed. Brendan Dooley and S.A. Baron (2001), 46; Peter Fraser, *The Intelligence of the Secretaries of State and Their Monopoly of Licensed News, 1660–1688* (Cambridge, 1956), 115.

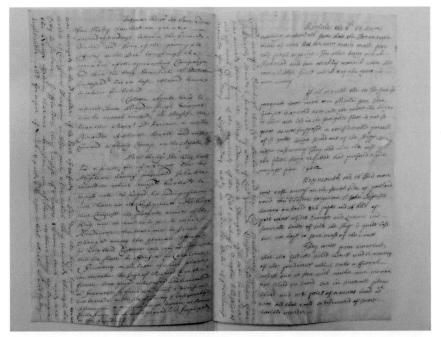

Figure 2: Newsletter employing a bifolium layout showing the usual organisation of items, moving from foreign news on pages one and two through port/shipping news on page three and local London and court items in the margins. 19 April 1694. Pole Family News Collection, MS 1951.021, Box 2, Folder 11, William Andrews Clark Memorial Library, University of California, Los Angeles.

of manuscript news to the Continent... most written news concerned foreign parts'.[14] Similarly, while Alex W. Barber argues that 'the reason for the survival of scribal news can be found... in the difficult relationship between press and parliament,' the persistence of newsletters cannot be fully explained by a desire for parliamentary reporting.[15] In 1660, the house of commons banned reporting of its votes and proceedings, a proscription that remained mostly in effect until the late 18th century.[16] However, this ban was intermittently reversed or unenforced, and it applied to manuscript as well as printed news, although printed sources were easier to track and control; newsletter writer John Dyer, for example, was arrested at least five times in the 1690s for reporting on parliamentary activity.[17] But while newsletters did not exist solely because of restrictions on printing parliamentary debates and votes, the circulation of such news was an important one of their functions.

[14] Atherton, ' "The Itch Grown a Disease" ', 42.

[15] A.W. Barber, ' "It is Not Easy What to Say of our Condition, Much Less to Write It": The Continued Importance of Scribal News in the Early 18th Century', *Parl. Hist.*, xxxii (2013), 295.

[16] Sutherland, *Restoration Newspaper*, 7.

[17] Sutherland, *Restoration Newspaper*, 15; H.L. Snyder, 'Newsletters in England, 1689–1715, with Special Reference to John Dyer –A Byway in the History of England', in *Newsletters to Newspapers: Eighteenth-Century Journalism*, ed. D.H. Bond and W. Reynolds McLeod (Morgantown, WV, 1977), 5.

Alongside foreign reporting and details on ships departing and arriving, newsletters from this period include extensive information about parliamentary elections, debates, negotiations, and votes, often in greater detail than in the printed newspaper.[18] This is true of the newsletters that Madam Pole and Mrs Newey received from the 1680s to 1710s.

These female news customers neatly deconstruct many of the implicit binaries, and often hierarchies, that undergird scholarship on the histories of news and letter writing at a crucial time in the development of both: the turn of the 18th century. They were women who engaged with the apparently masculine sphere of manuscript newsletters and consumed – or at least received and preserved – copious amounts of parliamentary news, but their newsletters were also part of the world of print. Both collections include handwritten documents with reverse-image impressions of offset type, showing that newsletters and freshly printed newspapers were folded up and mailed together; in both cases the contents of the letters make constant reference to printed papers, either citing print as a source or referring the reader to printed gazettes. From a number of directions, therefore, such documents upset associations of women with manuscript and privacy and of men with print, political activity and publicity. Despite the fact that the documents are almost universally superscribed 'Sir' while addressed to Madam Pole or Mrs Newey – although in a few telling instances, 'Sir' is struck through in favor of 'Madam' (see Fig. 3) – no one involved in the exchanges seems to have found it unusual for women to subscribe to these news services. In this article, I will first detail the parliamentary news that was included in Pole's newsletters, arguing that it helps elucidate manuscript newsletters' broader role in the developing media environment of the period. I will go on to argue that Newey, as the recipient if not necessarily the reader of the newsletters addressed to her, played a crucial role in the circulation of parliamentary news in the vicinity of Tamworth, a fact that shows more broadly how news was consumed within communities of readers. The Pole newsletters illustrate the production side of manuscript news, while the Newey ones reveal networks of circulation and consumption. In both cases, we see that manuscript newsletters projected a national or international news community that could and did include provincial women.

2

Madam Pole was a voracious news consumer. From at least the 1690s until the 1710s, she received manuscript newsletters on a tri-weekly schedule at her home of Radbourne Hall, about five miles outside of Derby, as well as at other locations where she was presumably visiting.[19] The Clark Library's Pole Family News Collection includes about 300 manuscript

---

[18] This situation began to reverse in the second half of the 18th century, when newspapers increasingly reported parliamentary news. Newspapers began regularly reporting on parliament in the 1770s and the process became more rapid and systematic in the 1780s, at which point letters and newsletters could not match the circumstantial detail of newspaper reports, although parliamentary news continued to circulate by letter. Christopher Reid, 'Reporting by Letter: The 2nd Earl of Hardwicke and His Parliamentary Correspondents', *Parl. Hist.*, xxxix (2020), 248–51.

[19] There are three letters to Pole directed to her 'At Sr Richard Newdigates in Arbury near Coventry'. Newdigate also amassed a collection of newsletters now held at the Folger Shakespeare Library, some of which feature the same hand as that on some of Pole's newsletters. The Pole and Newdigate families were related by marriage. Beinecke Library, Yale University [hereafter cited as Beinecke], OSB MSS 60, Box 3: Newsletters addressed to Madam Pole, 28 Aug. 1694; 30 Aug. 1694; 1 Sept. 1694.

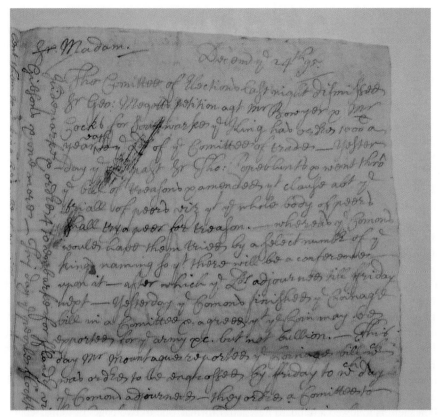

Figure 3: Manuscript newsletter addressed to Madam Pole showing 'Sr' struck through in favour of 'Madam', followed by parliamentary news. 24 December 1695. Pole Family News Collection, MS 1951.021, Box 3, Folder 38, William Andrews Clark Memorial Library, University of California, Los Angeles.

newsletters and 500 printed newspapers with manuscript additions, while the Beinecke Library's collection of newsletters addressed to Madam Pole contains about 300 newsletters and ten print-manuscript sheets. Pole seems to have received letters from multiple news providers, although there is only one signed note in the collection: on 25 January 1694, one John Sims wrote:

Madam I was ordered by Mr Smith to send you this Letter as allso to acq[uain]t you that 4 lb. per annum is the price that all men have that desires to live and perform their business diligently I shall continue the Letter unless I receive an order to the contrary pray order the Letter directed for me to be left at the Widow Humphreys Coffee house in St Peters alley Corn hill.[20]

---

[20] Beinecke, OSB MSS 60, Box 3: 25 Jan. 1694.

It may be that at this point Pole's purveyor changed or she began receiving an additional newsletter, since the format of the letters switched from quarto to bifolium and the folios featured a variety of new hands. Pole sometimes received two letters covering the same time period, again indicating a subscription to multiple news services. Other than Sims's note, there are only a few other, unsigned lines personalised to Pole, for example thanking her for paying her bill or wishing her a happy new year. This was a commercial service – not the official newsletter released by the secretary of state's office, but a third-party operation providing a compendium of public and private letters, foreign printed reports, court gossip and local reporting.

The letters contain no information about Pole or how she engaged with them. We cannot know for sure that she, or anyone else, even read them; there are no marginalia or endorsements.[21] Despite scholars' assumptions that one of the reasons for the continuance of manuscript newsletters was that they provided, in James Sutherland's words, a 'personal service,' there is no personalisation in Pole's letters, to the extent that the vast majority of them are superscribed 'Sir'.[22] It may therefore seem irrelevant that their recipient was a woman. But the apparently unremarkable subscription by a woman to these letters, particularly with regards to her access to parliamentary content, offers important insights into the developing news industry at the turn of the 18th century. It shows the central role that manuscript media and epistolary transmission continued to play in the media marketplace, and how news was beginning to be consumed as narrative and entertainment rather than as useful information. It elucidates the restrictions, or lack thereof, on both handwritten and printed news and shows that parliamentary details were circulating to a greater extent than scholars of the news and of parliament have often assumed. Overall, it shows a news industry that was standardising procedures and becoming an assumed part of everyday life, even for provincial women.

Pole's letters followed a standard newsletter format: one to two pages of items, separated into paragraphs, gleaned from the 'foreign mails,' followed by another page of domestic and London news, with an address panel on the blank fourth page. When parliament was in session there were at least a few lines relating to the previous day's activities, usually located on page three, and often multiple paragraphs providing the latest updates. In total about 30% of the Beinecke's Pole newsletters contain parliamentary news.[23] The newsletters often followed 'stories' from day to day, for example providing updates on bills under debate or describing the Houses' responses to the monarch's annual speech. Even when no decisions were made or material business conducted, the news writer includes an update. For example, on 25 November 1693, the letter noted, 'The H. of Coms was yesterday in a Gr. Committee on the Trienniall Bill & went thro' the same; they divided upon the word declare, whether it should be inserted before the word enacted, it being alledged that it was declarative in an other law, but was carried in the Ney by 165 agt. 110'.[24] Ten days later an update came on the topic: 'The H. of Peers yesterday read the engrossed Trienniall Bill againe & passed the same & sent it to the H. of Coms,' and three days later, on 12 December, the letter

---

[21] A few letters in each collection are addressed to German Pole and Samuel Pole.

[22] Sutherland, *Restoration Newspaper*, 8.

[23] I have not been able to perform a complete inventory of the Clark's collection, but the ratio appears to be roughly the same.

[24] Beinecke, OSB MSS 60, Box 2: 25 Nov. 1693.

continued, 'Yesterday the H. read the Trienniall Bill the 1. time, (which came from the Lords) & then went into a Gr. Com[mi]ttee upon the ways & means to raise mony for the fleet'.[25] In this way, the newsletter offered a breakdown of parliamentary procedure, rather than simply reporting outcomes. The style begins to feel like the 'inside baseball' political coverage that we now take for granted; it is unlikely that Pole would derive much advantage from knowing that the House, by a vote of 165 to 110, rejected the insertion of the word 'declare' before 'enacted' in a bill for triennial parliaments, but the writer included this detail anyway. In the letters, we see news becoming a narrative, providing the reader with entertainment as much as 'need to know' information. This is true even in manuscript newsletters, which we often associate with a more circumscribed audience and insider knowledge.

But although the letters' parliamentary reporting is often dense, it lacks what to us seem like crucial details. Speeches are rarely reported and votes are also scarce; when they are included, they are simply given by number without names attached. This style accords with what Ian Harris has documented of newspapers' parliamentary reporting: 'the character of parliamentary debate as a process by which a decision was reached was one that required that reporters focus on what tended to this end... A report therefore conveyed the writer's conception of what mattered in a debate'.[26] Harris, however, is discussing the 1780s and '90s, when parliamentary reporting became more extensive in newspapers, while we can see similar dynamics in the manuscript newsletters a century earlier. The writers assumed that parliamentary news was one of the standard categories of news, but rarely included details of members and speeches. Even when speeches and debates were reported, it was often in general terms. For example, in December 1693 the newsletter reported on 'a great debate in the H. upon the land estimates' and, unusually, included a rundown of the debaters' various positions on supplying the allied forces with more troops. 'Some men are for employing the said mony for our whole Navy, till wee are masters of the sea it was in vain to endeavor that of the land,' the letter noted. 'An other Gent[le]man answered, that that methode had been more practicable in the beginning but now... that wee are so farr in the war, that there was no looking backward'. The newsletter captured oral turns of phrase along with the result that 'the main Q. whether the kings forces should be increased' was carried 'in the Affir[mativ]e by a great Majority,' but did not identify the speakers or the breakdown of votes.[27] The newsletters show standards for parliamentary reporting developing much earlier than in newspapers.

At the same time, while there is more parliamentary information in the newsletters than in contemporaneous newspapers, the letters reveal that manuscript documents also were subject to regulation and that the writers may have self-censored to avoid oversight. The writers frequently documented cases of censorship and punishment for both printing and writing material that was objectionable to the government. In May and June 1694 the letter included frequent updates on the investigation of a pamphlet in favour of the exiled King James II. As the letter noted on 4 May:

[25] Beinecke, OSB MSS 60, Box 2: 9 Dec. 1693; 12 Dec. 1693.

[26] Ian Harris, 'What Was Parliamentary Reporting? A Study of Aims and Results in the London Daily Newspapers, 1780–96', *Parl. Hist.*, xxxix (2020), 264.

[27] Beinecke, OSB MSS 60, Box 2: 14 Dec. 1693.

On Tuesday afternoon the Missenger [sic] of the Press seized at Parksplace in St. James street one Anderson a notorious Jacobite & in a closet artfully contrived beyond the head of a Bed, which was pulled away on occasion running upon wheeles found a great number of virulent Libells with a private press which he printed them with.[28]

The conspiracy, however, went beyond Anderson, as the letter updated two weeks later: 'On Sunda[y] morning a great number of treasonable Jacobiticall papers were scattered about, entit[le]d K. J. declaration, being the same that lately was seized with the 2 printing presses'.[29] Those involved faced various punishments: a 'Mrs. Lettis was tryed for dispersing libels & fined 200 lb. to stand twice in the pillory & to continue in prison, till she payed the fine,' while Anderson was hanged at Tyburn.[30] Although this case concerned printed pamphlets, at other times manuscript documents caused problems. In 1693, the newsletter noted that 'One Buttlar, that writes news letters, was seized 3 dayes agoe at the Posthouse in Lumbard Street by order of the Ld Major [sic], having counterfeited the hands of several Parlt. men & in their names carried the Letters to the Posthouse to franke them'.[31] And in a December 1694 letter, the writer included in his parliamentary news a complaint 'that Dyer the newes writer misrepresented the proceedings of this House,' adding that it was 'ordered that he attend this day'. Three days later, he included the outcome: 'upon Dyers writing the votes false the house of Comons ordered that none should be writ and reprimanded him upon his knees'.[32] The newsletters make clear that official oversight of the burgeoning news industry was common and that it applied to both handwritten and printed news.

From multiple angles, then, the Pole newsletters show manuscript and printed sources working together to develop norms for news-gathering, writing and circulation. Both media were assuming a standard layout where local news followed foreign items, teaching readers to expect the news to come in a certain order. Even when there were major domestic events – which a newsletter writer could have added to the opening of a letter much more easily than could a newspaper printer, since there would be no need to reset type – this information came on page three after several paragraphs of foreign items. For example, on 29 December 1694, after items from Turin, Vienna, Venice, Paris, Brussels and Edinburgh, the letter announced, 'Yesterday morning some few minutes after one a Clock her Ma[jes]ty departed this life the Archbishop of Canterbury being with her to the last which occasioned that universall sorrow that no pen can indite all things at Court appearing Melancholy and deserted'.[33] The foreign-to-local organisation was the result of both newsletter writers and newspaper printers waiting as late as possible to include any recent local news in their documents, but it also became a norm that readers could use to navigate the newsletter or newspaper – an embryonic form of the sections of the present-day newspaper. The newsletters also helped establish norms by sticking to a strictly periodical schedule, like the newspapers. They featured a variety of clerks' handwriting and used the tri-weekly schedule that the era's leading newspapers, the *Post Boy* and *Post Man*, also

[28]Beinecke, OSB MSS 60, Box 2: 4 May 1694.
[29]Beinecke, OSB MSS 60, Box 2: 22 May 1694.
[30]Beinecke, OSB MSS 60, Box 2: 16 June 1694; 17 June 1694.
[31]Beinecke, OSB MSS 60, Box 2: 2 Feb. 169[3?].
[32]Beinecke, OSB MSS 60, Box 3: 22 Dec. 1694; 25 Dec. 1694.
[33]Beinecke, OSB MSS 60, Box 3: 29 Dec. 1694. Mary II died at Kensington Palace.

employed. The Pole news writer makes clear the priority placed on periodicity. On 25 December 1693, he opened his letter, 'Madam/ I pray your Ladys[hi]p to excuse the Brevity by reason of the day,' before including two pages of foreign and local news.[34] In early January, the writer apologised:

> The sudden Indisposition which this day was sevennight by stoppage of urine violent ague, a great paine in the side &c. ˆdidˆ put a stopp to my duty in serveing you with my letter these holly dayes for which I begg your favourrable excuse, & having gott God be thanked this day some reliefe I hoape I will recover my strength as to be able to serve you as formerly if you please.[35]

The note shows that, unlike in a personal letter, even a week's delay in the correspondence would be considered a serious breach for the news consumer.

In the Pole newsletters, the discrepancy between the female recipient and the 'Sir' that heads most of the letters demonstrates an orientation toward a 'mass,' or at least large-scale audience, even in a handwritten letter. There is evidence that some newsletters circulated in hundreds of copies, and that John Dyer, for example, employed up to 40 clerks.[36] These figures are comparable to those of an influential print periodical such as Daniel Defoe's *Review*, whose circulation was around 400.[37] If, according to Benedict Anderson, a defining feature of print capitalism – whose paradigmatic product is the daily newspaper – is that readers imagine themselves engaging the same news 'world' as their fellow unknown-yet-known readers, then we can certainly see such a standpoint in the manuscript newsletters.[38] The newsletters' lack of personalisation and multiple clerks' hands reveal an assembly-line approach to news-gathering and reporting: cutting and pasting from public and private letters and foreign gazettes, in addition to some information observed at court or in the law courts. On their own, the letters tell us much about the news industry at the turn of the 18th century. But the fact that they were sent to a female subscriber deepens our understanding of how this industry was standardising and professionalising at the time. Whether in manuscript or print, the news was expected to cover certain topics, to adhere to regulations for reporting on parliament and to stick to a periodical schedule. Madam Pole's newsletters show how written and printed sources worked together to create a more publicly oriented news industry.

3

Susannah Newey of Tamworth, Staffordshire, leaves even less of a mark on the newsletters addressed to her than does Anne Pole. This is despite the fact that the letters feature an

---

[34] Beinecke, OSB MSS 60, Box 2: 25 Dec. 1693.

[35] It is unclear whether these notes come from the same newsletter writer or two different ones. They feature different hands and formats. Beinecke, OSB MSS 60, Box 2: 4 Jan. [1694?].

[36] Barber, 'It Is Not Easy What to Say of our Condition, Much Less to Write It', 298.

[37] James Sutherland, 'The Circulation of Newspapers and Literary Periodicals, 1700–30', *The Library* (4th ser., xv, 1934), 111.

[38] Benedict Anderson, *Imagined Communities: Reflections on the Origin and Spread of Nationalism* (London and New York, 1991), 34–5.

incredible variety of marks: multiple hands, marginalia and underlining, stamps and seals, and franks from different members of parliament (see Fig. 4). It is unclear whether Newey was the intended reader of the letters: most of them are addressed 'for Mrs. Newey' or 'to Mrs. Susannah Newey in Tamworth' but a few are directed to other people, 'to be left with Mrs. Newey'. Perhaps Newey was the postmistress or an innkeeper, or a sort of human entrepot for news distribution in Tamworth.[39] But as with Pole, Newey's name on the letters tells us much about the status of manuscript newsletters in the broader media environment of the turn of the 18th century. The producers and consumers of the newsletters left traces that show how they were valued and how they circulated within communities of readers. Featuring additional notes, lines copied from newspapers and other newsletters, and endorsements summarising their contents, the letters reveal how 18th-century news consumers were learning to compile and compare different sources to draw a full picture of the facts. With parliamentary news in particular, the newsletters' reader annotated and added material from a variety of news documents to flesh out the details included in the newsletter. Although we cannot be sure whether Newey herself read or subscribed to the letters – there are no personal notes from the news writer even of the minimal kind found in the Pole collections – as the letters' recipient she played a pivotal role in the news community that centred on them.

The letters feature extensive underlining and marginalia by a reader who continued the practice from at least 1690 until 1710 (the handwriting, pictured in Fig. 4, is consistent in these notes while the newsletters display a number of clerks' hands). Often, the reader used the newsletter as a space to gather news on the same topic from different newspapers and newsletters. He or she also added brief headings summarising the news that read like present-day headlines: 'Papist Lord turns Protestant', 'Lord Griffin reprieved', or, once, simply, 'Sodomy'.[40] There is only one note offering a solid clue to the annotator's identity: a letter, or a copy of a letter, dated 1 March 1693, to one John Browne that is added to the end of a newsletter whose date has been torn away. The letter, which apologises for the author's sisters' apparent rejection of Browne, is signed 'Robert Burdett'.[41] This note is written in the same hand as the other notes and headings added to the collection's newsletters. However, it is not clear whether Burdett is the note taker or whether this is simply a copy of Burdett's letter; it is possible that the writer was adding a personal letter to Browne to the end of the newsletter, but this seems unlikely given that the address panel reads only, 'For Mr. Caine Bailiff of Tamworth in Staffordshire'. And at other times, the note taker copies verbatim from other sources without changing first-person pronouns. For example, in April 1710 the reader quoted from the 'Newes letter April 8 1710. I hear ˆaˆ low church

[39] A Susanna Newey, daughter of Josiah and Susanna Newey, was christened in St Editha's Church in Tamworth on 23 Apr. 1672. A Shushannah Newey was married to Thomas Knight in the same church on either 5 or 8 Aug. 1703; if this is the same Susanna Newey as that of the newsletters, it would mean that Mrs Newey and Mrs Hobson are not the same person. There is a burial record for Susannah Newey, also in St Editha's Church, on 19 Aug. 1716; however, the fact that her surname is listed as Newey rather than Knight suggests this may be the mother of the Susanna Newey christened in 1672. 'Susanna Newey', England Births and Christenings, 1538–1975. 'Thomas Knight', England Marriages, 1538–1973. 'Susannah Newey', England, Staffordshire, Church Records, 1538–1944. FamilySearch. Accessed 16 Oct. 2020.

[40] Henry E. Huntington Library, San Marino [hereafter cited as HL], MSS HM 30659, ff. 95, 97, 94: manuscript newsletters from London, 13 Jan. 1708; 17 June 1708; 14 October 1707.

[41] HL, MSS HM 30659, f. 4: 24 Feb., no year.

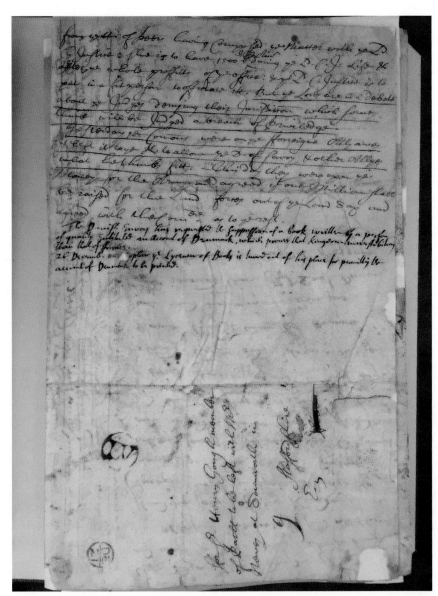

Figure 4: A newsletter addressed 'for Sr. Henry Gough member of Parlt to be left with Mrs Newey at Tamworth in Staffordshire' and featuring underlining in the body of the newsletter, annotations in the collection's 'note' handwriting, and a variety of postal marks. 21 December 1693. Manuscript newsletters from London, 1689–1710, MSS HM 30659, f. 33, The Huntington Library, San Marino, Calif.

ˆaddressˆ is carrying on in [corner torn]…'[42] This note, and others like it, indicate that the writer received or had access to multiple newsletters, which he or she collated in the margins and blank pages of the newsletters addressed to Newey. But as we have already seen with the address to Mr Caine, Newey is not the letters' only addressee. The address panels also include the names of Francis Wolfreston, owner of Statfold Hall in Tamworth, 'to be lefte with Mrs Woodcocke'; Mr Hobson; Mrs Hobson; Sir Henry Gough, Tory member of parliament for Tamworth who franked many of the letters but who was also the addressee of some (e.g., 'For Sr. Henry Gough member/ of Parlt to be left with Mrs/ Newey at Tam-worth in/ Staffordshire'); and Thomas Guy, Whig member for Tamworth who also both franked and received letters 'to be left' with Newey.[43] It is unclear if any of these people can be identified as the person who made such extensive notes in the letters' margins. But the variety of names, of both men and women, demonstrates the scope of the news community that circulated these newsletters between London and Tamworth.

The kind of news that the note-taker highlighted also signals the community at stake. In 1709 and 1710, the writer consistently underlined, commented on and added information about the controversy surrounding Henry Sacheverell's inflammatory high church sermon preached at St Paul's Cathedral on 5 November 1709. The newsletters' extensive coverage and lack of critical commentary of Sacheverell indicates that this is likely the newsletter service provided by Dyer, who was known for his high church and Tory sympathies.[44] The note-taker underlined almost all of the news relating to Sacheverell and also added updates from other newsletters and newspapers, providing more detailed information about Sacheverell's impeachment in the house of commons and trial before the house of lords. For example, on 22 December the newsletter offered in its parliamentary news:

> The Lds read a 3d time & past the Malt Bill & to Morrow the Queene will come to the House & give the Royall Assent & then tis sd both Houses will adjourn to the 9th pro & till which time Dr. Sacheverell [will] continue in the Custody of the Serj[ean]t att Armes.

The reader underlined this passage and added immediately after it, 'He has retained for counsel Sr. Prat, Sr. Simon Hare [corner torn]… he is visited by A great many of the principall clergy and gentry'.[45] On 14 January 1710, the newsletter reported that Sacheverell had been granted bail on £6,000 surety, while the note-taker included a day-by-day account of the ongoing negotiations, listing the articles of impeachment and adding on 12 January that 'Mr Harly spoke well and long'.[46] This close coverage in both the newsletter and the notes continued through the summer of 1710, with updates on Sacheverell's reception in the countryside following his conviction and suspension from preaching for three years.

However, while the newsletters may have featured more information on this topic than would be found in a printed newspaper, they also included the usual mix of foreign news, which the note-taker also underlined at times. The letters follow the standard layout of

---

[42] HL, MSS HM 30659, f. 121: 4 Apr. 1710.
[43] HL, MSS HM 30659, ff. 2, 33: 20 Jan., no year; 21 Dec. 1693.
[44] *The State Trial of Doctor Henry Sacheverell*, ed. Brian Cowan (Oxford, 2012), 45.
[45] HL, MSS HM 30659, f. 106: 22 Dec. 1709.
[46] HL, MSS HM 30659, f. 113: 14 Jan. 1710.

foreign items followed by port and shipping news, and then London and parliamentary news on page three or in the margins. On 23 January 1689, the letter included paragraphs datelined Brussels, Rome, Edinburgh, Plymouth and Portsmouth before closing with the 'discourse att Court'.[47] The newsletters, like those in the Pole collections, hewed to readers' expectations for where certain types of news would be found; even its specialised domestic news, such as that on Sacheverell, was located at the end of the letter. As in newspapers, domestic news was secondary to foreign; in 1710, when interest in Sacheverell was at its height, the news writer noted, 'My foreign Newse today is run to so great a length that I cannot give you the further progress of Dr. Sacheverall, but must postpone it to my next'.[48] In this way, once again, the newsletters indicate that the reason for the persistence of manuscript news into the 18th century was not to circulate otherwise unavailable domestic information, but because they were an established part of the news ecosystem and consumers valued access to a variety of sources. The Newey letters also show evidence of mass production, indicating that while this reader may have been particularly interested in parliamentary and church politics, his or her letters were not tailored to this topic. Occasionally we see the clerk hurriedly miscopying a letter, as on 17 June 1708, when the text, discussing the trial of Edward, Lord Griffin, read:

> her Ma.ty was pleased to say that he was a faithfull servant to her father & uncle & some Lords said that he was a faithful servant forced over agt his own consent from France & that it was very rare to execute a man upon an outlawry without allowing him a tryall.[49]

The repeated phrase shows a clerk getting lost in the lines he was copying from a master copy or another newsletter (this item appears almost verbatim in Narcissus Luttrell's *Brief Historical Relation of State Affairs from September 1678 to April 1714*, demonstrating its use by another reader). Once again, we see newsletters operating as professional news media, issuing standard reports of parliamentary information while keeping readers apprised of a variety of foreign, British and local news.

The annotations on the Newey newsletters offer evidence of how 18th-century readers were learning to sift and layer sources of news, and how the circulation of news within information communities cut across manuscript–print, private–public and feminine–masculine spheres. The note-taker used the newsletters to compile and preserve a variety of perspectives on the topics he or she found significant. For example, on 4 April 1710, he or she added information from both the 'Newes letter April 8 1710' and the 'Post man Apr. 1 to Apr. 5. 1710,' elaborating on the drier accounts often provided by the newsletter itself. In addition to using the letters to bring together several sources, the note-taker also returned to the newsletters years after first receiving them. On an undated letter, he or she added the heading, 'Portlands Pompous Embassy to France about 1697 or 1698 or 1699,' indicating a much later re-perusal.[50] Another letter includes a paragraph of notes on historical events:

[47] HL, MSS HM 30659, f. 3: 23 Jan. 1689.
[48] HL, MSS HM 30659, f. 98: no date [1710].
[49] HL, MSS HM 30659, f. 97: 17 June 1708.
[50] HL, MSS HM 30659, f. 76: no date.

Ch[arles] 2 K. of Spain died Nov. 1. about 3 in the afternoon. 1700. See Post boy Decemb. 3. 1700 Numb. 883 Note K. James died September 1702 K. William died March 8: 1701/2... Pope Clement 11 was elected and proclaimed Pope his name was Francis Albani of Pesaro in Decemb. 1700. See Post boy Decemb. 3. 1700. Numb. 883. his age 52. See ibid and also in a publick newes letter dated 1700.[51]

As this indicates, the note-taker referred variously to the 'newes letter,' the 'publick newes letter,' and the 'publick Tam[worth] Newes letter'.[52] Just as we do today, readers in the 17th and 18th centuries interpreted news based on its origins and sourcing and they contextualised individual items within a complex matrix of news genres. Although we cannot know whether Newey personally read this news, as at least the recipient and circulator of the newsletters she served as the hub of a news community that cut across several circles in Tamworth. In this role she shows again how women's participation was both central and uncontroversial within news networks.

Half a century later, two other women's correspondence revealed that newsletters continued to serve as a model of news writing. In 1740, Frances Seymour, countess of Hertford, wrote to Henrietta Louisa Fermor, countess of Pomfret, 'I foresee that this letter will be very much in the style of Dyer's News-writer: which I dare say your ladyship was acquainted with in the days of your youth'. Referring to her forthcoming information about changes in court places, she continued, 'The end of a session of parliament always furnishes a great deal of matter for the journalists and gazetteers' – and, apparently, for female correspondents.[53] The Newey and Pole newsletters help us understand the news ecosystem at a crucial moment in its development, showing how women could play important roles in both the consumption and circulation of newsletters and newspapers. There was a complete interleaving of manuscript and printed news: the newsletter writer referred the reader to information 'already in print,' the newsletters displayed offset type from the printed items with which they were mailed, and the recipient used the letters to record news from other newsletters and newspapers. Commercial newsletters such as these were periodical, ephemeral, mass-produced documents like printed newspapers. But they were also, in the much later words of *Washington Post* publisher Phil Graham, the 'first rough draft of history,' providing the basis for retrospective analysis and confirmation of facts. These letters show the thoroughly communal nature of news from the sides of both production and consumption, as they were written by stables of clerks based on information gathered from letters, diplomatic circulars and gazettes, and then addressed to multiple interconnected people. They contain a multitude of parliamentary details but, from the other direction, their parliamentary news clarifies their status as significant news media of the era. Newsletters addressed to women show how 18th-century news, in both manuscript and print, was becoming more public and professionalised even as it continued to operate through personal networks of correspondence.

---

[51] HL, MSS HM 30659, f. 85: no date.

[52] HL, MSS HM 30659, f. 85: no date.

[53] Frances Seymour, countess of Hertford, to Henrietta Louisa Fermor, countess of Pomfret, 8 May 1740. *Correspondence Between Frances, Countess of Hartford, (Afterwards Duchess of Somerset,) and Henrietta Louisa, Countess of Pomfret, Between the Years 1738 and 1741* (1806), i, 263.

Wodrow's News: Correspondence and Politics in Early 18th-Century Scotland[*]

ALASDAIR RAFFE

This article examines the creation and consumption of scribal news by the early 18th-century Scottish Presbyterian minister Robert Wodrow (1679–1734). It argues that Scottish news culture depended on the interaction of printed newspapers, professionally produced newsletters from London, personal letters and oral communication. For Wodrow, at least, personal letters were the most important source. No widely circulated commercial newsletter was produced in Scotland, and personal letters were vital for communicating information about the Scottish parliament, the church courts and the Westminster parliament after the Anglo–Scottish Union. News provided as a gift, rather than a commodity, served social functions. The article explores two moments at which Wodrow paid particular attention to parliamentary news: the ratification of the Union in 1706–7, and the passage of the Episcopalian Toleration, Patronage and Yule Vacation Acts in 1712.

Keywords: news; letters; Scottish parliament; British parliament; Church of Scotland; Robert Wodrow

Around the end of January 1707, Robert Wodrow, minister of Eastwood, Renfrewshire, received a letter from Edinburgh. After acknowledging receipt of a letter from Wodrow, his correspondent gave a detailed account of the previous day's business in the Scottish parliament. Having recently ratified the Treaty of Union with England, parliament had proceeded to consider how Scotland's towns would be represented in the British legislature when the Union came into force on 1 May. The burghs were to be classed into single-member districts, and parliamentarians discussed several possible schemes. Acknowledging that he could not remember how the burghs were grouped, the writer referred Wodrow to the printed minutes of parliament. Wodrow's correspondent then discussed rumours that the Stuart claimant of the throne ('the P[retended] K[ing] J[ames]') planned to invade Scotland. Mentioning the 'great deal of talking here about it', he summarised a report on Jacobite preparations from another source, the London newsletter of John Dyer.[1]

---

[*]I am grateful to Adam Fox and the editors for their helpful comments on drafts of this article.

[1]NLS, Wod.Lett.Qu.IV, f. 180: John Maxwell to Robert Wodrow, 30 Jan. 1707. Cf. *Minuts of the Proceedings in Parliament* (1706–7), no. 67, 29 Jan. 1707. On the projected invasion, see: Daniel Szechi, *Britain's Lost Revolution? Jacobite Scotland and French Grand Strategy, 1701–1708* (Manchester, 2015), 176–80.

The writer, John Maxwell, was not a professional newsmonger, but rather a friend who wrote as a favour to Wodrow. His residence in Edinburgh allowed him to converse with members of parliament and other eyewitnesses to its business, though in principle he was not entitled to observe sessions himself.[2] He sent his letter via Glasgow, where it was opened by Wodrow's father, James Wodrow, professor of divinity at Glasgow University. In a note to his son, written on the letter, Professor Wodrow explained that he 'opened this for newes'. He said that he had heard similar reports in a letter to his academic colleague, Principal John Stirling, which was read out in his company. Because there was 'no newes in the prints' – printed newspapers – Professor Wodrow had nothing to add.[3] By opening his son's letter, he demonstrated his anxious interest in the passage of the Union, and the contemporary habit of sharing personal correspondence containing news. As James Daybell has remarked, it was common throughout the early modern period 'for letters to be read by persons other than the addressee'.[4] Indeed, in October 1706, Robert Wodrow had sent a similar letter from Edinburgh on to his patron, the judge Sir John Maxwell, Lord Pollok, adding a note containing information derived from Dyer's newsletter and from 'privat letters' concerning the business of the commission of the general assembly.[5] Wodrow and his correspondents cited manuscript newsletters in conjunction with printed and oral sources, using their personal letters to summarise and assess stories drawn from the range of media making up the period's news culture.

The papers of Robert Wodrow allow us to explore the production and consumption of scribal news, and its interaction with other media, in early 18th-century Scotland. Wodrow (1679–1734) was born in Glasgow and studied at that city's university. After completing the divinity course under James Wodrow (1637–1707), Robert served as the university's librarian. Following a short period as chaplain and tutor in the household of Lord Pollok, he was ordained to Eastwood in October 1703. He remained in this small rural parish, a few miles south-west of Glasgow, for the rest of his life.[6] Wodrow is best known as the author of *The History of the Sufferings of the Church of Scotland from the Restoration to the Revolution* (1721–2), an extensively documented chronicle of Presbyterian dissent under Charles II and James VII and II.[7] His letters and journals reported on Scotland's ecclesiastical affairs throughout the first third of the 18th century.[8] Wodrow also collected accounts

[2] The orders of parliament sought to limit those observing its proceedings to noblemen's sons, senators of the college of justice and a few other specified officials and servants: *Records of the Parliaments of Scotland to 1707*, ed. K.M. Brown et al., http://www.rps.ac.uk/, 1662/5/6, 1685/4/13, M1689/3/16, 1693/4/15, 1698/7/14, 1705/6/20 (accessed 10 Dec. 2020).

[3] NLS, Wod.Lett.Qu.IV, f. 180v: Maxwell to Wodrow, 30 Jan. 1707, undated postscript by James Wodrow.

[4] James Daybell, 'The Scribal Circulation of Early Modern Letters', *HLQ*, lxxix (2016), 365–86, at 371.

[5] NLS, Wod.Lett.Qu.IV, f. 78v: Robert Wodrow to Lord Pollok, n.d.. On ministers as communicators of news, compare Sheila McIntyre, ' "I heare it so variously reported": News-Letters, Newspapers, and the Ministerial Network in New England, 1670–1730', *New England Quarterly*, lxxi (1998), 593–614.

[6] W.J. Couper, 'Robert Wodrow', *Records of the Scottish Church History Society*, iii (1927–9), 112–34; *Oxf. DNB*, s.v. Robert Wodrow (1679–1734).

[7] Robert Wodrow, *The History of the Sufferings of the Church of Scotland from the Restoration to the Revolution*, ed. Robert Burns (4 vols, Glasgow, 1828–30). On Wodrow as historian, see: A.M. Starkey, 'Robert Wodrow and the History of the Sufferings of the Church of Scotland', *Church History*, xliii (1974), 488–98; W.J. Couper, 'Robert Wodrow and his Critics', *Records of the Scottish Church History Society*, v (1933–5), 238–50.

[8] *The Correspondence of the Rev. Robert Wodrow*, ed. Thomas M'Crie (3 vols, Wodrow Society, 1842–3); Robert Wodrow, *Analecta: or, Materials for a History of Remarkable Providences* (4 vols, Maitland Club, Edinburgh, 1842–3).

© 2022 The Author(s). Parliamentary History published by John Wiley & Sons Ltd. on behalf of Parliamentary History Yearbook Trust.

of special providences, his contribution to the defence of Christianity against scepticism.[9] Especially in the early part of his career, he had wide-ranging antiquarian, geographical and philosophical interests.[10] Throughout his life, he was an enthusiastic reader and writer of news.[11]

Historians have not yet assessed the place of scribal communication in 17th- and 18th-century Scotland's culture of news. Existing works largely neglect professionally written newsletters and personal letters in favour of tracking the emergence of printed news. Some scholars of print have incorrectly assumed that manuscript newsletters were superseded soon after the appearance in 1699 of the first enduring Scottish newspaper.[12] Elsewhere there are only brief comments on newsletters in Scotland.[13] There has been no systematic search for them in Scottish archives, though it is clear from published correspondence that noblemen received newsletters.[14] Nicola Cowmeadow has discussed the circulation of news in personal letters, but other social historians have assumed that news in the 18th century came in printed papers.[15] There is much to be discovered about scribal news in early modern Scotland.

In mapping a course through this uncharted terrain, this article proceeds in three parts. It first surveys the news media available in Scotland around the start of the 18th century, their distribution and consumption. It then examines two short episodes in Wodrow's life of news, concentrating on his interest in parliaments and the church courts. It first considers the passage of the Union through the Scottish parliament in 1706–7, and then the adoption in the British parliament in 1712 of the Episcopalian Toleration Act, the Patronage Act and the Yule Vacation Act. These case studies suggest that Wodrow relied largely on personal

---

[9] Wodrow, *Analecta*. On this aspect of Wodrow's work, see: Martha McGill and Alasdair Raffe, 'The Uses of Providence in Early Modern Scotland', in *The Supernatural in Early Modern Scotland*, ed. Julian Goodare and Martha McGill (Manchester, 2020), 160–77.

[10] A.J. Mann, 'A Spirit of Literature – Melville, Baillie, Wodrow, and a Cast of Thousands: The Clergy in Scotland's Long Renaissance', *Renaissance Studies*, xviii (2004), 90–108, at 101–4; C.W.J. Withers, 'Reporting, Mapping, Trusting: Making Geographical Knowledge in the Late Seventeenth Century', *Isis*, xc (1999), 497–521, esp. 504–5; Thomas Ahnert and Martha McGill, 'Scotland and the European Republic of Letters around 1700', in *Scottish Philosophy in the Seventeenth Century*, ed. Alexander Broadie (Oxford, 2020), 73–93, at 78–9.

[11] Wodrow's communication of news across the Atlantic is discussed in David Parrish, *Jacobitism and Anti-Jacobitism in the British Atlantic World, 1688–1727* (Woodbridge, 2017), 144–9.

[12] See esp. W.J. Couper, *The Edinburgh Periodical Press* (2 vols, Stirling, 1908); A.J. Mann, *The Scottish Book Trade, 1500–1720: Print Commerce and Print Control in Early Modern Scotland* (East Linton, 2000), 20, 103, 147–8, 174, 218; S.W. Brown, 'Newspapers and Magazines', in *The Edinburgh History of the Book in Scotland*, vol. 2: *1707–1800*, ed. S.W. Brown and Warren McDougall (Edinburgh, 2012), 676–702; Karin Bowie, 'Newspapers, the Early Modern Public Sphere and the 1704–5 *Worcester* Affair', in *Before Blackwood's: Scottish Journalism in the Age of Enlightenment*, ed. Alex Benchimol, Rhona Brown and David Shuttleton (2015), 9–20. The fullest account of cheap print (including newspapers) in early modern Scotland is now Adam Fox, *The Press and the People: Cheap Print and Society in Scotland, 1500–1785* (Oxford, 2020).

[13] Couper, *Edinburgh Periodical Press*, i, 71–6; Alasdair Raffe, *The Culture of Controversy: Religious Arguments in Scotland, 1660–1714* (Woodbridge, 2012), 20.

[14] E.g., *HMC Hamilton Suppl.*, 11–12; *Seafield Correspondence from 1685 to 1708*, ed. James Grant (Scottish History Society, 2nd ser., iii, 1912), 68–9.

[15] N.M. Cowmeadow, 'Scottish Noblewomen, the Family and Scottish Politics from 1688–1707', University of Dundee PhD, 2012; R.K. Marshall, *The Days of Duchess Anne: Life in the Household of the Duchess of Hamilton, 1656–1716* (1973), 118; Katharine Glover, *Elite Women and Polite Society in Eighteenth-Century Scotland* (Woodbridge, 2011), 61–3.

letters, which in turn sometimes drew on professionally written newsletters, to understand parliamentary and ecclesiastical developments.

1

Scotland's news culture around 1700 depended on the interaction between four sources of news: printed newspapers, professionally authored newsletters, personal letters and oral communication. Scotland's first domestically produced printed newspapers were short-lived. A single issue of *Ane Information of the Publick Proceedings of the Kingdom of Scotland, and their Armies* appeared in August 1648. *Mercurius Scoticus* started in July 1651 and ran for almost six months. *Mercurius Caledonius* (1661) reported for three months as parliament determined the character of the Restoration settlement in Scotland. The first *Edinburgh Gazette* – unlike the *London Gazette*, a privately run paper – was published in at least four issues in late 1680.[16] Before the end of the century, however, the main printed newspapers circulating in Scotland came from London. After the *Edinburgh Gazette* was relaunched in 1699, there was an almost continuous succession of Scottish titles. From 1705, there was sometimes significant competition between Edinburgh papers.[17] Like the London press, the Scottish newspapers gave more attention to foreign news than to domestic occurrences; they were often frustratingly brief or evasive about sensitive political matters.

In Scotland as in England, manuscript newsletters continued to supplement and some-times to contradict printed newspapers during the early decades of the 18th century.[18] Edinburgh postmasters, keepers of the letter office and other agents wrote newsletters from the Scottish capital to provincial towns. But there does not seem to have been a profes-sionally produced Scottish newsletter on anything like the scale of John Dyer's London newsletter. The reasons for this must have included the small size of the Scottish market for news and the fact that, even after 1689, the Scottish parliament's sessions were shorter and less frequent than those of its Westminster counterpart. After the Union, the most influ-ential commercial newsletter in Scotland was that of Dyer, which furnished fuller accounts of parliamentary debates than appeared in printed papers. As a country minister of modest means, Wodrow did not himself subscribe to this expensive product. But he saw copies of Dyer's newsletter in Glasgow and Edinburgh; his correspondents in those towns regularly communicated stories from Dyer to Wodrow at Eastwood.[19]

[16]David Stevenson, 'Scotland's First Newspaper, 1648', *The Bibliotheck*, x (1981), 123–6; Couper, *Edinburgh Periodical Press*, i, 166–9, 174–87, 188–9; R.S. Spurlock, 'Cromwell's Edinburgh Press and the Development of Print Culture in Scotland', *Scottish Historical Review*, xc (2011), 179–203; J.M. Buckroyd, 'Mercurius Caledonius and its Immediate Successors, 1661', *Scottish Historical Review*, liv (1975), 11–21; Fox, *The Press and the People*, 99–100.

[17]Bowie, 'Newspapers'.

[18]A.W. Barber, ' "It is Not Easy What to Say of our Condition, Much Less to Write It": The Continued Im-portance of Scribal News in the Early 18th Century', *Parl. Hist.*, xxxii (2013), 293–316; R.S. King, 'The Manuscript Newsletter and the Rise of the Newspaper, 1665–1715', *HLQ*, lxxix (2016), 411–37; R.S. King, ' "All the News that's Fit to Write": The Eighteenth-Century Manuscript Newsletter', in *Travelling Chronicles: News and Newspa-pers from the Early Modern Period to the Eighteenth Century*, ed. S.G. Brandtzæg, Paul Goring and Christine Watson (Leiden, 2018), 95–118.

[19]Barber, ' "It Is Not Easy What to Say of our Condition, Much Less to Write It" ', 299. On Dyer's newsletter, see also: H.L. Snyder, 'Newsletters in England, 1689–1715: With Special Reference to John Dyer – a Byway in the History of England', in *Newsletter to Newspapers: Eighteenth-Century Journalism*, ed. D.H. Bond and W.R. McLeod (Morgantown, WV, 1977), 3–19.

More important than newsletters were personal letters containing news.[20] For Wodrow, news was typically a gift rather than a commodity, and this was not only for financial reasons. The exchange of news by personal letters served to strengthen friendships and to affirm relationships of patronage.[21] Wodrow's correspondents synthesised information from printed, manuscript and oral sources. Printed newspapers contained basic facts, which well-informed Scots could be expected to know. 'I need not suggest to you what is in the prints already', wrote one of Wodrow's friends in 1713.[22] Wodrow's personal correspondents sought to add to this elementary information, communicating the contents of letters sent to local magistrates and noblemen, stories they had heard in conversation and their own eyewitness reports on events. Concerning the anticipated results of the general election of 1713, one letter to Wodrow referred both to the coverage in the *Post Boy* and to more detailed testimony about local politicians' manoeuvring before the polls in the Glasgow burghs and Lanarkshire.[23] Moreover, personal letters were a vital source of intelligence concerning the institutions remaining in Scotland after 1707, notably the courts of the established Church. Until the appearance of the *Scots Magazine* in 1739, even the Edinburgh newspapers said little about the business of the general assembly and its commission.[24] Personal letters supplied the kind of news that could not be found in print or newsletters.

Much news originated in, or passed through, Edinburgh. The postal route from London to Edinburgh brought printed and manuscript news from England and the continent.[25] The keeper of the letter office and postmaster general in Edinburgh were thus essential conduits of information. As keepers during the Restoration period, Robert Mein and his son William supplied Edinburgh's town council with 'news letters and gazets'. In April 1690, the contract to provide the council's news was assumed by John Blair, postmaster general.[26] The councils of other royal burghs paid one of these officials or another newsletter writer in Edinburgh to supply regular printed and scribal news. John Nimmo, a writer to the signet (solicitor), provided this service for Glasgow and Dumfries in 1687.[27] Councils shopped

---

[20] For various perspectives on early modern letters, see e.g., S.E. Whyman, *The Pen and the People: English Letter Writers, 1660–1800* (Oxford, 2009); *Cultures of Correspondence in Early Modern Britain*, ed. James Daybell and Andrew Gordon (Philadelphia, PA, 2016); Alain Kerhervé, 'A Theory of British Epistolary Sociability?', in *British Sociability in the Long Eighteenth Century*, ed. Valérie Capdeville and Alain Kerhervé (Woodbridge, 2019), 145–62.

[21] On the newsletter as gift and commodity, see: Heiko Droste, 'How Public was the News in Early Modern Times?', in *Handwritten Newspapers: An Alternative Medium during the Early Modern and Modern Periods*, ed. Heiko Droste and Kirsti Salmi-Niklander (Helsinki, 2019), 29–44, esp. 33–5.

[22] NLS, Wod.Lett.Qu.VII, f. 164: John Williamson to Robert Wodrow, 8 June 1713.

[23] NLS, Wod.Lett.Qu.VII, f. 184: John Cross to Robert Wodrow, 19 Sept. 1713.

[24] The *Scots Magazine*'s reports on the assembly were collected in *Annals of the General Assembly of the Church of Scotland*, ed. Nathaniel Morren (2 vols, Edinburgh, 1838–40).

[25] Nikolaus Schobesberger et al., 'European Postal Networks', in *News Networks in Early Modern Europe*, ed. Joad Raymond and Noah Moxham (Leiden, 2016), 20–63, at 46–58.

[26] A.R.B. Haldane, *Three Centuries of Scottish Posts: An Historical Survey to 1836* (Edinburgh, 1971), 22–6; Couper, *Edinburgh Periodical Press*, i, 73; Bob Harris, *Politics and the Rise of the Press: Britain and France, 1620–1800* (1996), 6; *Extracts from the Records of the Burgh of Edinburgh, 1689 to 1701*, ed. Helen Armet (Edinburgh, 1962), 31–2 (quotation).

[27] Glasgow City Archives, Mitchell Library, C1/1/17, p. 279: Glasgow council minutes, 17 Dec. 1687; Dumfries and Galloway Archives, Ewart Library, Dumfries, WA2/5, p. 219: Dumfries council minutes, 14 Feb. 1687.

---

around in a competitive marketplace of news: at least three writers of newsletters can be identified in 1689, aside from William Mein.[28] Noblemen also employed agents to write the news from Edinburgh.[29] If some councils discontinued their contracts with Edinburgh newsletter writers after the reappearance of the *Edinburgh Gazette*, this does not indicate the rapid triumph of print implied by William Couper in 1908. Couper twice narrated that Stirling's town council subscribed to the *Edinburgh Gazette* in 1699 because it was cheaper than the news supplied by John Murray, the postmaster general in Edinburgh. In 1703, however, Stirling was paying for both the *Edinburgh Gazette* and Dyer's newsletter, which cost almost three times as much as the new newspaper.[30] Scribal news retained its value, even for cash-strapped Scottish burghs.

There were postal services from Edinburgh to many other Scottish towns, though some correspondents used other carriers, servants and friends. Postal deliveries between Edinburgh and Glasgow usually took two days, and Wodrow objected to news reports sent by slower carriers, 'because by the time they came to your hand they were stale'.[31] When the news from Edinburgh arrived in other parts of the country it was eagerly consumed. If landowners and burgh magistrates were among the first to read the news, inquisitive clergymen such as Wodrow were not far behind. Newspapers and burgh records refer to shops, coffeehouses and taverns at which papers and newsletters could be consulted.[32] 'I was not in the Coffee house yesternight so cannot give you the news', wrote Robert Yuill, a former bailie of Glasgow, to Wodrow in 1712. On this occasion, nonetheless, Yuill passed on information received by post to other members of the town's elite.[33] Because of the importance of scribal communication, contemporaries could learn the news by meeting well-informed individuals on the street or at social gatherings.

When he found contradictions between different sources, Wodrow did not always accept what he read in printed newspapers. Adjudicating between conflicting accounts of disorderly protests against the Union in late 1706, he preferred to believe parliament's proclamation against the disturbances. The *Edinburgh Gazette* suggested that demonstrations were less widespread than parliament alleged, but Wodrow considered it a 'Private Paper … not to be put in ballance w[i]t[h] [th]e proclamation'.[34] It was in their personal letters that Wodrow and his correspondents distilled the gist of the news and reconciled divergent reports. These letters communicated what was known in Edinburgh to other large towns and, more importantly, rural communities. Knowing that Wodrow had good connections, James

[28] Dumfries and Galloway Archives, WA2/5, p. 291: Dumfries council minutes, 16 Feb. 1689 (William Menzies); NRS, B48/9/4, p. 796: Linlithgow council minutes, 22 June 1689 (John Currie); Glasgow City Archives, C1/1/17, p. 343: Glasgow council minutes, 29 June 1689 ([blank] Muir).

[29] In the mid 1670s, James Johnston supplied Edinburgh news to James Hamilton, earl of Arran. See the letters between the men in NRS, GD406/1: correspondence of the dukes of Hamilton, 1563–1712.

[30] Couper, *Edinburgh Periodical Press*, i, 74–5, 207; *Extracts from the Records of the Royal Burgh of Stirling, A.D. 1667–1752*, ed. Robert Renwick (Glasgow, 1889), 90, 349.

[31] NLS, Wod.Lett.Qu.IV, f. 182: John Maxwell to Robert Wodrow, 3 Feb. 1707; cf. f. 119v: Robert Wodrow to James Wodrow, 28 Nov. 1706.

[32] Fox, *The Press and the People*, 212–14, 223; Karin Bowie, *Scottish Public Opinion and the Anglo–Scottish Union, 1699–1707* (Woodbridge, 2007), 24.

[33] NLS, Wod.Lett.Qu.VI, f. 93: Robert Yuill to Robert Wodrow, 29 Jan. 1712.

[34] NLS, Wod.Lett.Qu.IV, f. 138: Robert Wodrow to James Wodrow, 31 Dec. 1706; cf. f. 170: James Wodrow to Robert Wodrow, 27 Dec. 1706; *A Proclamation against All Tumultuary and Irregular Meetings and Convocations of the Leidges* (Edinburgh, 1706).

© 2022 The Author(s). Parliamentary History published by John Wiley & Sons Ltd. on behalf of Parliamentary History Yearbook Trust.

Rowat, minister of Dunlop, Ayrshire, beseeched him to send news.[35] Scribal communication enabled the full participation of men such as Wodrow and Rowat in early 18th-century Scotland's news culture.

2

There was intense public interest in the proceedings of parliament during the winter of 1706–7. Following the negotiation of a treaty of Union with England, parliamentarians met from 3 October 1706 to debate its terms. Other national bodies also gathered in Edinburgh to consider the Union. The convention of royal burghs addressed parliament with its concerns about trade and taxes in the projected United Kingdom. The commission of the general assembly submitted petitions and lobbied parliamentarians for measures to secure Scottish Presbyterianism after the creation of a predominantly Anglican British parliament.[36] Men and women across the country engaged in anguished debates about the Union, joining protests and signing addresses to parliament against the treaty.[37] Informing their discussions were numerous printed pamphlets, newspapers and broadsides, including the official record of parliament. As in several preceding sessions, the minutes of each sitting were printed at the command of the royal commissioner.[38] From 4 November, parliament also sanctioned the publication of voting lists in the main divisions.[39] Nevertheless, to understand the debates in detail, and to identify the principal speakers, contemporaries relied on manuscript letters.

In addition to two substantial memoirs concerning the passage of the Union,[40] the Wodrow papers include at least 58 letters from Edinburgh reporting on the parliamentary session of 1706–7. Wodrow's correspondence also contains letters from writers elsewhere in Scotland, all avidly following the news from Edinburgh. Wodrow later copied a set of more occasional newsletters, written from Edinburgh from October 1706 to January 1707. These were probably the work of his like-minded friend, Robert Wylie, minister of Hamilton.[41]

The letters illustrate the value of accounts of parliament from well-connected correspondents in Edinburgh. Before he arrived in the capital on 30 October, Wodrow received letters from his friend Robert Steuart, a regent (philosophy professor) at Edinburgh's town college and nephew of both Lord Pollok and the lord advocate, Sir James Steuart of

---

[35] NLS, Wod.Lett.Qu.VII, f. 185: James Rowat to Robert Wodrow, 22 Sept. 1713.

[36] *Addresses against Incorporating Union, 1706–1707*, ed. Karin Bowie (Scottish History Society, 6th ser., xiii, 2018), 37–68; Jeffrey Stephen, *Scottish Presbyterians and the Act of Union 1707* (Edinburgh, 2007).

[37] Bowie, *Scottish Public Opinion*.

[38] *Minuts of the Proceedings in Parliament* (1706–7). Serials with this title were published in 1693, 1698, 1700, 1700–1, 1702, 1703, 1704, 1705. Records of the convention of estates and parliament of 1689–90 were published unofficially at London: *An Account of the Proceedings of the Estates in Scotland, 1689–1690*, ed. E.W.M. Balfour-Melville (2 vols, Scottish History Society, 3rd ser., xlvi–xlvii, 1954–5).

[39] *In the Parliament Monday 4th November 1706, a Vote was Stated in thir Terms* (Edinburgh, 1706). The titles of the other published voting records were in the same form.

[40] John Bell, 'The Most Memorable Passages of the Life and Times of Mr J B, Written by Himself, 1706', ed. Jeffrey Stephen, in *Miscellany XIV* (Scottish History Society, 6th ser., iv, 2013), 139–228; *Addresses against Incorporating Union*, ed. Bowie, 295–334.

[41] NLS, Wod.Qu.XL, ff. 27–33; Karin Bowie, 'A 1706 Manifesto for an Armed Rising against Incorporating Union', *Scottish Historical Review*, xciv (2015), 237–67, at 247, n. 64.

Goodtrees.[42] Steuart of Goodtrees and his son (also Sir James) were members of parliament.[43] Robert Steuart's letters combined summaries of parliament's meetings – perhaps communicated to him by one of his uncles or his cousin – with predictions of the outcome of the session. Though it was expected that the Union would be approved, Steuart reported a rumour that members of the opposition would protest and secede from the chamber. Steuart also offered to supply Wodrow with pamphlets relating to the Union debates.[44]

Once in Edinburgh, Wodrow aimed to write to his father in Glasgow by every post. Professor Wodrow urged his son to '[con]tinou a narration of maters of fact … [tha]t we may know [wha]t to pray for'.[45] Robert also wrote to inform his ministerial colleagues in the presbytery of Paisley, who he anticipated would call on his father to read his letters.[46] The correspondence would serve as a record for the future. Wodrow had preserved selected outgoing letters since his early adulthood, and he recognised the significance of those he now wrote. He twice asked his father to 'keep all my letters till I come home'.[47] When Robert was about to leave for the west of Scotland in January 1707, James Wodrow encouraged him to 'engage some friend' in Edinburgh 'to write ane account of things to us after ye come away'.[48] Accordingly, Wodrow arranged to receive letters from John Maxwell, the correspondent with whom this article began.

Especially in his first weeks in Edinburgh, Wodrow produced copious and insightful commentary on debates in parliament. Two letters discussed parliament's approval on 12 November of an act providing security for the Church's Presbyterian government. This measure responded to the commission of the general assembly's fears for the future of Presbyterianism in the event of union. But the act was couched in general terms, leaving several of the commission's specific concerns unaddressed.[49] Wodrow narrated the main developments that were recorded in parliament's minutes for 12 November: the failure of an amendment to free Scots from the English sacramental test; a protest by John Hamilton, Lord Belhaven against the act as insufficient; the adherence to this protest of the dukes of Hamilton, Atholl and other members; the vote in favour of the act. But Wodrow added several important details. Not only did he specify the margin by which the amendment was defeated (28 votes),[50] but he mentioned that it was briefly suggested that Englishmen should be required to subscribe the Westminster confession of faith and accept Presbyterian government before holding office in Scotland. This would have served as a Scottish

---

[42] Alexander Grant, *The Story of the University of Edinburgh during its First Three Hundred Years* (2 vols, 1884), i, 262, 272, ii, 348–9.

[43] *Records of the Parliaments of Scotland to 1707*, ed. Brown et al., http://www.rps.ac.uk/, 1706/10/2 (accessed 10 Dec. 2020); *The Parliaments of Scotland: Burgh and Shire Commissioners*, ed. M.D. Young (2 vols, Edinburgh, 1992–3), ii, 667.

[44] NLS, Wod.Lett.Qu.IV, f. 81: Robert Steuart to Robert Wodrow, 21 Oct. 1706.

[45] NLS, Wod.Lett.Qu.IV, f. 153: James Wodrow to Robert Wodrow, 6 Nov. 1706.

[46] NLS, Wod.Lett.Qu.IV, f. 102: Robert Wodrow to James Wodrow, 2 Nov. 1706.

[47] *Early Letters of Robert Wodrow, 1698–1709*, ed. L.W. Sharp (Scottish History Society, 3rd ser., xxiv, 1937); NLS, Wod.Lett.Qu.IV, f. 100v: Robert Wodrow to James Wodrow, 1 Nov. 1706 (quotation); f. 102: same to same, 2 Nov. 1706.

[48] NLS, Wod.Lett.Qu.IV, f. 174: James Wodrow to Robert Wodrow, Dec. 1706/Jan. 1707.

[49] Alasdair Raffe, 'Petitioning in the Scottish Church Courts, 1638–1707', *Parliaments, Estates and Representation*, xxxviii (2018), 323–36, at 334–5.

[50] John Erskine, earl of Mar wrote that the court majority was 39: *HMC Mar and Kellie*, i, 318.

counterpart to the sacramental test, but the court was unwilling to accept such a measure. Whereas the duke of Hamilton's party, which included many Episcopalians and Jacobites, protested and voted against the Act of Security, Wodrow reported that the 'staunchest presbiterians' withdrew from the chamber, so as neither to vote for an inadequate act nor to appear opposed to the principle of security for the Church. Wodrow himself thought that the act was insufficient, and he continued to worry that the Union would undermine Scottish Presbyterianism.[51]

As his lengthy discussion of the Act of Security suggests, Wodrow was particularly attentive to religious dimensions of the debate about union. He sometimes admitted that he did not fully understand the treaty's economic provisions or his informants' reports about parliament's discussions of trade.[52] Like the newsletters probably by Robert Wylie, Wodrow's correspondence commented in detail on the commission of the general assembly, about which printed sources revealed little. In their letters, Wodrow and Wylie, who were both members of the commission, described its principal fault line – between a minority of supporters of union, and a majority with serious doubts. The latter group consisted largely of ministers, while the former was dominated by lay elders, many of whom also sat in parliament. These elders opposed the commission's petitioning parliament for measures to preserve Scottish Presbyterianism beyond those included in the proposed Act of Security. There was thus a significant struggle in the commission before the signing on 8 November of an address to parliament outlining several specific concerns about the Union. These included the complaint that the sacramental test barred conscientious Scottish Presbyterians from public office in the rest of Britain. The debate encapsulates the divergence between those Scots who prioritised settling the Protestant succession to the throne by means of the Union, and those who feared the consequences for the Church of any departure from the constitutional settlement of 1689–90. Many Presbyterians – Wodrow included – could not support a union that they saw as incompatible with the National Covenant (1638) and the Solemn League and Covenant (1643). The commission's reference to the Covenants – in the final clause of the address of 8 November – was strongly opposed by the leading elders.[53] By reporting on the commission's activities, Wodrow helped to reassure other Scots who shared his concerns that the highest church court then sitting had protested against the aspects of the Union that contradicted Presbyterian principles.

3

During the first four months of 1712, Wodrow and other Scottish Presbyterians closely followed the news of three bills then passing through the Westminster parliament. The

---

[51]NLS, Wod.Lett.Qu.IV, f. 110: Robert Wodrow to James Wodrow, 12 Nov. 1706; f. 107: same to same, 14 Nov. 1706 (quotation); *Minuts of the Proceedings in Parliament* (1706–7), no. 19, 12 Nov. 1706.

[52]NLS, Wod.Lett.Qu.IV, f. 116v: Robert Wodrow to James Wodrow, 23 Nov. 1706; f. 119: same to same, 28 Nov. 1706.

[53]NLS, Wod.Lett.Qu.IV, ff. 103–4: Robert Wodrow to James Wodrow, 5 Nov. 1706; f. 105: same to same, 7 Nov. 1706; f. 106, same to same, 9 Nov. 1706; NLS, Wod.Qu.XL, ff. 27–8: newsletters probably by Robert Wylie, 4 Nov., 11 Nov. 1706; NRS, CH1/3/8, pp. 271–6, Register of the Commission of the General Assembly, 7–8 Nov. 1706; *Addresses against Incorporating Union*, ed. Bowie, 48–50; Bell, 'The Most Memorable Passages', ed. Stephen, 191–3.

© *2022 The Author(s). Parliamentary History published by John Wiley & Sons Ltd. on behalf of Parliamentary History Yearbook Trust.*

Episcopalian Toleration Act, a statute reviving the Christmas vacation in the Scottish law courts, and the restoration of the right of lay patrons to present ministers to vacant Scottish parishes seemed to compromise the security for Presbyterianism that had been promised in 1706. At his manse in Eastwood, Wodrow relied on letters for accounts of the parliamentary progress of this alarming legislation.

In this period, Wodrow's main sources of scribal news were again correspondents in Glasgow and Edinburgh. The most important was John Cross (or Corse), a Glasgow merchant and probably the former bailie of that name.[54] From December 1711 to April 1712, he wrote to Wodrow at least once every four days. Wodrow received more occasional letters from Charles Morthland, professor of oriental languages at the University of Glasgow.[55] Cross and Morthland saw letters from Thomas Smith, Member for the Glasgow burghs, who corresponded regularly with his wife, the provost and other local magistrates in Glasgow, and sometimes with members of the university and the burgh's clergy. Though Cross supplied Wodrow with much information from Dyer's newsletter and printed newspapers, reports from Smith were his best source of parliamentary news. Cross frequently sent Smith's letters to Wodrow, but expected them to be returned.[56] Thus Wodrow copied Smith's news onto the letters he received from Cross.[57] Wodrow also acquired a small number of what appear to be professionally written newsletters from London.[58] Nevertheless, news about the parliamentary developments that concerned him most came from his personal contacts.

Wodrow's main correspondents in Edinburgh were similarly well informed, though it is less clear how they acquired information about parliament. Matthew Wood was minister of Old Greyfriars, Edinburgh, but a native of Glasgow, where he presumably came to know Wodrow.[59] Lieutenant-Colonel John Erskine of Carnock was a former provost of Stirling, a strict Presbyterian, opponent of the Union and an active ruling elder in the general assembly and its commission, including during the winter of 1706–7.[60] Knowing that Wodrow had other sources of news, letters from Wood and Erskine supplied private reports and Edinburgh gossip. 'I need not tell you whats publick … but you shall have whats talked',

[54] *Extracts from the Records of the Burgh of Glasgow, A.D. 1691–1717* (Scottish Burgh Records Society, 1908), 175, 278, 576; *Correspondence of Wodrow*, ed. M'Crie, i, 197.

[55] *Munimenta Alme Universitatis Glasguensis: Records of the University of Glasgow from its Foundation till 1727* (4 vols, Maitland Club, 1854), ii, 395–6.

[56] E.g., NLS, Wod.Lett.Qu.VI, f. 58: John Cross to Robert Wodrow, 29 Dec. 1711; f. 170: same to same, 25 Apr. 1712; *Correspondence of Wodrow*, ed. M'Crie, i, 252–3. At 252, the text's reference to 'J.S.' should read 'T.S.'. On Smith's career, see: *HPC 1690–1715*, s.v. Thomas Smith II (*d.* 1716), of Glasgow.

[57] E.g., NLS, Wod.Lett.Qu.VI, ff. 53–4: John Cross to Robert Wodrow, 24 Dec. 1711, with addition in Wodrow's hand dated London, 15 Dec. 1711. This is the letter referred to in *Correspondence of Wodrow*, ed. M'Crie, i, 252. Wodrow practised this habit over several years: David Hayton, 'Traces of Party Politics in Early Eighteenth-Century Scottish Elections', *Parl. Hist.*, xv (1996), 74–99, at 84, n. 44, 88, n. 61.

[58] NLS, Wod.Lett.Qu.VI, ff. 127, 128, 142–3, 154: newsletters, 1 Mar., 8 Mar., 22 Mar., 5 Apr. 1712.

[59] Hew Scott, *Fasti Ecclesiae Scoticanae: The Succession of Ministers in the Church of Scotland from the Reformation* (rev. edn., 8 vols, Edinburgh, 1915–50), i, 46, v, 109.

[60] *Journal of the Hon. John Erskine of Carnock, 1683–1687*, ed. Walter Macleod (Scottish History Society, 1st ser., xiv, 1893); *Addresses against Incorporating Union*, ed. Bowie, 66, 130, 166, 168; Bell, 'The Most Memorable Passages', ed. Stephen, 200. Erskine should not be confused with his first cousin once removed Lieutenant-Colonel John Erskine of Sand Haven, a supporter of the Union who sat in the Scottish parliament and in the house of commons until 1710: *HPC 1690–1715*, s.v. John Erskine (1660–1733), of Sand Haven, Culross, Fife.

wrote Erskine in January 1712.[61] 'I have no news at this time', admitted Wood, 'only I saw a letter from a p[er]son of good intelligence'.[62]

As well as including news of the peace congress at Utrecht and criticisms in parliament of the former commander-in-chief, the duke of Marlborough, Wodrow's letters in early 1712 provide a detailed narrative of the three bills' passage through parliament.[63] On 29 January, he received from the former bailie Robert Yuill an account, written by Thomas Smith, of parliamentary business on 21 January. That day, Sir Simeon Stewart, Member for Hampshire and part of the October Club of Tory backbenchers, moved for leave to bring in a bill for the toleration of Episcopalian services in Scotland using the English Book of Common Prayer. He was seconded by Sir Alexander Areskine, Member for Fifeshire. The Presbyterian Members John Pringle (Selkirkshire) and George Baillie (Berwickshire) objected, contending that such a measure would contradict the Claim of Right (1689) and the Act of Security. Stewart's motion passed in spite of these arguments. Gloomily, Smith wrote that 'if a motion be made by [tha]t party to over turn our Church establishment it would cary in [thi]s H[ouse] of C[ommons]'. Nevertheless, the ministers William Carstares, Thomas Blackwell and Robert Baillie were in London to represent the Church's concerns about the bill.[64]

Wodrow received a further account of the debate on 21 January from Wood. Wood's letter reported that Stewart, speaking in favour of Episcopalian toleration, had referred to a recent prosecution of an Episcopalian clergyman by the presbytery of Perth. This was probably the case of Henry Murray, whom the presbytery deposed from the ministry on 10 January for intruding on a parish settled with Presbyterian ministers and using the English Prayer Book. A summary of the presbytery's action was printed, helping to make the case for Episcopalian toleration.[65] Wood's letter went on to describe the bill's presentation to the Commons and its first reading. In response to a suggestion that Episcopalian ministers should swear allegiance to the queen, Wood claimed, the Episcopalian Member for Midlothian, George Lockhart of Carnwath, argued that Presbyterian ministers should have to renounce the Covenants and accept a royal ecclesiastical supremacy in Scotland. These measures would have been unacceptable to the Presbyterian clergy. A letter from Morthland questioned the veracity of this story, attributing it to Dyer.[66] In this case and others, Wodrow relied on his multiple sources of intelligence to sort fact from rumour. True or

[61] NLS, Wod.Lett.Qu.VI, f. 73: John Erskine to Robert Wodrow, 8 Jan. 171[2].

[62] NLS, Wod.Lett.Qu.VI, f. 151: Matthew Wood to Robert Wodrow, 10 Apr. 1712.

[63] For other discussions, see: Daniel Szechi, 'The Politics of "Persecution": Scots Episcopalian Toleration and the Harley Ministry, 1710–12', in *Persecution and Toleration*, ed. W.J. Sheils, *Studies in Church History*, xxi (Oxford, 1984), 275–87, at 283–5; Daniel Szechi, *George Lockhart of Carnwath, 1689–1727: A Study in Jacobitism* (East Linton, 2002), 94–7.

[64] NLS, Wod.Lett.Qu.VI, f. 93: Yuill to Wodrow, 29 Jan. 1712, with addition in Wodrow's hand dated London, 22 Jan. 1712; *CJ*, xvii, 33.

[65] NLS, Wod.Lett.Qu.VI, f. 94: Matthew Wood to Robert Wodrow, 31 Jan. 1712; *The Church of England still Persecuted or The Case of Mr. Murray, Depos'd by the Presbytry of Perth, on the 10th of January, for Reading the English Service* ([1712]); Ben Rogers, 'The House of Lords and Religious Toleration in Scotland: James Greenshields's Appeal, 1709–11', in *The Church and the Law*, ed. Rosamond McKitterick, Charlotte Methuen and Andrew Spicer, *Studies in Church History*, lvi (Cambridge, 2020), 320–37, at 335.

[66] NLS, Wod.Lett.Qu.VI, f. 94: Wood to Wodrow, 31 Jan. 1712; f. 99: Charles Morthland to Robert Wodrow, 2 Feb. 1712; *CJ*, xvii, 35.

not, the report was an early sign of the trouble that the Toleration Act would create for the Presbyterian clergy.

Wodrow learned of the bill's second reading in the Commons, on 25 January, in a letter from Smith, passed on by Cross.[67] Wood then reported that the three Presbyterian ministers in London were petitioning the queen, Lords and Commons against the bill, information he obtained from letters sent by the ministers to the moderator of the commission in Edinburgh.[68] By 11 February, the provost of Glasgow had received news of how Scottish Members voted at the bill's third reading. Erskine sent Wodrow a note of the voting record on the following day.[69] In the Lords, the bill was amended to require all Scottish ministers to swear an oath abjuring the Stuart pretender. Knowing that the Presbyterian clergy had expressed scruples about the abjuration oath in use in England, the Lords adjusted its text to make it more palatable. The amendment was an attempt to sabotage the bill, by ensuring that it would provide little benefit to the predominantly Jacobite Episcopalian clergy. Wood wrote that Carnwath and Areskine 'cursd & blasphemd' against the amendment, and the bishop of Edinburgh now urged Episcopalian parliamentarians to vote against the bill.[70] Unfortunately for the Presbyterians, however, the Commons restored the phrasing of the abjuration oath to which many ministers of the Kirk objected. The Lords then accepted the bill as amended by the Commons.[71] Wodrow heard that the October Club threatened to vote against new taxes unless the Commons' version of the bill was accepted.[72] The Episcopalian Toleration Act required Episcopalian ministers who sought protection and all the Presbyterian parish clergy to swear the abjuration oath.[73] As we shall see, this element of the legislation created serious divisions in the Church.

In mid March, Wodrow's correspondents wrote that bills to restore the Yule vacation and lay patronage were expected imminently.[74] Smith's reports of parliamentary business became briefer, perhaps because he expected the bills to pass without difficulty. He seemed demoralised by the momentum of the October Club and their Scottish allies, whom Cross characterised as 'a party of men in the hous [tha]t will stick at nothing [tha]t will give uneasiness to this Church'.[75] The fate of the commission of the general assembly's petition to the Lords against the Patronage Bill reflected the Presbyterians' weakness. Scrupulously refusing to acknowledge 'lords spiritual', the document was directed to 'the Peers of Great Britain, In Parliament Assembled'. This error of form prompted a complaint in the Lords, even though the commission's similarly addressed representation against the Toleration Bill

[67] NLS, Wod.Lett.Qu.VI, f. 97: John Cross to Robert Wodrow, with addition in Wodrow's hand dated London, 26 Jan. 1712; *CJ*, xvii, 38.

[68] NLS, Wod.Lett.Qu.VI, f. 101: Matthew Wood to Robert Wodrow, 8 Feb. 1712; *HMC Laing*, ii, 162.

[69] NLS, Wod.Lett.Qu.VI, f. 107: John Cross to Robert Wodrow, 11 Feb. 1712; ff. 108–9: John Erskine to Robert Wodrow, 12 Feb. 1712; *CJ*, xvii, 73.

[70] NLS, Wod.Lett.Qu.VI, f. 114: copy in Robert Wodrow's hand of letter by ?Thomas Smith, ? 15 Feb. 1712; f. 119: Matthew Wood to Robert Wodrow, c. 26 Feb. 1712 (quotation); *LJ*, xix, 379.

[71] *CJ*, xvii, 103–4, 113; *LJ*, xix, 384, 385; NLS, Wod.Lett.Qu.VI, f. 121: John Cross to Robert Wodrow, 28 Feb. 1712; f. 122: same to same, 3 Mar. 1712; f. 125: John Erskine to Robert Wodrow, 1 Mar. 1712.

[72] *Correspondence of Wodrow*, ed. M'Crie, i, 303; Wodrow, *Analecta*, ii, 28–9.

[73] 10 Ann. c. 7.

[74] NLS, Wod.Lett.Qu.VI, f. 129: John Cross to Robert Wodrow, 13 Mar. 1712; f. 131: John Erskine to Robert Wodrow, 14 Mar. 1712.

[75] NLS, Wod.Lett.Qu.VI, f. 136v: John Cross to Robert Wodrow, 22 Mar. 1712.

© 2022 The Author(s). Parliamentary History published by John Wiley & Sons Ltd. on behalf of Parliamentary History Yearbook Trust.

had been read without demur.[76] On 17 April, Wood reported that the Patronage Bill had passed in the Lords, with only four Scottish peers voting against.[77] The Yule Vacation Act, which was approved by both Houses on 12 April, placed no demands on ministers and ceased to be of much concern to Wodrow and his correspondents.[78] But the Patronage Act was a major blow to the Church's Presbyterian constitution, and the source of recurrent struggles for the next century and a half.[79]

In the spring, Scots awaited the reaction of the church courts to the three bills. As we noted earlier, observers relied especially on personal letters for news of these important bodies. In the absence of reliable reports, the church courts' business could be the subject of speculation and malicious rumours. When the synod of Glasgow and Ayr, meeting at Ayr in April 1712, called a fast day in terms critical of the perceived threats to the Church, some characterised its plain speaking as disloyalty. In Edinburgh, Erskine heard talk that the government would seek to prosecute members of the synod.[80] Wood was reassured when Wodrow sent him an eyewitness account of the synod, for its actions were 'sadly misrepresented here [i.e., in Edinburgh] by a letter frome some p[er]son in Glasgow'. Wood reciprocated by describing the next meeting of the synod of Lothian and Tweeddale.[81]

The most hotly anticipated response to the legislation was that of the general assembly, which met in Edinburgh on 1 May. Wodrow, who was present, described the assembly's proceedings in letters home to his wife, Margaret Warner, a practice he had begun in 1709 and would continue yearly until 1729. Debates in the assembly made clear that the most immediately problematic component of the recent legislation was the requirement that Presbyterian ministers swear the oath of abjuration. Lengthy conferences at the assembly considered various concerns about the oath, of which the most significant was the perception that, by swearing, ministers would endorse the Anglican conformity expected of successors to the throne, thus contradicting Presbyterian principles.[82] In March, when it became clear that the Toleration Act would impose the oath on Presbyterians, the commission of the general assembly had addressed Queen Anne, testifying the clergy's support for the Hanoverian succession, but warning that many ministers objected to the terms of the oath. Some members of the assembly thought that the commission's address had misinterpreted the oath, to suggest that it was compatible with Presbyterian values. As these

---

[76] *LJ*, xix, 422; NLS, Wod.Lett.Qu.VI, f. 101: Wood to Wodrow, 8 Feb. 1712; f. 157v: John Erskine to Robert Wodrow, 15 Apr. 1712; f. 162v: John Cross to Robert Wodrow, 19 Apr. 1712; *Correspondence of Wodrow*, ed. M'Crie, i, 307. The address was printed in *A Collection of Papers against the Scots Toleration and Patronages* (1712), second pagination sequence, 72–5. The three ministers amended the address and it was presented a second time: *LJ*, xix, 425.

[77] NLS, Wod.Lett.Qu.VI, f. 160: Matthew Wood to Robert Wodrow, 17 Apr. 1712; *LJ*, xix, 427.

[78] *LJ*, xix, 427; *CJ*, xvii, 184; 10 Ann. c. 13; NLS, Wod.Lett.Qu.VI, f. 148: Charles Morthland to Robert Wodrow, 5 Apr. 1712.

[79] 10 Ann. c. 12; L.A.B. Whitley, *A Great Grievance: Ecclesiastical Lay Patronage in Scotland until 1750* (Eugene, OR, 2013); Richard Sher and Alexander Murdoch, 'Patronage and Party in the Church of Scotland, 1750–1800', in *Church, Politics and Society: Scotland, 1408–1929*, ed. Norman Macdougall (Edinburgh, 1983), 197–220.

[80] NLS, Wod.Lett.Qu.VI, f. 158: Erskine to Wodrow, 15 Apr. 1712. See also: *Correspondence of Wodrow*, ed. M'Crie, i, 306. The synod's act was published, but probably arrived in Edinburgh after the rumours: *Act of the Provincial Synod of Glasgow and Air, for Keeping a Solemn Fast and Humiliation, on the 24th April, 1712* ([Glasgow, 1712]).

[81] NLS, Wod.Lett.Qu.VI, f. 160: Wood to Wodrow, 17 Apr. 1712; f. 167: same to same, 26 Apr. 1712.

[82] *Correspondence of Wodrow*, ed. M'Crie, i, 285, 288–9.

critics pointed out, only parliament, as the body imposing the oath, could authoritatively clarify its meaning. When the assembly came to approve the commission's actions regarding the oath, several members voted against and many more abstained, because of their scruples about the address.[83] A major split was avoided at the assembly. But it was clear that, as the deadline of 1 November for swearing approached, there would be a great controversy over the oath.[84] More than the competition of tolerated Episcopalian worship, divisions between Presbyterian jurors and non-jurors weakened the Church of Scotland for the rest of the decade.[85]

4

Like their English contemporaries, early 18th-century Scots who were fascinated by parliamentary developments relied on scribal sources of news. Robert Wodrow read about the Scottish and British parliaments in printed newspapers; he received accounts of Westminster's business deriving from professionally written newsletters. But he learned most about parliament by reading personal letters. Until 1707, Wodrow could ask his associates in Edinburgh to send him summaries of the Scottish parliament's deliberations. That he had access to eyewitness reports of proceedings in the Westminster parliament after the Union was a consequence of his friendships with important men in Glasgow, one of Scotland's leading burghs, to whose magistrates and councillors Thomas Smith was accountable. The letters of the minister Matthew Wood in Edinburgh suggest that he had similar connections, and prove that Wodrow was not unique among the clergy in seeing detailed parliamentary news. If Wodrow and Wood were unusually well-informed ministers, they nevertheless served as conduits of intelligence to clergymen in more remote locations. Further research would be required to establish whether Scotland's noblemen and lairds circulated news in similar ways.[86]

More than for some of his English contemporaries, then, for Wodrow, scribal news came freely from his friends, and was by no means fully commodified. Scotland lacked a widely distributed commercial newsletter comparable to John Dyer's, and Wodrow recognised the necessity of cultivating his correspondence with well-placed figures in Glasgow and Edinburgh. Another advantage of the personal letter was its capacity to filter and compare various sources of news. John Cross and others summarised Dyer's newsletter when it added to what was in the printed papers, but they prioritised Smith's reports whenever they were more accurate or complete. A further reason for Wodrow to rely on personal correspondence more than on newspapers or newsletters was his desire for reliable descriptions of the meetings of the church courts. Wodrow was a prolific reporter on the Kirk's general assembly, but he was not alone. His correspondents in other parts of Scotland sent him accounts

---

[83] *Collection of Papers*, second pagination sequence, 49–51; *The Principal Acts of the General Assembly of the Church of Scotland; Conveened at Edinburgh, the First Day of May 1712* (Edinburgh, 1712), 34–9; *Correspondence of Wodrow*, ed. M'Crie, i, 298–9.

[84] The deadline of 1 Aug. 1712 set by 10 Ann. c. 7 was extended to 1 Nov. by 10 Ann. c. 32.

[85] Raffe, *Culture of Controversy*, 90–1, 205–7; Alasdair Raffe, 'The Hanoverian Succession and the Fragmentation of Scottish Protestantism', in *Negotiating Toleration: Dissent and the Hanoverian Succession, 1714–1760*, ed. Nigel Aston and Benjamin Bankhurst (Oxford, 2019), 147–67.

[86] See the case study of the earl of Wigtown in Robin Eagles, 'Reporting Trials and Impeachments in the Reign of George I', in this volume.

of their synod and presbytery meetings, satisfying his demand for news of institutions that were not much discussed in print or newsletters. Finally, we can conclude that Wodrow's consumption of scribal news was part of his social life. Wodrow valued the sharing of news in personal letters and its tendency to reaffirm his social ties. Whatever the differences that future research might find between Wodrow's news-gathering practices and those of his contemporaries, epistolary sociability was surely at the heart of early 18th-century news culture.

Inscripting Rebellion: The Newdigate Manuscript Newsletters, Printed Newspapers and the Cultural Memory of the 1715 Rising[*]

LEITH DAVIS

In this essay, I bring a literary critic's perspective to the study of the continued use of manuscript newsletters in the 18th century. I suggest that by comparing and contrasting the treatment of political news in official manuscript newsletters and printed newspapers during a specific and limited time period in the early 18th century, the beginning of what became known as the 1715 Jacobite Rising, we can see in relief the different affordances of each medium, gain further information about what role scribal news played in conveying political information and understand why it eventually lost traction. Analysing the news coverage in the Newdigate manuscript newsletters and in five newspapers ranging across the political spectrum, I suggest that the 1715 Rising in fact presented an opportunity for newspapers to compete with manuscript newsletters' established authority as they conveyed news that was occurring in the locations of conflict in a more timely and thorough manner. At the same time, the affordances of the newspaper form also amplified the impression of the 1715 Rising as a disjointed and uncontrollable series of events. The essay concludes by examining the information management that took place in the printed histories produced in the aftermath of the conflict as they wove the newspaper reports together into narratives that minimised the danger that the events of 1715 had actually posed.

Keywords: manuscript newsletters; newspapers; media change; 1715 Rising; Jacobites; cultural memory

In his 2003 article in *Parliamentary History*, Alex Barber takes issue with the dominant historiographical narrative that suggests that 'the lapse of licensing in 1695 signalled the end of restraint' and that 'political elites, whilst at times sceptical of newspapers, largely embraced the new form and eschewed any form of systematic restraint'.[1] In contrast, he asserts, there were significant tensions in the relationship between parliamentarians and printed news so that 'parliamentarians, constituents and interested political observers, sought out snippets of information in handwritten letters and, most significantly, scribal news'.[2] In Barber's assessment, scribal news 'continued to be important well after 1695 and into the 18th century'.[3]

---

[*]An expanded version of this argument appears in *Mediating Cultural Memory in Britain and Ireland: From the 1688 Revolution to the 1745 Jacobite Rising* (forthcoming Cambridge University Press), ch. 4.

[1]A.W. Barber, ' "It Is Not Easy What to Say of our Condition, Much Less to Write It" ': The Continued Importance of Scribal News in the Early 18th Century', *Parl. Hist.*, xxxii (2013), 293–316 (p. 294).

[2]Barber, ' "It Is Not Easy What to Say of our Condition, Much Less to Write It" ', 296.

[3]Barber, ' "It Is Not Easy What to Say of our Condition, Much Less to Write It" ', 294.

Barber's argument about the continuity of manuscript newsletters in an era of printed news both reflects and is reflected in recent scholarship in the area of book history that reassesses the role of manuscript culture in general in 18th-century Britain. The work of Margaret Ezell, Rachael Scarborough King, David McKitterick and Betty Schellenberg, for example, rejects the model of media succession in which the 'new' medium of print displaced the 'old medium' of manuscript.[4] Instead, they acknowledge the continuing role of manuscript circulation even as the media landscape in Britain was moving to a point of print 'saturation' by the mid 18th century.[5] As Clifford Siskin and William Warner suggest, while print was coming to take 'center stage', it was doing so only within the context of an 'already existing media ecology of voice, sound, image, and manuscript writing'.[6] Key to this new perspective is an understanding of 18th-century media as a complex ecological system as well as an acknowledgment that particular media possess particular characteristics or, in the term taken from Ian Hutchby, 'affordances' which impacted their use, circulation and storage for later re-activation.[7]

In this essay, I bring a literary critic's perspective to the study of the continued use of manuscript newsletters in the 18th century, turning to the question of the 'affordances' of manuscript versus printed news. I suggest that by comparing and contrasting the treatment of political news in manuscript newsletters and printed newspapers during a specific and limited time period in the early 18th century, we can see in relief the different affordances of each medium and gain further information about what role scribal news played in conveying political information and about why it eventually lost traction.

The time period on which I focus is the beginning of what would become known as the 1715 Jacobite Rising, the most extensive conflict to occur within the British Isles since the 1688 Revolution, one which directly involved the citizens of all three kingdoms in actual and potential violence as well as raising the possibility of the reinstatement of a Catholic Stuart monarch.[8] Unlike the 1688 conflict, however, which was initiated by a foreign leader landing his troops on English soil and gaining support while marching to London, the actions that constituted the 1715 Rising were organised by diverse local leaders and took place at different times and in different locations within Britain.[9] If the temporal and spatial parameters of the crisis in 1715 were more complex than in 1688, so,

---

[4] Margaret Ezell, *Social Authorship and the Advent of Print* (Baltimore, MD, 1999); R.S. King, *Writing to the World: Letters and the Origins of Modern Print Genres* (Baltimore, MD, 2018); David McKitterick, *Print, Manuscript, and the Search for Order, 1450–1830* (Cambridge, 2003); B.A. Schellenberg, *Literary Coteries and the Making of Modern Print Culture, 1740–1790* (Cambridge, 2016).

[5] Multigraph Collective, *Interacting with Print: Elements of Reading in the Era of Print Saturation* (Chicago, 2018); *The Cambridge History of the Book in Britain: Vol. V, 1695–1830*, ed. M.F Suarez, S.J. and M.L Turner (Cambridge, 2010).

[6] Clifford Siskin and William Warner, *This is Enlightenment* (Chicago and London, 2010), 10.

[7] Ian Hutchby defines 'affordances' as 'functional and relational aspects which frame, while not determining, the possibilities for agentic action in relation to an object' ('Technologies, Texts and Affordances', *Sociology*, xxxv (2001), 444).

[8] Daniel Szechi, *1715: The Great Jacobite Rebellion* (New Haven, CT, 2006), 61. See also Éamonn Ó Ciardha, *Ireland and the Jacobite Cause, 1685–1766: A Fatal Attachment* (Dublin, 2002); Bruce Lenman, *The Jacobite Risings in Britain: 1689–1746* (1980); Frank McLynn, *The Jacobites* (1988); Murray Pittock, *Poetry and Jacobite Politics in Eighteenth-Century Britain and Ireland* (Cambridge, 1994); and *Loyalty and Identity: Jacobites at Home and Abroad*, ed. Paul Monod, Murray Pittock and Daniel Szechi (New York, 2010).

[9] Szechi, *1715*, 5.

similarly, were the media parameters. In 1688, there was one official newspaper, *The London Gazette*. The 1695 lapse of the Licensing Laws, however, led to an exponential expansion in printed periodical news, and the numbers of newspapers continued to grow in the early years of the 18th century.[10] During the eventful months of summer 1715, the newspapers in circulation included one daily and seven tri-weekly newspapers in London; at least 15 newspapers in the provinces; two newspapers in Scotland and one in Ireland.[11] The nation was hungry for information about the conflict, and there were multiple resources that were available to feed that hunger.

In the analysis that follows, I consider the unfolding of the news from the end of May to the end of September 1715 in five newspapers. The majority of examples that I use are drawn from *The Daily Courant*, the only daily paper at the time. As the *Daily Courant* was whig-leaning, I also include material from four other papers of different political persuasions: the *Post Man*, edited by John Fonvive, which was, according to Snyder, a 'non-partisan' journal; the *Post Boy* and *The Evening Post* which constituted the 'chief Tory organs'; as well as the whiggish *St James's Evening Post*, which was begun by Abel Boyer in June 1715.[12] I am less concerned with the specific political differences between the newspapers, however, and more focused on the ways in which the different affordances of the manuscript and printed forms of news affected perceptions about events in 1715 for particular audiences.

The newsletters that I examine are drawn from one of a small number of archives that contain a long-term run of manuscript newsletters beginning in the 17th and continuing into the early 18th century: the Newdigate family newsletters held at the Folger Library.[13] The Newdigate family manuscript newsletters were composed and copied out by a group of clerks in the secretary of states' offices at Whitehall and sent out to a limited number of individuals with whom the government wished to maintain connections. They were therefore what I call official manuscript newsletters rather than the commercial variety produced by men such as John Dyer and William Wye.[14] Like their commercial counterparts, official manuscript newsletters were 'confidential' documents, in Donald Reiman's classification, not 'intended for the eyes of a wide and diverse readership', but rather 'addressed to a specific group of individuals all of whom either [were] personally known to the writer or belong to some predefined group that the writer has reason to believe share communal values with him or her'.[15] The official manuscript newsletters sent out during the early

---

[10]Three thrice-weekly newspapers went into circulation within a year of the lapse. The 1712 Stamp Act caused some specific publications to cease production or to modify their price, form, or their frequency, but the genre continued to grow. See Michael Harris, *London Newspapers in the Age of Walpole: A Study of the Origins of the Modern English Press* (Rutherford, NJ, 1987); Michael Harris, 'London Newspapers', in *The Cambridge History of the Book in Britain: Vol. V, 1695–1830*, ed. M.F Suarez, S.J. and M.L. Turner (Cambridge, 2009), 413–33; Andrew Pettegree, *The Invention of News: How the World Came to Know About Itself* (New Haven, CT, 2014).

[11]See, Udo Fries, 'Newspapers from 1665–1765', in *News as Changing Texts: Corpora, Methodologies and Analysis*, ed. Roberta Facchinetti et al. (Newcastle upon Tyne, 2015), 57–8.

[12]See H.L. Snyder, 'The Circulation of Newspapers in the Reign of Queen Anne', *The Library*, ser. 5, xxiii (1968), 210–11. I derived my examples from the 17th- and 18th-century Burney Collection of Newspapers.

[13]Folger, MS L.c.1-3950.

[14]For more information on this genre, see Leith Davis, 'Mediating the "Sudden & Surprising Revolution": Official Manuscript Newsletters and the Glorious Revolution', in *After Print: Manuscript Studies and Eighteenth-Century Literature*, ed. R.S. King (Charlottesville, VA, 2020), 148–74. For more on William Wye see the chapter by Robin Eagles in this volume.

[15]Donald Reiman, *The Study of Modern Manuscripts: Public, Confidential and Private* (Baltimore, MD, 1993), 39.

stages of the 1715 Rising encouraged their readers to think about the events taking place as a narrative that they were experiencing together as a specific and limited elite community who were connected personally to government officials and received government-oriented news. As a genre designed to share political information and, in particular, news about the workings of parliament with this elite community, official manuscript newsletters were focused more on London and less on the active locations during the Rising. As the events constituting the 1715 progressed, this London-centred focus of the official newsletters made them consequently less valuable as sources of information about the developing domestic threat than newspapers. The 1715 Rising, then, provided an opportunity for the expanding newspaper press not only to attract new consumers from the less elite classes but also to increase their use value amongst more elite readers who purchased them.

In comparing the representation of news in newsletters and newspapers, I focus not only on the content of the news that is shared, but also on the material form of its representation. As Ronald Deibert suggests, citing Harold Innis, 'the medium is never neutral. How we organise and transmit our perceptions and knowledge about the world strongly affects the nature of those perceptions and the way we come to know the world'.[16] I suggest that the material representation of the news of the Rising on the pages of the newspapers amplified the senses of discontinuity and threat that were conveyed in both the newsletters and the newspapers. In the concluding section, I consider the way that printed works published shortly after the Rising focused on downplaying and containing the news as it was disseminated in the newspapers in order to retrospectively minimise the threat to the government. Newspapers consequently came to figure importantly in the shaping of what would become the cultural memory of the 1715 Rising.

1. *Gaps in the Story: Tracing the 1715 Rising in the Newdigate Manuscript Newsletters*

The first letters in the Newdigate archive were sent early in 1674 to Richard Newdigate (1602–78) of Arbury Hall, Warwickshire. Newdigate was a judge and serjeant-at-arms who served under Cromwell as well as Charles II, becoming a member of parliament briefly in 1660 and being granted a baronetcy in 1677. His son, Sir Richard Newdigate, 2nd bt. (1644–1710), an investor in innovative coal-mining technology, continued the practice of receiving the newsletters, as well as becoming an avid consumer of printed news.[17] The newsletters written during the summer of 1715 were sent to Sir Richard Newdigate, 3rd bt. (1668–1727) who had taken over the estate in 1710, the same year he was elected to parliament for Newark upon Trent, Nottinghamshire.[18]

The newsletters sent to the third baronet, like the newsletters sent to his father and grandfather, combine business, political and personal connections, often blurring the lines between the three. They maintain the sense of a formal exchange of letters that was typical

---

[16] R.J. Deibert, *Parchment, Printing, and Hypermedia: Communication and World Order* (New York, 1997), 8.

[17] See Elisabeth Chaghafi, 'The Newsy Baronet: How Richard Newdigate (Per)Used His Newsletters', The Collation: Research and Exploration at the Folger (2019), https://collation.folger.edu/2019/09/newsy-baronet/ (accessed 9 November 2020).

[18] See Richard Newdigate, *The Case of an Old Gentleman, Persecuted by His Own Son* (1707) and *An Alphabetical List of the Knights and Commissioners of Shires, Citizens and Burgesses, Elected in the Year 1710* (1711).

for the genre of manuscript news, beginning invariably with a stylized 'Sir' in the top left corner. As they were derived from information from a number of sources, the newsletters that travelled to the Newdigate family also served as vectors for other media, including other manuscript materials as well as printed works, as is indicated by occasional references to an enclosed 'gazette' as well as ink marks from a printed newspaper on the paper of several of the newsletters.[19] Individual newsletters frequently commence by acknowledging which foreign mails have arrived and what information has been gleaned from them. The newsletter for 19 July begins, for example: 'Last Night Arrived ye Maile due from H[o]ll[a]nd with ye foll[owing] News …'[20] Like other manuscript newsletters, the Newdigate manuscript newsletters employ expressions which signal the oral and scribal origins of the news being passed on. The 21 July newsletter relays information by indicating that 'There are Advices from [F]rance which *say*', for example, while other newsletters include phrases such as 'We *hear*' or 'It is *said*'.[21]

The manuscript newsletters in the Newdigate collection written in the summer of 1715 pay particular attention to identifying subversive activities. They pass on information obtained from domestic reports about 'ryots' and tumults in Manchester,[22] Kidderminster,[23] and Wolverhampton,[24] together with an account from Glasgow of the seizure of 'three Chests Laden wth Musquets, Bayonets, Swords and pistols said to belong to a Laird of a Highland Clan'.[25] A number of the newsletter writers' comments focus on cases of transgressions by and punishment of particular individuals. On 16 June 1715, for example, the writer indicates, 'We have an Acc[ou]nt. From Cambridge yt one Mr. Watson has been lately Expelled yt University for drinking ye Pretenders [sic] Health'.[26] As well as selecting accounts of events from provincial locations, the writers also offer information on items of concern within London. On 9 June, it is noted that 'a written paper' purporting to offer 'a declaration in favour of ye Pretender' was 'taken down & delivered by one of ye beedles to ye Justices of Peace for Westm[inste]r'.[27] On 16 June 1715, a 'ffrench Schoolmaster was whipt from Stocksmarket to Aldgate' for making disparaging remarks on the king, although the news writer also indicates that 'as soon as he was taken from ye Car abundance of people gave him money & others treated him w[i]th. Wine'.[28] Other individuals were apprehended by messengers for spreading seditious pamphlets. The newsletters represent a nation that is unsettled in its urban centres as well as in its remote regions, in its university towns as well as in the nation's capital.

While the clerks writing the newsletters provide details about the variety of questionable activities taking place within the nation, they also situate those activities within a narrative

[19] Chaghafi, 'The Newsy Baronet'.

[20] Folger, MS L.c.3921: newsletter to Richard Newdigate, 19 July 1715. Several letters, however, such as that sent on 20 Sept. 1715, begin with news of parliament, then announce the arrival of the foreign mails in the middle of the letter. Folger, MS L.c.3947: newsletter to Richard Newdigate, 20 Sept. 1715.

[21] My italics. Folger, MS L.c.3922: newsletter to Richard Newdigate, 21 July 1715.

[22] Folger, MS L.c.3909: newsletter to Richard Newdigate, 21 June 1715.

[23] Folger, MS L.c.3923: newsletter to Richard Newdigate, 23 July 1715.

[24] Folger, MS L.c.3915: newsletter to Richard Newdigate, 5 July 1715.

[25] Folger, MS L.c.3903: newsletter to Richard Newdigate, 7 June 1715.

[26] Folger, MS L.c.3907: newsletter to Richard Newdigate, 16 June 1715.

[27] Folger, MS L.c.3904: newsletter to Richard Newdigate, 9 June 1715.

[28] Folger, MS L.c.3907: newsletter to Richard Newdigate, 16 June 1715.

comprised of other information, including details from the foreign mails about the Great Northern War and the Ottoman–Venetian War. In addition, writers note the activities at the court of James Stuart, son of James II and VII, at Bar-le-Duc, including the comings and goings of visitors to the court. On 21 July, the writer notes, 'There are Advices from ffrance which say that the Lord Bolingbrook is come to Paris and that the Pretender was there and had frequent Conferrences with that Lord and that an Attempt would shortly be made on Great Brittain - It is further said that the Pretender has given that Lord a sham Garter -'.[29] Nine days later, however, the writer indicates the contradictory information that has been received: 'Some advices say yt ye Pretender is still at Paris and frequently sees ye L[or]d. Bolingbrook & others will have it yt he is gone back discontented to Bar Le Duc'.[30] Also contradictory is the news regarding the ill health of the French king that began to circulate at the end of August. News of Louis XIV's eventual death is at first denied in 'letters from France' then obtained in a circular manner, first by means of letters from merchants,[31] then conveyed in an express from France, then, on 25 August, confirmed by an express from the English ambassador to France, the earl of Stair, who sent 'an Acco[un]tt. yt ye ffrench King did not dye till Sunday last at 10 a Clock in ye Morning'.[32] Rather than expressing relief about the king's death dashing the hopes of the Jacobites for French aid, the writer, in a rare speculative comment, suggests that the nation of France will be unsettled, and indicates continuing suspicion of the new regent of France and his power. Such details in the manuscript newsletters put the Jacobite opposition to the Hanoverian government in Britain into a wider global perspective.

Considerable space in the Newdigate newsletters is also taken up with details about the bills being read and voted on in the house of commons and house of lords, a number of which are directly related to the disturbances conveyed by the newsletters. On 2 July, for example, four days after an indication about 'Rioters at Manchester',[33] the writer indicates that a 'Bill […] to suppress all Ryots & Tumults' is brought before the house of commons.[34] Three weeks later, a 'bill to impower the king to set aside ye Habeas Corpus Act' is approved to 'be in force to ye 24th of Jan. next'.[35] One particular narrative thread running throughout the newsletters' parliamentary accounts during the summer of 1715 concerns the charges against the earl of Oxford and Viscount Bolingbroke for 'High Treason & other High Crimes & Misdemeanors'.[36] The writer of the newsletter suggests the contentiousness of this issue as he includes information regarding the voting about whether to adjourn and postpone consideration of the report.[37] The newsletters also focus on the ongoing activity of the house of commons, the work of settling the elections which, frequently postponed by other pressing issues, is usually conveyed in the last line of the newsletters.

[29] Folger, MS L.c.3922: newsletter to Richard Newdigate, 21 July 1715.

[30] Folger, MS L.c.3926: newsletter to Richard Newdigate, 30 July 1715.

[31] Folger, MS L.c.3935: newsletter to Richard Newdigate, 20 Aug. 1715.

[32] Folger, MS L.c.3937: newsletter to Richard Newdigate, 25 Aug. 1715.

[33] Folger, MS L.c.3912: newsletter to Richard Newdigate, 28 June 1715.

[34] Folger, MS L.c.3914: newsletter to Richard Newdigate, 2 July 1715.

[35] Folger, MS L.c.3923: newsletter to Richard Newdigate, 23 July 1715.

[36] Folger, MS L.c.3905: newsletter to Richard Newdigate, 11 June 1715.

[37] See also the articles by Robin Eagles and Charles Littleton in this volume.

By the end of August, however, the focus of the newsletters sent to Richard Newdigate changes. Instead of devoting attention to detailing the crimes of specific disaffected individuals, the newsletters switch to providing information about the government's response to the Jacobite threats, including the mustering of troops in the camp at Hyde Park. In the midst of the reporting on events in London, the newsletter writers do attempt to find out about and transfer information about the activities of the Jacobites. But the reports that arrive are sporadic and are passed on in a discontinuous manner. On 25 August, for example, the writer indicates that 'Letters from Scotland bring advice that the Earl of Marr is in that Kingdom and that 3 Scotch Lords and one Commoner (viz) Mr. Lockhart Author of the Memoires of Scotland are confined in the Castle of Edinburgh on suspition of being in the Interest of the Pretender'.[38] More letters apparently arrived between the initial writing and the posting of the newsletter, and consequently the writer adds the more recent news further down the page: 'this day came in Letters from Scotland w[i]th an Acc[oun]tt. yt ye Highlanders attempt to take possession of ye Castle of Drummond, but were obliged to retire –'.[39] In addition to arriving irregularly, the reports are often contradictory, as is suggested by the newsletter writer's remarks on 30 August, correcting information he had provided previously: 'Last Tuesday it was Reported yt a Camp was forming in ye Highlands of Scotland in favour of ye Pretender, but ye Letters which came in yesterday from thence bring no acc[oun]tt. of it'.[40]

As the crisis deepened and concerns mounted, the newsletters came to rely more frequently on 'express' letters, those which were not sent by regular post but instead were sent by special messenger. On 22 September, for example, the newsletter writer indicates that 'yesterday arrived an Express from Scotland that the Highlanders have received reinforcements and have taken the town of Perth [...] and afterwards Entred the Town and Imprisoned the Magistrates and Appointed others in the Name of the Pretender'.[41] Information provided about this incident, however, is minimal, and no further details about the taking of Perth are forthcoming in later newsletters. Instead of trying to provide such information, the writer focuses instead on parliament's actions in regard to the alleged rebel leaders in England, noting that 'A motion was made in the House of Lords to secure Severall Lords and Commons'.[42] He confirms that 'the Lords Landsdown and Duplin' were 'taken into Custody Yesterday' and that 'Warrants for several others are out'.[43] Notably, however, the specific names of the other two lords concerned are blacked out. The writer does list the names of all the commoners in question, however, as well as the constituencies that they represent: 'S[i]r. W[illia]m Windham Knight of the Shire for Somerset, S[i]r John Packington, Knight of the Shire for Worcester, Edward Harvey of Combe Esqr. Member for Clithero[e] in Lancashire, Corbet Kynaston Esq[ui]r[e], Member for the Town of Shrewsbury, John Anstis Esq[ui]r[e] Member for Lancaston [sic][44] in Cornwall and

[38] Folger, MS L.c.3937: newsletter to Richard Newdigate, 25 Aug. 1715.

[39] Folger, MS L.c.3937: newsletter to Richard Newdigate, 25 Aug. 1715.

[40] Folger, MS L.c.3939: newsletter to Richard Newdigate, 30 Aug. 1715.

[41] Folger, MS L.c.3948: newsletter to Richard Newdigate, 22 Sept. 1715.

[42] Folger, MS L.c.3948: newsletter to Richard Newdigate, 22 Sept. 1715.

[43] Folger, MS L.c.3948: newsletter to Richard Newdigate, 22 Sept. 1715.

[44] Launceston.

Thomas [F]orster Esq[ui]r[e] Junn[ior]. Member for Northumberland –'.[45] The information contained in the newsletter makes it clear just how diffuse the English Jacobite resistance was, but it also provides minimal details about specific events in the actual locations of conflict.

Official manuscript newsletters such as those sent to the Newdigate family played a crucial role in communicating political London-based information to a specific elite segment of the population during the time of the Rising. They also implicitly affirmed their addressees' networked connections with each other as privileged readers of the same national narrative provided by the government. Nevertheless, by concentrating primarily on events in London, the official newsletters made their readers very aware that they were only receiving part of the story, and not the most active part at that. Consumers of official newsletters, like those of newspapers at this time, were used to a certain level of disorder in the communication of information and were arguably used to correcting for what Tony Claydon calls the gaps and numerous 'updates and expansions of stories' in the reception of information.[46] But as the events that would later be collectively viewed as the Jacobite Rising of 1715 unfolded in the remote parts of the nation, both the temporal and spatial gaps in the manuscript newsletters' conveyance of news took on more serious implications than ever before. Newspapers, as we will see, were able and eager to try to fill in some of those gaps.

2. *Fitting to Print: Newspapers and the Discontinuities of Form*

Like manuscript newsletters, newspapers represented themselves as multi-modal vectors of communication, conveying information derived from oral sources, letters and other newspapers. Also like their manuscript counterparts, the newspapers published in the summer of 1715 frequently signalled the oral origin of the news they conveyed with phrases such as 'we hear', and they identified material derived from manuscript forms by employing such phrases as 'Letters from Edinburg' [sic], 'They write from Newcastle', or 'From Edinburgh … it is advised'.[47] Information is relayed under headings that indicate not only the location from which it is derived but also the specific date when it was sent. In conveying this information, newspapers frequently employ the same kind of temporally relational language as found in the newsletters, referring to 'last night' or 'instant'. At times, this provision of information about the origin of the reports results in a dizzying layering of remediations. Under the heading '*London,* September 1', for example, the 1 September 1715 edition of the *Daily Courant* indicates that the news in question was originally conveyed in letters from '*Venice*, August 23', then printed in the *Amsterdam Courant* before being reprinted in its current form. Like the manuscript newsletters,

---

[45] Folger, MS L.c.3948: newsletter to Richard Newdigate, 22 Sept. 1715.

[46] Tony Claydon, 'Daily News and the Construction of Time in Late Stuart England, 1695–1714', *Journal of British Studies*, lii (2013), 55–78 (p. 63). According to Claydon, 'There could not be one present narrative, but rather there was a shattered series of events, inevitably reported out of their true order' (66).

[47] As King suggests, newspapers at this early stage adopted many conventions of manuscript newsletters in order to represent themselves as authoritative sources of news for a population more likely to credit the written than the printed word, 'The Manuscript Newsletter and the Rise of the Newspaper, 1665–1715', *HLQ*, lxxix (2016), 1–28.

the newspapers in 1715 represented themselves as part of the world of traditionally conveyed information.[48]

Importantly, however, newspapers, being considerably less expensive, were designed for a wider readership than the manuscript newsletters. True, elite readers like Newdigate consumed newspapers, but newspapers were also designed for those in the 'middling ranks' of society who were concerned with business and trade,[49] and, in addition, because there were so many varieties of newspapers which were readily available in public places such as coffeehouses, newspapers were also consumed by a significant number in the lower ranks.[50] Whereas the manuscript newsletters circulated between an exclusive readership who often knew and communicated with one another by other means, newspapers were one-way systems of communication for a wider and anonymous body of readers.[51]

The newspapers published in the summer and early autumn of 1715 provided this wider network of readers with details about the escalating crisis, starting with increasing acts of opposition during the early summer months. While describing in great detail the celebrations of George I's birthday on 28 May, the *Flying Post* of 11–14 June, for example, also includes a letter from London describing the actions of the Jacobite faction: 'witness their making a Bonfire; and ringing the Bells in White-Chappel [sic], and the strolling about of several Scoundrels, with Cockades in their Hats, on what they call the Pretender's Birthday'.[52] The newspapers also note occasions of drinking of toasts. The *St James's Evening Post* for 15–17 August 1715 gives notice that 'On Wednesday last, one William Way was committed to Newgate, for speaking certain Words reflecting on the King and Government; as was the next Day James Osborn, on the Oath of two Persons, for drinking the Pretender's Health, by the Name of *James the Third*'.[53]

The official manuscript newsletters, as productions of the secretary of state's office, had government support behind them. Newspapers however, needed to be wary of incurring government disapproval. While the changing censorship laws had opened up the option of printing news without obtaining prior government approval, authors and printers could still be prosecuted for conveying opposition to the government. The newspapers give an indication of the frequency of prosecutions of editors and publishers at the time. In early August, for example, the printer Edward Berrington and the publisher John Morphew of the *Evening Post* were 'taken into Custody … for printing a pamphlet' which 'reflect[ed] on King & Parliament'.[54] While the manuscript newsletters were at liberty to list anti-government behaviour without comment, newspapers attempted to contain or qualify any information regarding the growing crisis such information might convey. The *Daily Courant* for 5 July, for example, includes a letter dated 2 July from Manchester that refers to the recent riots: 'Several Justices of the Peace having received particular Orders from his Majesty to

[48] *Daily Courant*, 1 Sept. 1715.

[49] Harris, *London Newspapers in the Age of Walpole*, 41.

[50] Harris, *London Newspapers in the Age of Walpole*, 192–3.

[51] Harris suggests that there were approximately 'a quarter of a million' readers and users of newspapers around this time period (*London Newspapers*, 423).

[52] *Flying Post*, 11–14 June 1715.

[53] *St James's Evening Post*, 25–17 Aug. 1715.

[54] Folger, MS L.c.3914: newsletter to Richard Newdigate, 2 July 1715. See also Alexander Andrews, *The History of British Journalism from the Foundation of the Newspaper Press in England to the Repeal of the Stamp Act in 1855, with Sketches of Press Celebrities* (2 vols, 1859).

inquire into the late Riots in and about this Town, came hither on the 29th past, and Sit frequently to take Examinations'.[55] The writer is reassuring, however, concluding that, 'From the time that Major Wivill [Wyvill] with two Troops of Dragoons arrived here, we have not had the least Disturbance, and still continue in perfect Quiet'.[56] On 15 June, the *Daily Courant* published a statement from the vice-chancellor of Oxford University condemning a recent riot in their midst. The statement describes how a 'Multitude of Persons, who assembled together' wandered 'from one Part of the City to the other, breaking of Windows, rifling of Meeting-Houses, and committing other Outrages'.[57] The vice-chancellor is quick to note that the rioters were 'to Us unknown'.[58] The fact that this declaration is the first item appearing in the paper indicates its importance in the eyes of the editor as an indication of loyalty.

Although newspapers needed to be cautious about focusing too much on dissent, readers could infer growing cause for concern in other ways. Information that was included in the newspapers about the steps the government was taking in order to contain unrest, for example, offered insight into situations otherwise not discussed. On 28 July, the *Daily Courant* indicated the publication the day earlier of 'his Majesty's Royal Proclamation for suppressing Riots and Rebellious Tumults'.[59] The language of the proclamation itself describes the subversive activities that have been taking place:

> some of the meanest of the People have of late been Stirred up to Riots and Tumults to the disturbance of the Publick Peace, and are now carried into open Rebellion and levying War against the King and his Authority; they having with an armed Force in many distant Places, proceeded to pull down, burn, and destroy, the Houses and Buildings of peaceable Subjects, declared for the Pretender, and actually resisted with force of Arms such as by lawful Authority were endeavouring to disperse them.[60]

The reference to 'open Rebellion and levying War against the King' offers readers a glimpse into the escalating national threat.

Indications of the seriousness of the crisis that was brewing were also provided by the addresses of loyalty that began appearing in the newspapers at the end of July. These addresses assert the loyalty of specific towns, cities and organisations and portray confidence in the government's ability to quell any conflict. The king's replies to these addresses, which were also printed in the newspapers, further asserted the bond between monarch and subjects. Nevertheless, the addresses also raised the fears they sought to quell. The 'humble Address' of '*the Lord-Lieutenant and* [...] *the Deputy-Lieutenants and Justices of the Peace of the County of Middlesex*', printed in the 26–30 July edition of the *London Gazette*, for example, asserts 'our firm and unshaken Adherence to your Majesty and your Royal Family', but also draws attention to 'Seditious and Rebellious Tumults, raised and fomented in several Parts of this Kingdom by the Enemies to your Majesty's Person and Government, encouraged by the

[55] *Daily Courant*, 5 July 1715.
[56] *Daily Courant*, 5 July 1715.
[57] *Daily Courant*, 15 June 1715.
[58] *Daily Courant*, 15 June 1715.
[59] *Daily Courant*, 28 July 1715.
[60] *Daily Courant*, 28 July 1715.

Hopes of an Invasion from Abroad in favour of a Popish Pretender'.[61] As the addresses assuring the king of the loyalty of his subjects continued to pour in, it became apparent just how much of a threat to the nation actually existed.

With the deepening crisis, the newspapers, too, had difficulty obtaining accurate news about the conflict. Like the manuscript newsletters, the newspapers contained 'numerous updates and expansions of stories' which Tony Claydon discusses, reporting initially on information and then reporting about it again with more details or corrections later. In the 15 September edition of the *Daily Courant*, for example, the arrival of an express from Edinburgh is noted: 'Yesterday about Noon … with the News that a Party of about 80 Rebels had attempted to Surprize the Castle in the Night time by Scaling-Ladders, and that three of them were entred before the thing was discovered'.[62] Four days later, the event is reported again with further details, including details of the 'Design' of the attackers, which was 'to mount the Wall on the West Side of the Castle by Rope-Ladders provided for that purpose, which were to be pulled up by Lines let down from within by some Soldiers belonging to the Garrison who had been corrupted'.[63] The account indicates that 'the Government having had some Intimation of this Design, had ordered part of the Town-Guards and some Gentlemen Volunteers to Patroll on the West Side of the Castle: and the Officers within to double their Guards and to make diligent Rounds'.[64] This same edition of the *Daily Courant* also contains information that had just arrived from Dundee and Perth about the raising of the Pretender's standard there on 6 September, eight days before the attempt on Edinburgh castle.[65]

Although they represented the same kinds of temporal lapses, the newspapers were able to give readers more information about events occurring in the sites of action and provide more extensive coverage than the manuscript newsletters. In reporting on the Jacobites' seizure of Perth and the decision made in London to arrest a number of Jacobite leaders in England on 20 September, for example, the newspapers offered a more expanded perspective on events north of the border. The manuscript newsletter sent to Richard Newdigate on 22 September had provided details about the arrests, including the names and constituencies of the non-nobility who were arrested, but had included little information about the capture of Perth. In contrast, newspapers offered a condensed version of the arrests, but considerably more information about events at Perth. The *Daily Courant* for 22 September, for example, noted that 'We hear, that Yesterday two Lords were taken into Custody and a Warrant out against a third: And that by Order of the House of Commons, Sir W. Windham, and five more Members of that House, will be also taken into Custody'.[66] The issue also provides a full account regarding the events in the north:

> By Express from Scotland there is Advice, that the Rebels having received their Reinforcements, passed the River Tay and had seized the Town of Perth, before the Lord Rothes with his Vassals to whom the Duke of Argyle (who arrived at Edinburgh the

[61] *London Gazette,* 26–30 July 1715.
[62] *Daily Courant,* 15 Sept. 1715.
[63] *Daily Courant,* 19 Sept. 1715.
[64] *Daily Courant,* 19 Sept. 1715.
[65] See Claydon, 'Daily News'.
[66] *Daily Courant,* 22 Sept. 1715.

15th) had given Arms, could arrive there. Some Highlanders, as ordinary Passengers, came by one or two at a time, and loitering at the Gate, found an Opportunity to seize the Guard of Townsmen whom the Magistrates had placed there, and immediately a Body of 100 Horse appeared and enter'd the Town, where they imprisoned the Magistrates and created others in the Name of the Pretender. The Lord Marr has taken the Title of Lieutenant-General of the Troops of the Pretended King James.[67]

As this example suggests, although the newsletters trumped newspapers in their ability to provide details about court, city and foreign news, newspapers were able to convey to their readers more information regarding the conflict that was unfolding in numerous locations around the country. Indeed, as the crisis deepened, newspapers began to expand their coverage of the Jacobite fronts, sometimes reprinting entire letters from eyewitnesses. Ian Atherton suggests that 'Manuscript was the more important form of written news' right up until the early 18th century: 'it was more plentiful than printed news; it was more accurate, less censored, and regarded as more authoritative.'[68] But in 1715, newspapers were able to offer more 'timely, accurate and authoritative news' than their manuscript counterparts.[69] It was the newspapers that more readily satisfied readers' desires to find out details of the rapidly changing situations in the centres of conflict throughout Britain.

But the newspapers also shaped that news in distinct ways due to their physical layout and their material form. As domestic news, reports on the Jacobite Rising were presented on the back page alongside advertisements for goods and services designed for a nation that was experiencing a consumer revolution. Although the papers might feature addresses to the king on the first page, or occasionally, news about the conflict itself when an important battle had taken place, for the most part, readers got their information about the ongoing crisis in their nation on the same page to which they turned in order to find out about the latest opportunities for commerce or entertainment. Moreover, advertisements were taking up proportionately more space on those back pages of newspapers in relation to news. In the case of the *Daily Courant,* for example, the advertisements often occupied the entire last page; the 19 and 21 November editions of the *Daily Courant,* for example, feature only advertisements on the last page, despite the recent battle at Sheriffmuir on 13 November. The inclusion of news about the unfolding events on the same page as the advertisements had the effect of making the news seem even more discontinuous.

These advertisements both responded to and encouraged readers' interest in the conflict by featuring items that frequently had a thematic connection to the news reports. Maps were popular items in the newspaper advertisements of 1715. The 9 November issue of the *Daily Courant* indicates that the following item has been 'Lately Published': 'Mr. Moll's Map of Scotland, in two Sheets, with considerable Improvements, and many Remarks not Extant in any Map, according to the Newest and Exact Observations. Printed for D. Midwinter at the 3 Crowns in St. Paul's Church-Yard'.[70] Other advertisements worked in a closer dynamic relationship to the news items. The *Post Man* for 22–24 September,

---

[67] *Daily Courant*, 22 Sept. 1715.

[68] Ian Atherton, 'The Itch Grown a Disease: Manuscript Transmission of News in the Seventeenth Century', *Prose Studies*, xxi (1998), 39–65 (p. 40).

[69] King, 'Manuscript Newsletter', 2.

[70] *Daily Courant*, 9 Nov. 1715.

for example, features news from London about the 'Rebel' leaders taken into custody and news from Edinburgh about the 'necessary Precautions' the government is undertaking 'for defeating the designs of the Rebels' who have now 'proclaim'd the Pretender at Dundee and Inverness'.[71] Included in the 'Advertisements' sections on the same page is a notice about a work that promised to put events into context for readers: 'This Day is published, The Political State of Great Britain, &c. For the Month of August 1715 ... Printed for J. Baker at the Black Boy in Paternoster Row. Price 1 s.[72]

But in the case of newspapers in 1715, the vast majority of advertisements had no thematic connection with the news stories that preceded them, and because there were so many advertisements, the impact was to increase the general sense of disorientation. In the 17 November edition of the *Daily Courant,* information about the capture of Jacobites at Preston subsequent to the inconclusive battle at Sheriffmuir is squeezed into the upper left corner of the last page. The items on the rest of the page invite readers to engage with issues other than news. Theatrical advertisements encourage them to attend either the tragedy of *Timon of Athens* at Drury Lane or the comedy of *The Devil of a Wife* at Lincoln's Inn Fields. Notices regarding the letting of either 'large House and Garden ... furnished or unfurnished' and a 'Dye house ... with or without all the Utensils' and the purchase of a 'Convenient Tavern, with good Vaults' offer them opportunities for mobility. Lost items are also brought to readers' attention, including a 'Kerry-stone seal fix'd in gold' and a 'Pocket-Book with Green Vellum Cover'. Items for sale featured in this issue include 'Fifty Hogsheads of Tobacco, Sweet-scented', 'Peter's Famous Bill and Cordial Tincture', and several books such as *Clerk's Writing Improv'd* and *An Essay on the Theory of Painting* by Mr Richardson.

Joad Raymond comments in general on the way that newspapers' juxtaposition of 'unrelated items ... required the reader to recognize and synthesize diversity'.[73] In the case of the newspapers during the 1715 Rising, the juxtaposition of news regarding the Rising with the large number of goods and services advertised in the papers amplified the sense of discontinuity surrounding the events taking place. While readers might vary in the particulars of their individual acts of synthesis, they were nevertheless united in their experience of being distracted by the diversity of material that they were reading. Making things even more complex for readers was the sheer number of printed newspapers circulating at the time, often operating in competition with each other. Within the pages of the daily, tri-weekly, and weekly papers, news items were reprinted and circulated, often using the same language. The notice about the details of the Jacobite attempt on Edinburgh Castle published in the *Daily Courant* on 15 September, for example, was also repeated virtually verbatim in the *London Courant* of 13–17 September, the *Post Man* of 17–20 September, and *The Weekly Packet* for 17–24 September.[74] By replicating those items of news in multiple periodical locations, newspapers fostered a sense of the news as a constant circulation of disconnected units of information.

[71] *Post Man*, 22–24 Sept. 1715.

[72] *Post Man*, 22–24 Sept. 1715.

[73] Joad Raymond, 'The Newspaper, Public Opinion, and the Public Sphere in the Seventeenth Century', *Prose Studies*, xxi (1998), 109–40 (p. 132).

[74] The *Flying Post* also published an account which employs similar language, although the editor makes some adjustments. 'Care and Vigilance' becomes just 'Care'; names of the individual officers who thwarted the plan are supplied.

For readers both of manuscript newsletters and newspapers trying to keep up to date with the national conflict, then, the events of the 1715 Rising unfolded in a disturbing manner. Manuscript newsletters did not provide accurate and timely coverage of events in the north. Newspapers, for their part, conveyed the news of the Rising as a series of consumable, portable items circulating between print venues. Rather than helping to contain the crisis by giving information 'a precise location in space and in time' and providing 'a bogus closure in a developing reality', as early printed periodicals had done according to C. John Sommerville, newspapers in 1715 presented events as dispersed and discontinuous.[75] In its initial inscription on the pages of the manuscript newsletters and the newspapers, the 1715 Jacobite Rising was spread out before the reading citizens of Britain either as missing data or as endlessly circulating units of information. Although the newsletters and the majority of newspapers generally conveyed messages of loyalty, the forms in which those messages were represented suggested that the Rising was neither contained nor easily containable. Subsequently, in the aftermath of the rising, it was the containment of the newspaper coverage of the events of the Rising that became of particular consequence.

3. *The Information Management of the 1715 Rising*

The project of public information management of the events of 1715 took place through other works of print culture published during and shortly after the Rising. These works adopted different tactics in response to representation of the threat to the nation, targeting the newspapers' ongoing accounts of events in particular. Employing another new print genre of the time, the periodical essay, Richard Steele in *The Town Talk* and Joseph Addison in *The Free-Holder* make clear that their work is intended to serve as an antidote to the presentation of events in the newspapers. In Issue Number 7 (Friday, 27 January 1716) of *The Town Talk*, for example, Steele refers to 'all the prepense [sic] impertinencies' which are 'premeditate[d]' by 'authors of daily or weekly papers, who do not only gravely sit down, and take pen, ink, and paper, to communicate our crudities to our private friends, but also make the press labour to spread our errors among the rest of the people'.[76] Steele's narrator comments on the way in which news was constantly changing and was as likely to be 'muffled up' and inaccessible as to be understandable. Importantly, he also suggests a solution to the problems associated with reading news in newspapers: the reading of a different kind of 'paper', which, 'if attended to, cannot but, at the same time that it is an entertainment, be very serviceable to the public'.[77] That paper, he indicates, is *The Free-Holder* which 'comes out in the midst of the confusion and animosity, which are fomented by pamphlets and other loose papers, like a man of sense in a multitude, whose appearance among them suppresses their noise, and gains him an authority to be heard with attention for their common service'.[78] Steele is not only praising his friend Addison's work here, he is also articulating the goal of both their projects, as *The Town Talk* and *The Free-Holder* were

[75] C.J. Sommerville, *The News Revolution in England: Cultural Dynamics of Daily Information* (Oxford, 1996), 11.

[76] Richard Steele, *The Town Talk, the Fish Pool, the Plebian, the Old Whig, the Spinster, &c.* (1790), 79.

[77] Steele, *Town Talk*, 80.

[78] Steele, *Town Talk*, 79–80.

designed by their authors as sources of authority in contrast to the 'noise' of pamphlets and other 'loose papers' and the discontinuities of newspapers.

Other printed works at the time also attacked the genre of the newspaper, focusing in particular on its periodicity as an element preventing a true understanding of events, at the same time as they reworked the mobile and shifting units of information found in the newsletters and newspapers into a longer and focused narrative arc that suggested the inevitable containment of the rebellion. In 1716, for example, the Company of the Sun-Fire Office drew attention to its efforts to provide a long view on recent events, announcing that it was changing from printing the weekly *British Mercury* to producing a quarterly publication, *The Historical Register. Containing an Impartial Relation of All Transactions, Foreign and Domestick.*[79] The editors noted, 'News-Papers and Lies are become almost synonymous Terms'.[80] In order to provide 'an authentick Account of Affairs' and to avoid 'unsaying' what has already been printed, the editors indicate that they consider it necessary not only to publish less frequently, but also to dispense with the customary phrases used by the newspapers.[81] Phrases such as '*'Tis reported, 'Tis believ'd, Tis not doubted, We hear,* and the like', they suggest, only serve to introduce a 'Train of groundless Conjectures, and airy Speculations'.[82] Notably, these are exactly the expressions which newspapers, following the lead of manuscript newsletters, had used to assert their own authority. By omitting these expressions from their publication, the editors suggest a shift in the authority of news away from oral and manuscript sources.

The goal of providing an 'authentick Account of Affairs' connected with the events of 1715 also inspired the publication of four self-styled histories that appeared in print immediately after the suppression of the Rising: the anonymous *A Compleat History of the Late Rebellion* (1716), *A Faithful Register of the Late Rebellion* (1718), *The History of the Late Rebellion* by Robert Patten (1717) and *The History of the Late Rebellion* by Peter Rae (1718). All four of these histories incorporated newspaper reports into their historical record of recent events. *A Faithful Register of the Late Rebellion,* for example, includes newspaper accounts as well as the *Impeachments, Trials, Attainders, Executions, Speeches, Papers, &c. of All Who Have Suffered for the Cause of the Pretender in Great Britain* in an attempt to construct what the author suggests will be 'a lasting Monument' to the Rising.[83] Aware of the fact that his history contains passages similar to some in Patten's *History*, Peter Rae remarks generally that both accounts included 'many Things, which we had all collected from the publick Papers'.[84] While the newsletters and newspapers represented the conflicts with Jacobites which occurred in various locations at different times as separate events, however, these histories attempted to knit the separate threads of Jacobite activity at each site into a narrative of a single Rising.

---

[79] Sun-Fire Company, *The Historical Register, Containing an Impartial Relation of All Transactions, Foreign and Domestick* (1717), i.

[80] *Historical Register*, ii–iii.

[81] *Historical Register*, iii.

[82] *Historical Register*, i.

[83] *A Faithful Register of the Late Rebellion: Or, An Impartial Account of the Impeachments, Trials, Attainders, Executions, Speeches, Papers, &c. of All Who Have Suffered for the Cause of the Pretender in Great Britain* (1718), iv.

[84] Peter Rae, 'Preface', in *The History of the Late Rebellion* (1718) n.p.

The text of *A Compleat History* consists of reprinted accounts from the newspaper reports woven together virtually verbatim, although the traces that link the information to the oral and manuscript media through which it was originally conveyed have been removed. The newspaper account of the attack on Edinburgh Castle published in the *Daily Courant* for 19 September 1715, for example, indicates that 'Letters from Edinburgh of Sept 10 bring an Account of a Conspiracy being formed to surprise the Castle on the 8th between 11 and 12 at Night; which was happily prevented by the Care and Vigilance of the Government there'.[85] *A Compleat History* includes the same account, but it removes the references to the letters that were the source of the information: 'Besides the Measures concerted among the Chiefs of the *Highland-Clans*, a Conspiracy was form'd at *Edinburgh,* to surprize the Castle there, on the 8th of September between 11 and 12 at Night; which by the Care and Vigilance of the Lord Justice *Clerk,* who had early Notice of it, was happily prevented'.[86] The rest of the long account is identical in both texts. *A Compleat History,* in other words, extracts advices that the newspapers derived from letters and repositions the information as objective information, not as a communication event. Moreover, whereas the newsletters and the newspapers presented information as it was received, creating, as we have seen, a disjointed series of individual daily news items (that appeared even more disjointed in the newspapers by the fact that they competed with advertisements on the last pages of the newspapers), *A Compleat History* provides connections between the disparate pieces of information, linking them in time and space in a narrative arc of the rise, progress and suppression of the 'Rebellion'. *A Compleat History* essentially creates 'History' by 'un-mediating' information from the newsletter and newspaper reports in which it had originally appeared.

4. Conclusion

In his article 'The Print Culture of Parliament, 1600–1800', Jason Peacey suggests that the investigation of 'the ways in which print impacted upon practical political life and political processes' is an area in which 'the interests of parliamentary historians intersect with those of scholars of print culture'.[87] In this examination, I have extended Peacey's focus on print culture to include a consideration of print's relationship to manuscript culture in the early 18th century. I have suggested that understanding the contemporary affordances of the manuscript newsletter and the printed newspaper as well as the way in which each has fared over the long term tells us much not just about the political culture of the time, but also about how the cultural memory of that political culture has been shaped by its representation within a shifting media ecology.

The 1715 Rising was initially inscribed within both manuscript and print news genres then 'reiterated' and 'adapted to new circumstances' – and to new genres – in the years following the Rising.[88] As I have suggested, the 1715 Rising in fact presented an opportunity for newspapers to compete with manuscript newsletters' established authority as they conveyed news that was occurring in the locations of conflict in a more timely and thorough

---

[85] *Daily Courant*, 19 Sept. 1715.
[86] *A Compleat History of the Late Rebellion* (1716), 22.
[87] Jason Peacey, 'The Print Culture of Parliament, 1600–1800', *Parl. Hist.*, xxvi, part 1 (2007), 2.
[88] Ann Rigney, *The Afterlives of Walter Scott: Memory on the Move* (Oxford, 2012), 19.

manner. At the same time, the affordances of the newspaper form also amplified the impression of the 1715 Rising as a disjointed and uncontrollable series of events. Newspapers made information more widely available to a wider and more diverse audience, providing storage for that information for use in the later construction of the cultural memory of the '15. In *1715: The Great Jacobite Rebellion*, Daniel Szechi argues that the 1715 Rising has been consistently perceived as a 'damp squib' in relation to the other 'major attempts by the Jacobites to resist or overthrow the "Glorious Revolution" '.[89] My research suggests that the attempt to downplay the threat of the 1715 began with the printed histories that were produced in the aftermath of the conflict as they wove the units of information from newspaper reports together into accounts that ultimately minimised the danger that the events of 1715 had actually posed.

[89]Szechi, *1715*, 1–2.

Reporting Trials and Impeachments in the Reign of George I: The Evidence of the Wigtown and Wye Newsletters[*]

ROBIN EAGLES

This article will examine how two newsletter collections reported the impeachments of the former ministers of Queen Anne in 1715, the trial of the earl of Oxford in 1717 and that of Francis Atterbury, bishop of Rochester in 1723. It will also consider how the two collections relate to one another and touch on the way the newsletters' reporting of proceedings across parliamentary business during the reign of George I compares with that presented in the printed press. It will thus attempt to offer insights into why people continued to subscribe to manuscript news services in a period where print had traditionally been seen to be rapidly overtaking the older, more intensive news form.

Keywords: newsletter; parliament; trials; impeachments

On 10 January 1733 the duke of Newcastle was sent a copy of one of William Wye's newsletters by an official at the general post office, who advised that it was 'not fit to be sent around the country'.[1] This was not the first time Wye had come to the notice of the authorities. *The Historical Register* for 1728 recorded how in the spring of that year Edward Cave, future publisher of the *Gentleman's Magazine*, had been called before the Commons and examined at the bar about sending information relating to the House's proceedings to Robert Raikes, printer of the *Gloucester Journal*.[2] Cave admitted sending Raikes various 'written news-letters' and named the various sources as William Wye, John Stanley, John Willys and Elias Delpeuch.[3] The House resolved that Cave had infringed the Commons' privileges and ordered him into custody of the serjeant at arms; it was also resolved that the named news providers Wye, Stanley, Willys and Delpeuch, should also attend at the bar on 2 April.[4] Having done so, they were all ordered into custody. On the 5th Raikes

---

[*] The collections on which this piece is based were studied while I was the holder of a David Walker Memorial Fellowship in Early Modern History at the Bodleian Library. I am grateful to everyone at the Bodleian for facilitating my access to these collections and to members of the Senior Common Room at Lincoln College, Oxford, for their hospitality. I am also grateful to the staff of General Register House, Edinburgh, for facilitating access to the collections held by the National Records of Scotland.

[1] TNA, SP36/29/9: E. Carteret to duke of Newcastle, 10 Jan. 1733.

[2] Edward Cave had commenced his own newsletter in about 1725, which was similar in format to John Dyer's. Andrew Sparrow, *Obscure Scribblers: A History of Parliamentary Journalism* (2003), 11.

[3] This would appear to be the only occasion Delpeuch, who had first come to England as a Huguenot refugee, featured in the House's journals under such circumstances. When he died in the 1730s he left a will describing himself merely as a 'gentleman' from St Martin's in Middlesex. TNA, PROB 11/680.

[4] For more on Cave see Sparrow, *Obscure Scribblers*, 11–12.

appeared before the Commons, where he was reprimanded on his knees by the Speaker before being discharged.[5] The remaining prisoners petitioned for their release on the 8th, each expressing 'hearty sorrow' for the offence and 'promising a future good behaviour'.[6]

Wye was clearly not disheartened by his experience and persisted in his activities. As late as 1741 his newsletter was being cited by the *Norwich Gazette* as that paper's source for particular information.[7] Neither was he the only purveyor of manuscript news to come to the attention of the ministry or parliament.[8] As such he was just one of several providers of news, whose activities were of concern to the authorities, many of them continuing the work begun by John Dyer in the 1690s.[9]

The parallels between the careers of Dyer, Wye and the other purveyors of manuscript newsletters are striking and say much about the relationship between parliament and information management, and the continuing prominence of the handwritten newsletter in circulating information in the first half of the 18th century.[10] They also demonstrate (as Rachael Scarborough King notes in her piece in this volume) that the continuing success of the manuscript newsletter was not necessarily solely down to issues of privacy, since purveyors of handwritten news were just as susceptible to investigation by the authorities as the producers of printed newspapers.[11]

In spite of his lengthy career, Wye has not been much noticed by historians.[12] Such a lack of interest is the more surprising given his prominence in the world of newsletter writing in the period, and his evident entrepreneurialism. His operation may not have been quite as

---

[5] Both Raikes and Stanley appear to have come to the attention of the House only the previous month, again over inserts in the *Gloucester Journal*. On that occasion, Raikes, suffering from poor health, had insisted he was ignorant of the insertion, asserting that it had been done by Robert Gythens or his assistant. The House had questioned Gythens (or Giddins), clerk of the Bristol roads, and John Stanley, and the latter confessed to being the author. See Alexander Andrews, *The History of British Journalism from the Foundation of the Newspaper Press in England, to the Repeal of the Stamp Act in 1855, with Sketches of Press Celebrities* (2 vols, 1859), i, 206.

[6] *CJ*, xxi, 108, 115, 119.

[7] *Norwich Gazette*, 13–20 June 1741. For more on the extent of Wye's influence, see Jeremy Black, 'The House of Lords and British Foreign Policy, 1720–48', in *A Pillar of the Constitution: The House of Lords in British Politics, 1640–1784*, ed. Clyve Jones (1989), 118.

[8] In 1747 Edward Cave was again brought before the House and ordered into Black Rod's custody for printing accounts of Lord Lovat's trial in the *Gentleman's Magazine*. He appeared at the bar of the Lords on 1 May, where he was reprimanded. *LJ*, xxvii, 109. Abel Boyer was another perennial offender. In 1711 he was fined by the Lords for breaching privilege, but, like Wye, continued to produce a variety of news media. Sparrow, *Obscure Scribblers*, 10–11.

[9] According to Mark Knights, Dyer's output 'appealed particularly to bigoted Tory country parsons and fox-hunting squires', Mark Knights, *Representation and Misrepresentation in Later Stuart Britain: Partisanship and Political Culture* (Oxford, 2005), 227n. For more on Dyer, see H.L. Snyder, 'Newsletters in England, 1689–1715, with Special Reference to John Dyer –A Byway in the History of England', in *Newsletters to Newspapers: Eighteenth-Century Journalism*, ed. D.H. Bond and W.R. McLeod (Morgantown, WV, 1977), 3, 5, 7–9.

[10] For more on this see Alex Barber, ' "It Is Not Easy What to Say of our Condition, Much Less to Write It": The Continued Importance of Scribal News in the Early 18th Century', *Parl. Hist.*, xxxii (2013), 293–316.

[11] Some newspapers took pleasure in reporting the travails of rival producers. Thus in July 1715, one paper reported how 'Mr Berrington, Printer of the Evening Post, surrender'd himself to the Serjeant at Arms... for printing a Libel said to be a letter from R. Walpole Esq; to the Earl of Sunderland', *Weekly Journal with Fresh Advices Foreign and Domestick*, 16 July 1715.

[12] An exception is Jeremy Black, who has noted that in the 1730s Wye's printed paper was 'the most influential newsletter' relied on by the provincial press as a source for parliamentary news, though Wye did not include reporting of Commons' proceedings, which were perhaps harder to come by. Jeremy Black, *Parliament and Foreign Policy in the Eighteenth Century* (Cambridge, 2004), 149.

extensive as that of Dyer, but there is evidence that his was more than a one-man business and he employed a team of copyists to produce the letters sent out to his clients.[13] His work was often cited in the local press as their source for national news and, strikingly, by the 1730s he was producing both a printed newsletter and a manuscript newsletter.[14] His willingness to provide a service in both media also tells much about the way in which manuscript news continued to flourish hand-in-hand with printed newspapers well into the 18th century.[15]

This article will consider what might be thought of as a golden age of reporting the inner workings of Westminster following the death of Dyer in 1713, by comparing the reporting of the early years of George I in two collections in the Bodleian Library: one a set of Wye letters covering the early 1720s,[16] the other an even less noticed set conveyed to a Jacobite Scots peer, John Fleming, 6th earl of Wigtown between 1715 and 1725.[17] It will concentrate on two important events covered by these collections: the trial of Queen Anne's former chief minister, Robert Harley, earl of Oxford, in 1717 as reported in the Wigtown letters; and second that of the suspected Jacobite plotter, Francis Atterbury, bishop of Rochester, in 1723 as reported in both the Wigtown and Wye collections. By doing so, it will seek to do two things. First, it will consider why such manuscript newsletters continued to be used, whether on their own, or in combination with other sorts of news media. Second, it will consider the nature of the two collections themselves, the information contained in each issue, and the extent to which they may have drawn on common sources to assemble their respective offerings.

1

Wigtown had succeeded to the peerage aged about eight in 1681 and at some point prior to the Revolution of 1688 he had been despatched to France with his younger brother, Charles. An adherent of the exiled Stuarts, he had spent time at St Germain in the early 1690s before returning to his family estates. From the late summer of 1691 he had been under pressure to return home but refused, citing his relations' refusal to allow him the 'wherwithal to doe my exercises'.[18] By the mid 1690s some sort of resolution had clearly

---

[13] For example, in one newsletter of 22 Oct. 1722 the hands clearly change mid-way through, suggesting one scribe handing over to another: Bodl., MS Rawlinson C. 151, ff. 7–8.

[14] Wye's move into print while maintaining his manuscript new services further emphasises the argument made by Rachael Scarborough King that 'the newsletter and newspaper flourished together in the epoch of the early state post as the rhythm of postal delivery became the characteristic trait of periodical publication'. R.S. King, 'The Manuscript Newsletter and the Rise of the Newspaper, 1665–1715', *HLQ*, lxxix (2016), 414. It is also interesting when considered in the light of Daniel Defoe's earlier ventures, who, as Alan Downie has pointed out, proposed changing the *Review* into a manuscript newsletter in 1712. Alan Downie, *Robert Harley and the Press: Propaganda and Public Opinion in the Age of Swift and Defoe* (Cambridge, 1979), 70.

[15] Wye's experience was at odds with that of the author of the London *News-Letter*, who had been forced to cease circulating a handwritten newsletter and turned to print to retain his customers. Knights, *Representation and Misrepresentation*, 228.

[16] Newsletters sent by William Wye to various recipients, Bodl., MS Rawl. C. 151. The collection comprises 120 letters, the first two directed to Lord Lansdown, in Paris, and the remaining 118 to a Mr Dorvall, a merchant, also resident in France.

[17] Newsletters sent from London to John Fleming, 6th earl of Wigtown, Bodl., MS Eng. hist. c. 1039–1042.

[18] NRS, GD24/1/1075A: Wigtown to 'My Lord', 7 Sept. 1691.

been reached and he was certainly back in Scotland by 1697 when he engaged in correspondence with a distant kinsman, Placid Fleming, abbot of the Scots monastery at Ratisbon.[19] The Union reminded him of his former loyalties, and his Jacobite identity was no doubt reinforced by his second marriage to one of the daughters of the 8th Earl Marischal. His third marriage to Euphemia Lockhart then further consolidated his reputation as a Jacobite sympathiser.[20] In 1713 he appears to have been considered as a candidate for a pension, no doubt to try to bind him to the ministry,[21] but the following year he was one of the earl of Mar's allies in seeking to have the Anglo-Scottish Union overturned.[22]

It is quite clear from his personal correspondence, that Wigtown valued being kept informed. In May 1711 he wrote to Harry Maule of the imminent ending of the parliamentary session at Westminster:

> I had by last post a letter from Kilsyth who says this session of parliament draws now very near a close and that it was expected to rise gainst Saturday nixt and that dayly it was expected Mr Harley should be made E. of Oxford and Ld high Threasurer after which all the change that were to be made in england would be declared as likewais there would be several made amongst the places of this nation and so far as he could get any certainty he would not faill to acquaint me…[23]

The collection which bears his name emphasises still further how important a regular supply of news must have been to him. It covers a vital period in the early years of Hanoverian Britain, which also proved a dramatic period for Wigtown himself. In 1715 he was arrested and imprisoned on suspicion of Jacobite activities around the time of the rebellion, so it is to be assumed that for some of the time the newsletters were being despatched to him he was under guard. The flow of letters continued throughout the period of his incarceration, and as he continued to subscribe until at least 1725 when the run ends, he clearly found the service valuable.

Wigtown's movements during the late summer of 1715 are slightly uncertain. On 23 August he was one of two Scots earls mentioned in a letter by secretary of state, Viscount Townshend, who were to be arrested.[24] A month later at least one newspaper reported that he was one of a number of Scots grandees called on by the authorities to surrender, who had failed to do so.[25] By this time, however, he was clearly already under guard as the bishop of Edinburgh noted him at the beginning of September among those Scots notables who were in prison in Edinburgh.[26] This did not prevent later confusions, such as the report in a paper of 3 December listing him among those Scots nobles taken prisoner at Preston.[27]

---

[19] NRS, GD45/14/323/2: Placid Fleming to Wigtown, 8/18 Apr. 1697.

[20] *Letters of George Lockhart of Carnwarth 1698–1732*, ed. Daniel Szechi (Scottish History Society, 5th ser. ii, 1989), xvi.

[21] *HMC Portland*, v, 314.

[22] Daniel Szechi, *1715: The Great Jacobite Rebellion* (New Haven, CT, 2006), 41.

[23] NRS, GD45/14/323/7: [Wigtown] to Harry Maule, 30 May 1711, Cumbernauld.

[24] TNA, SP55/3/91.

[25] *Weekly Packet*, 17–24 Sept. 1715.

[26] NRS, CH12/12/1835: Alexander, bishop of Edinburgh to [?], [1] Sept. 1715.

[27] *Weekly Journal with Fresh Advices Foreign and Domestick*, 3 Dec. 1715.

After his period of incarceration, Wigtown appears to have kept his head down. He appeared fleetingly in a letter to the earl of Dundonald from a contact in Edinburgh in the spring of 1719,[28] and was noticed in the press in 1726 as lieutenant-colonel of the company of archers (and the winner of that year's silver arrow).[29] He ultimately accepted a minor official role following the accession of George II and died, conveniently enough, in 1744: a year before Charles Edward Stuart's rebellion threatened his repose and may have forced him to declare his hand to either side.

The 'Wigtown newsletter' on which he relied for over a decade, was a more limited, or at least a more focused, production than the kind of letters produced by Dyer or Wye. It comprised a single sheet, occasionally made up of just one side of text, offering a concentrated compendium of the key events of the moment, with in-depth reporting of a few themes per issue. Most of the letters are dated from London, though one of them bears a heading of Edinburgh.[30] The author's (or authors') identity is unknown, but it seems unlikely that it was compiled by one of the better-known news providers of the period such as George Dormer, who continued to work in the same vein as Dyer, and whose work was also regurgitated in the printed press. How many were produced and how much they cost Wigtown is also matter for speculation.[31]

Like many newsletters of the period, the information in the reports sent to Wigtown followed a reliable format with international news compiled from a variety of 'foreign mailings' posted first, followed by domestic political information. Occasionally, the bulletin might be rounded off by minor social tittle-tattle. During the period when parliament was not sitting, foreign news predominated; when parliament was in progress, the balance of reporting altered accordingly. As will be argued below, the later issues of the 1720s bear close resemblance to what was available in Wye's newsletters of a similar date.

2

Along with the progress of the 1715 rebellion,[32] reporting the proceedings against the former ministers of Queen Anne dominated the newsletters' coverage in 1715 and again in 1717 when the much-delayed trial of the earl of Oxford finally came on. The handwritten news service relied on by Wigtown was sometimes able to improve on what was available in the printed press, though it was by no means the only source of news available for those wishing to follow the course of Oxford's impeachment and trial.[33] Some papers, though,

---

[28] *HMC Portland*, v, 578–9.

[29] *Daily Post*, 19 July 1726.

[30] It seems likely that this letter is not from the same source as the remaining issues in the collection. As well as the different place of origin, it was composed by a different hand and follows a different format. Bodl., MS Eng. hist. c. 1039, f. 3.

[31] It is unlikely that this was produced on the same scale as a Dyer newsletter, which involved numerous scribes and despatched hundreds of copies. Prices also seem to have varied according to quality. Brian Cowan has pointed out that Ephraim Allen informed a Lords committee that he paid the owner of a coffee shop 18 pence for information, while another news provider called Hancock charged his clients between £4 and £6 p.a.. Brian Cowan, *The Social Life of Coffee: The Emergence of the British Coffeehouse* (New Haven, CT, 2005), 173, 214.

[32] For more on the 1715 Rebellion see Leith Davis's article in this volume.

[33] For example, the *Evening Post* of 29 Nov.–1 Dec. 1715 carried an advertisement for the recently published *Whole proceedings against Robert Earl of Oxford*.

were shy of offering too detailed an account of what was transpiring in Westminster. For example, when the articles of impeachment against Oxford were debated in parliament and clearly widely distributed outside of Westminster, one printed newspaper made much of its refusal to publish the information and thus to abide by the secrecy demanded by parliament:

> The six additional Articles of Impeachment against the Earl of Oxford, are handed about; but it solely and wholly belonging to the House of Commons, to publish them when they shall think fit, we shall not venture to incur their Displeasure by a Breach of Privilege, in making them see the Light.[34]

The author of the 'Wigtown newsletter' had no such compunction about not only sending his reader the articles in detail, but commenting on which ones were considered the most significant.

At the heart of the coverage was Robert Harley, earl of Oxford.[35] He had occupied the position of lord high treasurer from 1710 until just a few weeks before the queen's death in the summer of 1714.[36] Cast aside by the dying queen, Oxford saw his prospects further threatened by the accession of George I. In 1715 parliament moved to impeach him and some of the other key ministers involved with negotiating the Peace of Utrecht.[37] Oxford was committed to the Tower, where he was made to wait for almost two years before parliament finally moved to proceed against him in Westminster Hall.

The newsletters conveyed to Wigtown recorded much of the detail of the way in which the former ministers of Queen Anne were targeted and some of the inner workings of the proceedings against them. Two of Oxford's former colleagues, James, duke of Ormond, and Henry St John, Viscount Bolingbroke, were dealt with first, with the case against Ormond coming before parliament in June 1715.[38] Ormond's case centred on his role as commander of the British forces in the closing years of the War of the Spanish Succession, after Marlborough had been turned out, and his role in sharing information with his enemy opposite numbers. As the newsletter reported:

> Mr Secretary Stanhope moved for Impeaching the [aforesaid] Duke chiefly for his having acted by the orders of the marq[ui]s de Torcy and Ma[rsha]ll Villars discovering to the Enemy the Secret of the Confederate Generals and sending the said ma[rsha]ll a particular account of what number of forces marched with him at the tyme of the

[34] *Weekly Packet*, 30 July–6 Aug. 1715.

[35] The first letter in the collection, lacking a date owing to a damaged top but clearly from some point in the summer of 1715, concludes with the information: 'The E. of Oxford is closer confyned'. Bodl., MS Eng. hist. c. 1039, f. 1.

[36] For one of the best accounts of the Oxford ministry see Geoffrey Holmes, *British Politics in the Age of Anne* (rev. edn, 1987), passim.

[37] In June 1715 Jonathan Swift commented on the anticipated proceedings against Oxford and the others: 'They say the Whigs do not intend to cut of[f] Lord Oxford's head but that they will certainly attaint poor Ld Bolingbroke'. *Correspondence of Jonathan Swift DD*, ed. David Woolley (4 vols, Frankfurt, 2001), ii, 130.

[38] According to the newsletter, the Commons debated the issue of Ormond's impeachment during a marathon sitting of 11 hours. A subsequent effort to impeach the earl of Strafford lasted nine hours. Bodl., MS Eng. hist. c. 1039, f. 6.

separation of the British forces from those of the confederates, and [thereby] giving the Enemy aid and comfort[39]

The formal proceedings against Bolingbroke were delayed until August, but on 6 August the Commons finally sent up the articles they had agreed on to the Lords for their consideration. Like Ormond, Bolingbroke was accused of having exceeded his instructions (in his case in diplomatic terms) and having fraternised with the enemy. Both men were suspected, quite fairly as it turned out, of having sympathies with the exiled Jacobite dynasty and of working to thwart the succession of the Hanoverians. On receipt of the charges against him, the Lords made out the usual order for Bolingbroke to be taken into custody, delegating the matter to Black Rod. By then, Bolingbroke had been resident in France for several months, so several peers were heard exiting the House jovially wishing Black Rod a pleasant voyage.[40] The following month, with neither Ormond nor Bolingbroke answering the calls for them to appear, the Lords ordered nem. con. that both Ormond and Bolingbroke should be stripped of their titles. As the newsletter sent to Wigtown relayed it, both men were:

> razed out of the list of peers and degraded according to the usual form in law by which the first [Ormond] is now styled James Butler yeoman and the latter Henry St John labourer

Ormond's disgrace did not end at being downgraded in society to below the rank of a gentleman; his coat of arms displayed in St George's chapel, Windsor, was also ordered to be removed from its place and smashed to pieces.[41]

Following on from the impeachment of Ormond, the house of commons turned their attention back to Oxford. An experienced and formidable propagandist in his own right, on the eve of the proceedings against him Oxford had been engaged in a print war with various pamphleteers, who were intent on depicting him in the worst possible light. As one newspaper reported:

> Whereas for some months since a Pamphlet entituled, The Secret History of the White Staff; and lately another Pamphlet entituled, An Account of the conduct of Robert Earl of Oxford, have been Printed and Published: These are therefore to inform the Publick, that neither of the said Pamphlets have been written by the said Earl, or with his knowledge, or by his Direction or Encouragement; but on the contrary he has Reason to believe from several passages therein contained, that it was the intention of the Author or Authors to do him a Prejudice… [4 July 1715][42]

Oxford's efforts made no difference to the inevitable production of articles of impeachment against him. Initially comprising 16 articles, of which two amounted to treason and the remainder to the lesser charge of high crimes and misdemeanours, a further six were later

---

[39]Bodl., MS Eng. hist. c. 1039, f. 6.
[40]Bodl., MS Eng. hist. c 1039, ff. 22, 23.
[41]Bodl., MS Eng. hist. c 1039, f. 29.
[42]*Post Man and the Historical Account*, 2–5 July 1715.

added to make a grand total of 22 articles complaining of Oxford's proceedings as head of the ministry.[43]

The articles brought against Oxford were printed, and it seems reasonable to assume widely distributed through coffee shops and taverns. However, parliament remained protective of the details of debate within the chambers, and this is where manuscript news reporting was perhaps able to offer additional insights to what was commonly available. The newsletter of 9 July provided in-depth reporting of the events of the day before in the Commons reporting on some of the personalities involved and the procedure followed by the lower house in its proceedings against Oxford:

> The Commons yesterday read the 2nd time the articles of Impeachment against Robert Earl of Oxford after which Mr Walpole took the chair and the house in a committee went through them and ordered them to be engrossed… There were three divisions on the following questions but the party for his lordship were overpowered in number in every one of them…

The newsletter then went on to record the size of the relative divisions: on the question whether the charge against Oxford amounted to high crimes and misdemeanours: yeas 180, noes 125; whether they amounted to high treason: yeas 248, noes 131; and finally whether the word 'traitor' should stand as part of the impeachment: yeas 247, noes 126.[44] It also offered an insight into just how hard fought this all was, noting that the debates lasted from 11 in the morning until midnight. Oxford was provided with a chair to sit on while the impeachment articles were read out as they took an hour to go through, and the clerks were left sitting up all night writing them out in time for their third reading next day.[45]

Time was a recurring feature of the newsletters. Later on in the proceedings, when the Commons' articles had been presented to the Lords, the compiler was forced to excuse himself to his audience (Wigtown) as the debates had pressed on so late that he was forced to curtail his reporting: 'sitting late we can not send ye Result'.[46] Accordingly, the next letter opened with 'My last left the Lords sitting on the articles of impeachment against Robert Earl of Oxford on which they continued to debate till three next morning', a statement that went some way towards explaining just why the writer had felt unable to continue his account in the previous piece. The outcome was Oxford's commitment into custody. According to the newsletter the division in favour of imprisoning Oxford was 81 to 51 (the actual tally was 81 to 52), a slight error that emphasises both the author's close grasp of detail and the way in which a service that prided itself on speed of reporting was vulnerable to small slips. The report, though, captured the mood of the House as Charles Spencer, 3rd earl of Sunderland, a man with a very definite axe to grind against Oxford, insisted that no one bar Oxford's immediate servants, his physicians and relatives should be allowed to visit him.[47] Anyone reliant on the printed newspapers would have gleaned little of the

[43]Bodl., MS Eng. hist. c. 1039, ff. 12, 20.

[44]For insights into the accuracy of some of the newsletter reporting of divisions, see the article by Charles Littleton in this volume.

[45]Bodl., MS Eng. hist. c. 1039, f. 13.

[46]Bodl., MS Eng. hist. c. 1039, f. 13.

[47]Bodl., MS Eng. hist. c. 1039, f. 14.

bad-tempered nature of the debates in the Lords over the decision to commit Oxford, since normally these confined themselves to reports of the state of Oxford's health and the public information surrounding his commitment first to house arrest and ultimately to his being lodged in the Tower.[48] It is suggestive, then, that it was this additional detail and 'atmosphere' that a manuscript newsletter was able to convey that may have been particularly attractive to those wishing to receive them.

Following almost two years of impasse, the next stage of the impeachment process against Oxford finally returned to Westminster in the early summer of 1717. News of the trial and some of the details of the arrangements were gazetted in print newspapers. For example in its issue of 30 May to 1 June 1717, the *Evening Post* reported the Lords' address to the king for appointing a lord high steward to preside at the trial and a few days later, the *Post Boy* reported Oxford's own petition to be permitted counsel in the forthcoming proceedings.[49] One weekly newspaper also offered a detailed account of proceedings for the end of June, including the numbers involved in one division.[50] But, once again, the value to be found in the handwritten newsletters was speed, as the issues strove to despatch information from inside the court as quickly as possible, while also tending to offer readers detailed insights not normally to be found in the press. Thus, on 2 July the newsletter reported the debates of the day before and how at one point during the toing and froing between Lords and Commons, one anti-ministry member of parliament, Thomas Miller, gave a 'long speech' calling on Oxford to be brought to justice:

> After Reciting the whole transactions of the late ministry in which he [particularized] the abandoning the Catalans breaking of alliances Mardyke Commerce &c laid the whole of it on the E[arl] of Oxford who he said had been in effect as well as lord High Admiral & Archb[isho]p of Canterbury as L[or]d High Treasurer & Secretary of State.

Miller then closed his harangue by hoping that 'some method would be taken for bringing the said Earl to justice advising that all Europe as well as this nation called for it'. He was not alone in wanting Oxford brought to account. Sir William Strickland was also eager to see Oxford humbled, proposing bills of attainder, banishment or of pains and penalties, but to no effect.[51]

Unable to prevent the Lords from proceeding with their intention of acquitting Oxford, many of those of the contrary view chose to stay away from the remaining moments of the proceedings. But once again the atmosphere was well captured by Wigtown's correspondent, who reported how:

---

[48] For example, the reporting in the *British Weekly Mercury*, 9–16 July 1715. The Jacobite Tory commentator and antiquarian, Thomas Hearne, recorded Oxford's imprisonment in the Tower in his own records: 'Yesterday sennight the Earl of Oxford was put in the Tower for High-Crimes & Misdemeanours. There is no doubt but he is a Villain. Yet no body thinks that he is guilty of Treason'. *Remarks and Collections of Thomas Hearne*, ed. D.W. Rannie (11 vols, Oxford, 1885–1921), v, 80–1.

[49] *Post Boy*, 6–8 June 1717.

[50] *Weekly Journal or Saturday's Post*, 29 June 1717.

[51] Bodl., MS Eng. hist. c. 1039, f. 93.

after the Lord High Steward had given the said judgement three huzzas were made in the Court – Thus you have an account how this great affair which has made so much noise & occasioned the imprisonment of the said Earl for above two years besides other ignominious circumstances which he has undergone is at last terminated.[52]

This was far from the only account of the trial available to the interested public.[53] Many printed newspapers reported the manoeuvring around the opening of the trial, with one recording Oxford's petition to be assigned legal counsel early in June.[54] Besides, in the aftermath of the trial the Lords ordered the proceedings to be printed and a variety of private letter writers communicated details of the events to their correspondents.[55] Some newspaper reporting was relatively terse, as can be seen from the following three notices:

Yesterday the Earl of Oxford appear'd again in the Court at Westminster-Hall, and, as we hear, was at Night acquitted and discharged[56]

We hear the Earl of Oxford was discharged last Night; but it being late, we refer a further Account thereof to our next[57]

On Monday last, about at 11 at Night, the Earl of Oxford was acquitted by the Lords, of all the Articles of Impeachment that were exhibited against him.[58]

Only one of these papers promised a more in-depth account in due course. And yet, much more information was available as was made clear by the announcement in the *Weekly Journal or Saturday's Post* of a 'Very Full Account of the Proceedings' against Oxford. This newspaper's willingness to risk censure by parliament and to commit a detailed account to print, not to mention the existence of detailed reporting such as that offered by Abel Boyer, thus raises the question why some people continued to choose to subscribe to a handwritten news service when apparently equally detailed reporting was available elsewhere?

3

Examination of the accounts of both the Oxford trial, and that of Francis Atterbury, bishop of Rochester, suggest that the continuing popularity of manuscript news services may have

---

[52] Bodl., MS Eng. hist. c. 1039, f. 93.

[53] It is also worth noting that other private communications carried news of the event, one important example being the 'memorandum' of William Wake, at that point bishop of Lincoln. See Clyve Jones, 'The Opening of the Impeachment of Robert Harley, Earl of Oxford, June to September 1715: The "Memorandum" of William Wake, Bishop of Lincoln', *eBLJ*, (2015), article 4.

[54] *Post Boy*, 6–8 June 1717.

[55] The official printed account, published by order of the Lords, provided substantial detail of the event, even including the complaint of the lord high steward that his place was so far away from the bar that he was struggling to hear the evidence presented. Bodl., Don. c. 156, *The Tryal of Robert Earl of Oxford and Earl Mortimer… Published by Order of the House of Peers* (1717), 58.

[56] *Post Boy*, 29 June–2 July 1717.

[57] *Post Man and the Historical Account*, 29 June–2 July 1717.

[58] *Weekly Packet*, 29 June–6 July 1717.

been owing to a combination of reasons. Perhaps most of all, they offered an apparently personalised type of news reporting, speedily delivered and tailored to the individual subscriber with helpful summaries of the principal themes. This is most clear in the early stages of the proceedings against Atterbury, shortly after his initial arrest on suspicion of being at the head of a Jacobite conspiracy.[59] The newsletter conveyed to Wigtown of 25 August 1722 offered the following exposition:

> You must needs imagin[e] the surprise of the Town to [be] great on this oc[c]asion and that it[']s endless to give you the p[ar]ticulars of what passes in publick Conversations but the Gen[era]ll inference is that numbers of persons of Rank and distinction are in the Confederacy...[60]

As well as summarising the principal features of a case, newsletters like that sent to Wigtown also endeavoured to provide behind-the-scenes information, often introduced with the telling phrase 'we hear' to indicate privileged, though unsubstantiated knowledge. Thus, a matter of weeks after his commitment, Atterbury was reported to have been suffering poor health and eager to press on with his trial:

> Very heavy charges are s[ai]d to be fixed ag[ain]st the Bishop of Rochester, meanwhile we hear that Prelate seems not very [anxious] concerning the Event & is not at all for deferring but on the Contrary desireous of Comeing to a speedy tryall – accordingly a petition was presented yes[ter]day at the old Bailly & a motion was [there]upon made by Constantine Phipps in the name of Mrs Morris, daughter of the s[ai]d Bishop praying that her father in consideration of his ill state of health occasioned by his Closs [sic] Confinement might be either put to a tryall or Comitted to bail...[61]

The following month, the newsletter was able to communicate the details of Lord Carteret's address to the house of lords, seeking the Lords' agreement to the commitment of Atterbury, Lord North and Grey and Charles Boyle, 4th earl of Orrery. This appears to have passed with little dissension in the House, but a few days later the newsletter was still able to report the ongoing support for Atterbury in the City of London, where prayers were given in many churches for his recovery from gout.[62] Evidence of more dangerous agitation on Atterbury's behalf was indicated in the issue for 30 October, which reported how a procession of the lord mayor and court of aldermen in London was disrupted by a group 'crying out high church and a Steward [sic] for ever'. Their demonstration was considered threatening enough to warrant calling out the guard, who were 'sent for to Qualifie them'.[63]

How newsletter writers compiled their information, what their sources were, and how quickly they were able to despatch news was no doubt one set of considerations that enabled

---

[59] For more on Atterbury and the Atterbury plot see G.V. Bennett, *The Tory Crisis in Church and State, 1688–1730: The Career of Francis Atterbury, Bishop of Rochester* (Oxford, 1975); and Eveline Cruickshanks and Howard Erskine-Hill, *The Atterbury Plot* (Basingstoke, 2004).

[60] Bodl., MS Eng. hist. c. 1041.2, f. 105.

[61] Bodl., MS Eng. hist. c. 1041.2, f. 111.

[62] Bodl., MS Eng. hist. c. 1041.2, f. 130.

[63] Bodl., MS Eng. hist. c. 1041.2, f. 133.

them to continue in business alongside, and presumably for some readers, in preference to printed newspapers and newssheets. A comparison of the coverage of the Atterbury trial in the Wigtown newsletters with those compiled by Wye shows both a degree of overlap, which suggests that both may have been reliant on a common source, and a degree of distinctiveness indicative of the choice available for those interested in subscribing to a manuscript news service. On 11 October 1722, both services compiled letters and it is instructive to compare how closely each followed the other in reporting that day's proceedings in parliament.

Wye newsletter, sent to Lord Lansdown[64]	Anonymous newsletter sent to Lord Wigtown[65]
The King came this day to the house of Peers and in a Speech Signif[yed] his Concern of being obliged to accquaint them with ye Discovery of a Conspiracy w[hi]ch was formed and is still carrying on in favour of a Popish Pretender, that these Discoveries were made by Informations from his Ministers abroad & upon Ample proofs - That ye Conspirators had applyed to forreign Powers for assistance but this being refused ym they designed to attempt ye Conspiracy on yr own strength having raised money and Engaged officers from abroad & if their Designes had not been timely discovered the City of London would ere this have been in Blood and Confusion. That on these Discoveries ye Standing forces had been Encampt 6 Regiments sent for from Ireland & ye States Generall had given assurances yt a Body of their forces should be ready to Embark on ye first Notice [his Maty] That some of ye Conspirators had been taken up & search was making after the rest Left it to ye consideration of ye Parliament to doe what they should think necessary for ye safety and security of ye Kingdom Recomending that they would Exert ymselves on this occasion	This day the king came to the house of peers and was pleased in a most gracious speech to signifie his concern of being obliged to acquaint them with a discovery of a Conspiracy which was formed and is [still] carrying on in favour of a popish pretender That those discoverys were made by informations from his Min[iste]rs abroad and from ample proof that the conspirators had aplyed to forraigne powers for assistance but this being refused them they designe to attempt the Conspiracy in yr own strength having raised mony and engaged officers from abroad and if ye designes had not been timely discovered the City of London would ere this have been in blood and confusion That on these discoverys the Standing forces had been encreased Six regiments sent for from Ireland and the States Gene[ra]ll had given assurances yt a body of yr troops should be ready to embarque on the first notice His maty being intent of laying no burdens upon his people but what are absolutely necessary That some of the Conspirators had been taken up and Search was making for the rest and his maty left it to the consideration of the parlia[men]t to do what they should think necessary for the safety and security of the kingdome Recomending that they would [assert] themselves on this occasion

The close correlation between both letters suggests that each relied on a common source; or perhaps that one scribe had seen the other's work. Only on one small point, the king's eagerness not to lay 'burdens upon his people but what are absolutely necessary', did the

[64]Bodl., MS Rawl. C. 151, ff. 1–2.
[65]Bodl., MS Eng. hist. c. 1041.2, f. 125.

Wigtown letter vary from that compiled by Wye, and as the phrase 'his Maty' was struck out from the latter, it seems likely that time or editorial policy led to that small additional detail being excised. The king's speech would later have been made public, so drafts may have been available in the coffee shops around Westminster, which were then transcribed for insertion in the newsletters, likely more swiftly than in the press. For example, on 20 February 1716 the Lords presented the king with an address, which was reported back next day with the king's answer and ordered to be printed. It was published in the printed newspaper called (confusingly) the *News-Letter* of 25 February, suggesting some slight delay in getting it into print.[66]

Even more strikingly similar was the following section, which concluded with both letters informing their readers that the lateness of the hour made it impossible to complete the day's account.

Wye newsletter, sent to Lord Lansdown	Anonymous newsletter sent to Lord Wigtown
The Lords having been presented by ye Duke of Grafton with a Bill for Suspending the Habeas Corpus Act went into a Committee there[on?][67] [f.1r margin] The Duke of Wharton[68] in ye Chair - The Arch Bishop of York[69] Earls of Anglesy[70] Cowper[71] and Lord Couningsby[72] made long Speeches ag[ain]st[73] it But ye 2 Secretaryes of State & divers other Lords[74] argued that there never was more occasion than at present for ye suspension of ye sd Act for 12 months on wch great debates arose and are like to sit soe late as not to send you ye Result this post	The Lords having been presented by the D[uke] of Grafton w[i]t[h] a bill for suspending the habeous Corpus act all went into a [Committee] the D[uke] Wharton in the Chair The archbishop of York E[arl] of anglesea and Cowper L[or]d Coningsby made speeches[75] ag[ains]t it but the two Secretarys of State[76] and diverse other Lords argued that yr was never more occasion then at present for the suspension of the afors[ai]d act for 12 moneths on which great debates arose and are like to sitt so late that we cannot give the result this post

[66] Heiko Droste has emphasised that speed was one of the likely benefits of the handwritten newsletter over its print counterpart: 'handwritten newspapers' advantages lay in their speed, exclusivity, and adaptability to their readers' particular interests'. Heiko Droste, 'How Public was the News in Early Modern Times?' in *Handwritten Newspapers: An Alternative Medium during the Early Modern and Modern Periods*, ed. Heiko Droste and Kirsti Salmi-Niklander (Helsinki, 2019), 40.

[67] There is some disparity between this account and that in Timberland. This account misses the detail of the debate over whether to give the bill a second reading 'which was strenuously oppos'd', while Timberland makes no mention of the contributions made during the committee stage. *The History and Proceedings in the House of Lords from the Restoration in 1660 to the Present Time*, ed. Ebenezer Timberland (7 vols, 1742), iii, 244.

[68] Philip Wharton, duke of Wharton.

[69] Sir William Dawes.

[70] Arthur Annesley, 5th earl of Anglesey.

[71] William Cowper, Earl Cowper.

[72] Thomas Coningsby, earl of Coningsby.

[73] Timberland lists the opposition Lords speaking as Anglesey, Cowper, Strafford, Coningsby, Trevor, Bathurst and Bingley. Timberland, *History and Proceedings*, iii, 244.

[74] Timberland lists those speaking in favour as Harcourt, Townshend, Carteret (the secretaries of state), Argyll, Grafton, Wharton and Newcastle. Timberland, *History and Proceedings*, iii, 245.

[75] Bodl., MS Rawl. C. 151, f. 1 (margins) has 'long Speeches'.

[76] Carteret and Townshend.

Here, the availability of a common source is not enough to explain the overlap and one is left wondering whether one of the scribes had borrowed his information from the other.

Once again, a comparison of two letters from 18 October appears to make plain that both the Wigtown compiler and Wye correspondent were reliant on common information. It should be emphasised that the services were distinct. Wigtown's letter did not look like Wye's, nor do they appear to have followed the same schedule for release. Yet on the occasions when papers overlapped, and events in parliament were reported in detail it seems hard to conclude otherwise than that both compilers were using the same source, or that one may have had sight of the other.[77]

Wye newsletter	Anonymous Newsletter sent to Lord Wigtown
The Substance of the Debates last Tuesday[78] in the house of Commons for and agst the Bill for Suspending the habeas Corpus Act for 12 months were to this Effect vizt	The substance of the debates in the house of Comons last [tuesday] for and ag[ain]st the bill to suspend the habeas Corpus act were to this effect vizt[79]
Those who were ag[ain]st ye Bill said that though they did not doubt of a Conspiracy having been formed ag[ain]st the Governm[en]t yett as ye same was now discovered they thought there was noe Necessity to continue it for soe long a time as to ye 24 of October 1723	Those who were against the bill s[ai]d yt tho they did not doubt of a Conspiracy having been formed ag[ain]st the Governmt yet as the Same was discovered they thought yr was no necessity to Continue the Suspension of the s[ai]d act for so long a time as 12 months
But those on ye other side and particularly Mr Walpole said there were Designes at the Demise of the Queen by some Great Men to proclaim ye Pretender, that as to ye present Plott an Insurrection was Intended during the Election of this Parliament as ye most proper time to gett a Parliam[en]t on their side and if that had not been discovered a Parliament might perhaps have been now Sitting for ye Pretender	But those on the other side particularly s[ai]d[80] yr was designes at the demise of the Queen by some G[rea]t men to Proclaime the Pretender that as to the Plott ane Insurrection was intended dureing the Election of this Parliament on yr side[81] and if that had been discovered a Parliam[en]t [might have perhaps have] been now sitting for the Pretender

As one further example of the clear debt each paper owed to the other or to a common source, reporting of the events of 1 March 1723, when the Commons turned their attention

[77] It does not seem to be the case that the more selective Wigtown newsletter merely filtered the longer issue released by Wye, as on occasion Wigtown's reporting was in advance of the other. For example, one Wigtown newsletter of 8 Dec. 1722 offered a similar account of affairs in Scotland to that covered by Wye two days later in his letter of 10 December. See Bodl., MS Eng. hist. c. 1041.2, f. 150 and MS Rawl. C. 151, f. 35. On other occasions, Wye anticipated Wigtown, for example in reporting Bishop Atterbury's assault on Colonel Williamson, with Wye leading with a report on 31 Dec. 1722, and Wigtown following suit on 1 Jan. 1723. Equally, there were occasions when the letters shared a date of composition, emphasising that while distinct, they were drawing on a common source.

[78] 16 October.

[79] This opening statement is word for word that contained in Bodl., MS Rawl. C. 151, f. 5, 18 Oct. 1722.

[80] Bodl., MS Rawl. C. 151, f. 5 states 'But those on ye other side and particularly Mr Walpole said...'

[81] Bodl., MS Rawl. C. 151, f. 5 has 'an Insurrection was Intended during the Election of this Parliament as ye most proper time to gett a Parliamt on their side...'

to details of the Atterbury plot, demonstrates how closely allied these services were. In his letter of 4 March, Wye related that the report from the Commons' committee investigating the plot comprised 120 sheets of paper and took William Pulteney six hours to read out. The report in Wigtown, dated two days prior to Wye's, was word for word the same.[82]

In May 1723 the long process against Atterbury, that had begun the previous summer, reached its inevitable conclusion. Before parliament voted to pass the bill of pains and penalties against him, though, Atterbury was able to deliver a final oration in his defence. This was later printed, so became widely available to the public,[83] but an immediate glimpse of its tone was available in Wye's newsletter of 13 May:

> the Bishop of Rochester Concluded his defence & made a Speech of 2 houres long where in he made the strongest asseverations of his Innocency and Concluded with these words of Scripture Vizt. Naked came I into the World and naked shall I Return out of it the Lord giveth & ye Lord taketh away Blessed be ye name of ye Lord[84]

Atterbury's pathetic conclusion had no effect on the majority of his brethren, who joined in arguing for the bill against him to be passed. Leading the way was the bishop of London, who concluded his oration by insisting:

> if the Unfortunate Prelate[s] Designs had taken Effect and ye Pretender been advanced to the Throne he should have thought it an Easy punishmt to have been Subjected [to] the same pains and penalties as contained in this Bill and hoped the Bench of Bishops would think it their Duty as he did to Contribute all in their power to support the present happy protestant Government[85]

Publication of Atterbury's speech was advertised in the issue of the Wye newsletter for 24 June 1723, which also took upon itself to reproduce sections of the address for the benefit of the reader. Once again, it served as a compendium as well as offering prompt early notice, maintaining its reliable function as a crafted snapshot of what was most pertinent in the week's news.[86]

4. Conclusion

How important was manuscript reporting of high-profile state proceedings, such as trials in parliament? Much of what was covered in the newsletters was later printed, sometimes with the authority of the house of lords. Speeches were later published by Ebenezer Timberland, derived from a variety of sources that help indicate how much was available for perusal for the interested consumer.

---

[82]Bodl., MS Rawl. C. 151, f. 61; MS Eng. hist. c. 1042, f. 18.

[83]The same was true of the speech made by the famously unstable Philip, duke of Wharton, whose address was appended to his life, which was published shortly after his death in exile. For more see Mark Blackett-Ord, *Hell-Fire Duke: The Life of the Duke of Wharton* (Windsor, 1982), passim.

[84]Bodl., MS Rawl. C. 151, f. 99.

[85]Bodl., MS Rawl. C. 151, f. 101.

[86]Bodl., MS Rawl. C. 151, f. 115.

It would seem reasonable to conclude, however, that four significant advantages attached to subscription to a private news service. First was the question of privacy. At times of high political tension, both the publishers and recipients of more public, printed newspapers may have found themselves too exposed to official interest. Certainly, in August 1722 it was sufficiently newsworthy for the author of the Wigtown newsletter to alert his audience that copies of Nathaniel Mist's journals had been seized that morning by government messengers.[87] However, as has been indicated in this piece and elsewhere, handwritten newsletters were not immune from investigation and some newspapers as well as taking advantage of information gleaned from newsletters, made their own political postures clear by reporting on what was being circulated in handwritten news.[88] Elsewhere, newsletters were thought of as instigators of trouble. In March 1716 Mary Cocks received a letter from a Mrs Rogers referring to 'a most impudent written newsletter', which Rogers believed contained information 'calculated to raise the mob'.[89]

Second was the question of immediacy. A handwritten letter could be compiled and sent out by courier very speedily, offering to the recipient the promise of advance knowledge of important events. Occasional slips in the numbers of those engaged in divisions and scrambling of individual's names, seems to be clear evidence of the rapidity with which manuscript newsletters were compiled and it seems likely that their recipients were willing to accept a degree of error in return for early notice of the substance of news. The inaccuracy of manuscript newsletters was certainly something the printed press was keen to underscore when trumpeting their own more precise reporting. For example, in July 1715, one newspaper reported with evident pleasure: 'We kill'd Dr. Higden in our last, by the means of a written News-Letter, and are very joyful to bring him to Life again from more authentick Vouchers…'[90] However, it is also worth noting that the compiler of the Wigtown newsletter evidently took such matters to heart, and in the issue of 6 July 1721 brought to the reader's attention that in a previous letter they had 'Transcribed some spurious Coppy of Mr Gibbons Examination before ye Secret Committee' and so undertook to remedy the mistake.[91]

A further reason, perhaps harder to pin down but possibly just as important, may be that it was simply a question of taste and choice. For some, there was clearly something to be gained by being able to rely on a tailored news service, offering a focused compendium of the most salient points without needing to wade through the myriad items the 18th-century press included within its columns. For example, in April 1723 the Wye newsletter covering reaction to the Atterbury trial informed the reader clearly about the editorial policy taken in supplying details of one protest over another: 'There are some other Reasons wch we have to Insert of the protest mentioned in our last wch however we think fitt to omitt to make

---

[87] Bodl., MS Eng. hist. c. 1041.2, f. 99.

[88] For example, in the summer of 1715 one newspaper complained about reports in other papers and newsletters, noting in particular the content of Dormer's letters and printing an excerpt to make the point. See the *Flying Post or the Post Master*, 30 July–2 Aug. 1715. The following year, another paper complained of Mawson who, 'though absconded from justice' assaulted the ministry 'with his weekly News-Letter'. *Weekly Journal or British Gazetteer*, 24 Mar. 1716.

[89] Surrey History Centre, 371/14/O/2/102: D. Rogers to M. Cocks, 9 Mar. 1716.

[90] *Weekly Packet*, 2–9 July 1715.

[91] Bodl., MS Eng. hist. c. 1040, ff. 67, 76.

room for that Entred by the Duke of Wharton agst passing the Bishop of Rochesters Bill'.[92] A personalised, private and fast service seems to offer a fairly comprehensive explanation for the survival of manuscript news in general and of collections like that sent to Wigtown or despatched by Wye in particular. It is also clear from William Wye's experience as a producer of news and his willingness to continue to distribute a manuscript newsletter alongside of his printed one, that a substantial market remained for the older form.[93]

A final explanation is that men like Wye operated as much as distributors as compilers of news. A telling endorsement to one of his letters explained that the newsletter was only part of the package he was despatching, while setting out the reason for him sending something other than what was clearly expected: 'Sr ye Last Gazette having little or no news In it I send you instead of it ye House of Comons Addresse'.[94] Just as Wye himself later embraced a printed newsletter alongside of his more traditional handwritten one, he was by no means inimical to the idea of printed news and evidently acted as an agent, conveying a variety of types of information to his clients.

It is no great surprise to discover that different varieties of news outputs fed other news media, but it is significant nonetheless to emphasise the way in which commercial news services were repurposed according to taste and demand. Both the Wye and Wigtown collections make plain that manuscript news remained a successful example of news media alongside and often in partnership with their better-known print competitors. It is also apparent that some recipients clearly believed there were advantages to be gained from subscribing to these and similar news services whether in preference to, or in addition to, printed newspapers.

---

[92] Bodl., MS Rawl. C. 151, f. 107.

[93] The career of Abel Boyer, mentioned in Charles Littleton's article in this volume, also emphasises that a market remained for both forms of media well into the 18th century.

[94] Bodl., MS Rawl. C. 151, f. 6.

The Formidable Machine: Parliament as Seen by Italian Diplomats at the Court of St James's in the First Half of the 18th Century

UGO BRUSCHI*

To the representatives of Italian states in London, early 18th-century Britain often remained a puzzle. The Revolution Settlement presented them with the problem of identifying the real source of power, both in order to send home reliable information and to try to secure support for the interests of their princes, who were sometimes desperate for the friendship, or at least the lack of hostility, of Great Britain. An analysis of the weekly despatches and of the final reports drafted by Italian diplomats (namely the representatives of the Savoyard state, the republics of Genoa and Venice, the Duchy of Modena and the Grand Duchy of Tuscany) in the first half of the 18th century offers evidence on their sources of information and on their vision of the political system of the country. Parliament loomed large in their correspondence. News on the activity of the Houses as well as forecasts on the challenge they posed to the ministry were a recurrent theme. To Italian diplomats, parliament was a source of instability. In their eyes, only the rise of a strong premier minister – of which Sir Robert Walpole was the epitome – could tame the fickle assembly in Westminster and bring order, though precariously, to the British polity.

Keywords: diplomatic correspondence; 18th-century Italian states; instability; constitution; premier minister; Sir Robert Walpole

1. *Context*

In the first half of the 18th century, a post in London was undoubtedly a place of high responsibility for a diplomat coming from one of the various Italian *ancien régime* states. Not only was Britain one of the superpowers of the time, events had also led to a greater involvement on the part of British forces, both in the Mediterranean and in central Europe, especially in the Wars of the Spanish (1701–14) and Austrian (1740–8) Successions. Such conflicts, and the peace treaties that brought an end to them, also had an impact on the balance of power between the states of the Italian peninsula. Most Italian states were on the receiving end of transformations in the political landscape of Europe, on which they had

*I would like to thank the participants in the 2018 'Scribal News and News Cultures in Late Stuart and Early Georgian Britain' conference in London for a very pleasant and fruitful experience and Michael Schaich and Robin Eagles for their precious comments on a first draft of this essay.

Unless otherwise specified, all dates are given in Old Style, but the new year is always taken to begin on 1 January.

an extremely limited influence, and London was one of the places where decisions were made and news and diplomatic gossip circulated. On the other hand, that period saw the rise of the Savoyard state to a regional power, a rise in which the relations between the courts of Turin and London played a crucial role.[1] This implied both the need for the duke of Savoy (later king of Sicily and, eventually, of Sardinia) to keep British monarchs under constant watch and the necessity, for other Italian states, to keep an eye on the success of their troublesome neighbour. Other reasons for a constant diplomatic vigilance at the court of St James's were specific to certain Italian states. The republics of Genoa and Venice, with their long commercial tradition, were obviously interested in keeping relations with an international trading power such as Great Britain. Moreover, being Mediterranean maritime powers, albeit in decline, they had at times occasion to complain of the behaviour of British fleets and merchants; or, conversely, it was the turn of Whitehall to take offence with what was perceived as an excess of leniency on the part of Genoese and Venetian naval authorities towards French or Spanish ships. Likewise, the status of Leghorn and of its thriving community of English merchants was a recurrent issue in the correspondence of the agents of the Duchy of Tuscany.

Although the reasons were many for Italian states to have a reliable and efficient agent in London, a serious problem constantly emerges, namely the difficulty on the part of Italian diplomats of understanding a country and a political system utterly different from anything with which they were familiar. Most of them were baffled by the peculiarities of the Revolution Settlement, and the shock of the Glorious Revolution did not seem to subside with the passing of time, as if the removal of a king 40 years after the beheading of another had made an axiom clear: uneasy lies the head that wears St Edward's crown, and in Britain, chaos and revolution can always be a few steps away. The instability of the political system was connected with two interplaying factors: the centrality of parliament in the constitution, and the endless struggle of parties for the control of the Westminster assembly and consequently of the balance of power in the realm. The aim of this chapter is to discuss, in the light of diplomatic reporting, how the role of parliament was perceived by the agents of Italian states as well as to survey the sources of information on which they built their knowledge. Naturally, each agent sent to London with a tough job to undertake had his own sensibility, and the length of experience in his post or his rank in the diplomatic world could affect each vision. Still, the work on archival sources relating to five Italian states – the Kingdom of Sicily (later of Sardinia), the republics of Genoa and Venice, the Duchy of Modena and the Grand Duchy of Tuscany – in a time span that goes from the accession of Queen Anne in 1702 to Sir Robert Walpole's fall in 1742, has highlighted recurring patterns of behaviour.

2. Parliament and Instability

A prominent factor was the perception of Britain – or rather *England*, so scarce was the attention normally paid to Scotland or, even less, Ireland – as a country with an unusual

---

[1] Cf. Christopher Storrs, *War, Diplomacy and the Rise of Savoy, 1690–1720* (Cambridge, 2000), 122–70; Christopher Storrs, 'Savoyard Diplomacy in the Eighteenth Century (1684–1798)', in *Politics and Diplomacy in Early Modern Italy: The Structure of Diplomatic Practice, 1450–1800*, ed. Daniela Frigo (Cambridge, 2000), 210–53; Enrico Genta, *Princípi e regole internazionali tra forza e costume: Le relazioni anglo-sabaude nella prima metà del Settecento* (Napoli, 2004).

constitution and a stormy, extremely unstable political life. Diplomats with a reduced experience of the English political way of life were naturally more exposed to feelings of confusion; this included ambassadors, whose stay in London was generally shorter than the many years spent by agents, secretaries and envoys. Even veterans, however, betrayed feelings of perplexity. Giuseppe Riva had been living in England since 1715 and acting in an official capacity as the envoy of the duke of Modena since the beginning of 1718, but when he left the country in 1729 and presented his final report to his master, the picture he painted of the British polity was rather unsettling:

> In the kingdom of England a monstrosity not deformed shows the Monarchy depending from the Aristocracy, a King who cannot make laws, a Parliament that can do everything while in existence, but that cannot exist unless the King wants it to exist, a Nation that does not accept laws or burdens, unless the Nation itself imposes them. There is sovereignty, but no real control.[2]

Riva's perception of Britain as a state unlike any regular form of commonwealth, and the language of his comments, echo Samuel Pufendorf's description of the Holy Roman Empire as 'an Irregular Body, and like some misshapen Monster, if it be measured by the common Rules of Politicks and Civil Prudence'.[3] This can perhaps help to explain why Riva's puzzlement was voiced in stronger terms than most of his colleagues were ready to use; still, it expresses a common concern.[4] Italian diplomats usually strove to understand the British constitutional and political system, sometimes alternating between puzzled fascination and desperate mistrust. Not only were they baffled by the interplay of a range of antagonistic political forces more complex than the ones they had been accustomed to in their native countries, but the constant alteration of the political landscape made their task more difficult. The king of Sicily, Victor Amadeus II, was at pains to repeat it to every new man he sent to London: Britain was 'a country subject to frequent mutations' and it was

---

[2] '[Nel] regno d'Inghilterra […] una mostruosità non deforme fa vedere la monarchia dipendente dall'aristocrazia, un monarca senz'autorità di far leggi, un parlamento, che tutto può unito e non può da sé unirsi, una nazione che non vuol ricevere leggi, né sopportar pesi, e se gli impone, le signorie senza dominio', BEUMo, manoscritti italiani [hereafter cited as MS it.] 678, f. 1v: 'Descrizione di Londra fatta l'anno 1729'. For the first two years of his stay, Riva had acted as secretary to the Modenese envoy, count Fabrizio Guicciardi, who died on 20 December 1717 NS and was immediately succeeded by his former aide, cf. Lowell Lindgren, 'Gioseffo Riva (1682–1739), a Diplomatic Arbiter of *Buon Gusto* in the London of George I', *Il Saggiatore musicale*, xxiii (2016), 280, 286–7. Guicciardi's death actually brought forward a substitution that had been planned since March, when the Modenese scholar Ludovico Antonio Muratori had written Riva that Duke Rinaldo of Este intended in due course to recall Guicciardi and leave Riva as the representative of the Duchy in London, BEUMo, Archivio Muratoriano [hereafter cited as AM], 48/23*bis*, f. 17v: Muratori to Riva, 24 Mar. 1717 NS; see Lindgren, 'Gioseffo Riva', 287, note 33.

[3] I am quoting from *The Present State of Germany: Written in Latin by the Learned Samuel Puffendorff, under the Name of Severinus de Monzabano Veronensis. Made English and Continued by Edmund Bohun* (1696), 152; the original Latin text reads thus: 'irregulare aliquod corpus, & monstro simile, siquidem ad regulas scientiæ civilis exigatur', Severini de Monzambano Veronensis [alias Samuel Pufendorf], *De Statu Imperii Germanici ad Lælium fratrem, dominum Trezolani, Liber Unus* (Genevæ [but actually The Hague], 1667), 157 [ch. VI, § 9].

[4] It must be mentioned, however, that while for Pufendorf the irregular, divided nature of the Empire was the main reason for its weakness ('Causa primaria mali est ex inconcinna, maleque digesta Reipubl. Compage': Pufendorf, *De Statu*, 176 [ch. VII, § 7]), one of the reasons of Riva's confusion was that, for all its oddness, the British constitution appeared somehow to be working. A 'constitutional deadlock' like the one Pufendorf had identified in Germany (Peter Schröder, 'The Constitution of the Holy Roman Empire after 1648: Samuel Pufendorf's Assessment in His Monzambano', *The Historical Journal*, 42 (1999), 967) did not seem imminent.

necessary to be ready to react, if and when the wind changed.[5] In 1706, back in Venice after his embassy, Alvise Mocenigo stated to the duke and senators that it is always difficult to give a correct idea of any foreign government, but:

> giving a detailed view of England and of the British kingdoms must be most difficult and beyond belief, since the fickleness of the weather and of the nation, the different character and the inconsistency of personal conduct prevent a full understanding of the true principles and of the foundations that give existence and movement to that part of the world.[6]

Parliament, as the den of parties and factions, lay at the heart of this perception of instability and even danger.[7] This sensation was particularly strong at the beginning of the century and until the 1720s, but it did not disappear altogether when the ministry seemed to take a firmer control over parliament. The experience of William III, who in the eyes of some Italian envoys had ended up as a political hostage of parliament after having been greeted as a saviour in 1688–9, cemented the idea that the assembly in Westminster was the machine where real power was wielded and that everybody, the monarch included, had to come to terms with it.[8] Mocenigo, after having explained at some length the organisation of Queen Anne's court, the influence exerted on the queen by the lord high treasurer (Sidney Godolphin, Lord Godolphin) and by the duke and duchess of Marlborough, and the role of the privy council, underlined that any authority was 'circumscribed and affected by that of Parliament'.[9] That coming to terms with this reality was no easy task is exposed when the Venetian ambassador later underlined that the influence of the crown and the royal prerogative were, however, great; on the other hand, parliamentary control of the purse acted as a brake, meaning that supplies could be granted to the crown only under certain conditions. The resulting contradiction was made worse by the desire of great authority on

---

[5] 'Una nazione sottoposta a frequenti mutationi', ASTo, Corte, Materie politiche per rapporto all'estero, Negoziazioni (Gran Bretagna) [hereafter cited as C/MPE/N/GB], 4/1: Victor Amadeus II's instructions to marquis de Trivié, 1713; similar instructions were given to count della Perosa in 1716 and to marquis di Cortanze in 1719: ASTo, C/MPE/N/GB, 5/5–6. De Trivié remarked that circumstances changed so often in England that no less than 14 (former and present) secretaries of state were alive at the time, ASTo, C/MPE/N/GB, 4/2, f. 100: de Trivié's final report, c. 1717.

[6] 'Difficilissimo oltre ogni credere deve riuscire il fare un dettaglio dell'Inghilterra e de' regni britannici, dove l'instabilità del clima e della nazione, il temperamento diverso e l'irregolarità della condotta non lasciano ben comprendere li veri principii e li fondamenti che danno moto e sussistenza in quel tratto di mondo', Luigi Firpo, 'La relazione inedita di Alvise Mocenigo sull'Inghilterra (1706)', *Atti dell'Accademia delle Scienze di Torino: Classe di Scienze Morali, Storiche e Filologiche*, xcix (1964–5), 489. In the same year, the Tuscan resident Iacopo Giraldi wrote that confusion and the violence of factions were the real character of the British government, ASFi, Mediceo del Principato [hereafter cited as MdP], 4234: Giraldi to Duke Cosimo III, 1 Jan. 1706 NS.

[7] At first, some reports wrote about *parliaments*, but the singular soon prevailed. Both upper and lower case were used.

[8] *Le relazioni degli stati europei lette al senato dagli ambasciatori veneti*, ed. Nicolò Barozzi and Guglielmo Berchet (4th ser., *Inghilterra*, Venice, 1863), 508–12: 1696 final report of the Venetian ambassadors Lorenzo Soranzo and Girolamo Venier. In 1699, the Genoese envoy extraordinary, Giovanni Antonio Giustiniani, had foretold that soon the monarchy would be just a shadow and England a republic in all but the name, *Relazioni di ambasciatori sabaudi, genovesi e veneti durante il periodo della grande alleanza e della successione di Spagna (1693–1713)*, ed. Carlo Morandi (Bologna, 1935), 163.

[9] The Italian text sounds thus: 'resta circoscritta e dipendente in certa tal qual forma da quella del Parlamento', Firpo, 'La relazione'. 'In certa tal qual forma' can be translated in two rather different ways, either as 'up to a certain extent' or as 'in a certain way'.

© *2022 The Author(s). Parliamentary History published by John Wiley & Sons Ltd. on behalf of Parliamentary History Yearbook Trust.*

the part of the monarch and by jealousy on the part of political parties; civil strife was thus a possible outcome.[10]

It is not surprising that parliamentary affairs were usually predominant in the weekly despatches sent by Italian agents to their courts. Despatches show a pattern of seasonality: when parliament was not in session, political activity seemed to stop, and diplomats were forced to resort to gossip or to wild guesses about its conduct when it would assemble again. Reporting about parliament took different forms and different levels of detail, depending both on the political circumstances and on the attitude of a specific diplomat. Many of them, such as the Tuscan secretary Vincenzo Pucci, or the Genoese secretary Domenico Maria Viceti, went for a constant scrutiny of what happened in Westminster. They offered facts on the discussion of the most important bills and motions as well as interpretations of their political significance; sometimes they gave the numerical result of crucial divisions, and occasionally they mentioned speakers in a debate or outlined the position they had taken. For some time, Pucci even included a sort of sketchy parliamentary journal, a by-the-day report of the business transacted in parliament. Usually, the attention was balanced evenly between the house of commons and the house of lords: the impression is that, if anything, despatches were more concerned with the house in which the court faced an uphill task.

Parliamentary acts that could be useful in order to understand the king and government's policy, or the attitude of the two houses, such as the speech from the throne and addresses of thanks, were frequently attached, either in the original or in a translation, to diplomatic correspondence. On the one hand, they evidently acted as a sort of barometer of the political weather; on the other, through them Italian governments had precious information on the agenda of the ministry as well as hints of the difficulties that they were facing. Similar acts, which were regularly dealt with in a despatch but only occasionally attached to it, were motions passed or rejected by each house, or protests transcribed in the journal of the house of lords. It was very unusual for the contents of a specific bill to form part of any attachment sent home, although there were a few exceptions.[11]

The attention to parliament, and the awareness of how easily the balance might change in either house, led Italian diplomats to a careful consideration of political parties. This mainly had the aim of weighing the strength of each party and assessing whether the court could implement its policy, but sometimes attention was also paid to the ideological background of both factions. Occasionally popular support for the different positions was discussed, although how correctly it could be assessed is open to question. Nevertheless, the representatives of the Italian states were usually quite sceptical about the good faith of politicians, and described transitions from Tories to Whigs (or vice versa) in terms of a struggle for power, money and honour. Actually, when they concluded that the ministry could widen its support in parliament, they often thought this could happen thanks to patronage. Lying under their description of political struggle is an idea of parliament as a formidable machine that creates the possibility of wielding great power, but that at the same time resembles a wheel of fortune. Successful politicians are pressed by those eager for office, but once the

[10]For a similar perspective, cf. ASTo, C/MPE/N/GB, 4/2, ff. 531–2, 541: de Trivié's despatches 7 Feb. and 6 June 1715 NS.

[11]The plan for a national lottery passed by parliament in 1712 and sent by Viceti to the senate of Genoa (ASGe, Archivio Segreto [hereafter cited as AS], 2279: despatch 25 Apr. 1712) is possibly the weirdest example. Did he expect senators to buy some tickets?

latter are in charge, it is their turn to feel under siege. As cynically observed by the Venetian ambassador Nicolò Tron in 1716, there were simply not enough positions in the administration to satisfy everybody.[12] This condition of instability and possibly sudden change also led to a constant interest in the opposition. Generally speaking, in their letters diplomats showed their support for the incumbent administration, and at times politicians who stood against the court were ostensibly described in negative terms in official, not ciphered correspondence.[13] This of course might have been a matter of caution, since correspondence was at risk of being intercepted, but there was also an awareness that any desirable stability in the British political system was provided only by a long-lasting administration. Still, the most expert or brilliant agents of Italian states knew that neglecting members of parliament who sided against the government would be, in the long run, a serious mistake. They were aware that the overthrowing of an administration had to be expected in Britain, or that politicians forcefully opposing the ministry might later decide to join it.[14] They might be explicitly advised to do so by their master, as in the case of Victor Amadeus II.[15] Remarkably, there is also an evolution in the language used to describe the opposition. Sometimes a neutral tag is used, typically 'the party contrary/opposed [to the Court]'.[16] The most usual expression, however, is 'the Malcontents'. In time, most diplomats shifted to 'the oppositions', and later (normally in the second half of the century) to 'the opposition', at times with a capital O. This can also reflect a transition from a perception of opposing members of parliament as saboteurs of the policy carried out by the crown, to their acknowledgment as participants in a wider political game. Naturally, when – as often during the reigns of George I and II – the reversionary interest was a factor, there was a major inducement to keep a channel of communication open, since the prince of Wales 'one day will be the Master', as a Modenese diplomat wrote in 1737.[17]

Tactics on either side of the political divide are often openly discussed in diplomatic correspondence. Some are also aware of how parliamentary procedure can be used to achieve a political goal, for instance with the Commons' attempt, in King William's reign, to force unpalatable measures onto the Lords and the crown by 'tacking' them onto supply bills.[18] In 1712, the Venetian ambassador Pietro Grimani discussed in similar terms a possible prorogation after Queen Anne's creation of 12 peers, or the queen's decision to promise parliament a discussion on the articles of peace.[19] Viceti observed that the introduction of a bill in favour of the elector of Hanover and the passing of a motion on the negotiations of peace in the house of lords on 22 December 1711 were made possible by the cunning move of the Whigs, who had taken advantage of the fact that most Tories, supposing that the business

[12] ASVe, Senato, Dispacci degli ambasciatori e residenti (Inghilterra) [hereafter cited as S/DAR/I], 91, f. 168v: despatch 1 May 1716 NS.

[13] Some of them (notably the Savoyard representatives) usually wrote in cipher the parts of their despatches where political gossip took a more serious character.

[14] The Venetian ambassador Grimani wrote that many who were fighting the court actually longed to be won by it, ASVe, S/DAR/I, 87, f. 613: despatch 25 Dec. 1711 NS.

[15] ASTo, C/MPE/N/GB, 4/1 and 5/5–6.

[16] 'Il partito opposto' or 'il partito contrario'; 'to the Court' is usually implied, not written explicitly.

[17] 'un giorno poi sarà il Padrone', ASMo, Carteggio Ambasciatori (Inghilterra) [hereafter cited as CAI] 21: despatch 11 Oct. 1737 NS (Abbot Pareti's remark about Prince Frederick is in cipher).

[18] *Le relazioni*, ed. Barozzi and Berchet, 509.

[19] ASVe, S/DAR/I, 87, ff. 662, 680–1: despatches 22 Jan. and 5 Feb. 1712 NS.

of the day was concluded, had left the House once the Occasional Conformity Bill had received the royal assent.[20] Conversely, in the following spring, the call of the House for members impatient to return to their homes was postponed until the administration could show parliament the result of the negotiations at Utrecht.[21] Every transformation in the composition of the houses of parliament was seen in the light of advantage for one faction. This was, unsurprisingly, the case in the creation of 12 peers by Queen Anne in 1712 in order to change power relations in the upper house, but the same view was adopted both for the Septennial Act in 1716 and the Peerage Bill in 1719.

As to the first act, it was explained by Italian diplomats as a trick of the Whigs, in order to avoid defeat in the forthcoming elections. Tron wrote that the ministry would stop at nothing in order to remain in office.[22] Pucci reported that the Tories realised it would be 'a deadly blow'. They also feared that the passing of such an act might lead, in seven years' time, to a further renewal of the sitting parliament, to be carried on repetitively as long as the crown and the majority in the house of commons would agree.[23] Italian diplomats, however, knew that the Whigs were taking a chance.[24] According to Pucci, the feelings of the nation were against the bill and parliament was going through it at breakneck speed in order to prevent the arrival of too many petitions from all over the country.[25] The decision to bring the bill into the house of lords, even though the outcome there was in doubt, was explained with tactical reasons.[26] Even if the bill should be rejected there, it would be less of a political reverse than a defeat in the upper house after it had been passed by the Commons. Besides, the Whigs were able to pretend that they were simply agreeing to something decided by the Lords and so, hopefully, annoy their constituents less.

The passing of the Septennial Act was considered a Whig triumph, the proposal of the Peerage Bill as a sort of plan B on their part, in order to secure a majority in the house of lords even after George II's accession to the throne. But diplomats were aware of the problems raised by the bill, both on the constitutional level (specifically, whether the provisions on Scottish peers violated the Act of Union) and on the parliamentary level, since the Commons were very reluctant to pass it.[27] That, Pucci observed, was why the Court Party, after having tried its best to manage enough members to pass it, at first decided to 'smother' the bill in the house of lords rather than risk defeat in the lower house.[28] It is significant that the decision to re-introduce the bill in late autumn 1719, after it had been abandoned before the summer recess, was read by some diplomats as evidence of the fact that now the

[20] *LJ*, xix, 351; ASGe, AS, 2279: despatch 28 Dec. 1711.

[21] ASGe, AS, 2279: despatches 2, 9 and 23 May 1712.

[22] ASVe, S/DAR/I, 91: despatches 3 and 17 Apr. 1716 NS.

[23] ASFi, MdP, 4222: despatches 6, 13 ('un colpo mortale') and 27 Apr. 1716 NS.

[24] De Trivié, though favourable to the measure, sarcastically remarked that the Whigs were thus repealing the Triennial Act they had forced on William III, ASTo, C/MPE/N/GB, 4/2, ff. 568–9: despatch 20 Apr. 1716 NS.

[25] ASFi, MdP, 4222: despatches 11 and 18 May 1716 NS.

[26] ASFi, MdP, 4222: despatch 27 Apr. 1716 NS.

[27] ASFi, MdP, 4223: despatch 13 Mar. 1719 NS; on the Scottish factor, cf. Clyve Jones, ' "Venice Preserv'd; or A Plot Discovered": The Political and Social Context of the Peerage Bill of 1719', in *A Pillar of the Constitution: The House of Lords in British Politics 1640–1784*, ed. Clyve Jones (1989), 87.

[28] 'ha stimato à proposito di soffogarlo nella Camera Alta ove ebbe origine', ASFi, MdP, 4223: despatches 10 and 24 Apr., 1 May 1719 NS.

government was sure that it would pass.[29] At the time, Pucci had just arrived from Rotterdam, after a dreadful crossing that lasted seven days, with rough seas and contrary winds. One suspects he was still sick when he wrote to the grand duke of Tuscany, because his mistake was quite unusual in a man who displayed a good knowledge of English politics: 'everything will go as the Court wishes, both in these reigns, and abroad', and, as to the bill, 'those who wish for it and support it must have taken steps to secure its approval, as they would not present it again, were they not certain of success'.[30] As it turned out, the Commons sank the bill and Pucci tried to excuse his mistake in his following despatch. He mentioned that there had been a widespread sensation that the bill would pass, but above all, he underlined 'the uncertainty of those deliberations that depend on so many, and so different humours'.[31] Thus the outcome was basically blamed on the nature of parliament.

3. *Taming Parliament*

The fact that parliament was perceived as a formidable centre of power did not necessarily imply that it was beyond control. As a matter of fact, there was a growing consciousness among Italian diplomats of the possibility of something else at the heart of the political system of Britain, something able to rein in even the tumultuous assembly in Westminster. This alternative source of power was identified in a strong (premier) minister. At first only a minority of Italian agents shared this opinion, so convincing was their idea of parliament as potentially unmanageable, and so great was usually their shock at the clamour surrounding some elections. An exception was Benedetto Viale, envoy from the Republic of Genoa, who, writing just before the 1708 elections and forecasting a Whig victory, stated that this prospect, not relished by a queen whom he saw as more on the Tories' side, could really vanish in a day. If the queen changed her lord treasurer before parliament met, the new minister, provided he was clever enough, would easily win many members of parliament on the court's side and induce them to leave their party.[32] In this view, royal prerogative and patronage could control parliament. This idea was shared by a restricted number of diplomats and had greater chances to prevail when a strong figure was acting as chief minister, such as Robert Harley, later earl of Oxford. At other times, trusting someone with the skills to keep parliament under control might be harder, but still, it was worth trying. Victor Amadeus II suggested that his men in London should take special care in identifying who the actual premier minister was, bearing in mind that the real holder of the place might not depend on the prestige of the office he was holding in the counsels of the sovereign. If such a man existed, however, he was unquestionably 'the driving force of government'.[33]

---

[29] ASMo, CAI, 10: despatch 11 Dec. 1719 NS.

[30] 'Tutto anderà come vuol la Corte sì riguardo al di fuori, che al di dentro di questi regni. [...] quei che lo bramano, ed appoggiano averanno prese le loro misure, e [...] non lo riproporrebbero senza esser sicuri d'un buon evento', ASFi, MdP, 4223: despatch 11 Dec. 1719 NS.

[31] 'quanto siano incerte le deliberazioni che dependano dalla diversità, e pluralità di tanti umori' ASFi, MdP, 4223: despatch 27 Dec. 1719 NS.

[32] *Relazioni di ambasciatori*, ed. Morandi, 182.

[33] E.g. ASTo, C/MPE/N/GB, 4/1: Victor Amadeus II's instructions to Marquis de Trivié, 1713 ('il principal mobile del ministero').

The quest for such a man was over in Walpole's time, and with the consolidation of the Robinocracy from the 1720s Italian diplomats seemed to take a more relaxed attitude. In their eyes, Sir Robert was the man who had tamed parliament, and consequently the endemic instability of the British polity was becoming less appalling.[34] Even Riva, who in his report to Rinaldo III, duke of Modena, painted the rather chaotic picture of the constitution quoted above, explained that the king of Great Britain was not a figurehead, a duke of Venice, since 'the clever and cunning ministers administer the two houses at their discretion'.[35] Supreme in this skill, according to him, was Walpole, whom he described as 'the oracle of England', master at court, in the house of commons, and in the nation as well, to the point that he 'will be minister and arbiter of Great Britain as long as he wants to'. Riva was really struck by the fact that when a year before the rumour had spread that Walpole was going to retire from politics, there had been a ten per cent loss in public funds.[36] Trust in Sir Robert's skills was a constant element of diplomatic reporting throughout his tenure of office. Still, it is noteworthy that not all diplomats who believed that Walpole was in control of parliament were aware of the fact that an important pillar of his predominance was his decision to remain a member of the house of commons and thus to keep in check, both through the force of sheer numbers and his talent in debate, the attempts of an opposition vocal in its criticism of the ministry. Some tend rather to focus on George II's support for his minister or on the strength of patronage, if not open corruption, as the source of Walpole's power. There is thus, sometimes, a blatant contradiction between the view of the prime minister as a supremely crafted politician and the idea of a power resting not on his talents, but on the royal resources on which he was able to draw.

Solid as the foundations of the Robinocracy were, it was forced to admit defeat in the Excise Crisis, which offers an outstanding example of how the representatives of Italian states had by that time taken for granted that Walpole would always manage parliament according to his aims. This is even more striking, since it is one of the few cases in which diplomats rid themselves of their London-centred perspective and paid attention to the great turmoil in the country; they wrote that petitioning had been carried on and towns were presenting addresses to the king or instructions to members of parliament.[37] Still, they continued to believe that the fate of the scheme would be decided in Westminster and that the ministry would never risk defeat there. At the time, the chargé d'affaires from the duchy of Modena was Giovanni Giacomo Zamboni. A man with a long experience of Britain, he was well aware of the opposition to the excise scheme and thought that passing the bill would not be worthwhile, the nation being so strongly prejudiced against it.[38] To his surprise, the bill was brought forward; he concluded that if that was the ministry's choice, there would possibly be a great uproar, but the excise would pass without the shadow of

---

[34] Contrariwise, even during the Walpolean era French diplomats perceived the British system as unstable: see, Jeremy Black, *Debating Foreign Policy in Eighteenth-Century Britain* (Farnham, 2011), 49–50.

[35] 'gli avveduti, e scaltri ministri regolano a loro talento le due Camere', BEUMo, MS it. 678, f. 1v: 'Descrizione di Londra'.

[36] 'l'Oracolo d'Inghilterra […] questi sarà il ministro arbitro della G. Bretagna sino a che vorrà esserlo', BEUMo, MS it. 678, ff. 82–84: 'Relazione della corte britannica'. Cf. also ASFi, MdP, 4229: despatch 19 Feb. 1731 NS.

[37] ASFi, MdP, 4230: despatches 9, 16 and 23 Feb. 1733 NS; ASVe, S/DAR/I, 99: despatch 6 Apr. 1733.

[38] ASMo, CAI, 20: despatches 2 and 23 Jan., 20 Feb. 1733 NS.

a doubt. Zamboni repeated this statement at least eight times, in his letters home.[39] His surprise when Walpole was forced to abandon the scheme is echoed in the despatches of his colleagues, but Zamboni went a step further and realised that it had been a victory of 'the people', rather than of the opposition.[40]

In spite of his setback in 1733, Walpole continued to be seen as the man in charge of the kingdom, with Zamboni describing him as basically *the* ministry.[41] Sometimes, such as in the despatches of another agent from Modena, Abbot Pareti, the praise is so openly bestowed on 'the most wise minister'[42] that one wonders whether the writer was contemplating the possibility that his letters would end in Walpole's hands. Consequently, his fall in 1742 was considered a serious moment of crisis. Despatches usually give a detailed account of the events in late 1741 and early 1742: the unsatisfactory outcome of the general election, the attempts on the part of the ministry to muster a working majority in the Commons and the fierce determination of the opposition, the failed attempts of the court to reach an agreement with the prince of Wales or the duke of Argyll or to buy off enough members,[43] and Walpole's confidence even when his majority grew thinner. Diplomats offered their interpretation of the reasons that weakened the administration. The representative of the Republic of Genoa, Giambattista Gastaldi, mentioned both the dismissal of Argyll in 1740 and a sort of overconfidence on Walpole's part, which had led to an insufficient employment of the king's money in the election.[44] The opposition had thus spied an opportunity and produced an enormous effort at the polls, while in Scotland Argyll's defection had meant the loss of 28 members on the government's side. At first, some thought that the prime minister, backed by the crown, would still get over the difficult situation, possibly taking advantage of the Christmas recess or of the support of the Independents. In the meantime, everything seemed deadlocked. The Sardinian envoy, Chevalier Osorio, wrote to his king that he could not follow his instructions: 'one does not know with whom one has to deal'.[45] With the passing of weeks, however, the sensation set in that what diplomats were witnessing was the showdown between two long-contending factions and that Walpole would fall. When at last this happened, the news was hailed as a real revolution and immediately Italian diplomats started worrying about the dreadful consequences this might have. Apocalyptic predictions seemed the order of the day. Gastaldi

---

[39] ASMo, CAI, 20: despatches 9 Jan., 13 and 20 Feb., 13, 20 and 27 March, 3 and 17 Apr. 1733 NS. Zamboni's adamantine belief was shared by the Venetian resident Giovanni Domenico Imberti, ASVe, S/DAR/I, 99: despatches 2 and 16 Mar., 6 Apr. 1733.

[40] 'o per dir meglio il Popolo', ASMo, CAI, 20: despatch 1 May 1733 NS.

[41] ASMo, CAI, 20: despatch 22 May 1733 NS.

[42] E.g. ASMo, CAI, 21: despatches 27 July ('questo saviissimo ministero') and 21 Sept. ('prudentissimo ministero') 1736 NS.

[43] The Genoese secretary Gastaldi wrote that £4,000 had been offered each and commented that many had not accepted, perhaps out of fear, perhaps because they hoped to gain more with a place in the new administration, ASGe, AS, 2285: despatch 1 Feb. 1742.

[44] ASGe, AS, 2285: despatch 18 Jan. 1742. However, Argyll's dismissal was not, according to Gastaldi, Walpole's fault: he had come too late to prevent the king's decision, stage-managed by Harrington and Newcastle. Cf. Eveline Cruickshanks, 'The Political Management of Sir Robert Walpole, 1720–42', in *Britain in the Age of Walpole*, ed. Jeremy Black (Basingstoke, 1984), 42: 'Walpole could have been saved had it not been for the obstinacy of George II'.

[45] 'On ne sçait avec qui traiter', ASTo, Corte, Materie politiche per rapporto all'estero, Lettere ministri (Gran Bretagna) [hereafter cited as C/MPE/LM/GB], 48: despatch 5 Feb. 1742 NS.

drew a radical agenda for the parliament that had defeated Walpole: triennial parliaments, no more standing armies, ejection of placemen, 'in short, such measures will be taken, that Parliament will no longer be dependent upon the Court, but the Court upon Parliament'. Osorio had already described secret committees as 'the most absolute power in the constitution of this country' and written that an administration forced to follow the will of parliament 'would cause such confusion that everybody is afraid of the consequences, since it cannot be foreseen how far they will go, or when they will be stopped'.[46] Parliament unchained, no longer under the skilful management of a prime minister, was back as a sort of nightmarish creature, ready to thrive on chaos and confusion: 'new revolutions can be born every day'.[47] It would take some time before this image of parliament as an untamed entity and of the British polity as intrinsically unstable[48] disappeared. The flop of the secret committee the Commons had selected to inquire on Walpole's tenure of office was a first signal, but it was not until the outcome of the 1746 struggle between George II and his ministers that Italian diplomats came back to the idea that the ministry was the driving force in the British constitution – a force that, as a rule, was even able to keep parliament at bay.

4. *Sources of Information*

The sensation that in Britain everything might change so quickly proved a constant, nagging suspicion for Italian diplomats; their need to find reliable sources of information appears therefore all the more pressing. Obviously, each man sent to the court of St James's had to fend for himself and try to find which were the most useful sources upon which he could rely, but there are some recurring elements. A rather important factor seems to elude the historian: to what extent did these men have a good command of English? Evidence is, at best, patchy. Those who spent many years in London probably spoke English well, as can be inferred by the fact that sometimes they directly provided Italian translations of some texts.[49] In the case of Zamboni, who spent most of his life in England, his fluency in English is evident from his vast correspondence that survives in the Bodleian library.[50] Other cases are less clear-cut. Complaints about the fact that Sir Robert Walpole's knowledge of foreign languages was limited to a smattering of French, and that interactions with him implied the

[46] 'Insomma si prenderanno misure tali, che il Parlamento non dipenderà più dalla Corte; ma la Corte dal Parlamento' ASGe, AS, 2285: despatch 22 Feb. 1742 (in his 25 Jan. 1742 despatch, Gastaldi had even evoked Charles I's fate). For Osorio's words ('il n'y a rien de plus absolu dans la constitution de ce Gouvernement', 'ce qui causeroit des confusions dont il n'y a personne qui n'en craigne ni les consequences, n'etant pas possible de prevoir jusqu'où elles pourroient aller, ni quand on pourroit les arreter') cf. ASTo, C/MPE/LM/GB, 48, despatches 5 and 12 Feb.1742 NS.

[47] ASGe, AS, 2285, despatches 15 and 22 Mar., 3 May ('da un giorno all'altro ponno nascere altre rivoluzioni') 1742.

[48] In Osorio's words: 'il est impossible de predire quel sera le succès de tant de brigues entre des gens si capricieux, et si extraordinaires', ASTo, C/MPE/LM/GB, 48: despatch 13 Apr. 1742 NS.

[49] Giraldi boasted that he opened a channel with Queen Anne's new favourite, Abigail Masham, thanks to his command of the language (and the recommendation of the duchess of Shrewsbury), ASFi, MdP, 4234: Giraldi to Duke Cosimo III, 17 Apr. 1711 NS.

[50] Bodl., MS Rawl., letters 116–38. I am very grateful to Robin Eagles, who directed me to the treasure trove of Zamboni's papers.

assistance of members of his staff, hint at the fact that some diplomats were not able to address the great man in English.[51]

A common feature is the variety of sources Italian diplomats used in their correspondence home. The fact that they were serving their masters in a bustling town was very helpful: one was surrounded by different sources of information, both public and confidential. First of all, the post played quite an important role. In the despatches sent by diplomats, London appears as the centre where news from different parts of continental Europe were collected, and from where the acquired information was spread to Italy. However, it is not easy to understand exactly which was the source of the news, as official correspondence was usually vague about that. Reading between the lines, one sometimes understands that the ultimate source was a newsletter or a gazette. At other times, it appears that information came from the net of diplomatic correspondence, with envoys in other European towns reporting about the most important events (or simply rumours) in their place of residence. In spite of possible rivalry, news circulated also among foreign ministers in London. After all, they spent tense hours together in the waiting rooms of the mighty, and shared official or friendly meals. Some Italian diplomats seemed to meet rather frequently, but it was possible to develop a confidential relation also with agents coming from north of the Alps: apparently one of the Imperial ministers was ready to show the drafts of his despatches to the resident of the Duchy of Modena.[52]

Although news from outside Britain played an important part in diplomatic correspondence, it was intelligence about the British court and political world that constituted the most prized knowledge an envoy to London could acquire. It was also – they felt – the most difficult one, in light of the ever-changing character of the political landscape. Once more, diplomats relied on a variety of sources. Newspaper accounts were mentioned in despatches, usually to confirm news, and even press clippings were sent to Italy. Regrettably, these attachments have often disappeared from archives. During the first decades of the century, it is also quite difficult to identify exactly which newspapers diplomats were referring to, even though the *London Gazette* is sometimes cited. This changed in the late 1720s and early 1730s, at the time of the struggle of opposition newspapers against Sir Robert Walpole: *The Craftsman* came then to be mentioned in diplomatic correspondence, and even caricatures against 'the prime and sole minister' were alluded to.[53]

Alongside newspapers, newsletters were a valuable source of information, although the details about them prove elusive. Newsletters (sometimes in French) played a vital role, especially when it came to one of the key elements in the reports to Italy: the activity of parliament. Newsletters were sometimes explicitly used as the source of knowledge on this subject;[54] on the other hand, our sources reveal that diplomats from time to time attended parliamentary sittings, even bringing their own guests. On the whole, they seemed well

[51] BEUMo, MS it. 678, f. 84: 'Relazione della corte britannica'.

[52] ASMo, CAI, 10: despatch 17 Feb. 1719 NS.

[53] Branding the most influential member of the administration as prime and/or sole minister had been a traditional opposition tactic at least since Oxford's times. Walpole was particularly open to this kind of accusation, which was frequently echoed in the pages of *The Craftsman*. For a few examples, cf. A.F. Robbins, 'Prime Minister', *Notes and Queries* (8th ser., xi, 1897), 69–73.

[54] If no political commentary was needed, Zamboni sometimes simply referred his readers to the French newsletter on parliamentary business he attached to his despatches.

informed on what was going on in Westminster. A case study offers valuable insights into the sources on parliamentary activity. If the papers that were once attached to despatches usually have not survived, the correspondence of Vincenzo Pucci is a notable exception. When Pucci sent parliamentary acts such as the king's speech, the addresses of thanks and the reply of the sovereign, they came in the original English text, usually in an official publication, together (always for the king's speech) with a translation, which could be either in Italian or French. The first case is self-explanatory: Pucci translated the text himself (or had it translated) in the same language he used in his correspondence with his superiors. But why in French? One suspects that sometimes, to spare time, he used a translation that was already available in London, where there was a market for French translations of these sorts of documents. This impression is strengthened by the evolution of the reports on parliamentary activity in Pucci's correspondence. When parliament was in session, he wrote, in a separate sheet, what is called 'a diary' on the activity of both houses. At first this account had been in Italian, and in Pucci's hand. At a later date, however, he attached a very similar document but in French, and written by another hand: this does look like a newsletter specifically dedicated to parliament, and probably a similar source can be claimed for the French translations of the documents mentioned above.[55] A specific entry for 'divisions, and other parliamentary papers' appears constantly in the accounts Pucci sent to Florence. His correspondence shows examples of further interesting material. In 1730, many despatches lingered on British foreign policy, and the attacks on Walpole over the Treaty of Seville. Pucci sent to Florence no fewer than five pamphlets on this topic, as well as copies of two issues of the opposition newspaper *The Craftsman*, containing articles condemning the government's foreign policy; he observed that, even though he dismissed the newspaper as 'Pulteney's outbursts', it was a vain attempt to discredit the ministry.[56]

Naturally an insider would have been the best possible source of information, but unfortunately diplomats were seldom explicit in their correspondence about how and from whom they got the information they sent home. This has also something to do with the nature of the historical sources that have survived. Diplomatic reporting was in fact based on two different genres: the weekly despatches sent by diplomatic agents to their princes, and the *Relazione finale* (final report), which ambassadors mostly presented at the end of their mission. While despatches usually still form an identified – and often catalogued – archival series in the 'Court', 'Senate' or 'Secret' archive of the pre-unification Italian states, finding a final report is quite a different matter, and only a few of them have emerged so far. The problem is that, whereas the final report was presented or discussed when the ambassador had come back, and with all guarantees of secrecy, a weekly despatch was in danger of being intercepted, and thus writing down one's source of information was usually avoided. Rather vague phrases such as 'a friend', or 'someone in the know' or 'a person of quality' were usually preferred. There are some exceptions though, and in the ciphered parts of

---

[55] It is interesting that the plan of the 1712 lottery Viceti sent to Genoa (cf. above, note 11) had likewise been printed in French: 'A Londres, de l'imprimerie de Jean Barber, dans la rue de Lambeth-Hill, 1712'. However, according to Paul Mantoux, *Notes sur les comptes rendus des séances du parlement Anglais au XVIIIe siècle conservés aux archives du Ministère des Affaires Etrangères* (Paris, 1906), 63–6, *précis des débats* were added to the correspondence of French diplomats only from the 1730s.

[56] E.g. 'parte, e sfogo principalmente di Pulteney avversario dichiarato del Cavaliere Walpole', ASFi, MdP, 4229: despatch 18 Dec. 1730 NS.

despatches, reserve could be dropped. Sometimes one was forced to do so: in 1719, Riva pressed his duke for extraordinary funds in order to pay the intelligence he acquired from Sir Luke Schaub, presented as 'Mr Scob, [...] a man who is in the secret of everything'.[57] Tight-fisted as Italian princes seemed to be when it came to providing money for their agents abroad, it was evidently necessary to be quite explicit in order to be granted more, even for such a vital aim.

If sometimes second-string members of the administration could be managed, acquiring knowledge from ministers was a more difficult task. First of all, getting their attention might not be easy. To their surprise, diplomats perceived another peculiarity of the English government: the predominance of domestic rather than foreign policy. Except when a great crisis was looming or taking place, foreign policy was not appealing, and when the administration was under attack over domestic reasons, diplomats candidly wrote that ministers were better left alone. In any case, they simply did not have any time to spare for foreign envoys. Circumstances were worse during parliamentary recess, when in London there seemed to be basically nothing to do for members of the cabinet, with the result that they disappeared into the country, beyond the reach of all but the most stubborn and ingenious foreign agents. When at last it was possible to get a minister's ear, diplomats had to be cautious: they were aware of the differences inside the ministry, and of the possibility of being enlisted in the support of one of the factions that were fighting for supremacy in the administration. Italian residents did not limit themselves to the minister who was in charge of their area (i.e., the southern secretary), but they tried to be in touch with many at a time. Gaining the confidence of the chief minister would have been the ultimate prize, but it was extremely difficult. A remarkable exception is the *Relazione Finale* of the envoy extraordinary of the duke of Savoy to England, Pierre de Mellarède, in 1713. The report deals at length with what Oxford had told Mellarède at their meetings. This is valuable in itself, but a further statement is even more telling: the lord treasurer mentioned a Savoyard diplomat who had previously served in London, Count Maffei, as the only foreign minister who had not conspired to topple the ministry. In return, Oxford had taken Maffei into his confidence and told him everything he needed to know to serve his master, while other diplomats were left in the dark: 'While the others knew only what they read in the Gazettes'.[58] One wonders whether Oxford's original words and meaning were specific (the *London Gazette*) or more generic ('gazettes' as a synonym for newsletters or newspapers). The fact that Mellarède's final report contains insights into the thorniest issues of the time, including the possibility of a Jacobite succession and the existence of a will of Queen Anne in which she acknowledged the rights of the Pretender, makes one wonder if he received this sort of intelligence from the same source that had served his predecessor so well.

British ministers usually tended to be close-mouthed. This was not true, as a rule, for the Hanoverians, and to them diplomats appealed when they wanted information. Members of the Hanoverian entourage were often playing a different game than the one played by the

---

[57] ASMo, CAI, 10: despatches 5 and 20 Jan. ('quest'uomo ch'è nel segreto di tutto') 1719 NS. Schaub was private secretary to Lord Stanhope. A ciphered remark in Riva's 28 Apr. 1719 NS despatch styles him as 'our Scob' ('il nostro Scob').

[58] 'pendant que les autres ne sçavoient que ce qu'ils lisoient dans les Gazettes', Domenico Carutti, '*Relazione sulla corte d'Inghilterra del consigliere di Stato Pietro Mellarède*', Miscellanea di storia italiana, xxiv (1885), 235–6.

© 2022 *The Author(s). Parliamentary History published by John Wiley & Sons Ltd. on behalf of Parliamentary History Yearbook Trust.*

administration, and so they could be open to interaction with foreign diplomats. Moreover, they were always keen on foreign policy, which was at times neglected by their British counterparts. Gaining their confidence was therefore worthwhile, and so it does not come as a surprise that among the sources quoted in despatches appear the names of the likes of Bernstorff and Bothmer:[59] even if Hanoverian statesmen did not betray secrets, they seemed to be more available than British ones when a foreign envoy sought an interview. At a later date, when the influence of Hanoverian ministers vanished, diplomats could try the same move with the English politicians who chose to uphold George II's Hanoverian interest.

There are two further sources of information that at least some Italian diplomats were ready to use. One was the opposition: for the reasons explained above, cultivating the friendship of members of the opposition was a sort of insurance policy. It was also useful to gain knowledge, and sometimes one is tempted to guess that members of the opposition were hidden behind the anonymous 'friends' who were acknowledged in the despatches as the source of juicy political gossip, or of behind-the-scenes details about negotiations on a reshuffle in the ministry or on parliamentary activity.[60] Another source is public opinion. The regard shown by Italian diplomats to the feelings of the people is, in a way, surprising. Was it possibly because of their perception of the British constitution as constantly on the brink of collapsing into dangerous democracy? This aside, a view of the general feeling of the nation is mentioned in diplomatic correspondence when both foreign and domestic policy issues are under discussion. It is difficult to tell on what the judgment was founded. Of course, they might have read newsletters or the press, but often one is under the impression that they based their sensations mainly on what happened in London, and that the behaviour of London crowds mattered a great deal in their judgment of the situation. Yet there are exceptions, such as in the case of the Excise Crisis, when it appears that foreign ministers secured newsletters in order to be informed of what was happening throughout the kingdom.

A final remark can be made on the occasions when the sources of information used by Italian diplomats did not prove reliable. They seldom simply believed 'fake news', but sometimes too strong a dependence on a specific kind of source led to failure. The fact that this happened especially when the ministry eventually met with a disappointment is telling; possibly some diplomats relied too much on their sources in the administration. The rejection of the Peerage Bill and the withdrawal of the Excise Scheme, two of the bitterest defeats suffered by the court and ministry in the early 18th century, coincided with drastically wrong forecasts on the part of some of the veterans of the Italian diplomatic corps in London. Perhaps this shows that a faith in the ability on the part of the ministers to control even parliament sometimes led to excessive dependence on their word. Alternatively, it confirms that, in spite of the many sources they used, Italian diplomats were still at risk of ending up puzzled by all the forces at work in the British polity.

[59] E.g. ASFi, MdP, 4223: 'Minuta' 28 Jan. 1718 NS; ASMo, CAI, 10: despatches 3 Nov. and 22 Dec. 1719 NS.

[60] In 1727–8, Zamboni, who however at the time was not serving an Italian prince, but Ludwig IV, landgrave of Hesse-Darmstadt, even intrigued with Pulteney, among Walpole's fiercest opponents, to put his hands, or at least his eyes, on a copy of the 1721 treaty between Britain and Spain, Bodl., MS Rawl., letters 119, ff. 200–1 and letters 123, f. 467.

Appendix: Giuseppe Riva and Samuel Pufendorf's *De Statu Imperii Germanici*[61]

As mentioned above, one of the most striking examples of an Italian diplomat's mystified judgment on the British political system, namely the one included in the final report of the Modenese Giuseppe Riva, was couched in a language reminiscent of Samuel Pufendorf's analysis of the Holy Roman Empire in his *De Statu Imperii Germanici*. If – as it is very plausible – this is not a coincidence, it seems more probable that Riva had come across the text of the Saxon philosopher in London rather than in Italy. *De Statu* was enormously successful, with 18 Latin editions before 1734, printed in 30,000 – or perhaps even 300,000 – copies.[62] None had seen the light in Italy, since the typographical data of the 1667–8 Veronese edition of *De Statu* are almost certainly spurious.[63] Actually, no other book published by the alleged printer, Franciscus Giulius, is recorded in the central catalogue of Italian libraries.[64] In contrast, most of Pufendorf's works had been enjoying a long fortune in Britain. *De Jure Naturae* had been favourably discussed (and quoted at length) by James Tyrrell in 1681,[65] the same work had been recommended by John Locke in the first edition of *Some Thoughts Concerning Education*,[66] to which *De Officio Hominis et Civis* was added in 'The third edition enlarged'.[67] By the time Riva was living in England, and even more so by the time he wrote his final report, literally dozens of editions and translations of the Saxon jurist had been published in Britain.[68] As far as *De Statu* is concerned, Edmund Bohun published two editions of his translation (and slight adaptation) of Pufendorf's pamphlet, in 1690 (but the name of the translator was kept anonymous) and in 1696. It has been argued that they must have been especially popular among the diplomats at the court of St James's.[69] Even as a Catholic, Riva would not have been prevented from reading most of Pufendorf's works by their inclusion in the *Index Librorum Prohibitorum*. It is true that the

---

[61] I am very grateful to Michael Schaich for calling my attention to Pufendorf's text and to Bernardo Pieri who introduced me to the reception of the Saxon philosopher in 18th-century Italy.

[62] Cf. Samuel Pufendorf, *The Present State of Germany; Translated by Edmund Bohun, 1696*, ed. M.J. Seidler (Indianapolis, 2007), xiii, note 10.

[63] Andreas Osiander, 'Irregulare aliquod corpus et monstro simile: Can Historical Comparisons Help Understand the European Union?' (Aug. 28, 2010), 6, note 13, available at SSRN: http://doi.org/10.2139/ssrn.1648807 (accessed 5 Dec. 2020).

[64] https://opac.sbn.it/ (accessed 13 Jan. 2021).

[65] James Tyrrell, *Patriarcha non Monarcha: The Patriarch Unmonarch'd. Being Observations on a Late Treatise and Divers Other Miscellanies, Published under The Name of Sir Robert Filmer, Baronet: in Which The Falseness of Those Opinions That Would Make Monarchy* Jure Divino *Are Laid Open, and the True Principles of Government and Property (Especially in our Kingdom) Asserted. By a Lover of Truth and of His Country* (1681), 236–9.

[66] John Locke, *Some Thoughts Concerning Education* (1693), 221 [§ 175].

[67] (1695), 322 [§ 186]. On Locke's admiration for Pufendorf see also M.P. Thompson, 'Significant Silences in Locke's Two Treatises of Government: Constitutional History, Contract and Law', *The Historical Journal*, xxxi (1988), 275–94 and Colin Heydt, *Moral Philosophy in Eighteenth-Century Britain: God, Self and Other* (Cambridge, 2018), 5–6.

[68] Cf. Klaus Luig, 'Zur Verbreitung des Naturrechts in Europa', *Tijdschrift voor Rechtsgeschiedenis / Revue d'Histoire du Droit / The Legal History Review*, xl (1972), 539–57; David Saunders and Ian Hunter, 'Bringing the State to England: Andrew Tooke's Translation of Samuel Pufendorf's De officio Hominis et Civis', *History of Political Thought*, xxiv (2003), 218; Guglielmo Sanna, 'La fortuna di Pufendorf in Inghilterra: il contributo del clero anglicano nella prima metà del Settecento', *Rivista Storica Italiana*, cxviii (2006), 82–3; Michael Seidler, 'Pufendorf's Moral and Political Philosophy', *The Stanford Encyclopedia of Philosophy*, ed. E.N. Zalta, https://plato.stanford.edu/archives/spr2018/entries/pufendorf-moral/ (accessed 12 Dec. 2020).

[69] Heinz Duchhardt, 'Pufendorf in England: Eine unbekannte Übersetzung von Pufendorfs Reichsverfassungsschrift aus dem Jahre 1690', *Archiv für Kulturgeschichte*, lxxii (1990), 152.

Einleitung zu der Historie der vornehmsten Reiche und Staaten was put on the list in 1693, but it was followed only in 1714 by *De Jure Naturae*, while his other works had to wait much longer, until 1754 for the book of our interest, *De Statu.*[70]

The situation was completely different in Italy. Historians have highlighted the delay of the first appearance of Italian editions of Grotius's and Pufendorf's works, with the first adaptations of *De Officio Hominis et Civis* coming out no earlier than 1746, while the first translation, Giambattista Almici's version of *De Jure Naturae* (heavily indebted to Jean Barbeyrac's French edition), started appearing in Venice in 1757.[71] Even if educated persons like Riva could read the Latin originals, such a delay speaks volumes about the absence of a discussion on Pufendorf in early 18th-century Italy. Besides, to my knowledge no Latin edition of the works of the Saxon jurist had been printed in Italy at the time. Pufendorf appears more frequently in the private correspondence and libraries of Italian intellectuals.[72] Alongside the Neapolitan philosopher Giambattista Vico, Ludovico Antonio Muratori is often credited with circulating Pufendorf's ideas in Italian culture and in a letter to Canon Agostino Pantò he celebrated the Saxon thinker among a very restricted number of representatives of the modern school of natural law ('great men, who won rare praise').[73] Still, it took many years before Pufendorf's texts were publicly discussed. It can be argued that Muratori is a possible channel of Riva's familiarity with the Saxon philosopher: they were both from Modena and had been in constant correspondence since 1715 at the latest; moreover, their letters were rather frequent, the tone constantly warm and books a recurrent topic. It is nonetheless true that, while Muratori harshly criticises Thomas Hobbes,[74] I could not trace any reference to Pufendorf in his letters to Riva (at least up to the time of the diplomat's final report).[75] Pufendorf is not mentioned in Muratori's correspondence with Riva's friend and successor Giovanni Giacomo Zamboni, either.[76]

Naturally, in the light of the pamphlet war that had followed the appearance of *De Statu*, the Italian diplomat might have discovered that book during the short stays in Vienna that punctuated the first years of his career. Nonetheless, Riva's choice of words, especially

---

[70] Cf. Franz Heinrich Reusch, *Der Index der verbotenen Bücher: Ein Beitrag zur Kirchen- und Literaturgeschichte* (2 vols, Bonn, 1883–5), ii/1, 173, who cites *De Statu* as one of the most striking examples of a work that reached the list of prohibited books inexplicably late (Reusch, *Der Index*, ii/1, 168).

[71] Luig, 'Zur Verbreitung', 543, 555–6; Diego Panizza, 'La traduzione italiana del "De Iure Naturae" di Pufendorf: giusnaturalismo moderno e cultura cattolica nel Settecento', *Studi Veneziani*, xi (1969), 483–528; Maurizio Bazzoli, 'Giambattista Almici e la diffusione di Pufendorf nel Settecento italiano', *Critica storica*, xvi (1979), 3–100.

[72] Cf. Bazzoli, 'Giambattista Almici', 51; Emanuele Salerno, 'Giusnaturalismo e discussione politica nella Toscana della prima metà del Settecento: Neutralità, indipendenza e governo giusto da Sutter a Buondelmonti (1703–1755)', University of Pisa PhD, 2012, 22–3, 29, 36–9, https://core.ac.uk/download/pdf/14704128.pdf (accessed 12 Dec. 2020).

[73] Bazzoli, 'Giambattista Almici', 51–4; for the quotation, cf. BEUMo, AM, 47/33A, f. 1: Muratori to Pantò, 10 July 1722 NS ('vi hanno atteso grandi uomini, con rara lor lode').

[74] BEUMo, AM, 48/23*bis*, f. 45v and f. 47: Muratori to Riva, 1 Apr. and 24 Dec. 1728 NS.

[75] Muratori's letters to Riva can be found in BEUMo, AM, 48/23*bis* or published in *Epistolario di L. A. Muratori*, ed. Matteo Càmpori, (15 vols, Modena, 1901–22), v–vii, and Ercole Sola, 'Curiosità storico-artistiche-letterarie tratte dal carteggio dell'inviato estense Giuseppe Riva con Lodovico Antonio Muratori: Con giunte e note illustrative', *Atti e memorie della R. Deputazione di storia patria per le provincie modenesi e parmensi* (3rd ser., iv, 1886), 197–392. Checking Riva's inedited letters to Muratori (with the exception of those in BEUMo, AM, 82/58 and 83/63, the only available in digital form) was prevented by the COVID-19 pandemic.

[76] *Edizione nazionale del carteggio di L.A. Muratori* (24 vols so far, Firenze, 1975–), xlvi, *Carteggi con Zacagni … Zurlini*, ed. Anna Burlini Calapaj (Firenze, 1975), 42–104.

his 'una mostruosità non deforme', seems an allusion to Bohun's translation of another passage in Pufendorf's text, 'all kinds of mixture can produce nothing at last but a monstrous deformed Government',[77] rather than to the original Latin version, 'qualiscunque mixtura non nisi monstrum aliquod civitatis producere apta sit'.[78] If this is correct, there is some irony in the fact that Riva, a subject of a prince who acknowledged the suzerainty of the emperor, ended up finding the key to his interpretation of the British political system in the English translation of a work by a Saxon philosopher offering one of the most controversial views of the Holy Roman Empire.

Acknowledgement

Open Access Funding provided by Università degli Studi di Bologna within the CRUI-CARE Agreement.

---

[77] *The Present State of Germany*, ed. Bohun, 150.

[78] Pufendorf, *De Statu*, 154–5 [ch. IV, § 8]. Seidler observes that 'some monster of a state' would have been a more correct translation, *The Present State of Germany*, ed. Seidler, 173, note *e*.

Philip Yorke and Thomas Birch: Scribal News in the Mid 18th Century*

MARKMAN ELLIS

This article examines the newsletter-writing practices of the Hardwicke circle, the intellectual coterie centred on Philip Yorke, 2nd earl of Hardwicke (1720–90), and Thomas Birch (1705–66). It begins by examining the 'Weekly Letter' written between Birch and Yorke from 1741–66 (BL, Add. MS 35,396-35,400). This comprised a letter written by Birch every Saturday when Yorke was not in London, describing the political and literary events of the week, together with Yorke's less regular replies. In form the Weekly Letter was modelled on a historical example of the scribal newsletter, itself a significant focus of the historical research of the Hardwicke circle. Yorke and Birch collected and preserved historical collections of 17th and 18th century scribal newsletters, as well as conducting research into the history of printed news. Yorke's interest in scribal news, encouraged by Birch's regular Weekly Letter, saw him subsequently establish an extensive network of newsletter correspondents on parliamentary affairs. As a case study of those interests, the article examines Yorke's 'Paris alamain', a commercial *nouvelle à la main* he secured from Paris through personal connections in France.

Keywords: Hardwicke circle; *nouvelle à la main*; newsletter; Thomas Birch; Philip Yorke, news history

1.

Scribal news was an important aspect of the news culture of the 'Hardwicke circle', the intellectual and sociable coterie associated especially with Philip Yorke, 2nd earl of Hardwicke (1720–90), and Thomas Birch (1705–66), secretary of the Royal Society. In the mid 18th century, the coterie developed sophisticated interests in a wide spectrum of news culture, including the history of scribal and printed news; the collecting of early newspapers and newsletters; and refining their own practices of scribal news. Birch, for example, wrote a manuscript weekly newsletter to Yorke on political and literary topics, the 'Weekly Letter', from 1741 to 1766; and Yorke wrote and published creative essays and hoaxes in news history.[1] David Miller has shown how the 'Hardwicke circle', so named for the first time in the 20th century, exercised considerable influence in intellectual institutions in London in

---

*In writing this article I would like to thank Christopher Reid and Rebecca Beasley, my colleagues in newsletter studies including Joad Raymond and Alex Barber, and the editors of this volume, Robin Eagles and Michael Schaich, for their help and assistance. All the mistakes I made by myself.

[1] Markman Ellis, 'Thomas Birch's "Weekly Letter" of "Literary Intelligence" (1741–1766): Correspondence and History in the Mid-Eighteenth Century Royal Society', *Notes and Records: The Royal Society Journal for the*

the mid-century, holding high office in or influencing the proceedings of the Royal Society, the Society of Antiquaries and the British Museum.[2] Although their activities in these institutions often focused on administrative reforms and secretarial diligence, rather than the kind of research outputs and projects to which the institutions were dedicated, both Birch and Yorke were also historians, writers and literary patrons of some influence. In this mode, they were also significant innovators in history writing, especially in their methodological insistence on the value of original documentary evidence, which they privileged over grand historical narrative.[3] In this sphere of activity, their innovative contribution to the history of news, both printed newssheets and manuscript newsletters, is contiguous with their history-writing practice. But, as this article explores, Yorke's experience with a commercial French *nouvelle à la main* service in the early 1750s, showed to him that not all scribal news was equal. In particular, he discovered that the *nouvelle à la main* from Paris, as a commercially driven enterprise, privileged scandal over news, and was operated in a distinctly different cultural and regulatory regime in France that severely constrained its contents.[4] As such, the Paris alamain, as he called it, failed to provide him with the private insight to literary and political news that he desired, especially in comparison with the Weekly Letter from Birch. In subsequent decades, in the 1760s and 1770s, Yorke, having learned from his experience with the Paris alamain, developed, as Christopher Reid has described, an extensive network of personal contacts and informants who wrote for him private letters of news reporting on debates in the house of commons.[5]

2. *The Weekly Letter Collaboration*

Yorke's interest in newsletters and scribal news emerged when he was still an undergraduate at Corpus Christi College, Cambridge, just before he first met Thomas Birch in 1740. Birch was a historian and clergyman who had benefited from the patronage of Yorke's father, also called Philip Yorke (1690–1764), later the 1st earl of Hardwicke.[6] Birch had been born a Quaker in Clerkenwell in London, the son of a coffee-mill maker, and had been educated in Quaker schools, where he also subsequently taught as an usher. After the death of his wife and son in 1729, Birch was baptised into the Anglican church in 1730, and ordained in 1731. Hardwicke presented him to the vicarage of Ulting in Essex in 1732, a parish in the gift of the lord chancellor, the first of a series of preferments made by Hardwicke.[7] Birch's skills in history writing, and in the management of scholarly projects, were demonstrated in his role as one of the chief editors of the *General Dictionary, Historical and Critical*, an expanded

---

[1] *(continued)* *History of Science*, lxviii (2014), 261–78; Markman Ellis, 'The *English Mercurie* Hoax and the Early History of the Newspaper', *Book History*, xxii (2019), 100–32.

[2] D.P. Miller, 'The "Hardwicke Circle": The Whig Supremacy and its Demise in the 18th-century Royal Society', *Notes and Records of the Royal Society*, lii (1998), 73–91, at 76.

[3] Laird Okie, 'Birch and the Historians', in *Augustan Historical Writing: Histories of England in the English Enlightenment* (Lanham, MD, 1991).

[4] *De Bonne Main: La communication manuscrite au XVIIIe siècle*, ed. François Moureau (Oxford and Paris, 1993).

[5] Christopher Reid, 'Reporting by Letter: The 2nd Earl of Hardwicke and his Parliamentary Correspondents', *Parl. Hist.*, xxxix (2020), 239–54.

[6] For the sake of clarity, this essay will refer to Philip Yorke, 2nd earl of Hardwicke, as Yorke, and the lord chancellor, Philip Yorke, 1st earl of Hardwicke, as Hardwicke.

[7] Birch was rector of St Margaret Pattens, a wealthy City parish, from 1746 to his death in 1766.

ten-volume edition of Pierre Bayle's *Dictionnaire Historique et Critique* (1697) that appeared between 1734 to 1741, for which Birch completed more than 600 biographies. While Yorke was still an undergraduate at Cambridge, Birch offered assistance to him as a tutor, and as a literary agent in London, undertaking a variety of roles including research and proof correction, literary advice and bibliographical services, as well as searching for and buying books and manuscripts for Yorke's library. Birch assisted in the publication of Yorke's ironic historical essay on Roman news writing, eventually published as 'On the *Acta Diurna* of the *Old Romans*' in the annual preface to Edward Cave's *Gentleman's Magazine* in 1740.[8] Birch also helped with the publishing arrangements for his prose fiction, *Athenian Letters* (1741–3), a collaborative work mostly written by Philip and his younger brother Charles Yorke, assisted by at least ten others including Birch, that anachronistically repurposed the scribal newsletter to relate the history of the Peloponnesian War between Greece and Sparta in the 5th century BC, as recorded by Thucydides and Plutarch.[9] Yorke left Cambridge (without completing his degree) on his marriage, on 23 May 1740, to Lady Jemima Campbell, *suo jure* Marchioness Grey, whose inherited property included a substantial country house, Wrest Park, near Bedford. Yorke and Lady Grey had an affectionate marriage, sharing interests in landscape gardening, architecture, natural philosophy and scientific institutions.

From 1741, Birch was closely engaged in the Yorke household's literary and intellectual life. When Yorke was in London, he attended breakfast with Yorke and Lady Grey at their townhouse in St James's Square. When the Yorkes were at Wrest, as they were for at least six months of the year, following the parliamentary calendar, Birch began a habit of writing a regular Saturday newsletter to Yorke. Birch's Weekly Letter was initiated on Tuesday 18 August 1741, apparently without any contractual negotiation or agreement, and was continued until 2 January 1766. It comprises 680 letters (1741–66), of which 428 are written by Birch, and 252 replies by Yorke.[10] Birch's newsletter summarised the political and literary events of the week: or, as Yorke described it in 1747, it mixed 'the occurrences of the literary with those of the political world'; Yorke's shorter response made 'observations' and responses to Birch's news and information.[11]

In format, Birch's newsletter was deliberately modelled on his understanding of 17th-century scribal news, derived from his research, noted below. In this way, it was typically a half-folio sheet folded in two to create four pages (bifolium), although there was some variation that saw it extended by another bifolium to five or six of potentially eight pages. Birch habitually added postscripts vertically to the fourth page, and occasionally to the central margin of page three, reflecting the high regard he had for filling his page. Yorke's reply comprised a letter of up to four pages, but often less, on the same format paper, usually every week or second week. The hebdomadal regularity of Birch's Weekly Letter, to which

---

[8] Philip Yorke, 'On the *Acta Diurna* of the *Old Romans*', *Gentleman's Magazine*, x (1740), preface, iii–viii.

[9] *Athenian Letters: or, the Epistolary Correspondence of an Agent of the King of Persia, Residing at Athens during the Peloponnesian War. Containing the History of the Times, in Dispatches to the Ministers of State at the Persian Court* (4 vols, 1741–3).

[10] Correspondence of Philip Yorke, 2nd earl of Hardwicke, with Rev. Thomas Birch, D.D., Secretary to the Royal Society, Hardwicke Papers, vols XLVIII–LII, BL, Add. MSS 35,396-35,400. The term 'Weekly Letter' appears to have been coined in the only extant book-length treatment of Birch's life: A.E. Gunther, *An Introduction to the Life of the Rev. Thomas Birch D.D., F.R.S., 1705–1766: Leading Editor of the General Dictionary … 1741, Secretary of the Royal Society and Trustee of the British Museum* (Halesworth, 1984), 45–6.

[11] BL, Add. MS 35397, ff. 64–5: Yorke to Birch, 4 Aug. 1747.

he was very committed, recalled the scribal newsletter. Furthermore, he used some of the typical formations of the scribal newsletter — notably the paragraph as a unit of news or information — but also borrowed framing structures from the familiar letter, including extensive polite salutations and humilific personal closing statements. There is evidence that Birch took some care over the compilation and composition of the Weekly Letter: for example, between 1759 and 1761, he used a small notebook to record potential topics and memoranda. As each topic was used, he scored a line through it, to gauge his progress through both the information and the material letter.[12] Birch's archive also preserves some rough drafts of his newsletter, demonstrating that on some occasions at least the letter sent to Yorke was a fair copy, improved by emendations and corrections to expression and style. A small number of his Weekly Letters were also copied and sent to other members of the Hardwicke circle, including Yorke's brother Charles, Daniel Wray and John Lawry.[13] Yorke was also in the habit of reading aloud from Birch's 'weekly Dispatch' to 'the good company' gathered at Wrest.[14]

Birch's weekly newsletter followed a distinctive pattern. Broadly, the first two or three pages were devoted to political news, which included information gleaned from other newsletters, printed newssheets and gossip or rumour collected by Birch. The latter half of the newsletter contained literary news and information from the intellectual culture of London, including notices of book publications, meetings of learned institutions and summaries or abstracts of learned journals. An important source for both, at least imaginatively, was Birch's London life, especially his visits to the coffeehouses, dining societies and theatres. Birch figured himself as, and probably was, a regular habitué of several 'literary' coffeehouses in London: notably Rawthmell's in St Martin's Lane, and George's and Tom's in Devereux Court, near to the Royal Society in Crane Court, as well as, on occasion, visiting other coffeehouses in search of news, such as Lloyd's in the City, and the Chapter in St Paul's Churchyard. His closeness to this associational world of intellectual culture in London was an important part of his value as a *nouvelliste*: even if his assiduity in collecting and reporting intelligence from these sources to some extent allied him with the calling of the Grub Street newsmonger.[15] Richard Flecknoe's 'Character of a Common Newsmonger' (1677) describes how the newsmonger or journalist picks up rumours and spreads them as true news in the gazettes and the coffeehouses.

In my 2014 article on the Weekly Letter, I argued that evidence from the material text, and internal evidence, suggested that for Birch there was a profound psychological dimension to completing the newsletter. In material terms, there is evidence that he took great care with the preparation of the Weekly Letter, that he aimed to fill his page, parcelling out his material to exactly fill the space available, squeezing in felicitations and greetings at

---

[12]BL, Add. MS 4471, ff. 143–56: Thomas Birch, memorandum book and diary combined, 1759–61. On the paragraph see Will Slauter, 'The Paragraph as Information Technology: How News Traveled in the Eighteenth-Century Atlantic World', *Annales (English Ed.)*, lxvii (2012), 253–78. On the memorandum book, see John Guillory, 'The Memo and Modernity', *Critical Inquiry*, xxxi (2004), 108–32, and Richard Yeo, *Notebooks, English Virtuosi, and Early Modern Science* (Chicago, 2014).

[13]References to reading Birch's 'Weekly Pacquet to Wrest', BL, Add. MS 4322, f. 95v: Daniel Wray to Birch, Queen's College, Cambridge, 23 Nov. 1744; Add. MS 4312, f. 103: John Lawry to Birch, Rochester, 28 Nov. 1756.

[14]BL, Add. MS 35396, f. 226: [Yorke] to [Birch], note, endorsed by Birch 'July 24 1744'.

[15]Richard Flecknoe, 'Character of a Common Newsmonger', in *Seventy Eight Characters of so Many Vertuous and Vitious Persons* (1677), 6.

the end. Chronologically, Birch was remarkably committed to the regular Saturday slot of
the letter, and equally remarkable for his assiduous application to its completion for over
26 seasons.[16] Although the newsletter writer is habitually demeaned or diminished in contemporary ideations, and their output is considered as a low or vulgar production, hastily
hammered out by a kind of Grub Street hack, Birch found a kind of historical nobility in his
calling. The relationship between Birch as *nouvelliste* and Yorke as client, was clearly marked
by their difference in status and class. However, there is no evidence that Birch was directly
remunerated for the Weekly Letter. Rather he was careful to maintain his self-construction
as an independent gentleman of some means, as a rector of a wealthy parish in the City
of London, with his own intellectual interests. Preferment was the wages of Birch's allegiance to the Hardwickes, and even that remained a largely unspoken debt. Birch figured his
newsletter as a service to the Hardwicke family, voluntary, unpaid and as such genteel. The
framing language used to describe the Weekly Letter correspondence helped to regulate
this social equilibrium, especially phrases that located it in the 'republic of letters' and 'the
literary world', suggesting that they met there as equals.[17] Furthermore, Yorke's letters were
larded with professions of friendship and equality, well in excess of the conventional polite
discourse of correspondence. He also repeatedly phrased his commands and requests using
a gentle self-deflecting irony, undercutting his social precedence. Rather than the simple
contractual and commercial arrangement of a newsmonger and client, Birch and Yorke's
Weekly Letter correspondence was managed in and through complicated patterns of emotional entanglement, signalling of gentlemanly virtue, and notions of equality between men
of letters.

The nomenclature of the Weekly Letter is further contextualised by the Hardwicke circle's historical interest in newsletters, which informed the way the letter was described and
preserved. Both Birch and Yorke, but especially Yorke, laced their discourse on the Weekly
Letter with a kind of self-deprecating irony intended to complicate and mystify the debts
of obligation and deference embedded in the correspondence. Yorke in particular enjoyed
describing his research and writing using the diction of its 17th-century antecedents, ex-
tending this to Birch and his more extensive writing projects whenever he could. In this
way, Yorke referred to Birch's Weekly Letter using a series of technical terms associated
with the early modern newsletter. He repeatedly used the term '*aviso*' or '*Avisi segreti*', for
example, an Italian word for a newsletter in 17th-century diplomatic correspondence: in
1743, for example, he comments that he had 'just perused your weekly *Avisi segreti* with
great pleasure, but am sorry they brought no more decisive news'.[18] As this suggests, one
of the qualities Yorke liked about his newsletter was that the knowledge of public affairs
it contained was private or secret, or at least, not known publicly. 'I wish you could pick
out a little, what is said to be going on behind the Curtain — we see enough of public
appearances in the Papers'.[19] In 1747, Yorke had compared Birch's newsletters to those of

[16]Ellis, 'Thomas Birch's "Weekly Letter"', 261–78.

[17]Birch used the phrase 'the Republic of Letters', BL, Add. MS 35398, f. 1: Birch to Yorke, London, 29
June 1751; and Add. MS 4322, ff. 109–10: Birch to Wray, Wrest, 23 Oct. 1752. Yorke referred to 'a free literary
Republic', Add. MS 35396, ff. 207–8: Yorke to Birch, 'Rest', 24 June 1744. Birch used the phrase 'the literary
world', Add. MS 35396, ff. 13–14: Birch to Yorke, London, 29 Aug. 1741; and Add. MS 35396, ff. 184–5: Birch
to Yorke, London, 29 Oct. 1743.

[18]BL, Add. MS 35396, f. 109: Yorke to Birch, 'Rest', 19 June 1743.

[19]BL, Add. MS 35396, f. 109: Yorke to Birch, 'Rest', 19 June 1743.

three 17th-century 'novelists', by which he meant the *nouvelliste* or newsletter writer: 'I shall set you far above those illustrious Novelists your Predecessors, Rowland White, Mr Chamberlain, & Master Garrard'.[20] In this letter, Birch was compared to an unrelated group of newsletter writers uncovered in Birch's own historical research: Rowland White, a secretary and news writer for Sir Philip Sydney in the period 1598–1600; George Garrard, master of the charterhouse and a gossipy newsletter writer to the earl of Strafford, 1633–5; and John Chamberlain, secretary in the household of Sir Dudley Carleton in the period 1598–1625. This is a somewhat precarious compliment of course, as these men, although in the service of great men of state, were themselves hired pens not so distant from the disreputable and vulgar trade of the newsmonger. Yet another historical analogy was coined by Yorke when he referred to his archive of Birch letters at Wrest as his 'Paper Office', recalling with some irony the government office of the secretaries of state that controlled the 17th-century newsletter system.[21] The deliberate archaism and foreignness of these terms helps Yorke associate Birch's weekly letter with an historically enduring practice of news writing.

3. *Historical Newsletter Research in the Hardwicke Circle*

Yorke's historicised descriptions of Birch's newsletter writing practice located it within the context of Birch's own historical research on early modern news systems. Birch's historical research was directly concerned with 16th- and 17th-century newsletters and their writers. Both Birch and Yorke were avid collectors of early modern correspondence collections when they found them, and Birch especially went to considerable lengths to consult early modern English correspondence in private and public collections. In 1740–1, for example, he took on the compilation of a seven-volume folio edition of the correspondence collection of John Thurloe (1616–68), secretary (1652–8), first, to the council of state, and afterwards to the two Protectors, Oliver and Richard Cromwell. In the course of his duties, Thurloe had organised a considerable and efficient network of correspondent newsletter writers, both domestic and foreign, and a comprehensive system for collating and managing the correspondence. Thurloe's papers were found concealed in the wainscot of a garret in his chambers in Lincoln's Inn in the 1690s: in 1740, Birch was commissioned to publish a selection of them by the bookseller Fletcher Gyles.[22] Birch's seven volume folio publication, *A Collection of the State Papers of John Thurloe, Esq* (1742) was at the forefront of a new innovation in history writing, the compilation of 'State papers'. This was a new term for official papers concerning government, first seen in a title in Samuel Haynes's publication of *A Collection of State Papers* from William Cecil's archive in 1740.[23] In the 'Preface' to *Thurloe*, Birch argued for 'the importance of state-papers, as the most solid and

---

[20]BL, Add. MS 35397, f. 77: Yorke to Birch, Wimpole, 22 Sept. 1747.

[21]BL, Add. MS 35397, f. 206: Yorke to Birch, Paris, 29 Aug. (OS) / 9 Sept. (NS) 1749.

[22]Birch's preface details the provenance of Thurloe's papers from their rediscovery to their purchase by Gyles in 1739. Most of the originals are now held in Oxford at Bodl. MS Rawl. A 1–73.

[23]*A Collection of State Papers: Relating to Affairs In the Reigns of King Henry VIII, King Edward VI, Queen Mary and Queen Elizabeth: From the Year 1542 to 1570*, ed. Samuel Haynes (1740). The term 'state papers' is also seen in *Letters, Memoirs, Parliamentary Affairs, State Papers, &c. […]. Publish'd from the Originals of the Lord Chancellor Bacon*, ed. Robert Stephens (1736).

useful foundation of history'.[24] As well as Thurloe's own correspondence, Birch included a large number, estimated at 350, of newsletters or 'letters of intelligence', albeit sometimes in truncated extracts, from Thurloe's extensive network of paid but otherwise unrecognised intelligence-gatherers.

Birch also assembled his own personal collection of newsletters. These were relevant to Birch's publication of the correspondence and papers of the Elizabethan spy Anthony Bacon (1558–1601),[25] assembled primarily from the 16 volumes of Bacon manuscript letters that Birch located in the Library at Lambeth Palace.[26] In the summer of 1750, Birch was permitted by the archbishop to borrow the volumes, one by one, to make relevant transcripts.[27] These papers were central to two publications: his *Historical View of the Negotiations between England, France and Brussels* (1749), and his two-volume *Memoirs of the Reign of Queen Elizabeth* in 1754.[28] In the course of this work, Birch acquired or transcribed a series of letters and papers on state affairs, related to Bacon, now in the Birch collection in the British Library. Additional Manuscript 4125 includes, for example, several series of manuscript newsletters: two French '*nouvelles*' from 1586 and 1588; 62 bifolium weekly newsletters in Italian in a variety of hands relating news of events in Venice, Rome and Antwerp from January 1593 to February 1594; and another series of 53 newsletters from April 1597 to March 1598.[29] The same volume also contains a newsletter from France from 1657, detailing the movements of Charles Stuart (Charles II) and the conflicts between the king of France and the *parlement*.[30] Another collection of 17th-century newsletters assembled by Birch is found in Additional Manuscript 4182, described in the catalogue as a 'Collection of Newsletters 1665–1746', including both printed and manuscript news. These manuscript newsletters include, for example, a continuous series in one hand describing domestic and foreign events from January to November 1665; and another series, dated from London, addressed to John Ellis, secretary of the revenue in Ireland, records domestic English occasional news from 9 September 1684 to 17 February 1695.[31] No record of the provenance

[24] *A Collection of the State Papers of John Thurloe, Esq; Secretary, First, to the Council of State, and Afterwards to the Two Protectors, Oliver and Richard Cromwell. In Seven Volumes. Containing Authentic Memorials of the English Affairs from the Year 1638, to the Restoration of King Charles II. Published from the Originals [...] The Whole Digested into an Exact Order of Time. To which is Prefixed, the Life of Mr. Thurloe: with a Complete Index to Each Volume* (1742), p. v.

[25] BL, Add. MS 4125, f. 11: Newsletter from Narbonne, 12 Nov. 1586; ff. 17, 21: From France, 24 Dec. 1590, 15 June 1591; ff. 24–37b: From Venice, 1 Jan.– 19 Feb. 1593/4; ff. 44–359b: From Antwerp, Rome, Venice, 27 June 1593–28 Feb. 1598. The origin of these newsletters is not clear.

[26] *Index to the Papers of Anthony Bacon (1558–1601) in Lambeth Palace Library (Mss. 647–662)* (Lambeth Palace Library, 1974).

[27] BL, Add. MS 35397, f. 249: Birch to Yorke, London, 23 June 1750.

[28] *An Historical View of the Negotiations between the Courts of England, France, and Brussels, from the Year 1592 to 1617. Extracted Chiefly from the MS. State-Papers of Sir Thomas Edmondes, Knt. Embassador in France, and at Brussels, [...] and of Anthony Bacon, Esq; [...] Never before Printed* (1749); *Memoirs of the Reign of Queen Elizabeth, from the Year 1581 till Her Death. In which the Secret Intrigues of Her Court, and the Conduct of Her Favourite, Robert Earl of Essex, both at Home and Abroad, are Particularly Illustrated. From the Original Papers of His Intimate Friend, Anthony Bacon, Esquire, And Other Manuscripts never before Published*, (2 vols, 1754).

[29] BL, Add. MS 4125, ff. 11–12: 'nouvelles' from Narbonne; ff. 24–37, 44–156: Newsletters from Venice etc., 1593–4 series; ff. 180–305: 1597–8 series [interspersed with other items].

[30] BL, Add. MS 4125, ff. 385–6.

[31] BL, Add. MS 4182, ff. 1–56: 1665 newsletter; ff. 57–81b: Ellis newsletter 1684–94. There are further series: Add. MS 4182, ff. 93–5, 97–8: Affairs in parliament, 29 May 1646–11 Feb. 1647; and Add. MS 4182, ff. 99–110: another set of newsletters from Paris, Rome and Vienna, 1654–8.

of these collections of newsletters has yet been located, and of course, their primary utility, for Birch as for now, is as historical sources relevant and interesting to the diverse historical periods of their production. But it is also relevant to note that their acquisition, collection, organisation and preservation in Birch's archive testifies to Birch's intense interest in original documents in the writing (or compilation) of history, including those by unlettered Grub Street newsmongers.

Christopher Reid has recently shown, in relation to newsletter reports of the proceedings of the house of commons, the extensive network of correspondents Yorke assembled to give him accounts of proceedings of the House in the 1760s and 1770s.[32] Yorke, while the member of parliament for Reigate (1741–64), had maintained a parliamentary journal for the sessions 1743–4 and 1744–5.[33] He also occasionally solicited reports on parliamentary debates when he was not able to attend himself. Birch's Weekly Letter included reports of parliamentary gossip whenever available. When Yorke was elevated to the Lords on the death of his father in 1764, Reid demonstrates how he made a 'more organised and sustained effort to establish a reporting network'.[34] For example, he received 135 letters reporting proceedings in the Commons in the 1768–74 parliament alone. Correspondents in his network included family members: his brother John Yorke (member of parliament); his nephew Philip Yorke (member of parliament); his cousin Charles Cocks (member of parliament); his son-in-law Thomas Robinson, 2nd Baron Grantham; and his second cousin Philip Yorke of Erthig (member of parliament). But he also requested and commanded parliamentary news from others, including the members of parliament Soame Jenyns and Sir John Hynde Cotton, and his exchequer clerks, E. Langton and Samuel Wilde.[35] Reid describes how Yorke could be a demanding master to his newsletter writers, even though it is not always clear what he did with the intelligence, as his own political career was nugatory. But for Yorke, the medium of the newsletter was itself of considerable value, not only for its historical resonances, but for the aura of private and inside knowledge it gave him. As a case study of Yorke's enthusiasm for scribal newsletters, this article will now turn to Yorke's efforts to establish and maintain a foreign correspondence in the form of a *nouvelle à la main* from Paris in the early 1750s. This was Yorke's first attempt to subscribe to (or perhaps establish) a newsletter on a commercial and contractual footing: in that sense it was a precursor to, or trial run for, the later more successful and sustained networks described in Reid's work, focused on parliamentary reporting in the period from the late 1760s to the late 1780s.

4. *Yorke's Paris Alamains: A Case Study in Hardwicke Newsletter Culture*

Yorke's 'Paris alamain' was a *nouvelle à la main*: a handwritten newsletter, distributed privately using the postal system, to a limited set of subscribers.[36] The context for it was established

---

[32] Reid, 'Reporting by Letter', 239–54

[33] BL, Add. MS 35337: parliamentary journal of the Hon. Philip Yorke, M.P. for Reigate, for the sessions 1743–4 and 1744–5.

[34] Reid, 'Reporting by Letter', 243.

[35] E. Langton's first name is not known.

[36] In this article, I refer to Yorke's newsletter from France, which he conceived in 1749 and received in sporadic series from 1751 to 1755, as his 'alamain' or 'Paris alamain', retaining the spelling he used, so as to distinguish it from wider discussion of the *nouvelle à la main*.

© 2022 *The Author(s). Parliamentary History published by John Wiley & Sons Ltd. on behalf of Parliamentary History Yearbook Trust.*

in 1749, when Yorke undertook a visit to Holland and France, his first to the continent. His immediate impetus was the appointment in 1749 of his younger brother, Lieutenant-Colonel Joseph Yorke (1724–92), to the post of 'secretary of embassy' to the new British ambassador to Paris, William Anne Keppel, 2nd earl of Albemarle (1702–54). While Yorke was away in Europe, travelling first in Holland, and then via Ghent and Lille to Paris, Birch sent him three Weekly Letters, care of Joseph Yorke at the Hôtel Anspach in Rue Jacob, and received three replies, two from Paris and one on Yorke's return, sent from Wrest. In addition, Birch maintained the regular flow of the Weekly Letter to Wrest, addressed to Jemima, Lady Grey, so that the Wrest file would be a complete record of the political and literary events in London while Yorke was away. Yorke complimented him on his diligence, noting that 'My Lady writes me word that you have shewn your regard to the Paper Office at Wrest by continuing the Lines of your *Avisi* through her hands.'[37] In order to meet these competing requirements, on two occasions Birch sent one letter to Yorke in Paris, and another to Lady Grey at Wrest for the library file. (The two versions have numerous points of similarity, although they are different).[38] On Yorke's return to London on or before 21 October, he complimented Birch on his faithful weekly newsletter: 'You have taken care to continue the History of the Times in your Letters to my Wife, she will be as good as her word, & paste them into the bound Collection—'.[39] The bound collection of the Weekly Letter was kept in Yorke's study at Wrest, where it could be consulted not only by Yorke but by other visiting literati.

In Paris, where he was staying in the Rue de Colombiers, Faubourg St Germain, Yorke undertook the kind of activities appropriate to a man curious in natural philosophy and *belles lettres*, supplemented by a busy round of social engagements facilitated by the embassy. He complained to Birch that this left little time for correspondence: 'Between the hurry of travelling & the dissipated Life one leads here, I have had but little time for keeping up even the most necessary Correspondences'.[40] In fact, Yorke's letter writing home to the friends in his coterie adopted a more expansively descriptive style, distinct from the usual mode he adopted in his replies to Birch, in which he made brief observations and responses. Yorke's travel letters may also have been informed by the style of the *nouvelle à la main* he encountered in Paris in the embassy, with paragraphs addressing politics, natural philosophy, literature and social events (in that order), embedded within the framing structures of gentlemanly sociability and intellectual equality of Enlightenment correspondence. An example of this newsletter mode is found in a letter he wrote to Daniel Wray FRS from Paris dated 1 September (old style) and 12 September (new style) 1749, which is notable for its description of his visits to French scientific and literary institutions.[41] Wray was a member of Yorke's intellectual coterie, a good friend and a regular guest at Wrest: his blend of

---

[37] BL, Add. MS 35397, ff. 206–8: Yorke to Birch, Paris, 29 Aug./9 Sept. 1749.

[38] Birch wrote three letters to Yorke in Paris in 1749: BL, Add. MS 35397, ff. 211–12: 8 Sept. 1749; ff. 217–18: 21 Sept. 1749; ff. 225–6: 2 Oct. 1749. Birch's news and commentary contained in the first two of these was replicated in the Weekly Letter sent to Jemima, Marchioness Grey at Wrest: Add. MS 35397, ff. 213–14: 9 Sept. 1749; ff. 219–20: 23 Sept. 1749.

[39] BL, Add. MS 35397, ff. 233–4: Yorke to Birch, Wrest, 2 Nov. 1749.

[40] BL, Add. MS 35397, ff. 206–8: Yorke to Birch, Paris, 29 Aug./9 Sept. 1749.

[41] BL, Add. MS 35401, ff. 117–20: Yorke to Wray, Paris, 1/12 Sept. 1749. The letter is printed in: P.Y. and J.J. Champenois, 'A Visit to Paris in 1749', *The Modern Language Review*, ix (1914), 514–16, erroneously referencing a copy at BL, Sloane MS 4325, ff. 10–12.

intellectual curiosity and witty good humour endeared him to both Yorke and Lady Grey. Yorke's letter begins with a section praising Wray's own letters ('choise Closet Pieces') and his intellectual activities ('your Literary Repasts in Kew Lane'), which Wray had humbly disavowed in his own letter.[42]

In his letter, Yorke describes to Wray his visit to the Abbé Sallier (Claude Sallier, 1685–1761) at the Bibliothèque Royale, an institution which he praises for its noble foundation, the large number of volumes in its collection, and the 'great method' with which most were ordered (all aspects of the library of the British Museum project in which the Hardwicke circle took a leading role in the following decade).[43] He also describes a visit to the Collection of Prints in the Hôtel de Nevers in Rue de Richelieu, where again he is most impressed by the large folio catalogue, but was unable to see the Cabinet of Medals, as the 'keeper', Claude Gros de Boze (1680–1753) was 'out of Town'. He visited Réaumur and his collection, although with such a large group that he expresses a wish to visit again alone 'en philosophe'. And he visits Fontenelle and the Académie Royale, presenting him with a letter of introduction from Martin Folkes, president of the Royal Society in London. Although Fontenelle is gracious and welcoming, speaking to him with 'great Politeness' and 'very Honourably of the English & their productions', Yorke is also mortified to hear that Folkes has failed to reply to one of Fontenelle's letters: in doing so, he has broken the gentlemanly gift exchange code of correspondence. Yorke after this reports on a meeting of the Academy of Belles Lettres, where he heard two papers, neither of which he thought merited publication.

In Paris, Yorke was also acquiring materials and curiosities for his own collections: 'I am picking up Books, Prints, & maps as well as I can, I wish you would enquire about the best way of sending them over'.[44] He sent Birch requests for copies of recent Birch publications to make use of in gift exchanges with French philosophes. He reported encountering what he called a 'Cologne Alamain', which contained diverse information, including news of a rebellion in the Dutch East Indies colony of Java, which had been suppressed by Baron Gustaaf Willem van Imhoff, governor of Batavia.[45] Yorke describes to Wray some recent literary publications, albeit noting that as he is visiting in the 'dead season' of summer, there are not many publications — 'even Novels and Plays' are kept back until 'the Town is fuller'.[46] The letter ends with a rather racy anecdote about Lord Londonderry, seen leaving the opera with three women in his chaise, evidently courtesans of the demi-monde – an anecdote that he is unlikely to have included in a letter to the Reverend Birch.[47] Yorke's Paris newsletter is a very good example of a *nouvelle à la main*, mixing gossip and ironised gentlemanly politeness with notices of intellectual endeavour, and literary production and critical remarks. In relation to scientific endeavours, Yorke is, as ever, light on detail

---

[42] Wray's house, Mount Ararat Lodge, was in Kew Lane, Richmond.

[43] Yorke asked Birch to send Sallier 'in sheets the 10th Volume of ye General Dictionary; I will be responsible for the money' (BL, Add. MS 35397, f. 207v: Yorke to Birch, Paris, 29 Aug./9 Sept. 1749).

[44] BL, Add. MS 35397, ff. 223–4: Yorke to Birch, Paris, 19/30 Sept. 1749.

[45] BL, Add. MS 35397, ff. 211–12: Birch to Yorke, London, 8 Sept. 1749.

[46] Yorke describes a work in preparation by Voltaire (*Catiline*, published later in 1749), and notes that Voltaire's *Nannine* (1749), though based on Richardson's *Pamela* (1742), has not met with the same success. He further assesses the performance of comedies by Dumenil and Gaussin, finding them inferior to Garrick.

[47] Champenois, 'Visit to Paris in 1749', 514–16. Lord Londonderry was the Irish peer, Ridgeway Pitt, 3rd earl of Londonderry (1722–1765), member for Camelford in Cornwall (1747–54).

© 2022 The Author(s). Parliamentary History published by John Wiley & Sons Ltd. on behalf of Parliamentary History Yearbook Trust.

of the actual natural philosophy, and more interested in administrative method, especially catalogues.

After his return to England in 1749, Yorke retained his curiosity about news from Paris, as is shown in the Weekly Letter correspondence. In May 1750, having read in the London press of strange 'Tumults and commotions' in Paris, Yorke pressed Birch for any news he could obtain about these events.[48] Birch replied with a juicy detail not contained in the newspaper reports, gleaned, he said, from a personal letter from an unnamed old friend who was resident there: the tumults had been occasioned by a 'popular Notion, that certain children had been seiz'd, in order to the making of a Bath with their Blood for the Cure *d'un Prince Cadre*'.[49] Yorke requested a copy of the letter in his next reply.[50] Birch returned to the spectacle of popular unrest in Paris in November 1750, the source for which he ascribes to 'A Letter from Paris', without specifying further the correspondent.[51]

It is in this period that Yorke conceived of the idea of commissioning or subscribing to a regular newsletter, a *nouvelle à la main*, from Paris. The occasion to do this occurred in September 1751, when his brother Joseph was promoted to the post of minister-plenipotentiary at The Hague, a post which he held until 1780. Although this promotion meant that the supply of Paris news from his brother would end, nonetheless, Yorke saw an opportunity in the change of personnel in Paris. As a consequence of Joseph's move, Yorke announced to Birch that Mr Shalkin was to be 'succeeded by the Abbé Jeffreys as his library Chargé', noting that 'I am very clear that I shall be no loser by the exchange'.[52] Birch may have been acquainted already with Rev. John Jeffreys (1718–98), who had been appointed rector of a City church, St Nicholas, Cole Abbey, London in 1746, and moved in some of the same circles. Jeffreys had been educated at Westminster and Christ Church, Oxford, graduating MA in 1746. He was appointed chaplain to Lord Albemarle's embassy, and resided in Paris from 1752 to 1755, until the time at which the embassy was withdrawn. Yorke's term 'library Chargé' is typically ambiguous and allusive, but suggests that Shalkin had been asked to perform various bibliographic tasks for Yorke, such as buying and transmitting French books for Yorke's library. Shalkin (perhaps under Joseph Yorke's direction) had supplied Yorke with a Paris alamain, in a run of 34 letters dated from 15 December 1750 (NS) to 25 May 1751 (NS), in French, now in the Hardwicke Papers in the British Library (Additional Manuscript 35445). It contained political information and 'news' collected from correspondents in a wide range of European states, some of which may have been gleaned from newsletters or printed newssheets received by the embassy.[53]

---

[48]BL, Add. MS 35397, ff. 243–4: Yorke to Birch, Wrest, 31 May 1750. 'Tumults and commotions' in Paris were reported in the *General Advertiser*, 23 May 1750. In 1752, Yorke reported that 'M. Grafigny's account of the Tumults at Paris in 1750 is the best I had seen of them, & is writ with spirit, I have ventured to copy what relates to that affair, & have enclosed the original.' (Add. MS 35397, ff. 100–101: Yorke to Birch, Wimpole, 4 Oct. 1752, the quotation at f. 100.) The enclosure has not been located.

[49]BL, Add. MS 35397, ff. 245–6: Birch to Yorke, London, 2 June 1750.

[50]BL, Add. MS 35397, ff. 247–8: Yorke to Birch, Wrest, 17 June 1750. The letter in question is not included in the Weekly Letter volume.

[51]BL, Add. MS 35397, ff. 320–1: Birch to Yorke, London, 17 Nov. 1750.

[52]BL, Add. 35398, ff. 28–30: Yorke to Birch, Wimpole, 20 Sept. 1751. The identity of 'Mr Shalkin' and his place in the embassy remain unknown, although the context here suggests he was a clerk of some kind.

[53]BL, Add. MS 35445, ff. 1–66: 15 Dec. 1750 (NS) – 25 May 1751 (NS).

© *2022 The Author(s). Parliamentary History published by John Wiley & Sons Ltd. on behalf of Parliamentary History Yearbook Trust.*

While Yorke was frustrated by Shalkin, he held Jeffreys in higher esteem. Jeffreys was the key to the supply of Yorke's Paris alamain over the next three years. This amounted to 213 newsletters, sent from 30 May 1751 (NS) to 8 April 1754 (NS), with a significant interruption from 9 November 1752 (NS) to 22 June 1753 (NS). The alamains were sent twice a week, following an irregular pattern (there are eight or nine in most months, and fewer in some, although some alamains may be missing from Add. MS 35445). Two postscript notes added by Jeffreys give evidence that the alamain was sent to him at the embassy and redirected from there to Yorke in London, perhaps by the diplomatic post.[54] The Paris alamain contained anecdotes and gossip in French about the French court and Parisian society, mixed with information about the literary and artistic world in Paris, such as notices of new books, anecdotes about writers and their compositions, and transcriptions of verses, songs and epigrams by French poets.

Yorke's *nouvelle à la main* from Paris was an orthodox example of the product: a bifolium manuscript letter, covering news and gossip not otherwise recorded in the published press, copied in significant numbers and sent by post to a range of subscribers. As Yorke was aware, the information environment for news in France was very different from that in Britain. In France the state authorised a small number of print newspapers, which by and large filtered out domestic news that was not authorised. The demand for additional domestic political information was catered for by private *nouvelles à la main*.[55] As their distribution was not authorised, *nouvellistes* could be prosecuted, and their *nouvelles à la mains* suppressed, at any time. While at some periods in the 18th century they were tolerated, at others they were more rigorously suppressed: in 1745, for example the parlement de Paris determined to suppress them altogether.[56] They had a reputation for gossip and rumour, reflecting their status outside authorised information, and their writers were considered as scandal mongers and hacks.

Yorke seems to have set considerable value on his Paris alamain, but at the same time, was frustrated by its frequent interruptions and its vapid contents. This is not necessarily a contradiction, as the conditions of production for a *nouvelle à la main* were trying. The long interruption in service between December 1752 and July 1753, noted above, was explained by Jeffreys on 14 November 1752, that the *nouvelliste* had been arrested. Jeffreys explained:

> I am sorry to tell you they will probably be the last you will receive, at least from the same Author: the poor fellow was last week sent to the Bastile [sic] and all his papers seized. He has lately made too free with certain persons about the Court, and not a fortnight ago I advised him to be more prudent or he would certainly meet with his present fate.[57]

---

[54] BL, Add. MS 35445, ff. 68–527: 30 May, 1751–8 Apr. 1754. Jeffreys's brief postscripts are appended to f. 256v and 296v.

[55] François Moureau, 'Les nouvelles à la main dans le système d'information de l'Ancien Régime', in *De Bonne Main*, ed. Moreau, 117–34.

[56] Christopher Todd, *Political Bias, Censorship, and the Dissolution of the 'Official' Press in Eighteenth-century France* (Lewiston, NY, 1991), 158–61. See also Gilles Feyel, *L'Annonce et la Nouvelle: La presse d'information en France sous l'Ancien Régime (1630–1788)* (Oxford, 2000).

[57] Jeffreys to Yorke, Paris, 14 Nov. 1752, quoted L.L. Bongie, 'Les nouvelles à la main: la perspective du client', in *De Bonne Main*, ed. Moureau, 138. Jeffreys's letters to Yorke are BL, Add. MS 35630.

After this interruption, Yorke pressed Jeffreys to secure another writer. In December, Jeffreys wrote that he too hoped 'to be able to get you another *à la main* soon, for since the suppression of the last I am ignorant of the common occurrences of Paris'.[58] In July 1753, Yorke reported to Birch that:

> The Abbé Jefferys [sic] has at last procured me an Alamain, & I judge from the hand, the style, & the matter that it comes from my Bastile Friend, who if he cannot get bread by his pen, might as well dine upon the King's Allowance in the Bastile.[59]

Yorke's response to his *nouvelliste*'s incarceration is rather insouciant, indicating that to his mind, the world of the Paris *nouvellistes* was closer to that of the Grub Street hacks that Birch and Yorke studiously avoided in London, with their penchant for rumour, gossip and scandal.[60] By August 1753, Yorke had reconsidered, and had decided that his new *nouvelliste* was in fact a different correspondent.

> My A la mains come regularly, I think the Writer of them is more prudent with regard to Perfidy than the last, & gives much the same Account of Parliamentary matters.[61]

Yorke had recognised by this time that his *nouvelliste* had changed, and was less prepared to record scandal, or was perhaps just more prudent with regard to persecution by the police. Eventually this reluctance to write about the more contentious news cost the *nouvelliste* his employment. The final alamain in Yorke's collection is dated 8 April 1754. In May 1754, Jeffreys assured Yorke that he had 'frequently told my mind very freely to the Author and my utmost endeavours have not been wanting to procure you another'.[62] In October 1754, Yorke recorded that Jeffreys has ended the contract with the alamain writer: 'I have not heard from Jeffreys these 3 weeks, He has dismissed the A la Main writer, whom he thought not worthy of the hire'.[63] To some extent Yorke's response inscribes the *nouvelliste*'s double bind of gossip and scandal, the inclusion of which was commercially valuable, but also legally risky and morally demeaning.

Although the writer of Yorke's Paris alamain remains unknown, Laurence Bongie has argued that it was François Jérôme Bosquet (or Bousquet) de Colomiers, a former lawyer and *subdélégué* at the Parlement de Toulouse. Bosquet had left his wife and family in Toulouse in the 1730s for the urban excitements of Paris, where he became a *nouvelliste*. Bosquet's *nouvelle à la main* was a well-known information product, whose subscribers included prominent members of Toulouse society, including the presidente Riquet and the archbishop of Narbonne, and also the ambassadors of Britain and Holland. But life as a *nouvelliste* was risky, and in late 1752, Bosquet was imprisoned in the Bastille. The Paris police were aware of Bosquet's activities as a *nouvelliste*, and had tolerated his *à la main* as long as it remained at the level of social and literary gossip. Bosquet's clients, however, valued his coverage of

---

[58]Jeffreys to Yorke, Paris, 5 Dec. 1752, quoted in Bongie, 'Les nouvelles', 139.

[59]BL, Add. MS 35398, ff. 130–1: Yorke to Birch, Wrest, 12 July 1753.

[60]L.L. Bongie, *From Rogue to Everyman: A Foundling's Journey to the Bastille* (Montreal, 2004), 155.

[61]BL, Add. MS 35398, ff. 149–50: Yorke to Birch, Wrest, 23 Aug. 1753.

[62]Jeffreys to Yorke, Paris, 29 May 1754, quoted in Bongie, 'Les nouvelles', 140.

[63]BL, Add. MS 35398, ff. 240–1, 241v: Yorke to Birch, Wrest, 30 Oct. 1754.

'les affaires du temps', which is to say political controversies and scandals.[64] On 9 December 1752, Bosquet, despite being warned by a collaborator in the police, was arrested as a *nouvelliste*, and incarcerated in the Bastille. After his release, Bosquet was exiled to Toulouse, where his life as a *nouvelliste* was over. It is Bosquet's arrest that ties his story to Yorke. Bongie's attribution rests on the near coincidence of Bosquet's arrest as a *nouvelliste*, and the subsequent period of interruption to the alamain.[65] But although Jeffreys confirmed to Yorke in November that his nouvelliste had been 'sent to the Bastile', Yorke himself believed for some time that his alamain was written by the same hand, before and after the interruption caused by Bosquet's arrest.[66] So although the attribution remains conjectural, Bongie's account of Bosquet's career as a *nouvelliste* sheds relevant light on Yorke's commercial newsletter correspondent.

Yorke's consumption of his Paris alamain was enthusiastic, but undertaken with a kind of weary irony about its limitations. He took note of, and followed closely, some of the political information it contained. Among 'les affaires du temps' covered was an account of the struggle between the French King Louis XV and the parlement de Rouen over the imposition of an income tax to the clergy. The alamain gave reports of speeches to the parlement, and the various proceedings, remonstrances and registers, of this controversy in 1752–4, including several transcribed in extended enclosures.[67] Yorke's response to this news is explored in detail below. It also included gossipy anecdotes about the court of the Young Pretender, Charles Edward Stuart, then at Paris. One such was the story of the marriage of the 'Princesse Radzivil' to 'Prince Edward' — a story that rehearsed a rumour first heard in 1749, that Charles Edward Stuart had married his cousin, the Princess Teofila Konstancia (1738–80), daughter of Michal Kazimiercz Radziwill, prince of Lithuania, and they had borne a son.[68] Another was the report of the death aged 80 years in Paris in November 1753 of Charlotte O'Brien, widow of Charles, self-styled Viscount Clare, an Irish officer in the service of the French army.[69] At the end of the same year, on 31 December 1753 (NS), the alamain noted the death of Voltaire, to which Jeffreys added a postscript on first page: 'The Report of Voltaire's death is contradicted'.[70]

Light and occasional verses by court poets and satirists also filled Yorke's Paris alamains. The *nouvelliste* transcribed verses by and about Pierre-Charles Roy (1683–1764) and Michel de Bonneval (*d*.1766), best known as librettists for the spectacular French operas of the period. As a courtier in charge of masquerades and other large scale public entertainments at

---

[64]Bongie, 'Les nouvelles', 135–42; Bongie, *From Rogue to Everyman*, 188–9.

[65]Bongie, 'Les nouvelles', 137–40.

[66]Furthermore, Robert Dawson reports that the copies of Bosquet's *à la main* in the Arsenal Library bear a stamped heading 'Le courrier de Paris', whereas Yorke's copies do not (Paris, Arsenal Library MS 7082, f. 33), quoted in Robert Dawson, 'The *Mélange De Poésies Diverses (1781)* and the Diffusion of Manuscript Pornography in Eighteenth-Century France', in *'Tis Nature's Fault: Unauthorized Sexuality during the Enlightenment*, ed. Robert Maccubbin (Cambridge, 1988), 229–43, at 240n. John Rogister also cast some doubt on Bongie's attribution to Bosquet, in *Louis XV and the Parlement of Paris, 1737–1755* (Cambridge, 1995), 267.

[67]BL, Add. MS 35445, ff. 220, 237, 345–61.

[68]BL, Add. MS 35445, f. 98. The rumour had been reported, for example, in a letter from Sir Horace Mann to Horace Walpole, Florence, 21 Mar. 1749 NS: *The Yale Edition of Horace Walpole's Correspondence*, ed. W.S. Lewis (48 vols, New Haven, CT, 1937–83), xx, 35.

[69]BL, Add. MS 35445, f. 453b.

[70]BL: Add MS 35445, f. 481.

Versailles, Bonneval had access to the gossip of the French court.[71] The *nouvelliste* transcribed a verse satire on the *Encyclopédie* entitled 'Dialogue entre M. Diderot, un Libraire, et un Colporteur'.[72] Verses, satires, songs and epigrams by a range of minor poets were transcribed: Pedro Clemente de Arostegui, bishop of Osma in Spain (1692–1760),[73] Charles Marie de La Condamine (1701–74),[74] Abbé François Joachim de Pierre de Bernis (1715–94).[75] These writers include some figures already known to Yorke and Birch, as in the case of the traveller and natural philosopher La Condamine, who had been elected a Fellow of the Royal Society in December 1748. There is however little evidence that Yorke found these literary offerings interesting, as he never commented on them to Birch. It was as if he considered them little more than filler in the space of the alamain.

It is in this way difficult to measure how useful or entertaining Yorke found the Paris alamain. His commentary on it in his letters to Birch in the period suggests that although he received it regularly, it only occasionally intruded into his reflections. One recurring topic that he found relevant was evidence of domestic unrest, political dissension or internal fiscal deficiency in the French state — all elements that played into the 'Great Power' rivalry of the early 1750s. Yorke's curiosity was piqued sufficiently by the *vingtième* crisis in the period 1750–5 to mention it to Birch repeatedly. As Yorke said in October 1752,

> My Paris alamains have not of late contained any material Advices, the Parliament's being adjourned puts a stop to the Church Controversy, the Court seems to have now declared in favor of the Clergy, & it is supposed that the Controller intends to squeeze a large free Gift from them, as an Equivalent for this step.[76]

The *vingtième* was a form of income tax, levied at the rate of five per cent of income (or one twentieth, a *vingtième*), proposed by the minister of finance, Jean-Baptiste de Machault, comte d'Arnouville, in 1749, in order to repay the national debt incurred by the War of the Austrian Succession. The crisis was of interest to Yorke because it arguably gave some evidence of fiscal weakness in the French state. But he may also have enjoyed the spectacle, in this letter to Birch, of the role of the clergy in resisting the tax.[77]

Throughout the summer in 1753, Yorke continued to make reference to the information in the alamain on these domestic troubles in France. In July 1753, he reported to Birch:

> The King lately sent the Declaration to the Grand Chamber at the Pontoise, & it passed by a majority of 24 voices against 18, that they would not deliberate upon it, without & the sense of their exiled Brethren, the *Enquete & Requete*.[78] It is thought this will greatly

---

[71] BL, Add. MS 35445, ff. 119b, 141, 163: Pierre Charles Roy; ff. 111, 141, 144, 145, 179b, 185, 189b, 214, 287, 309, 321, 323: Michel de Bonneval.

[72] BL, Add MS 35445, ff. 121–2.

[73] BL, Add. MS 35445, ff. 193, 202, 269, 277, 293, 301, 303, 307, 317.

[74] BL, Add. MS 35445, f. 303.

[75] BL, Add. MS 35445, f. 333.

[76] BL, Add. MS 35398, ff. 100–1: Yorke to Birch, Wimpole, 4 Oct. 1752.

[77] See Julian Swann, *Politics and the Parlement of Paris under Louis XV, 1754–1774* (Cambridge, 1995).

[78] The Chambre des Enquêtes ('inquiries') and the Chambre des Requêtes ('petitions') were courts of the parlement of Paris in the 1750s, subservient to the Grand Chamber. See Swann, *Politics*, 5–7. The Arrêts were the final decisions of these or other courts.

incense the Court. The Parliament of Rouen have so far given way to the Kings Order, that they have by 47 Voices agst 22 suspended all Proceedings agst the Comte & Vicars of Verneuil, but at the same time, they appointed a Committee to frame Remonstrances to the King agst the Tone of the Arrets of Council which he had just sent them, annulling their Decrees, upon the Complaint of some of the Parliament of Verneuil.[79]

But although Yorke's observations on the alamain in his reply to Birch's Weekly Letter indicates he found the question of French state finances relevant, it hardly suggests that he had a firm grip of the problem. He concluded 'You may judge from these Particulars, how well funded the Nation is, wch is got into our News-Papers, that the Court & the Parliament are very near an Accommodation'.[80] In August 1753, when Yorke also received from Jeffreys a copy of a recent letter from Voltaire detailing his fall from grace at the Prussian court, his report on the alamain to Birch remained focused on the contentions between king and the Parlement de Rouen.[81]

The Disputes between the King & the Parliament of Rouen run high, & it is thought will come to Extremities. Their Registry have been cancelled by Order of the Court, under the eyes of a Lieutenant General, & their Remonstrances wch are very strong, verge on the point of being presented. There seems no Probability of an Accommodation between the K. & the Parliament of Paris. They are determined not to take any steps for that purpose without the Return of their exiled Brethren of the other Chamber, & have rejected every Article of the Agreement proposed by the Pr. of Conti. One was that they shd register a Declaration of the King's concerning the Schism; & 2d, that they should resume their ordinary Functions; 3d, that they should depute to the King for the recalling of their exiled Brethren; & 4th that they shd register only provisionally the Declaration above mentioned.[82]

In September, having complained to Birch about the lack of news in London, Yorke reflected further on French domestic politics mentioned in the alamain:

The Deputies at the Parliament of Rouen were sent back with a pretty smart answer to the Remonstrances & Court being apprehensive that they wd not register it, has prorogued their meetings till they become more tractable. The Deputys were expressly forbid to take Pontoise in their Way.[83]

Yorke added further, in a postscript addendum to the opening page of his letter: 'Not having the Alamain by me, I mistook the purpose of Mr Fouger's Orders, wch were not to suffer the Parlmt to adjourn till they had registered the King's Answer etc.' He also noted that 'My alamain tells me that Mr Boze is dead, who is a great loss to the Fr. Academy of

[79] BL, Add. MS 35398, ff. 130–1: Yorke to Birch, Wrest, 12 July 1753.

[80] BL, Add. MS 35398, ff. 130–1: Yorke to Birch, Wrest, 12 July 1753.

[81] Voltaire, *Babouc; or, the World as it Goes. By Monsieur de Voltaire. To which are Added, Letters Concerning His Disgrace at the Prussian Court: With His Letter to His Niece on that Occasion. Also, The Force of Friendship, or, Innocence Distress'd. A Novel* (1754).

[82] BL, Add. MS 35398, ff. 149–50: Yorke to Birch, Wrest, 23 Aug. 1753.

[83] BL, Add. MS 35398, ff. 161–2: Yorke to Birch, Wimpole, 20 Sept. 1753.

© 2022 The Author(s). *Parliamentary History* published by John Wiley & Sons Ltd. on behalf of Parliamentary History Yearbook Trust.

Belles Letters'.[84] De Boze, of the Académie des Inscriptions et Belles-lettres, was one of the philosophes he had visited in Paris in 1749. By October 1753, Yorke reported the *vingtième* crisis was still not resolved.

> The A la Main informs me that the King's letters Patents have been registered at the Chatelet in a pretty extraordinary manner, viz – in the presence of a Deputation from the new Chamber of Vacations, attended by a Detachment of Archers wth their Muskets shouldered. I suppose after this step, the Chatelet will look upon its self no longer in a situation of acting.[85]

As his summary to Birch suggests, Yorke maintained a kind of tactical interest in French domestic politics. He summarised for Birch a complicated dispute, whose relevance to British interests he had trouble determining, beyond his desire for evidence of French military and fiscal fragility.

In 1754, the French king's continuing dispute with the clergy was joined in the alamain by a more ominous story recording the French view of a series of minor disputes and conflicts between French and British forces in India, the Caribbean and North America. Yorke wrote to Birch:

> I had lately a letter from Mr Jeffreys, wch brings but little News. Moderate Men (He says) wish some peaceable End may be put to our E & W Indian Disputes, but of that there seems no Possibility at present. I do not find, that these Church Disputes in France make so much noise as they did, but till the Parliament resumes its sittings after the Vacation, we shall not be able to form any Judgment about it. The Fr. King's Answer to the Clergy when they attended him with some Remonstrances agst his Edict was sharper than usual.[86]

Yorke's observations in his letters to Birch, about the French news in the alamains in 1754 show that they gave him some insight into the worsening relations between France and Britain in the period. 'The French are eternally giving us fresh Provocations in all parts of the World'.[87] These conflicts were focused on colonial rivalries unresolved by the Treaty of Aix-la-Chapelle (1748) that had brought an end to the War of Austrian Succession. These tensions were particularly acute in North America, where British forces clashed with French militia and First Nation warriors in the disputed Ohio Country. General Edward Braddock's attempt to seize the French position at Fort Duquesne (now Pittsburgh) in the summer of 1755 ended with a disastrous defeat at the Battle of the Monongahela on 9 July 1755.[88] But while Yorke's private alamains touch on these international affairs, they failed to give him any unique insight into the coming global conflict, the war now known as the Seven Years War (1756–63), of which these disputes were the immediate precursor. In July 1755, in a sign of the increasing tension between Britain and France, Jeffreys and

[84]BL, Add. MS 35398, ff. 161–2: Yorke to Birch, Wimpole, 20 Sept. 1753.
[85]BL, Add. MS 35398, ff. 174–5: Yorke to Birch, Wrest, 18 Oct. 1753.
[86]BL, Add. MS 35398, ff. 226–7: Yorke to Birch, Wrest, 15 Oct. 1754.
[87]BL, Add. MS 35398, ff. 161–2: Yorke to Birch, Wimpole, 20 Sept. 1753.
[88]T.C. Pease, *Anglo-French Boundary Disputes in the West, 1749–1763* (Springfield, IL, 1936), xx–lxi.

the embassy returned to London. The ambassador (Albemarle), had died suddenly on 22 December 1754, and the embassy was left in the hands of Ruvigny Du Cosné, who was appointed chargé, and recalled on 22 July 1755. The embassy's final months were consumed by the negotiations caused by the disaster of the Braddock expedition. Yorke reported that though he was 'impatient for the Events of such Great Transactions as are now depending' he 'valued the quiet days we have enjoyed since the last Peace'.[89]

Yorke was also concerned about continued flow of French news after Jeffreys was recalled. When Jeffreys dismissed the *nouvelliste* in 1754, news from Paris became much less regular. Birch included a report from Du Cosné of his treatment in Paris before his recall in the Weekly Letter of 9 August 1755.[90] Yorke asked Birch to contact Jeffreys to ensure at least continued access to copies of *Le Mercure de France*, the long-running and authorised printed record of literary events in Paris.

> I desire my Compliments to Abbé Jeffreys, & wish you wd ask him if I can still have the Mercures sent over, if that is not practicable, our friend Sir Daniel will be deprived of his favourite Lecture.[91]

However, even this proved impossible, especially after the opening of hostilities between France and Britain in 1756, initiated by the French descent on Fort St Philip in Minorca in April 1756.[92] But by then the Paris alamain was long finished. It seems somehow appropriate that Yorke chose this moment to repurpose the term alamain, using it in 1755 to refer to Birch's Weekly Letter: at the beginning of the season, he commented that 'My chief Intent in writing to you now is to desire you would begin your usual *A La Mains* forthwith, for I am almost famish'd for want of Intelligence'.[93]

5. *Conclusion*

Yorke's experiment with the Paris alamain was inspired by the pleasure he derived from Birch's Weekly Letter, his own newsletter writing experiments and his historical interests in scribal news. As he perhaps discovered on his visit to Paris in 1749, Birch's account of the literary and political news of London was a distinctly superior entity to the scandalous information product of the *nouvelliste à la main*. Nonetheless, the idea of a foreign correspondence, undertaken in private, with access to secret knowledge, appealed to his sense of himself as a significant actor in British politics, even though this appears overestimated.

[89] BL, Add. MS 35398, ff. 276–8, 277v: Yorke to Birch, Taymouth, 20 Aug. 1755.

[90] BL, Add. MS 35398, ff. 271–2: Birch to Yorke, London, 9 Aug. 1755.

[91] BL, Add. MS 35398, ff. 276–8, 277v: Yorke to Birch, Taymouth, 20 Aug. 1755. 'Sir Daniel' is perhaps an ironic reference to Wray, who was not a baronet.

[92] Birch's accounts in the Weekly Letter in 1755 of the rivalry between British and French over their colonial possessions in North America were not based on the Paris alamain, but rather, British news outlets. In June 1755, for example, Birch noted that he had read an 'article' in the 'Book at Lloyd's Coffee House', that contained conflicting information about an encounter between the French and British fleet, under Admiral Boscawen, off the coast of Newfoundland, which, in Birch's description, 'heightens the Impatience of our Curiosity of knowing more'. (BL, Add. MS 35398, ff. 246–9: Birch to Yorke, London 21 June 1755.) See also Alan Houston, 'Benjamin Franklin and the "Wagon Affair" of 1755', *The William and Mary Quarterly*, 3rd ser, lxvi (2009), 235–86.

[93] BL, Add. MS 35398, ff. 256–7: Yorke to Birch, Berwick, 15 July 1755.

The information Yorke gathered from the Paris alamain was curious enough to mention to Birch in his letters, but never seems to have had more significant influence on Yorke or his wider circles. Although Yorke may have been piqued to know that the alamain was private, secret and illegal in France, the information it contained was not espionage. Yorke did not gain any unique or valuable insight from the Paris alamain into French politics, such as might have been useful in the run up to the most significant war with France for decades, the Seven Years War. Instead of intelligence, the Paris alamain delivered its paragraphs of literary and intellectual gossip, its transcripts of occasional verses and minor satires, and a modicum of social scandal — a mode as typical of a Paris *nouvelliste* as it was atypical of Birch.

Afterword

KATE LOVEMAN

Writers of scribal news in the 17th and 18th centuries were often keen to evade scrutiny of how their productions were created and transmitted but – as the articles in this volume have demonstrated – they certainly merit that scrutiny. The information that a political newsletter contained was not, and is not, confined to what the words on the page relay about events in parliament or other developments. As each manuscript was the product of a set of political interactions, it can be used to investigate the networks which produced, circulated and preserved it, rather than being treated only as a repository of reports. In adopting this approach to scribal news, the authors of this collection share a position with the investigators of the 17th and 18th centuries.

Those investigators well understood the value of examining a newsletter – and, where possible, its author – as a means to uncover information about the people and the motives behind its transmission. So, in 1683, the news writer William Cotton, having been arrested on several warrants, was pressed to offer up information on other news writers in order to win clemency. In response, he produced an account of 'those as are writers of newes', and he addressed letters to the king and privy council that touch on many of the themes considered in this collection. Focusing on commercial writers of political news, Cotton sketched a picture of highly interrelated, time-sensitive news services, with writers rapidly recycling each other's content for their own clienteles. A typical post day for Cotton began with gathering foreign news, including a trip to the Royal Exchange, the City's main trading forum. At 3pm he received the newsletter of 'Pike & Bill' who used 'to goe partners in Parliament time' to serve coffeehouses – the demands of the parliamentary session, Cotton indicated, prompted special, seasonal arrangements among news writers. Finally, at 8 or 9pm, Cotton would pay an intermediary in order to acquire Giles Hancock's newsletter, which was known for its coverage of 'Court & Councell', and then lift material from it.[1] As contributors have noted, the arrangement of items in both printed newspapers and scribal newsletters generally proceeded from the foreign to the domestic, and Cotton's collecting methods indicate his was no exception – it was also an arrangement governed by the timetables of other news writers, which in turn followed the post.

Once assembled, Cotton's newsletter therefore combined oral and scribal sources, providing foreign, parliament and court news drawn from different areas of what Jason Peacey

---

[1]TNA, SP 29/433, f. 323b: William Cotton, account of news writers [22 Oct?] 1683; SP 29/433, f. 319: William Cotton, petition to the king, [22 Oct?] 1683; SP 29/433, f. 322: William Cotton to the king and privy council, [22 Oct?] 1683.

© 2022 The Author(s). Parliamentary History published by John Wiley & Sons Ltd. on behalf of Parliamentary History Yearbook Trust.

and Rachael King have each characterised as a news 'ecosystem'. Cotton's own sense of how this ecosystem operated was distinctly hierarchical – along the lines of a reverse food chain where those at the top nourished those further down. At the very top were writers such as Hancock who could offer 'verry privett things' from inside sources at Whitehall, so that 'what ever is considerable, whether publique or privett, hee hath it with the first'. News writers at this level, Cotton was clear, could command 'great' prices precisely because they had 'that which is privett'. Their most eager readers therefore included other news writers, himself among them. Some writers, he suggested, were known for their specialisms in terms of content and for their literary talents – 'Mr Blackhall', for example, was well informed about Scottish news; while John Combes was 'in great request' because he combined private news from court with 'a good stile'. At the bottom of the ranks of news writers were men such as Mr Cleiypole who 'generally depends upon others for his newes for hee is one that will not take any paines for it but will word things well if not in drink'.[2] Apparently a news writer's rhetorical skill might help to compensate for both a lack of novel content and the unreliability of a writer prone to booze.

Cotton's account of the operations of political news writers is revealing while also being exemplary of the often problematic sources with which contributors to this volume, and indeed any investigation into political newswriting, have to deal. Cotton claimed to be one of the lowly news writers – a politically naive man who copied what others produced and who had taken up the job only temporarily to feed his family. Yet he simultaneously claimed to be an amazingly authoritative source on the news writers' activity, who was able to reveal 'as much of this Intreague as any man in London if not more'.[3] Writing to save his skin, Cotton's less than reliable account survives in the state papers because, unlike the majority of news writers, the steps he took to protect himself were unsuccessful. More than most early modern writers and readers, the many people who engaged with political newsletters often had reason to be cautious about the evidence they left of their involvement and views. Despite what was evidently a thriving culture of scribal news well into the 18th century, its participants are often hard to trace. As we have seen, letters go unsigned; writers omit the sources for their news; the many hands through which a letter passed leave no marks; or, where readers can be identified, they can be tricky to find in the archives (perhaps because, being women or labourers, they were not in a position to write or to preserve their papers, or because, as employees of a diplomatic service, the records of their activities are dispersed internationally across collections).

In contending with frequently elusive evidence, the essays in this collection have offered a wealth of insights for future work on parliamentary and political newswriting to develop. Collectively they have demonstrated how, when it comes to scribal newswriting, familiar terms and categories for considering early modern texts and activities tend to require refining in order to capture the complexities and nuances of these exchanges. While it is possible to study printed news to understand 17th and 18th-century politics, contributors have shown that this would have appeared a strange method of evaluation to many early modern readers – for print and manuscript news circulated alongside each other (sometimes literally in the same packet), fed each other, and were produced by the same news

---

[2]SP 29/433, f. 323b. Combes's first name is supplied in John Zeale, *A Narrative of the Phanatical Plot* (1683), 14.
[3]SP 29/433, f. 319; SP 29/433, f. 322.

writers. Although contemporaries like Cotton wrote of 'private' and 'public' news as if these categories required no explanation, contributors have illustrated how the gradations of 'private' (or privileged or confidential) information were many, shaped by factors ranging from access to reserved spaces (as with the Lords' and Commons' chambers), to the medium (what was not in print), to time (what news writers considered 'private' at the start of one day began to lose its exclusivity over a matter of hours as multiple news services circulated it around the town, the country and beyond).[4] In discussing newsletters, the classifications that have emerged to describe their types or genres refer not to the content as such, but the relationship between the writer and their readers: newsletters are 'sociable', 'commercial', 'diplomatic' or 'official', while the boundaries between these recognisable types are often less than firm.[5] Moreover, even standard terms such as 'writer' and 'reader' require consideration. A news 'writer' might range from someone who put considerable effort into seeking material and crafting sentences, to someone who acted principally as compiler of others' words, to someone who served as a straightforward copyist. Meanwhile to talk only of 'readers' can obscure the part played by the recipients of news and the addressees of letters who may *not* have been readers of the contents themselves but who nonetheless served significant roles in circulating scribal news.[6]

Examining scribal news therefore prompts closer attention to the words we use in describing early modern information exchange in political and literary cultures. It has also shown the importance of recognising that the meanings newsletters carried were not only borne by words: the material qualities of a newsletter shaped its interpretation. For example, the paper's format might align the work with a genre of news; the layout could be used to locate the type of news or identify a writer's priorities; while paratexts – including adverts, annotations, salutations and a letter's address – were part of the whole and potential influences upon the ways the news content was received.[7] Today, achieving literacy is understood to involve more than becoming fluent in recognising how letters form words: it also entails learning how the *mise-en-page* conveys meaning and how to use information derived from texts in ways that are endorsed by the reader's society.[8] A number of the articles in this collection have explicitly or tacitly proposed ways we can improve our own literacy in scribal news: by familiarising ourselves with newsletters' conventions and their material characteristics, we can better appreciate the range of signals that they provided to the more proficient of their early readers.

Those early readers of scribal news ranged from apex intelligencers such as Joseph Williamson in the secretary of state's office to sociable newsletter writers such as Robert Wodrow, and from the illustrious earl of Hardwicke to the anonymous annotator of the Newey newsletters.[9] The records of the responses of actual readers have to be set alongside what can be deduced from the newsletters themselves about their potential uses. William Cotton believed the value of a scribal news service was raised when the writer was able to provide customers with information that arrived speedily, was 'privett', written 'in a good

---

[4] For example, articles by Littleton and Raffe; TNA, SP 29/433, f. 323b, cf. f. 319.

[5] For examples of these terms, see articles by Peacey and Schaich.

[6] See article by King.

[7] See, for example, Ellis, Schaich, Davis and King.

[8] For example, B.V. Street, *Literacy in Theory and Practice* (Cambridge, 1984, repr. 1988), 154–5.

[9] These readers respectively feature in the articles by Peacey, Raffe, Ellis and King.

stile' and 'considerable' (i.e., significant), but he also conveyed that not all of these attributes were required for success. That a news writer had troubled to copy out an item implied it should have value to the intended reader or to a portion of the intended readership, even if it was not 'considerable' – yet identifying what exactly the value of that information was may have puzzled the actual readers, as it sometimes perplexes us. Contributors have discussed, for example, what readers might have gained from learning the extreme minutiae of parliamentary business, such as an account of a minor refinement to the wording of a bill. For foreign courtiers this kind of extensive detail on parliamentary divisions might cumulatively offer a pragmatic appreciation of Westminster politics that could not be had from other sources. For a Derbyshire gentlewoman such as Anne Pole, the opportunities to deploy this knowledge in political action are less apparent, but she might nonetheless have appreciated the sense of expertise and being 'in the know' that this detailed reportage offered.[10] In both cases the advantages may have lain, not in the usefulness of the information itself, but in being seen by others to be more fully informed on activities at the centre of power and as having information that – by virtue of being reported by a commercial or diplomatic news service – appeared to be of value and thus to hold out the potential of further exchange.

Although the value of news was generally dependent on its timely reception and news publications themselves were widely regarded as ephemeral, this was not always the case. For certain writers, such as Abel Boyer, news publications were written with an eye to posterity, as a form of history.[11] For certain readers, newsletters served as a means to store and preserve information – which is, of course, often how we come to have them at all. The literary qualities of some writers' letters and some news genres evidently helped encourage readers to collect them, binding the documents together or copying them into notebooks, as Edward Taylor has described with political verse. Meanwhile, Leith Davis has illustrated how one of the uses of newsletters and newspapers in the 18th century was as material to be woven together into a historical narrative. It was an approach that in the case of at least one historical volume, *A Compleat History of the Late Rebellion* (1716), involved removing references to the letters as sources, in order to recast communication acts as objective information. In investigating scribal political news, this volume of *Parliamentary History* has, rather aptly, reversed that process. It has urged appreciation of scribal accounts as communication events, as material objects and as texts which, in relaying parliamentary history, have other stories to tell about the politics, news and culture of the 17th and 18th centuries.

---

[10]Recipients who are discussed in articles by Schaich and King.

[11]See Littleton.

Index